WATCHING

THEM BE

WATCHING THEM BE

STAR PRESENCE *on the* SCREEN
from GARBO *to* BALTHAZAR

JAMES HARVEY

ff

FABER AND FABER, INC.
AN AFFILIATE OF FARRAR, STRAUS AND GIROUX
NEW YORK

Faber and Faber, Inc.
An affiliate of Farrar, Straus and Giroux
18 West 18th Street, New York 10011

The chapter "Charles Laughton" was originally published in different form as
"Quasimodo in America" in *The New York Review of Books*.

Illustrations on pages 22, 122, 199, 313, 331, and 347 appear courtesy of the author.
All other illustrations appear courtesy of Photofest.

Owing to limitations of space, all acknowledgments for permission
to reprint previously published material can be found on pages 379–80.

Library of Congress Cataloging-in-Publication Data
Harvey, James, 1929–
    Watching them be : star presence on the screen from Garbo to Balthazar / James
Harvey. — First edition.
        pages   cm
    Includes bibliographical references and index.
    ISBN 978-0-571-21197-5 (hardcover)
    1. Motion picture actors and actresses—United States—Biography.   I. Title.

PN1998.2 .H425 2014
791.4302'80922—dc23

                                                                            2013034423

Designed by Abby Kagan

Faber and Faber, Inc., books may be purchased for educational, business,
or promotional use. For information on bulk purchases, please contact
the Macmillan Corporate and Premium Sales Department at 1-800-221-7945,
extension 5442, or write to specialmarkets@macmillan.com.

www.fsgbooks.com
www.twitter.com/fsgbooks • www.facebook.com/fsgbooks

1   3   5   7   9   10   8   6   4   2

As before, as always—
for Betty Ann

CONTENTS

List of Illustrations   ix

Preface   xv

PART ONE: ICONS

1. Garbo   3
2. Dietrich and Sternberg   53
3. Bergman and Selznick   76
4. Wayne and Ford   89
5. Davis and Wyler   114
6. Charles Laughton   148

PART TWO: REALISTS

7. Robert De Niro   169
8. Altman's Nashville   202
9. Jackie Brown and Others   229
10. Godard's Close-ups   247

PART THREE: TRANSCENDERS

11. Bergman and Rossellini   265
12. Dreyer's Heroines   296
13. Balthazar   339

Selected Bibliography   361
Acknowledgments   365
Index   367

ILLUSTRATIONS

1   Greta Garbo in *Queen Christina*
5   The close-up before the final fadeout (*Queen Christina*)
6   At the beginning of *Camille*: Garbo's smile for the flower seller
9   Arnold Genthe's 1925 photograph of Garbo
11 Garbo with John Gilbert in *A Woman of Affairs*
15 Garbo with Conrad Nagel in *The Mysterious Lady*
17 *A Woman of Affairs*: Greta Garbo with Lewis Stone
19 Garbo in *Anna Christie*
22 *Susan Lenox (Her Fall and Rise)*: Garbo with Clark Gable
25 *Grand Hotel*: the Garbo mask
30 Garbo in *Queen Christina*
30 A Garbo close-up in *Queen Christina*
32 Garbo in *Anna Karenina* with Vronsky (Fredric March)
32 Garbo in *Anna Karenina* with Karenin (Basil Rathbone)
34 *Camille*'s Marguerite (Garbo) with her "friends" Olympe and Prudence
36 Marguerite at the entr'acte
36 Marguerite and Armand (Robert Taylor)
40 In front of her mirror: Armand is concerned about Marguerite.
42 Marguerite and the Baron de Varville (Henry Daniell)
44 Marguerite's renunciation scene
46 Marguerite listening to Armand

46 Marguerite at her end
51 *Ninotchka*: Garbo with Melvyn Douglas
56 Garbo as the condemned Mata Hari
56 *Dishonored*: Dietrich as the spy X-27
60 *Morocco*: Dietrich with Gary Cooper
62 *Shanghai Express*: on the train—Anna May Wong and Dietrich
64 *Blonde Venus*: the gorilla gets a look at Cary Grant
64 *Blonde Venus*: Dietrich sheds her monkey suit
64 *Blonde Venus*: Dietrich revealed
66 Dietrich and Cary Grant in *Blonde Venus*
71 Dietrich with John Wayne in *Seven Sinners*
71 Dietrich and Wayne in *Pittsburgh*, with Randolph Scott
74 Dietrich's memorable role in *Touch of Evil*
79 *Intermezzo*: Ingrid Bergman as piano teacher (with Ann Todd)
81 *Dr. Jekyll and Mr. Hyde*: Bergman as bar girl
82 *For Whom the Bell Tolls*: Bergman as guerrilla (with Gary Cooper, Arturo de Cordova, and Akim Tamiroff)
85 *Saratoga Trunk*: Bergman as adventuress (with Gary Cooper)
91 John Wayne with Claire Trevor in *Stagecoach*
94 "Welcome home, Ethan": Ethan (Wayne) and Dorothy Jordan in *The Searchers*
94 Ibid.
94 Ibid.
96 Ethan (Wayne) with Debbie the child (Lana Wood), as Martha (Dorothy Jordan) and family look on
101 James Stewart between Lee Marvin and John Wayne in *The Man Who Shot Liberty Valance*
104 *Rio Grande*: Wayne with Maureen O'Hara
106 The final image of *The Searchers*
112 Natalie Wood and Wayne in *The Searchers*
117 A "light meal" in *The Letter*: Herbert Marshall, Bruce Lester, Bette Davis, and James Stephenson
121 Davis in *The Letter*, after the crime
121 *The Letter*: confronting the moon
122 *The Letter*: Davis after the acquittal
128 *Marked Woman*: Davis with Jack Norton and Mayo Methot
133 *Jezebel*: Julie (Davis) and Pres (Henry Fonda) at the ball
136 Davis with George Brent in *Jezebel*

142 *The Little Foxes*: Regina (Davis), with Carl Benton Reid, Patricia Collinge, and Charles Dingle

145 "What a strain it is to be evil": Davis in *The Little Foxes*

150 Charles Laughton as the emperor Nero in *The Sign of the Cross*

154 Laughton with Ella Raines in *The Suspect*

157 Laughton with Robert Mitchum on the set of *The Night of the Hunter*

159 *The Night of the Hunter*: Lillian Gish guards her ward and her home, while Mitchum, beyond the scrim, menaces them.

162 Laughton does comedy in *Ruggles of Red Gap* (with Mary Boland and Charlie Ruggles).

167 Pam Grier in *Jackie Brown*

173 De Niro with costar Gérard Depardieu in Bertolucci's *1900*

180 A mutual delight: De Niro with Liza Minnelli in Scorsese's *New York, New York*

182 Jimmy (De Niro) kisses Francine (Minnelli) good night.

185 "I'm sorry, too," she says: De Niro and Minnelli in *New York, New York*

189 The epic scale and style of Sergio Leone's *Once Upon a Time in America*

197 Elizabeth McGovern as the grown-up Deborah in *Once Upon a Time in America*

199 Noodles (De Niro) watching the departing train in *Once Upon a Time in America*

200 Noodles's final close-up

206 *Nashville*: Barbara Jean (Ronee Blakley) greeting her fans, with Haven Hamilton (Henry Gibson) and Lady Pearl (Barbara Baxley)

208 Linnea (Lily Tomlin) with her son, Jimmy (James Dan Calvert); her daughter (Donna Denton); and her husband, Delbert (Ned Beatty) in *Nashville*

210 *Nashville*: Tom (Keith Carradine) of Tom, Bill and Mary in bed with Mary (Cristina Raines)

213 Linnea (Tomlin) at the Exit Inn as Tom (Carradine) sings to her

213 Ibid.

213 Ibid.

218 Barbara Jean sitting on her hospital bed in *Nashville*

222 *Nashville*: Kenny (David Hayward), PFC Kelly (Scott Glenn), and Opal (Geraldine Chaplin)

224 Barbara Jean singing "My Idaho Home"

231 *Jackie Brown*: Robert De Niro with Bridget Fonda

235 Jackie (Pam Grier) argues with her sometime boss, Ordell (Samuel L. Jackson).

238 Jackie with Ray the Fed (Michael Keaton), who'd like to think he can trust her

241 Jackie approaches Max (Robert Forster).

241 Ibid.

241 Ibid.

243 Jackie and Max together at Jackie's place

245 "Are you scared of me, Max?"

249 *Masculine Feminine*: Madeleine and Paul (Chantal Goya and Jean-Pierre Léaud)

252 Paul (Léaud) is attacked by a man with a knife.

255 Paul and Robert (Michel Debord) at the Laundromat

258 Elisabeth (Marlène Jobert) at center, with Madeleine and Paul

261 Madeleine at the police station

261 Madeleine: Will she smile? She begins to . . .

263 Anne Wiazemsky in *Au hasard Balthazar*

269 Ingrid Bergman as Karin in *Stromboli*

273 Karin's long and awful climb

276 *Europa '51*: Bergman as Irene, with Alexander Knox

278 Irene: "We must change our way of living—we have to . . . !"

281 Irene in the mental hospital, comforting the afflicted

289 *Journey to Italy*: Katherine (Bergman) at the museum

292 *Journey to Italy*: Katherine with Alex (George Sanders)

300 Maria Falconetti as Joan in *The Passion of Joan of Arc*

300 Joan and the fat monk

300 Joan in exaltation

302 Joan and guard

302 Antonin Artaud and fellow monk in *The Passion of Joan of Arc*

302 Joan at the stake

307 *Day of Wrath*: Herlofs Marte (Anna Svierkier) hiding from the witch hunters

309 Lisbeth Movin as Anne in *Day of Wrath*

313 Anne: "But who would wish you dead?"

316 Anne abandoned by her lover

319 *Ordet*: Borgen, the family patriarch, with his sons Mikkel and Anders and his daughter-in-law, Inger

324 Anders (Preben Lerdorff Rye) in *Ordet*

326 Priest (Ove Rud) at Inger's casket

326 Mikkel (Emil Hass Christensen) and his wife, Inger (Birgitte Federspiel), reunited

328 Nina Pens Rode as Gertrud

331 Gertrud at home with her prominent husband

334 Gertrud with Gabriel (Ebbe Rode)

335 Gertrud with Erland (Baard Owe), consenting to be his lover

342 Jacques and Marie (and friend) playing with Balthazar in *Au hasard Balthazar*

345 Gérard (François Lafarge) and his gang in *Au hasard Balthazar*

347 The grain merchant's stable in *Au hasard Balthazar*

349 *Au hasard Balthazar*: Marie (Anne Wiazemsky) and Jacques (Walter Green)

349 Marie kisses Jacques's hand.

353 Marie watches Balthazar in the moonlight while Gérard reaches out from the dark.

353 Ibid.

358 Balthazar's death

PREFACE

"ONE DOES NOT go to see them act," wrote James Baldwin about the great iconic movie stars Wayne and Davis and Bogart, "one goes to watch them *be*" (italics his). Of course. It seems obvious, you think, once he's said it (in *The Devil Finds Work*, 1976). That's what we do at the movies—what we still do. We watch our fellow human beings, but in a special way. The theater actor, however magnetic, however "good" your seat is, is always at an impersonal distance. At the movies, that distance is banished—and for all the seats. The stage star may be real, but the one on the movie screen, who is *not*, feels even realer. Where else besides the movies do you get to see other persons so intimately, so pressingly, so largely even? Where else such intense and close, such sustained and searching *looks* as you have of these strangers on the screen, whoever they really are? In life you try not to stare, but at the movies that's exactly what you get to do, for two hours or more—safely, raptly, even blissfully. The actor in the theater "disappears" into a role, at least ideally; the movie star, never. Just the reverse—even if he is an actor, even if he's a great one. There's always that close-up. "The screen performer is essentially not an actor at all," says Stanley Cavell; instead, "he *is* the subject of study, and a study not his own."

PART ONE

ICONS

1

Garbo

I.

SO WHAT WAS it about Garbo? In her time she evoked more widely felt and declared awe than any movie star ever has, before her or since. She was never the most popular star, at least in the United States (she was too austere for that). She was nevertheless for most people then the definitive one, even for those who had never seen her movies. Her counterparts at the time were not Gish or Gable or Fairbanks but Charlie Chaplin and Mickey Mouse—icons beyond their movies. But where the latter two offered fantasy versions of the commonplace, Garbo—as she came to be seen—offered something that approached sublimity. Not an easy thing to pull off, at least persuasively, not only in a realist medium but in a Hollywood whose truest and most reliable bent was for a cinema of common sense, for the reductive and the comic. She could do the latter, as it later turned out, but only at the end (*Ninotchka*, her next-to-last movie).

She was famously, even pathologically, shy. Where other screen stars would try to make up for the distance between themselves and their fans—giving interviews, making public appearances, telling their carefully prepared "stories"—Garbo only compounded the remove by refusing all publicity. Her celebrity became a kind of public privacy as a result. By the time of her talkies, "I want to be alone" was the line that everyone knew her by—like Mae West's "Come up and see me sometime," or Charles Boyer's "Come with me to the Casbah"—though in fact she had said it for the public record only twice, once to intrusive shipboard reporters and then once as a character in a movie (Boyer never said that Casbah line at all).

Her fame was inseparable from her riddle. A widely circulated photocollage from the mid-1930s showed her face imposed on the Egyptian Sphinx. She had become the most famous woman in the world—and her enigma seemed to haunt it. And no wonder. You take your secret with you when you die, it's said: Garbo seemed to have taken hers—safely enough as it turned out—into the movies.

Camille (1937) was her greatest film and performance, but it was an earlier and lesser movie in which she had her most celebrated and most epiphanic single close-up: in the final shot of 1933's *Queen Christina*. Where the eponymous heroine, having renounced her Swedish throne and then lost the lover she had renounced it for (killed in a duel over her), now gives the orders to the crew of the great ship to set sail nonetheless for the exile in Spain that she had meant to share with him. Now rising from her grief over his body, laid out on the deck by the sailors, she slowly crosses the ship's length, as the men of the crew shout and climb the riggings and the enormous sails rise billowing around her. Until she reaches the prow—and the famous close-up.

It begins as a medium close shot (see preceding illustration), which frames her as she moves into place and stands, resting her elbows on the railing above the figurehead, leaning on her forearms and looking out to sea, her uncovered hair lifting gently in the wind (a mistake: even in old movies you don't normally sail directly into the wind—but never mind). But then the camera tracks slowly in on her, with movie music swelling, to her face in extremest close-up, to her unblinking gaze, which the film holds until the final fadeout.

It was partly the duration of this shot, unusual for the time, even for a Garbo movie, that made it famous. A testament to the power of the Garbo image. But it was something more than that, too . . .

I first saw her on the screen in 1955, twelve years after she had retired from it altogether, in *Camille*, which MGM had rereleased that year with all the fanfare of a first-run movie and to wide acclaim. I remember the crowded theater in Chicago's Loop, a mostly young audience, as new to her probably as I was at the time, and a feeling in the place like revelation: So this is what a movie star is . . . or was, at any rate.

The close-up before the final fadeout (*Queen Christina*)

You first see her in that movie inside a carriage as she lowers her face into a bouquet of camellias, smiling with her eyes at the motherly little flower seller who has just handed it to her with a blessing: "For the lady of the camellias." What strikes you at first is not so much her beauty—which was then legendary—as her brimmingness, her feeling of eager life. It is that, as the movie goes on, which makes the beauty seem ravishing, irresistible. It's a classically "perfect" face, without a single bad angle, according to those who photographed it. But its lack of sensual emphases—the lips are thin, the nose prominent, as far from being pretty as a beautiful face could be—could also make it look plain. Not everyone, even at the time, saw its beauty. Graham Greene, a movie reviewer in the 1930s, imagined his descendants puzzling over it, looking for something more obvious. For Roland Barthes, writing in the fifties ("The Face of Garbo"), its perfection evoked a Platonic heaven, "the Divine Garbo," as she was called, seeming to him more of an ideal of beauty than a sensuous specific of it. That account of it at least might help to explain how she could be so moving in these first *Camille* close shots—descending to us, as it were, just as she "descends," inclining her head, to those flowers.

It was the year after this that I saw *Queen Christina*, in a Harvard

At the beginning of *Camille*: a smile for the flower seller

Square revival house. But I had already heard or read about the final shot. And when I did see it, I had no trouble understanding why it was famous. It was *still* overwhelming. Partly because it was so surprising—by the usual movie standards. Here was the tragic heroine getting her final big close-up—and what was she showing on the screen? None of the things we could have expected from the film we'd just seen—some stage of grief or prayerfulness, of desolation or heroic restitution. But no—instead something like impassivity, refusing the usual emotions, inviting us to do the same. But offering what instead? Blankness?—as her director Rouben Mamoulian later suggested in interviews. He had instructed her to empty her mind.

But Garbo doesn't do vacancy. And Mamoulian's story hardly touches the fact that we cannot help—especially at the end of the movie—but "read" this Garbo-Christina face. Somehow, and however uncertainly. That uncertainty is part of the effect. The real surprise is how exactly and deeply right the effect feels. She has gone beyond the narrative of her film, beyond the movie itself. Where then? To a kind of profound and mysterious acceptance—at the locus of the mystery itself? That she leaves us behind is one of the things that makes it moving. Definitively Garboesque.

"All art," said Walter Pater, "constantly aspires to the condition of music"—to its combination of specificity and abstraction. And similarly, you can say that all movie stardom—even in all its diversity—aspires to Garbo. To her mystery and ambiguity and transcendence—to her near incarnation (closer than anyone else's) of the hieratic visionary power of movies themselves.

II.

IT WAS THE director Mauritz Stiller who found her—and almost immediately christened her Garbo (as opposed to Gustafsson)—when she was just a plump, shy (of course) teenage drama student in Stockholm. He was the one who saw her specialness when it was invisible to everyone else. Stiller was at that time one of the two most revered filmmakers in Swedish silent film (the other was Victor Sjöström) when he cast her in his *The Saga of Gösta Berling* (1924), an epic melodrama based on Selma Lagerlöf's famous novel. It was the girl's performance in this film that persuaded Germany's G. W. Pabst, another first-rate filmmaker (though unlike Stiller, a novice one), to cast her in a leading role (an innocent girl almost lured to prostitution by poverty) in his *The Joyless Street* (1925), about the corruption and malaise of post–World War I Vienna.

And while she was thus occupied in Berlin, accompanied by Stiller, now her full-time mentor and manager, Louis B. Mayer, who had been impressed by *Gösta Berling*, tracked them down there and signed them both to come to Hollywood. There is still some controversy about which of them he really wanted, but for them it was either both of them or neither one.

First to New York, however—as always in those ocean travel days—where they languished in neglect, victims of a studio absent-mindedness that made them look and feel even more like the long shots they surely were. They might even have returned to Berlin if it hadn't been for the German-born photographer Arnold Genthe offering to do some portraits of her and then selling one of the results to *Vanity Fair*—where it appeared in full-page splendor in November 1925. Garbo was then nineteen.

You'd hardly know her from this photo. With frizzy hair and thick eyebrows, she's in extreme soft focus, her outlines blending into the darkness behind, her face with hair swept back thrusting toward us out of the shadows, her rouged lips slightly parted, her hand clasping her throat, her eyes with a drugged, sensual look—at once inward-looking and fronting the storm, both moony and intrepid. And she was elusive even to Genthe. He took several photos of her at this session, "all so different," he said, "that you would hardly know they were the same girl." (Foreshadowings of the elusiveness to come.) At any rate, these photos got the studio's attention once again. And so the two Swedes entrained for the West Coast.

She had been Stiller's property. Now she would be Metro-Goldwyn-Mayer's—even more irrevocably. Stiller himself seems to have alienated almost everybody in the studio from the start. The genius type, as he was quickly seen to be, and a pain in the ass. He couldn't get used to their methods, nor could the studio—especially the studio of Irving Thalberg, as it mostly was—get used to him. (He not only carried on, he did it in Swedish.) She, however, was more malleable. And the audience responses to her first picture, and then to her second one (from which Stiller, at first the director, had been quickly fired), told the studio which Swede they wanted to keep. Stiller left for Paramount, to direct Pola Negri, before returning to Sweden for good.

But they weren't yet sure what they'd got in *her*. Neither of her two European films offered much help: two versions—the Stiller epic-romantic, the Pabst grim-realist—of virginal fragility at risk. But they seem to have seen (the Pabst film gave clues) that she was sexy. And so she is a vamp in her first three American pictures—each one ratcheting up her badness a notch or two. In the first, *The Torrent* (1926), she goes from being a rural innocent (the first twenty minutes) to the "woman whose amours are the talk of all Europe" (the last sixty), having been jilted in the first reel by her hometown sweetheart (Ricardo Cortez). In *The Temptress* (also 1926), her excuse for her abandoned lifestyle is a dissolute unloving first husband who sells her to a millionaire, which is then meant to account for the havoc she wreaks on susceptible males "from Paris to Argentina." And what she does by way of aggressive lovemaking (the top position, the open-mouthed kiss) to the two lumpish leading men in these films (Antonio Moreno in the second) she does even more so to John Gilbert in the third, *Flesh and the*

Arnold Genthe's 1925 photograph: she was nineteen.

Devil (1927). No excuses here: she is simply out of control. Even flirting with blasphemy, kneeling at the communion rail and turning the cup around to savor the place where Gilbert's lips (he is her husband's best friend) had touched before hers—in front of a startled priest.

What was MGM doing to her? Stiller (by then at Paramount) wanted to know in his letter to Mayer. Hadn't the mogul first warmed

to her as the innocent young girl in *Gösta Berling*—wasn't her performance in that character why he had signed her in the first place? But
after her impact on audiences in *Flesh and the Devil*, and the sensation
of the teaming with Gilbert (and their consequent and highly publicized love affair), the studio could hardly suppose they were doing too
much wrong.

But they also had to deal with her growing unhappiness—at having
to play all those "bad women," as she put it, not to mention the scripts
they came in (and for the salary they were paying her). And in her next
movie, again with Gilbert of course, she is still adulterous but more
the reluctant pursued than the pursuer. *Love* (1927), directed by Edmund
Goulding, is a modern-dress reduction of *Anna Karenina* but with a
happy ending (Karenin dies)—except in Europe (she goes under the
train). The film was even more successful at the box office than *Flesh
and the Devil* had been. And never again would Garbo play so unsympathetic a heroine as she had in that earlier film.

She had held out to get Goulding as her director, but now, even
better, she got her compatriot Victor Sjostrom (billed as Seastrom in
Hollywood), and as her costar Lars Hanson, who had played Gösta
Berling in Stiller's film. It was called *The Divine Woman* (1928), and
she is a stage star (Bernhardt was the original idea, soon abandoned)
who gives up her career to marry Hanson's army deserter. It's the only
one of her films that's been lost. And though it sounds unpromising, a
fragment of it that turned up much later in Russia gives another impression: a ten-minute scene between her and Hanson where the soldier comes home on leave and they spend the night is gay and tender
and altogether magical. And *The Mysterious Lady*, which followed,
may represent the height of her youthful beauty and photographic
splendor. (It was during the shooting of this film that Edward Steichen
asked to photograph her between takes—arguably the most ravishing
portraits she ever sat for.) Like the *Divine Woman* fragment, it's
another buoyant performance (at least in the film's early scenes),
though in a more flamboyant mode: she is (it was only a matter of time)
a spy, falling in love with the one she's spying on.

But the talkies were looming; 1928 was nearly the last year a silent
film could be made in Hollywood. And MGM, wanting to get the most
out of their investment before or if she tanked in the talkies—as so
many would do (Gilbert did), especially if they, like her, had foreign

With John Gilbert in *A Woman of Affairs*

accents—rushed her through four films all released in 1929, the last year that silents could be widely marketed, at least domestically. The first was a bowdlerized adaptation of a scandalous novel and play, Michael Arlen's *The Green Hat*, with its daring modern-woman heroine, Iris March. It was a famous role, played by Katherine Cornell on the stage—too famous, however, for the censors. So the movie became A *Woman of Affairs*, the Garbo heroine became Diana Merrick, and her husband's syphilis (the most sensational element in the play) became his habit of committing embezzlement. It's Gilbert again (not as the husband but as the true love she never gets to marry) and director Clarence Brown (*Flesh and the Devil*)—neither of whom does it much good. Still, it was seen, as well as remembered afterward, as a triumph for her.

One could imagine she needed that to get through the next two—both of which subject her image to some domesticating. She is a faithful wife to an older husband in the first one, *Wild Orchids*—besieged throughout by a whip-wielding, eye-flashing Javanese prince (her friend and fellow Swede Nils Asther) who only desists once he gets shot by her husband. In the second one, *The Single Standard*, she is a free-woman type again, flouting convention in an affair with a boxer-poet-yachtsman (Asther again) who then dumps her, prompting her marriage to a decent man who yet requires a massive effort to remain faithful to (she finally succeeds) once the yachtsman returns and wants her back again.

Not that these films, though leadenly directed (by Sidney Franklin and John S. Robertson, respectively), are so much worse than her others—or even much different. But they demonstrate—especially after the others—that emptiness can have a weight. And that weight was beginning to seem like her specialty. "I don't see anything in silly love-making," she said in a rare interview (with *The New York Times*), after she had filmed *Wild Orchids*. A story she'd like to do, she said when asked, was Joan of Arc (she had seen and admired Dreyer's *La Passion de Jeanne d'Arc*). "But it probably wouldn't go so well," she added. She would be scheduled for *The Single Standard* next.

But then—and happily—came *The Kiss* (1929), her final silent. It's a dazzlingly made film by a first-rate director, Jacques Feyder. And though it puts her through familiar paces—a loveless marriage, an adulterous romance—it does so with such brio, with such sheer film-making skill (masterful tracking shots, inspired camera placements, exhilarating successions of high- and low-angle shots), all so far from the slow, relentless plod of most of her other films, that you almost don't feel the familiarity. Even her obligatory suffering (as when she is tried for her goatish husband's murder) is rather briskly gotten through, with an undercurrent of playfulness even that suits her nicely. Especially so in her scenes with the young Lew Ayres, who is not her lover (that's once again the improbable Conrad Nagel) but the one who gives her the eponymous kiss that causes all her trouble.

She is supposed to have said, when an MGM publicity man was urging her to endorse Palmolive soap, "I don't understand English very well. Wouldn't good pictures be enough?" But good pictures were exactly for the most part what she didn't get. And most of these early films of hers are bad enough to raise the question of how such a legendary career—as hers already was—could have come out of them. But then all you have to do to answer that question, so it seems to me, is to look at her in the kind of moments that people at the time would have left the theaters remembering—and would go on remembering long after the mechanical plots and would-be emotions were forgotten. And almost all these movies—and their directors—gave her such moments.

At the opening of *The Temptress* (directed by Fred Niblo, Stiller's replacement) she is a shadowed figure at a masked ball, in the midst of a festive crowd, running to escape an ex-lover, when she is seized and held by the hero. She is wearing the flimsiest of little masks, lacy, nearly transparent, and molded to the face, concealing it hardly at all. But when she removes it to oblige her savior, the impact is real. It's as if she really had been hidden before that, the force of her emerging is so emphatic. "You are beautiful," the hero gasps (in a title card) as she looks up at him, a how-about-*that* glint in her eyes, with the slightest fleeting smile. It's not only that she can show us her beauty—it's almost as if she can conjure it up as we watch her.

Her close-ups become like arias, they can negotiate so many meanings. The ground of all of them, of course—as in the one above—is her extraordinary beauty. In *The Kiss* (after she's broken off with her lover), Feyder fades into an early scene by an extreme close-up of her eyes—looking into ours, it seems for the first instant, until we recognize a mirror gaze: she's looking into her own eyes, coolly appraising, clearly pleased (why not?), looking down (that's enough) at her lips, lifting a fingertip to lighten the rouge, turning her head, even more pleased—as the camera pulls slowly back—and we suddenly see (so suddenly it's almost startling) her unhappiness: a darkening in the eyes, a tightening around the mouth—like a shadow falling and it's gone. As she turns to shake out a powder puff and go on, making dismissive little moues into her image in the hand mirror she's holding. She is giving a party for her husband, and a title card has already told us that she is "Striving To Forget"—as of course she is. But the banal meaning has been nearly transformed by her—and Feyder's—subtlety.

Of course her characteristic mode—it was what bowled over early reviewers—was understatement. Not that she couldn't be over the top at times, especially in her earliest silents—the arm-flapping, eye-rolling tantrum she throws in *Love* when Vronsky has his racing accident, or the even more embarrassing shitfit she flies into when a pious girl prays for her in front of her in *Flesh and the Devil*. But even in much quieter moments—and they multiply almost with each film—she could be too much if she wasn't cautious. Her face was almost haplessly expressive: a frown could feel like a shout-out.

But she had learned more than caution by the time of *The Mysterious Lady*—one of her most beautifully modulated performances, reuniting her with director Fred Niblo of *The Temptress*. She is sitting in an opera box watching a performance of *Tosca* as the hero (Conrad Nagel) enters unnoticed behind her. She is leaning forward toward the stage on her elbow, head in hand, her other arm extended in a long languorous line rightward. An image of both holding on and yielding, she has the look of someone being seriously moved. Then she does something only she would do, I think—as the lights go up and the spell breaks, she recovers and laughs. It's the laugh after great feeling—coming to herself, as it were, resuming her distance, rejoining that inner witness of hers who's been watching her watching all along.

No one—either then or now—seems to talk about her wit. But it's much in evidence here, when she is at the business (spy business) of seducing Nagel's German officer. The lights have gone out in her palatial quarters, and after showing herself to him from behind, as she looks out the window at the night rain, with her sinuous slouching posture, braless (very notably) in her clinging white silk gown, she goes with her taper to light some candles, so they won't be altogether in the dark. She moves in on a candelabra with four candles, and proceeds—very slowly and in several close-ups—to light each one. She knows how he's looking at her (and we can imagine)—we can see that on her face, which is poised in the frame between looking at him and looking at us. You half expect her to wink. Each careful illumination prompting another glance at him, another small sly smile—then a little frown, for the more serious business of lighting this next one. And voilà!—soon she is done, and turning to accept his approval as he comes charging to stand at her side. In close-up, she blows the taper out, in his (and our) direction, so that his burning gaze—in the next close-up—is literally smoking. She leans back, a laughing look now. "Happy?" she asks silently (there is no need for a title for this line). Is he happy?—is he ever! In the next shot she practically has to knock him down to get away from him. But she doesn't send him away. And the next day they go to the country together—a sure sign (as in *Camille* and the countless other such narratives at the time) of the real thing.

But it's not just her close-ups that dazzle you: she uses her whole body with the same witty expressiveness. After their lark in the country, she is standing with her back to us at her ceiling-high window, holding the drape with one hand and waving with the other to say goodbye to Nagel as he drives off. She is unaware of the uniformed

Between Conrad Nagel and a candelabra in *The Mysterious Lady*

and rather nasty-looking man (another spy) in the room—presumably there to recall her to her duties. As she waves out the window she stands with pelvis thrust forward, then pulls it in as the car departs (it's like a visualized sigh), her hand falling from the drape onto her hair and then to her hip as she turns to see her visitor, settling into an almost challenging stance, one hip cocked, the other clasped in a firmly placed hand. It's one long sinuous line, and you follow it almost with suspense to its conclusion (you almost want to applaud when it gets there). Especially when you notice that Tania (her spy name), in spite of her impressive control, is breathing quickly. And it's all there: *I love him and what can you do about it?* Except that that cliché formulation leaves out the grace of its unfolding, and the complication she leaves you with (her defiance is closer to wariness, and not unfriendly).

In *A Woman of Affairs*, a movie where everything is more serious (though no less incredible), she appears at another window—an ordinary hotel one—and we look at her front-on. Her young husband (Johnny Mack Brown) has committed suicide from the same window, and she has been confronted not only by the police but by his family survivors, who blame it all on her (here, she is a *fake* bad woman). When she looks toward John Gilbert, her real love, who should know better, and whose blustering father is her chief accuser, he only turns away, to follow his domineering parent out the door, leaving her behind in a close shot . . . and it's one of those moments she gives you when you can feel as if you're looking at the most grown-up person in the world. Her look after him is stricken but clear-eyed, devastated but honestly not all that surprised, as the small smile tells you.

And she goes to the window, first with her sidelong gaze, then in person—standing in it, settling on her hips, raising her arms with their trailing black sleeves, and propping herself with her hands in the frame, in order to look down, first with her eyes, and then with her head slowly dropping downward—to fadeout. This, too, is one pure continuous line, though the mode is more outsize, more glaringly theatrical—but done with such intentness and dignity, such inwardness, that it's transformed, from the banality of both its style and its "point" (a foreshadowing of her own suicide). She could do that.

But in this film it's "the scene with the flowers" that people remember more than any other. Her character lies near death in an alpine

A Woman of Affairs: a still from the scene with the flowers (with Lewis Stone)

hospital, tended by the inevitable nun in lip rouge and Lewis Stone as her doctor. Gilbert has arrived, but with his new bride. In the meantime he has sent Garbo a lush bouquet, which sits by her bed as she sleeps. Stone orders it removed and goes out to greet the Gilberts. They have gathered in the waiting room, the gift of flowers now prominently placed in a vase on a table at its center.

When suddenly into the corridor she comes out of her room—bursts out, really, staggering and holding her head, riven with confusion and distress: Where are they? She comes forward, fevered and delirious, sees them on the table, and comes down the long hallway toward them, stretching her arms out. Then, reaching them, like a desperate swimmer reaching shore—taking them in with her eyes, then with her arms, lifting them out of the vase, rocking backward with the contact, shutting her eyes and burying her face, then drawing back and gazing at them. Anxiety again: Hadn't she *lost* them, almost? But now they are here, as she touches and parts them again, hovering and then sinking into them again, tearful and laughing. "You are all I care about," she says in a title card. But then *he* is here, too, as it turns out. Oh— . . . She refocuses—it takes her a moment—hands the flowers off and goes to him, eagerly. (Until she's reminded of the wife, also standing nearby.)

All that—about flowers? It's almost as if *Gilbert* had become the metaphor, instead of them. The whole episode feels perilously over the top—and you see where and how far it's going almost as soon as she bursts out of that sickroom. And yet she carries you along to the end, with the anguish on her face, the animal intentness of her walk down the hall, the sensual relief and release when she reaches and claims this luxuriance they almost stole from her. Elia Kazan once described Marlon Brando as a kind of genius animal. And the description seems to fit Garbo, too—"the screen's great instinctual artist," as Pauline Kael called her. Except that at her greatest she has a generalizing power that exceeds even Brando's, it seems to me—the way that her sensuality shades into self-transcendence. As here, with these flowers— she seems to be registering the poignance of creation itself.

Did they really want her to talk—*too*? No one was too sure, in fact. Both she and the studio delayed the inevitable event as long as they could. Even her fans were nervous, it seemed. The box office returns made her final silent, *The Kiss*—filmed and released well after most U.S. pictures were talking—into her biggest hit since *Love*, three years before.

III.

BUT HER VOICE recorded on film—a plangent contralto, as expressive as her face—was everything they could have wanted. Her shrewdly chosen first talkie was a mostly faithful version of Eugene O'Neill's *Anna Christie* (1930). And her famous opening lines, spoken to a waterfront bartender—"Gimme a whiskey, ginger ale on the side, and

As Anna Christie—just off the street and needing a drink badly

don't be stingy, baby"—felt genuinely thrilling at the time: *that* was "talking" and then some. And her performance, as a Swedish American whore reunited with her runaway father and falling in love with an Irish sailor, both of them ignorant of her past, was greeted as an unqualified triumph.

In her next talking film (the only one she couldn't bear to sit through when they screened it for her at MOMA many years later), *Romance* (1930), she is an Italian opera singer whose attempt to seduce an English clergyman (the preposterous Gavin Gordon—his first and last leading man role) ends in her refusing him when he finally succumbs to her, all because of the newly virtuous woman he has turned her into by then ("My heart will always go with you, if you will only let me keep my soul").

The contrast between these, her first two talkies—both lamely directed by Clarence Brown—was of course designed. In spite of the popular success of *Anna Christie*, there was a felt danger in having the "new" and speaking Garbo become identified with such naturalist drabness. *Romance*, on the other hand, gave her Adrian's most sumptuous turn-of-the-century outfits to wear, some Big Moments in them in front of ornamental fireplaces, an "Italian" version of her Swedish accent, and not a single true or less than ludicrous moment, let alone a privileged one. It was far less popular than *Anna Christie* had been—which it followed into movie houses only a few months later—and it was curiously underpublicized. But it made its point.

And given the success she had made in the original, the studio decided to remake *Anna Christie* for the German market next—filming on the same sets with the same photographer (William Daniels, as nearly always with her) and many of the same camera setups, but with a different (German-speaking) cast and director, Jacques Feyder of *The Kiss*. Who would once again do well by her. (For the final time, unhappily—he would soon go the way of Stiller and Sjostrom and other of her friends before them: back to Europe to stay.)

She is more at ease in German, it seems, and her Anna this time has a gathering power the first one never quite finds—the character's exasperation rising into anguish over the two thick men, father and lover, who she knows in spite of her bravado hold her fate in their hands. Her baffled rage and sorrow at this almost leap off the screen.

The English-speaking Anna, on the other hand, had been a much softer sort, frailer and more damaged from the start. When she said "Don't be stingy, baby" to her bartender, it was with a plaintive inflection that would touch the whole performance. The German version eliminates the line and the plaintiveness: from her first entrance, this Anna is tougher, tartier—a more realistic version of a young but experienced streetwalker (she wears a more blatant getup as well, still by Adrian, by now as inevitable as Daniels her cinematographer was). But she is also, paradoxically, a marginally better-natured Anna— less prone in scenes with her delinquent old man to seem simply grudging or aggrieved. And she is more openly tender in their moments of rapprochement, which now become more genuinely touching as a result.

Partly because Feyder stages and directs them better, his framings and rhythms give the emotional currents more clarity, the conventional sentiments more conviction. Not to mention the relation of Anna to her sailor suitor, Matt—thanks to Hans Junkermann, who plays him, and who really seems hot for her (and she for him). Unlike the stentorian Charles Bickford in the earlier film, who performs the role with her at times as if he were practicing it in another room.

But it was the plush hokum of *Romance*, not the grim surface realism of *Anna Christie*, that signaled her future in MGM talkies. They put her back into vamping again. On the *Camille* model: regretting her lifestyle almost as soon as she meets (and, it's implied, deflowers) the virginal boy-man who is attracted to her—the pious clergyman in *Romance*, the stuffed shirt in *Inspirations* (1931), the gallant flyer in *Mata Hari* (1932). But when she was paired, to huge box office effect, with the more manly than boyish young Clark Gable—in *Susan Lenox (Her Fall and Rise)* (1931)—the pattern was slightly altered. He is the experienced one, launching Garbo's virginal farm girl on a course that takes her from homelessness to cooch dancing in a carnival to her name in Broadway lights (a quick montage) to a Park Avenue penthouse to a low dive in the tropics, all in her oblique pursuit of Rodney (Gable's most unfortunate character name), who turns up in each episode to reprove her for her newest career choice. Yet even in that sleazy off-the-map saloon she still sustains some options. Like the millionaire (John Halliday) who keeps hoping she'll visit his nearby yacht. "I'm not interested in yachts," she tells him. "You know," he says, "I'm beginning to believe you." If only Rodney would. In each of her films from *Anna Christie* on she has at least one big scene in which she has to reassure the hero that all those other men—even if they were "half the men in Paris," as in *Inspiration* ("and the other half are trying to forget her")—meant nothing before him.

Her voice may have enhanced her allure, but the words she was given to say rarely seemed to. And in those early talkies, actors were expected to talk a lot—in front of the newly immobile cameras. Long speeches like the climactic one she makes to Gable's Rodney, explaining to him (and to us) why the two of them should finally get together: "The hurt that we've inflicted upon one another became a bond, nothing

Susan Lenox (Her Fall and Rise): with Clark Gable

can break it. Just like two cripples, twisted—only together we can become straight," and so on. ("You have a queer way of looking at things," Gable replies.) And her discontent with her films was already something of a legend. While shooting *Inspiration*, a fan magazine reported, she refused to learn the lines she especially disliked ahead of time—requiring them to be given to her on the set when she got there—though always on time, they conceded.

"I tank I go home now," she supposedly said to her studio bosses at one point. Who took it calmly until they realized she meant Sweden. So the popular story went. And the line itself with its vaudeville dialect became as commonplace a way for the radio comics to evoke her as the ubiquitous "I vant to be alone." To most observers her discontent with the studio seemed warranted. Her reviews were still often rapturous, but almost never for her movies. "She never grows tiresome even in tiresome roles," wrote *The Nation*'s critic Margaret Marshall, "probably because unlike most of her rivals she has personality and intelligence as well as physical beauty."

But after the dreadful *Susan Lenox*, her next film, *Mata Hari* (1932), comes almost as a relief. As it may have done for her, too. A movie where the absurdity, at least for its first two-thirds, is flagrant and unapologetic, from her first appearance in it—as a celebrated exotic dancer (like the historical Mata) performing on a stage before "the god Shiva," a multiarmed golden idol, which she slowly advances upon, treading heavily forward, arms angled as if for flight, festooned with transparent veils and wearing a triple-tiered pagoda on her head (her pelvic grinds were done in long shots by a double). She seems, in fact, here and elsewhere, to be enjoying herself. And why not? For one thing (among many), she gets to mistreat Lionel Barrymore at his most querulous and repellent, as a thwarted lover—dodging his attempt at embrace with a little hand-pat to his uniformed chest and a saunter away: "I must help you to give me up," she says merrily.

But the fun is over, more or less, once the unlikely leading man, Ramon Novarro, gets permanently blinded in a plane crash. Mata is reunited with him—in front of the obligatory weeping nun—at his bedside hospital. When he is well again and the war is over, she tells him, they will see the world together. But he can't see, he reminds her, in his plaintive voice (much higher than hers). "*Here* are your eyes!" she exclaims, lifting the back of his hand to her own and pressing it into them. It became one of her most famous lines. And it manages—even near the end of this by now quite creepy movie—to be almost moving.

Okay—that's impressive. But you still have to feel—and more and more with each film—something like: What is she *doing* in this shit? Her authenticity at unexpected moments makes the surrounding falsity feel all the more oppressive, makes you resent all the more that she is serving such meretriciousness. She had a gift, her three-time costar Melvyn Douglas would later observe, for making the flattest banality sound like the profoundest truth. That was a gift, of course, that came to her with sound (you never quite blamed her for those titles between the visuals in her silents). But it was turning out to be a gift of doubtful value—both for her and for us.

Mata Hari was a huge success, of course—her biggest hit to date—but her next one was an even bigger hit, and one of her rare good films—and by her first good director since Feyder: Edmund Goulding (his second film with her—he'd also done *Love*, among her better silents). It was *Grand Hotel* (1932).

Poor as her talking pictures may have been up to then, in fact and by reputation, they were still building the legend. And in this Goulding film, she both plays the legend and confirms it by her performance as Grusinskaya the prima ballerina, like her a great and famous single-name artist—who wants to be alone. Or so she says—having bolted off the stage (we are told) in the middle of a performance and returned to her hotel, where her room is filled with people so alarmed about her disappearance that they at first don't see her standing right there, leaning against the open doorway, still in her Swan Queen costume. "I just want to be alone," she says.

The movie itself was a new thing in 1932: a multistar picture with seven names above the title. Garbo's at the top, of course—above Wallace Beery, Joan Crawford, and John and Lionel Barrymore. In a plot (from a Vicki Baum novel) of intersecting stories, all set in the great Berlin hotel. It was a characteristic MGM invention, the studio that specialized in "grand" moviemaking, in a certain kind of big movie experience, with the biggest stars—of whom Garbo was then the most resplendent. And Metro was the studio that had not only "created" her but sustained her unique prestige. Where another studio might have given her better pictures and directors (Lubitsch at Paramount, George Stevens at RKO), only MGM could give her a *Grand Hotel*.

A film she dominates, as reviewers said, without even being in most of it—in hardly thirty minutes of its two-hour running time. You wait twenty minutes before she even appears. And when she finally does, it's a moment so close to self-parody that it's a shock. Roused from her sleepless preperformance nap by her maid, she rises into a close-up, intoning the words: "I think, Suzette, I have never been so tired in my life." It's a glamour shot, as her close-ups usually are—artfully shadowed and molded and intense—but forbidding. It's the familiar Garbo mask of tragedy—the arched brows, lined forehead, drooping eyelids, sagging mouth—but at such a Kabuki-like extreme of dejection

Grand Hotel: the Garbo mask

and gloom that it's startling, almost like a challenge, the exaggeration all but daring you to scoff or to pull away. As it turns out, it's a marker laid down for the rest of the performance—as it goes on . . .

Almost embarrassingly at first. Now she rises and stands, doing an unconvincing little stretch at a chair (her ballerina impersonation), and then falls into gloom again: "So threadbare!" she growls, whipping around into another tight frontal shot—which holds on her as she recites a list of generic memories, with intensest feeling, and a pause between each portentous item: "Saint Petersburg . . . Imperial Court . . . Grand Duke Sergei . . ." And then with a break in her voice: "Sergei!" And finally, and direst of all, with a terrible grimace: "Grusinskaya . . .'S all gone . . ."

It doesn't work, of course. But those pauses, clumsy as they are, between the accumulating clichés—more like silent film titles than movie dialogue—are something like a foretaste of what Goulding will give her throughout the movie: space, both emotional and temporal, returning her to some of the freedoms of her best silent film work, restoring her powerful intimacy with the camera. Garbo's movie-star bigness in this film, her stylized intensity, whether in despair or in ecstasy (she will do both), takes some getting used to at first. But as in that scene with the flowers, she overcomes your resistance. Her acting is not "realism" but it's certainly not falsity.

When John Barrymore, as a disgraced aristocrat with criminal connections and gambling debts both, slips into her room to steal her pearls and finds instead that she is there herself (it's the night she fled the theater) and on the verge of a suicide attempt (the pills in the palm of her hand), he steps out from the shadows to save her. But what is he doing in her room? He invents a story: he comes when she is at the theater just to be near her somehow, to breathe her air. But now that he's found her in such a desperate state— Before he can finish, she begins to cry. "I was so alone," she says, "and suddenly you are here." But who is he? "I'm a man who could love you," he replies—she is so beautiful.

And as he pleads with her, in an extended and intimate two-shot, she turns her face away, her eyes filling with tears, listening to his words at her ear as if they were coming from far away at first, but then gradually coming nearer. His voice is kind—telling her how beautiful she is, with her life ahead of her, how she must forget and how she mustn't cry. Gradually her eyes brighten behind the tears, and you can even see an it-might-be-fun thought passing through her mind amid the fearfulness and confusion she's struggling with. Then she turns to look at him, with a melting smile. Above all, he is saying, you mustn't be alone tonight. "Let me stay," he says, "just for a little while. *Please* let me stay." "Well," she says, slowly giving way, "just for a minute, then." And he kisses her hand in joy and relief—though on her face, looking down at the back of his head, now, we see the fearfulness return. Fadeout.

(In Goulding's next MGM movie, *Blondie of the Follies*, just two months later, the director would do a very funny parody of this same scene, with Marion Davies—an accomplished mimic—and Jimmy Durante as the couple: "Please let me stay," implores Durante-as-Barrymore encircling Davies-Garbo in a clinch. "Well," she replies, after a hesitation, "just for a week, then." Prompting Durante to turn to the camera: "What a mama!" he says, rolling his eyes at us.)

She doesn't even know his name, she says the next morning—the postcoital scene—with a full and half-delighted registering of Just How That Must Sound. It's Baron Felix von Gaigern, he says, but his mother (an inevitable interest to Garbo about all her movie lovers) called him Flix. "No," she says crooningly. "Flix," she repeats, touching the side of his face, curling her voice around the word, proprietarily. He rests his head in her hand and she strokes his hair as he goes on to describe his black-sheep boyhood, all to her unflagging delight. "Garbo alone can be intoxicated by innocence," as Kenneth Tynan wrote—and she can even persuade us for a moment to see it in John Barrymore.

Until he gets to his black-sheep maturity—and returns the pearls he had meant to steal. Heartsick and angry, she throws them on the floor, and he must plead with her again. Again she is facing front as he does so, and we see the slow provisional relenting on her face, first firmly turned away from him, then turning, still troubled, to look at him again. With a slight bodily start (there he is again!) all her resistance to him leaves her. "Flix!" she says again, with infinite sweetness, and puts her hand on the back of his head, drawing him to her mouth for a kiss.

Before he leaves they make excited plans to leave together, to meet the next morning on the train to Vienna. Yet almost as soon as he's gone from the room she wants to speak to him again. And she goes to the elegantly attenuated black telephone we've seen her use before— and when she talks into it you feel, not for the first time in this film, that she has never *sounded* more beautiful—the voice itself like a caress. "Would you give me Baron von Gaigern please?" Pause—and she repeats the beloved name, lingeringly, accenting the long *o* in Baron: "Yes . . . Baron von Gaigern . . ." Then waiting . . . then there he is again, again there's the simple surprise of him: "Cheri, it's you . . . No, nothing . . . Good morning, good morning!" Then with a loving, poignant little break in her voice, her shoulders curling forward over this magical phone she has: "No-oo . . . Just to tell you . . . I'm happy . . ."

But except for a hurried goodbye before she goes to the theater that night, she will never see him again. There will be another phone call to his room, which he *won't* answer (he's been killed by Wallace Beery) before she departs the hotel (which provides a discreet hearse at the alley door for removal of the remains), all unawares, and going to "their" train. So that we never see her registering her final loss. Though in a sense we already have. Garbo's rhapsodic mode, even, or even especially, at its most intense, belongs to someone who remembers—and who will never not remember—desolation. It's what makes even her happiness a little harrowing.

But it's the happiness you remember best from *Grand Hotel*. Was anyone on the screen ever more radiant with it than Garbo is here—more exalted by tenderness? As in those close-ups? As the critic Charles Affron says, "No lover ever sees Garbo's beauty as the camera does." Her Grusinskaya is Garbo in her ecstatic-romantic mode—the Garbo with the flowers. But it was the last time she would commit herself so fully to that mode. She would later call her *Grand Hotel* work overacting. But then of course she had no very high opinion of any of her movie work ("I am not proud to be an actress"). Except for *Camille*.

Grand Hotel marked the peak of her American popularity—as well as the end of her MGM contract. So she finally went back to Sweden, as she had so long been threatening to do. But by that time she had finally given in and signed with the studio again. Something that was kept secret so that Metro could exploit the suspense while she was away and then proclaim her triumphant return for her next big movie—over which she had contractually secured, as it would turn out, an unprecedented degree of control of almost every aspect, including her director. No house hack like George Fitzmaurice (*As You Desire Me*) or Robert Z. Leonard (*Susan Lenox*). She wanted Lubitsch—if not him, Goulding. They were both unavailable. She then agreed to Rouben Mamoulian—classy enough (some well-reviewed earlier talkies like *Applause* and *City Streets*), even sort of arty (a distinguished theatrical career).

In *Queen Christina* (1933), as the androgynous seventeenth-century Swedish monarch, she gets to do a lot of new things—wear trousers and be taken for a boy, quell rebellious mobs and make speeches to her court, kiss another woman on the lips (her lady-in-waiting), ascend a throne and wear a crown and then remove it herself and step down, talk yearningly of her plans for world peace and universal justice. She also makes love, of course—after it's discovered that she's *not* a boy, when her improbable success at passing for one lands her in a room for the night with a male stranger: John Gilbert as the Spanish ambassador, and soon the one true love of her life (and her reason for taking that crown off). The most famous sequence in the film—other than the final close-up—is the postcoital one at the inn, a set piece to movie music as she slowly and silently, with her lover watching, goes about touching the various objects in the room they've spent the night together in—an icon, a spinning wheel, a bedpost, most notably a pillow—to fix each one in her memory. From now on, she says (the loneliness of rule), "I shall live a great deal in this room."

It's a Garbo "number"—virtually equivalent to that song she never sang for us. Both daring and sort of overwhelming—a demonstration of her ability to make meaning before your eyes, to invest it in objects and her relation to them. And to be powerfully sexy—as when she rests her face on that pillow and looks up at him, in extreme voluptuous close-up. Kenneth Tynan famously observed, "What when drunk one sees in other women, one sees in Garbo sober."

In a way it's her apotheosis movie—unlike *Grand Hotel*, it's all Garbo all the time. As was intended. All the 1933 ads and promotions blazoned *Garbo* (Greta is dropped), her name above the movie title and three times its size. In Times Square her image above the movie house marquee was a block long, under the words "She Returns!" And she had had almost her own way this time. Not the "bad woman" formula she detested, but a role that reflected not only her own regnancy but her well-known problems with it: a reluctant monarch—even foretelling her eventual abdication. And it made more money than any Garbo film ever had—a fact that MGM kept secret, particularly from her, in their unending struggle to control her.

But on the whole, unhappily, it's a dead thing—with its waxworks figures and performances, the funeral parlor chic of its sets and production, the leaden pacing (never a Mamoulian strength) and the dreadful writing ("Tonight I'm not a queen. Just a woman in a man's arms"). Even the contemporary reviews, which mostly praised it (she's wonderful again and even more so, etcetera), showed a certain queasiness: one of them even called it "clammy." Nor was she herself finally that pleased with it, it seemed—but whenever was she? It was considered a triumph for her—justly, if only for that final on-ship close-up. But the film itself looked and felt like a kind of embalming. An effect that touches even that famous scene after lovemaking.

Laurence Olivier, in his autobiography *Confessions of an Actor*, tells of his encounter with her when he was a new young movie actor in Hollywood. He was up for the Spanish ambassador role opposite her

Queen Christina: "I shall live a great deal in this room . . ."
By their bedpost—then (*below*) on their pillow

then, and was frankly scared of her. Seeing her alone on the set one day, he resolved to sit down beside her and talk. But after running out of his prepared remarks—and with no help from her silence—he began to babble, subjects ranging from (as he remembered) Will Rogers to Noël Coward. All to no response. "Oh, well," she said at last, "life's a pain anyway . . ."

Okay. But the Garbo mask of suffering on the screen—the down-turned mouth and stricken eyes—could be felt as a pain, too. Especially as she got more regal and less sexy. *Christina*, though a hit, had been more profitable abroad than in the United States. An ominous sign for the rest of her career, with war in Europe looming.

Almost equally ominous for her was the screwball comedy craze, with all its energy and irreverence, which began mid-decade, in films by Frank Capra and Howard Hawks, among others—the same year her next ponderous film would come out, *The Painted Veil* (1934), directed by Richard Boleslawski (a Stanislavskyite émigré from the Russian theater) and based on a Somerset Maugham novel, in which she marries doctor-idealist Herbert Marshall, then gets it on with playboy-cocksman George Brent. To her regret when he dumps her, leaving her behind in the tropics with an angry husband and a cholera plague. But Garbo is too large a presence for the realist register of discontent and frustration the role asks her to play in. (Also possibly too close to it personally.) And her trying to scale herself down to it only makes it more tiresome. (The realist actor Naomi Watts, in the 2006 remake, gets it exactly right, I think.) The saintliness the character attains by the end seems equally effortful, as she tends plague victims by the side of her even more saintly husband, not at all helped in these scenes by the churchy framing and lighting of her close-ups, nor by the white nun-like nurse's cowl she wears in them.

Her next, *Anna Karenina* (1935), was a big improvement, as appropriate to her legend and mystique as *Christina* had been. She'd already done the silent version with Gilbert of course, *Love* in 1927. But whereas that one was trashy and sexy (right after *Flesh and the Devil*), this was serious, David O. Selznick style (he was at Metro then, under his father-in-law, Louis B. Mayer). And in the movie's early scenes she is freshly wonderful again: in her genial seeress mode, among the troubled souls of her brother Stiva's large family when she first visits them in Moscow—or in her fatalist one, just after Karenin (Basil Rathbone),

Anna Karenina: at the ball with Vronsky (Fredric March); at home
with Karenin (Basil Rathbone)

his suspicions aroused, forbids her to see Vronsky again. "Too late," she says aloud, alone in front of her vanity, registering the sickening finality of what's already happened, and the likely road ahead of it.

It's a delicate and understated performance—as far away from the theatricalism of her Grusinskaya as she had yet gone. But the movie—although a spectacularly produced one—is another dead weight for her to carry. And yet almost the worst thing it does to her is Fredric March's Vronsky, with the actor giving one of his most irritable and reluctant (seemingly) young-hero performances. It's nearly her hollowest onscreen romance (she didn't like him offscreen, either: one of the stories had her putting a garlic clove in her mouth before the love scenes), and the movie never recovers from it. Nor from its own idle-seeming stateliness (director Clarence Brown again).

IV.

BUT THEN CAME *Camille* in 1937, and it was, by common agreement, beyond any Garbo experience so far. "Seeing her here," wrote Otis Ferguson in *The New Republic*, "one realizes that this is more than there are words for, that it is simply the most absolutely beautiful thing of a generation." And there was a lot more like this in most of the notices. (Not enough to get her an Academy Award, however.)

Irving Thalberg, the film's producer, and the main architect of her MGM career, saw it right away. She's never been quite like this before, he said, she's never been so good—as he watched the first rushes with the movie's director, George Cukor. But how could he tell? asked Cukor (as he would later recount)—"she's just sitting there." Thalberg's answer to this was that she was "unguarded," more than she had ever been. (Thalberg died just weeks later, at thirty-seven—it was the only big public funeral Garbo was ever known to attend.) And it's true: it's almost a new Garbo, relaxed into her role from the beginning with a freedom we have never quite felt in her before (compare her first appearance in *Grand Hotel*). Besieged as that freedom quickly is in the film, first by Prudence in the carriage (Laura Hope Crews—the "Aunt Pittypat" of *Gone With the Wind*), then at the theater by their fellow courtesan Olympe (Lenore Ulric), the one fussing at her about money, the other about men. Where Prudence is avaricious, Olympe is jealous

Marguerite sighting (she thinks) "the rich Baron de Varville." Her "friends"
Olympe (left) and Prudence (center) are helping.

and spiteful—and they are both noisy and quarrelsome, with Garbo's
Marguerite caught between them, laughing resignedly, but saying finally, "You really are a fool, Olympe," in simple sad acknowledgment.

The theater is an ornate Belle Époque music hall. It has gypsy
dancers on the stage and formally dressed gentlemen on the prowl in
the lobby. Garbo's Marguerite passes through it all at first, obliquely
but surely, a lovely leaning diagonal among the upright top-hatted men
and the pillow-shaped overdressed women—and then regards it gravely
from the top of a staircase (a private moment). Next you see her on
display in her box, seeming very gay—she is a pro, after all. And beyond that she has this deeply *humorous* presence, sitting there, biding

her time. Even her relation to her own finery—fingering the fur on her wrap, tapping her necklace with a fingernail, playing idly with her jeweled opera glasses—feels amused. This is the scene that Thalberg saw—and it's wonderful.

Prudence, now seated beside her, is pointing out to her the very rich Baron de Varbille (Henry Daniell) in the seats below them just at the moment when Marguerite is focusing her opera glass on the improbably handsome Armand Duval (Robert Taylor). "I didn't know that rich men ever looked like that," she says gutturally, lowering the binoculars and her voice at the same time. A lascivious sound.

Out in the lobby at the entr'acte, having turned to make sure that the young man has seen and followed her, she looks at him invitingly, head back, eyes widening, eyebrows arching: a *well-why-not?* look and smile, the most enchanting invitation you could imagine, reckless and gay. But as often with her at such moments, the enchantment has a surprising depth: a powerful benignity, a largesse of spirit that seems Garbo's alone. (It makes your own heart pound.)

They seem almost fated to meet, she says to him—sliding her arm into his and returning with him to her box. Inside, she steps away and leans back to look at him up and down—savoring her catch—then sits. He sits next to her. He tells her that he has been hoping for this meeting for a long time, adding: "You don't believe me?" "No," she says, looking straight ahead and laughing softly: she doesn't believe it, but she doesn't mind hearing it. Since he first laid eyes on her four months ago he's been following her around Paris, he tells her, and proceeds to give details of his sightings. But if all that is true, she says—beginning to be impressed—why hasn't he spoken to her before this? Because before this we hadn't met, he says—as she turns now to look at him. "And you hadn't smiled at me until now," he adds. "And now? Since you've met me?" she says, turning away again, with a smile that looks more like a wince (the kid's an innocent—what must he *really* think of her?). "Now I *know* that I love you," he answers gravely, "and have loved you since that first day." She turns to look at him again, with wonder—into his eyes, then above them, her gaze traveling over and around the face. That observing ironic distance of hers—something she somehow maintains through each encounter with others—seems to have been breached.

But then Prudence returns to the box and the confusion of identities

At the entr'acte: her *well-why-not?* look—and he joins her.

is cleared up: he is not the Baron. But stay, says Marguerite tenderly, to the mortified (and far from rich) Armand, "even if you're not the rich Baron." She is not sorry for the mistake, she says. But when he goes out before the curtain to buy her "some marrons glacés," the rich Baron enters and she goes off with him. When Armand returns, the box is empty. She has to live, after all (we've already heard about her bills).

"I'm not always sincere," she tells Armand in this same sequence—regretfully. "One can't be in this world, you know." But what she calls "insincerity" is really another name for her triumphant (as we register it here) worldliness, her social brilliance. She has fun with this skill in action, and so do we. But even "just sitting there" she seems remark-able enough. Her Marguerite is a virtuoso turn but not a diva one. Rather than overwhelming or overbearing you, she keeps her usual and essential distance. And her character becomes like those people in Shakespeare that Harold Bloom especially celebrates, the "heroic vitalists," as he calls them, the ones like Falstaff and Cleopatra, who are not larger than life but "life's largeness" itself. Like them, Garbo's Marguerite finally transcends even her own story. And within it, she comprehends everyone else: she simply *knows* more than anyone else, and knows *them* better than any of them (Armand included) could ever know her. And she is alive with this comprehension, making you feel that much more alive as you watch her.

When she encounters Armand again, it is after one of her long ill-nesses in bed. She is at an estate auction of another once high-living Paris courtesan (she wants to bid to keep Olympe from hiring—and inevitably abusing—the late woman's elderly coachman). Armand is there, too—and she finds out that he is the unnamed man who kept calling and leaving flowers for her while she was sick. And she offers him one of her little arias of feminine inconsequence, inviting him to the party the following night at her place. "It's my birthday," she says, covering her mouth with her kerchief, looking stricken-eyed at him. But his seriousness keeps intruding. As when he now makes her a pointed present of a leather-bound volume, *Manon Lescaut*, warning her that the story ("about a woman who lives only for pleasure") is a sad one: the heroine dies. "Then I'll keep it," she says, taking the book, "but I won't read it," adding, "I hate sad thoughts"—kittenish now. But then another thought comes: "However" (a beat) "we all die," she says, looking up at him brightly—he'd better know that any subject can provide her with a stage to be dazzling on. Though this one gets slightly out of her control with her next words: "But perhaps someday this book" (holding it and looking at it) "will be sold again at an auction after *my* death . . ." Armand is disturbed by this. "I thought you didn't like sad thoughts," he says. "I don't," she replies, brightening again, squeezing his forearm, and twinkling up at him, "but they come sometimes." And off she goes. She can handle *him*, all right—it's quite clear.

But at the birthday party, that's not so clear. Here—instead of the airhead Manon imitation we've just been watching—she seems truly like a girl, young and a little silly. Can those locks of Shirley Temple curls be meant to encourage that idea? In any case they suit her, however surprisingly. As does her alarmingly low-cut huge-skirted white party gown, exposing her beautiful eloquent shoulders more nakedly than ever. "I want to hear the joke!" she cries pettishly, at the head of her birthday table, when a dirty story starts to circulate around it behind cupped hands, greeted with whoops and howls of laughter, especially from the women, and disapproved of by Armand, who is seated next to her. Not, he says, that he doesn't know all the stories himself (Marguerite rolls her eyes at the others)—"In fact I told Gaston most of them," he adds, with an embarrassing lack of conviction. Then, lowering his voice: "But I'd rather they weren't told at your table." Now she seems embarrassed. "Oh come, come," she says softly. "You must remember"—lifting her glass to him—"I'm not a colonel's daughter just out of the convent." No indeed. But this concession to his decorum, with that curious toasting gesture, is touching.

But she is overexerting. And Armand seems the only one at her party who notices that she is, when she leaves the room where she has been dancing boisterously with Gaston (Rex O'Malley), coughing into the handkerchief she seems always to have clutched in her hand, and goes through the jolly crowd out of the light and into her darkened bedroom alone, where there is an Empire couch with two candles burning at its head, like a bier. She sinks onto the couch, into the darkness, the candlelight gleaming off her shoulders and hair, as she falls backward with open mouth to breathe, then sitting up again, bending forward, over and into that billowing white skirt, to reach for one of the candles, rising with it and going off right to her dressing table mirror. It's one slowly flowing movement—her long legato line, what Cukor called her plastique—both beautiful and disturbing.

But never mind: she's in front of her mirror now, darkness behind her, popping another pill from her little tin, sucking on it and pinning what looks (and sounds) like a paper flower to the top of her hair, and appearing, for the first time in the film, sort of tarty, even tough (coughing is hard). When Armand comes silently in behind her, she looks at him in her mirror. "You look ill too," she says. He tells her she is killing herself. "If I am," she replies, "you're the only one who objects." And when she gives him her hand to return to the party, he stands still in the shadows, lifts it to his mouth, and kisses it. "What a child you are," she says—seeming quite detached from what he is doing with the hand, sucking on her lozenge and observing him speculatively. "Your hand is so hot," he says, holding on to it. She comes closer, her tone is kinder: "Is that why you put tears on it? To cool it?" she asks playfully. But he doesn't want to be talked to this way, he wants her to take him seriously. Besides, somebody should be looking after her: "And I could if you'd let me," he says. This tears it. She draws away from him. "Too much wine," she says coldly, "has made you sentimental."

She, on the other hand, is *not* sentimental—she is not even romantic. Her "insincerity" is her lifeline: her need to stay on the surface when there is only meaninglessness below—or self-deception. She offers him "some good advice": he should be married, not hanging out with people like her friends and her—and she is no better than they are. He turns away. "What on earth am I going to do with you?" she says softly, kneading her kerchief in one hand and leaning toward him across the couch between them. The question is real, and he is encouraged, seizing her by the shoulders and declaring: "No one has ever loved you as I love you!" It's too much: his urgency seems to break against and over her like a wave, leaving her beached in his hands, her head lolling to one side, looking up at him. "That may be true," she says in a dead voice, "but what can I do about it?"

Still, she doesn't want to let him go, especially if he goes in anger. "Why don't you laugh at yourself as I laugh at myself? And come and see me once in a while in a friendly way?" But he can't be appeased in that way, and he is beginning to wear her down—until she makes a crucial concession: "I believe you're sincere at least," she says. Return

In front of her mirror: "You look ill, too," she says to Armand.

tomorrow, she says at last. No, tonight, he says—and she agrees. She will get rid of the party guests first, and then he can come back. This is not like the *marrons glacés* errand, is it? he says. She gives him her key. He kneels at her feet like a knight errant. Bending from the waist, she kisses him lightly all over his upturned face, roaming over it with her mouth the way she'd done with her eyes that first time in the opera box.

The problem, as both she and we are aware, is likely to be her current lover and supporter, the Baron. We've already seen her, in an earlier sequence with him, behaving like a mistress, saying goodbye to him as he leaves for Russia. They are affectionate with each other, but he would like her to be sorrier about his approaching absence than she is. The Baron is the one with whom she most clearly demonstrates her honest sort of insincerity, giving little moues of concern when he speaks of his going, half reclining on a lounge (she has been ill—this is before she encounters Armand at the auction) as the Baron sits beside and leans over her while she plays with the monocle that hangs from a chain on his neck, like a petted daughter with Daddy. She is not meaning to deceive him—nor does she—but only to play out with credit the necessary scene between them. We know that he is bad news—not only because the genre requires it but because he is played by Henry Daniell, who has a cruel mouth and who was already typed in movies as a suave villain.

And instead of Armand it's the Baron who turns up later that night. He hasn't gone to Russia after all. He has a key, too, and he lets himself in with it—just when she is expecting Armand. Who is the midnight supper laid out for? inquires the Baron. "You," she replies, without skipping a beat. "I have learned never to believe a man when he says he's leaving town." But she is panicked. She had been playing the piano when he came in—a waltz full of arpeggio excitement; now she asks him to play, he does it so beautifully. And knowing that Armand (with *his* key) may arrive at any moment, she whispers to her maid and surrogate mother, Nanine (the wonderful Jessie Ralph, who played Peggotty in Cukor's *David Copperfield*), to bolt the door. Marguerite leans on the piano as the Baron at the keyboard plays—with his nasty smile.

And as the tension between them grows, the scene gets uglier. She is committed to playing out her deception (a real one this time), even past the point, soon reached, where she can suppose she has any hope of fooling him. And he is reduced to taking whatever satisfaction he can from her growing discomfort. Each of them is angry at the other for the situation they are in, and at themselves. And the exacerbated feelings rise to an almost operatic pitch when Armand rings and knocks futilely outside, and the Baron plays with equivalent force and vehemence, and Marguerite keeps him playing, bantering with him rather than going to the door, where the noise is getting louder. "I'll tell you who it is," she says—then, with a hearty roguishness: "I could say" (a beat) "that there is someone at the wrong door . . ." And they both laugh unpleasantly—Varville's self-dislike finding an echo in her own, a hysterical one, mounting to something like a shared rapture between

"I have learned never to believe a man when he says he's leaving town"
(with Henry Daniell [Jesse Ralph] just behind him)

them. "*Or*—if not the wrong door—the great romance of my life!" The Baron likes this joke even more, his piano crescendos, the camera bears down on them (the only bravura camera move in the film) as she leans, almost falling, toward the keyboard and the Baron, laughing helplessly—laughing together as the scene fades out. "It might have been," she says (the guttural voice) and laughs some more.

Can she really come back from that? you wonder. It's a nightmare culmination of what we've seen (and admired) as her social brilliance, a kind of final "insincerity." But in the next sequence she seeks Armand out in his chambers and there they become lovers. But not before (a Garbo necessity) she has looked at his family pictures. Especially of his long-married parents: "And they loved each other all that time?" she asks. And now it's her turn to drop a tear. Why? he asks. "It's impossible to believe in such happiness," she says.

But she is tempted by belief. And it helps that he is almost as nice as he is handsome. You have only to look at her looking at him to feel her feeling for him (and Taylor, one of her less objectionable leading men, hardly distracts you from it)—the sheer fondness, as strong as a passion, both doting and distanced at once. He is, after all, *very* unworldly. As she registers once again when he tells her they can live together in the countryside on what he calls his fortune, seven thousand francs. She replies that she spends more than that in a month—"and I was never too particular about where it came from, as you probably know."

But this is just the sort of knowingness that he wants her to leave behind. And so she does. "It's heaven!" she tells him, waking in his arms when he first carries her into their country home. And later, together on their hillside, she presses her face against the earth. But the Baron's château is visible from that same hillside. And Armand, prone to jealousy, is growingly despondent. "I always know he's there," he tells her. "But I am always here," she says, pulling him toward her, her voice almost mewing with concern and tenderness. Before telling him that he has come to "mean everything" to her—"more than the world, more than myself." But when he asks her to marry him, she is frightened. She is almost *too* happy.

But the "brilliant" Marguerite reappears—after Duval père (Lionel Barrymore in his most unctuous mode) visits and prevails on her to give up his son for the sake of his future in society. She agrees, of course (does she ever *not?*), and resolves to make Armand believe she no longer loves him by returning to the rich Baron—proving her love (to *us* at least) by abandoning it. But the urgency of Garbo's suffering in these scenes makes you almost forget the formulaic contrivances. In her curls again, in another (or the same) naked-shoulder white dress, she joins Armand in their sitting room—where she performs an ugly caricature of her social self, repelling his concern with cynical rejoinders, even making him afraid, as he says, that she no longer loves him. "Well, perhaps I don't really," she replies, looking wan and drawn, pushing herself with hands on his shoulders up and out of his arms, leaning into her own heaviness to move away. "Only last night you were ready to give up everything for me," he says. "Well, that was last night," she says, biting off the words; "people sometimes say things they don't mean at night." And you feel all her revulsion at what she's having (as she sees it) to do—she's drawing on her bitterness just to get through it—until she tells him that she is leaving him tonight ("Baron de Varville is expecting me") and, throwing on her cape, scuttles from the room, a sudden crablike darting motion out the door, and over the hill in the moonlight to the Baron's château.

Marguerite's renunciation scene—pretending she doesn't love him

And from then on she really *is* killing herself—with the full com-
pliance of the Baron, who is getting his own back for what she's done
to him before this, as we see when the unhappy couple appear at a
Paris gambling club where Armand, equally embittered now, publicly
reviles Marguerite and challenges the Baron to a duel. They both survive, we soon learn, but as a consequence, Armand is exiled from Paris.
He gets back, in the final sequence, to reunite with the ailing Marguerite, but only just before she dies.

Before that, however, there's the struggle—in Nanine's strong but loving arms, with Marguerite begging, imploring her to let her get out of bed (he's here!). Being helped to a chair and then somehow managing to stand for him, she seems emptied of everything except that uncanny radiance—greeting Armand—who catches her in his arms just in time. And holds her: forgive me, he begs her—as she gazes up at him raptly—of *course* she forgives him (she makes a faint little "oh" sound). He knows now, he says, that no good can come to either of them apart. "I know that, too," she says—as if she has always known it, in spite of the suffering she's put herself through. Now, with her riveted moist-eyed gaze, her mouth-half-open smile, her total absorption in the face and voice above her, she's on a level of ecstatic "knowing" beyond even his—and it's almost enough. We'll go back to the country again, he says, and we'll go today. And she responds with delight to this—but then collapses. She dies in his arms while he's still trying to talk her around—opening her eyes and frowning slightly, as if a worried thought had come to her and passed. Then lapsing into serenity, her head thrown back—Armand relaxes his hold—just as it so often had been at the eagerest points of her life.

"You actually see her do it," said Cecilia Ager's *PM* review about Garbo's dying in this scene, "sense the precise moment when her lovely spirit leaves her fascinating clay." And so you can (that passing frown, I think). The "clay" goes without saying, of course. But it's as if the "spirit" had never been so lovely as here—it's as if all those other movies, all those finally redeemed whores, had been a rehearsal for this one, for this pinnacle. As if *now* you can see what she's been getting at—right? As Alistair Cooke saw it even before this in *Anna Karenina*—in the "protective tenderness" she wrapped around the other characters (even Fredric March, according to him). And the moral beauty of her Marguerite has its final, purest, and most piercing expression in these final scenes, in which this "tolerant goddess" (Cooke again)—who has always somehow seemed, even when at her most desperate, to have retained a goddesslike final control—is reduced here to a hapless humanity, even a piteous one. With Garbo trapped in confining close-up, tossing her head on the pillow as she struggles against Jessie Ralph's Nanine to get out of bed, and then being too weak to make it, then crying, even whimpering, until her friend and maid helps her, weeping herself as she does.

And she remains "Garbo" at such moments, never losing her essential

Marguerite at her end—listening to Armand as he tries to
talk her back from it

dignity—or her distance from us. She still inspires awe, but in *Camille* that is more than it ever has been before about the tragic magnamity she imbues the character with. Her Marguerite is above everything a kind of great soul—with a way of being in the world that feels rich and generous even when it's most challenged. She is moving even when she *isn't* dying. "Woman is the world and man lives in it," George Balanchine once said, gnomically and characteristically. And among the great stars of the past, it seems to me, it's Garbo who comes the very closest to showing us what that means.

V.

BUT NOT EVERYONE was (or is) a fan. Reviewer Graham Greene wasn't:

> A great actress—oh, undoubtedly, one wearily assents, but what dull pompous films they make for her, hardly movies at all so retarded are they by her haggard equine renunciations, the slow consummation of her noble adulteries.

The problem is, he concludes, that she is "a Houyhnhnm in a world of Yahoos"—and the equine analogies (not unapt) proliferate: "the finest filly of them all," "that magnificent mare's head of hers," and so on (a comparison you may think of again near the end of this book). He was reviewing *Conquest* (1937)—or *Marie Walewska*, as it was known in Britain and Europe—the movie she had done right after the triumph of Cukor's *Camille*. *Conquest* was not a triumph, but it was, unhappily, the most expensive sound movie MGM had made up to then—a commercial and critical disaster.

Greene compared watching a Garbo movie to reading Carlyle— something you want to put off as long as you can. He'd rather, he said, be watching Carole Lombard or Claudette Colbert in one of their bright new comedies. He was far from alone. "A Polish countess sacrifices her virtue to Napoleon to save her homeland," says the (entirely accurate) TV guide plot summary of *Conquest*. Who wouldn't want to see Carole Lombard instead?—"being Yahoos ourselves," as Greene says.

The plot of this latest Garbo film was not very different—nor was her disposition toward the day-to-day ordeal of filming it ("I have a psychiatrist now," she wrote to a friend in Sweden: "a little hunch-backed man who I am dragging down into the abyss of pessimism"). But she is different on the screen this time: open-faced and almost cheerful, with no trace of that gift to cartoonists of the time, the Garbo mask with its arched brows and downturned mouth. Nor is there any undertone of fatality—no undertones at all, in fact. It's her plainest performance yet—perhaps made easier by the fact that she has for her first and only time a brilliant leading man, Charles Boyer, witty and lively as Napoleon. But even the high you get from seeing them together on the screen, appreciating each other, is shortly done in by the movie's sluggishness, its massive final pointlessness.

It was time for Lubitsch—she would later call him the only great director she'd ever had. And time for a comedy, as she herself seemed to know—in spite of misguided friends urging her not only toward Joan of Arc again but toward Madame Curie (even Saint Francis of Assisi—"Replete with beard?" Aldous Huxley asked when she suggested it). But "Garbo Laughs" would soon become as famous a slogan as "Garbo Talks"—and was the idea preceding almost everything else about *Ninotchka* (1939). Even the original story (by Melchior Lengyel) about a Soviet Russian envoy sent by her government to Paris, where she falls in love with a capitalist playboy. Which was passed down through a succession of writers until Lubitsch agreed to take it on, and with his own screenwriters (Walter Reisch, along with Charles Brackett and Billy Wilder). Lubitsch had long wanted to work with Garbo—mainly because, he said (as recounted by Garson Kanin), she was so funny. Didn't they *know* her?—didn't they know how funny she was?

Of course she was "funny" in a particular Lubitsch way. The Garbo persona could be so easily flipped into the essential Lubitsch joke—the one about human isolation with all its terrible intensities. Who better than her? And though *Ninotchka* is a comedy—often a fairly low one—it still follows the pattern that Thalberg had long ago proclaimed for her movies: that the Garbo heroine should always be acted *upon* rather than herself acting decisively. Which became one excuse for all those faceless leading men having to rescue her from harlotry (and its vocational hazard of cynicism about love)—as in *Camille*. But in *Ninotchka* it's not loose morals or skepticism that she is saved from but ideology and literal-mindedness. The Garbo mask is back, and the humorlessness it had so often seemed to imply (both to detractors and to fans) is here made comically explicit.

She is a lovely young woman who is also implacably dour, as her entrance into the movie, getting off her train in Paris, shows—a scene that was surely meant to remind us of those other train arrivals, in *Flesh and the Devil* and *Anna Karenina*, both famously glamorous ones (in *Anna* her face in close-up appears from out of a cloud of engine steam). Here, however, she stands flat-footed and alone in long shot on the station platform, in a uniform-like dress and hat, holding her two suitcases, looking grim, as if waiting for the kind of people you expect to be late, if they come at all. But they are there—the movie's three comic "Russkies," Iranoff, Buljanoff, and Kopalski (Sig Rumann, Felix Bressart, and Alexander Granach). And she has been sent here because they have failed, it seems, in their mission to negotiate the return to the Soviets of a former duchess's priceless jewels (instead they are being conned and corrupted by the duchess's French boyfriend). But they *are* there to meet her now—and on time, too. It's just that they hadn't expected "a lady comrade." Oh, charming—they would have brought flowers had they—"Don't make an issue of my womanhood," she says, silencing them. "We are here to work."

They are of course terrified of her (a running gag through these early scenes)—when she praises the mass trials back home ("fewer but better Russians"), or sees a frivolous-looking lady's hat on display at their hotel as a sign of capitalism's imminent collapse, or when her request for a cigarette results in a rush into their lavish rooms of three squealing miniskirted cigarette girls. "Comrades, you must have been smoking a lot," she says dolefully. But there are real issues here, too. Don't they understand, she says to them, that they are wasting time and money that might otherwise help the desperate Russian people? It's only when she talks about *them* that the mask disappears.

Then she meets Leon, Count d'Algout (they tried for Cary Grant or William Powell—they settled for the skillful if uncharismatic Melvyn Douglas), at a traffic stop. Determined to educate herself about capitalist society, she is studying a large unfolded map. "Are you an explorer?" he asks. No—she is looking for the Eiffel Tower. And he follows her there. At the top she admits that the lights of Paris are beautiful but a waste of electricity. He shows her through the telescope—the lights of his apartment. "Does that mean you want me to go there?" she says. He's embarrassed. "You might be an interesting subject of study," she says, and they go there.

Although she doesn't believe in love, she acknowledges "a natural impulse common to all" about which too much nonsense gets talked and written. What can he do, he asks, to encourage that impulse in her now that they are here? Nothing, she says—"chemically we are quite sympathetic." But just as they are getting things on, the phone rings, and she discovers as a result that he is really her enemy, the Grand Duchess's consort. She leaves sorrowfully but firmly.

What's coming, of course, is the scene where he gets her to laugh, at a workingmen's bistro he's followed her to. And she laughs uncontrollably, not at all the feeble jokes he first tries on her (they only make the mask get grimmer) but at his pratfall when he loses patience with her and tips over in his chair. After this formulaic turning point she is no longer just very funny—plying her deadpan comedy with "the assurance of a Buster Keaton," as the *Times* said (reviewer Frank Nugent)—but touching, in her new divided self. Where we see her breaking into laughter at a business meeting the next day and going to the window to look out at the Paris spring (her three comrades, as usual, looking alarmed); actually buying that silly-looking hat and wearing it, awkwardly, to meet Leon that night; confessing to him that she knows his jokes are dreadful but still can't help laughing at them. And her embarrassment at herself, at what is happening to them both, is shown in unforgettable close-up: her brows knitting in dismay, her eyes tearing as she looks into his face next to hers. She has not only been delivered into love but into uncertainty, into imagination, almost into seeing the point (that hat) of pointlessness itself.

This is what Lubitsch did for her. Only for her—without her he wouldn't even have taken on the project, he later said—and she was "brilliant." The screenplay, though leagues beyond most of her others, is too facile, too gag-ridden. But she transforms it on the screen, not only with her unexpected comic flair but with her propensity, ever so lightly applied here, for emotional complication, as it shows in Ninotchka's feeling not only for Leon but for her socialist idealism (which she never really abandons). And the movie was a big success—two years after the calamitous tanking of *Conquest*.

Lubitsch, still at MGM, was eager to work with her again. But

Ninotchka: with Melvyn Douglas

Garbo withdrew—as she so often did—and they never talked. Worse even than that was what she let herself—after another two years of hesitation—be talked into: the disaster of her final movie, *Two-Faced Woman* (1941), directed by Cukor and written at least in part (there are two other credited writers) by her close friend Salka Viertel. In a double role, she's an athletic clean-living type who wins back her straying husband by masquerading as her sexy twin sister. Their idea was to Americanize her, now that she'd shown she could do comedy. She appears in a swimsuit, dances the rumba, bobs her hair, and so on—with an ad campaign that promised (not altogether falsely, alas) things like "Garbo wrestles her man while clad in filmy finery!" The film hit the screens nationwide to appalled reviews and a Legion of Decency condemnation, just a week or so after Pearl Harbor.

Of all the bad films she'd made, this was the first one that seemed actively to be humiliating her. It's still sort of shocking to watch. She had another film to go on her contract with Metro, but she released them from the "obligation" and left Hollywood to live in New York. "Your stock in trade is mystery," a supporting character in *Two-Faced Woman* had said to her. "We don't do that anymore . . ." Her dressing room, it's recorded, went to Lana Turner.

2

Dietrich and Sternberg

THEY CALLED HER Garbo's "rival." MGM had the original and Paramount had her—so the story went. And they even modeled her on the Garbo "look" (she wasn't the only female star so transformed at the time, only the most prominent), the round face of *The Blue Angel*'s Lola-Lola morphing into the hollow cheeks, the jutting cheekbones, arched brows, and gaunt close-up glamour of her "divine" predecessor—who had already made ten Hollywood movies by the time that Dietrich, who was five years Garbo's senior, made her first one: *Morocco* in 1930. Her movie career before that had been in German silents—twenty films from 1923 to 1929—and not very notable. But her "discoverer," Josef von Sternberg—unlike Garbo's Stiller—got to stay on her case in Hollywood, after the sensation made by those two films of hers, both by him, both in 1930. They would make five more films together at Paramount, until their breakup in 1936. (The only comparable constant in Garbo's career, early or late, was her cameraman William Daniels.)

Both stars were enigmatic, seductive, androgynous, emblems of sophistication and sexual allure. They mostly played sexual outlaws, prostitutes, or master spies betrayed by their hearts. Garbo would do that last one twice, in *The Mysterious Lady* and then in *Mata Hari*—with the same final result as in her other movies: her climactic redemption. No such ending for Sternberg's Dietrich—happily.

At the end of *Mata Hari* (1932), in a prison cell awaiting her execution (two weeping nuns keeping her company), Garbo receives her lover, Ramon Novarro, who is now blind, and who is under the impression (her contrivance) that she is in a hospital instead of a prison, and going to a surgery instead of a firing squad (don't ask). I'll wait here until they bring you back, he suggests, but she sends him away, just in time.

Too bad he couldn't see her before that: with her cropped slicked-down hair gleaming like a helmet, her regal black cloak fastened at the throat and flaring up behind, she's the height of dungeon chic. Now he's gone, and she steps from her cell into the squad of soldiers waiting with rifles to march her to her appointment. The movie's final shot shows her ringed by their shoulders as she walks to her death, kissing the ring on her finger—a gift from *him*—raising her eyes heavenward and smiling in exaltation.

Now take Dietrich in the same fix more or less—at the end of Sternberg's *Dishonored* (1931). Also in a cell but without the nuns or the visiting lover—only a sour-looking friar in a rope-belted cassock, who consents (last-request time) to get her the garish sort of clothing she prefers to die in: the "uniform," as she calls it, of her streetwalking days, "when I served my countrymen instead of my country" (she, too, is a captured spy). Somehow the friar seems also to have gotten her an upright piano to play in her cell—even retrieved her big-eyed black cat to sit on top of it, looking angry as she pounds the keys, also looking angry. Whereas the Garbo movie tries to finesse its absurdity, this one invites you to recognize and enjoy it.

As you do—as it mounts. When X-27 (her only name given in the movie) asks the callow and handsome young soldier who has approached to escort her to the firing wall if he has a mirror, he instantly unsheaths his sword and presents her with the reflecting blade—before which she arranges her little hat on her hair, pins on a black net veil, and is ready to go.

On high heels of course, and in a short tight skirt and a black feathered jacket, the cat in one hand (until she hands it off to the friar) and a black feathered muff on the other, she walks rather totteringly through the snow and proceeds to the wall, where she stands and quickly crosses herself. When the young soldier comes to offer her the obligatory blindfold for the eyes, she takes it and wipes *his* tear-filled eyes—like an impatient mother—then motions him back to his job.

Which is to give the final command to fire. And once he's in place again she offers him a slow private smile—clearly of sympathy, of even something more perhaps . . .

The drums rev up and the rifles are raised—and the soldier rebels, throwing his half-uplifted sword down into the snow. "I will not kill a woman!" he cries. "Do you hear! I will not kill any more men either . . . You call this war—I call this butchery!" And so on—and while he is ranting like this, she takes advantage of the delay to freshen her lip rouge. "You call this serving your country, you call this patriotism," he goes on, "I call this murder!"—as she lifts her skirt and slowly turns her leg, straightening the seam in her stocking. But then they push the soldier aside, someone else gives the command, and they shoot her. And it's a jolt—the sudden sharp fusillade of rifle fire (Sternberg took special care with this sound), and the way she gets flung suddenly backward into the snow—an image evoking Capa's photo of the Spanish soldier's death by gunfire, his rifle arm outflung at impact. Except that in this movie, the outflung arm has a feathered muff on it.

Sternberg's Dietrich is not just a rival to Garbo but an antithesis: the anti-Garbo. There is no transcendence for the Dietrich heroine— only a fantasy state of tough recognitions. The Garbo heroine may aspire to a kind of sublimity, but the Dietrich heroine aspires to it, too—in its skeptical materialistic form. What better thing could X-27 do while she waits than to check those stockings (she's already touched up her mouth)? Better than listening to that poor soldier's outburst. He's right, of course—about all of it. But really, what else is new?

As Amy Jolly in *Morocco*, her film before this, Dietrich is as far from the Lola-Lola of *The Blue Angel* (1929) as another saloon singer with a past could be. She is dreamy and mysterious, without the hard edges and the flaunting style of her predecessor in the German film. Private and withdrawn, she can be unnerving to talk to, as she seems to be for her boss at the café, the constantly sweating, face-and-neck-wiping Lo Tinto (Paul Porcasi), when he visits her dressing room and regards her top-hat-and-tails costume. She never once looks at him as he gabbles away at her side, extending her arm so that he can slip a tailcoat sleeve on it, handing him her palmetto fan so that he can cool himself a little while she adjusts her tie in the mirror and sings to herself the song she's going to sing for the crowd outside, in her first appearance before

Different ways of meeting the firing squad: grandly (Garbo as Mata
Hari) or casually (Dietrich as X-27—who will even refuse the
blindfold the soldier is offering her)

them. He is giving her advice about how to handle an audience of Foreign Legionnaires—not that she seems to need it.

But when they see her, sauntering out from the wings, smoking a cigarette, going to the center stage chair (Lo Tinto's, from which he has just introduced her) and sitting on its arm, in her male drag—they are *not* pleased. An outbreak of hisses and catcalls. A close-up of Legionnaire Tom Brown (her costar, Gary Cooper) registering the surprise, then narrowing his eyes, also with displeasure. But as the booing grows, and as the ragtag little band in the balcony above her begins to play, he takes her side, rising to quiet the gang around him, even his own Arab girlfriend, who seems angrier than any of them (and who unaccountably speaks Spanish). The crowd quiets—and Amy looks down at her defender, through her own cigarette smoke and in close-up, with a gaze as isolated as her lone position on that stage.

In this, her first American film, she (and Sternberg) had not yet artificialized her beauty: her eyebrows hadn't yet climbed her forehead, and her eyes, shadowed and underemphasized, still reflected depths. And her character's almost lazy effrontery here (the quality in Dietrich herself, Sternberg said, that first drew him to her), her casual sort of bravery, make her powerfully appealing. This is the Dietrich who could move us as well as divert us, and almost always unexpectedly.

The rest of this sequence has become famous. As the music plays, Amy strolls onto the runway above the pit with the Legionnaires and alongside the raised level against the wall where the small elite crowd in fancy dress are sitting at their tables (including Adolphe Menjou as her mega-bucks soon-to-be suitor). Half sitting on the railing between herself and them, she begins to sing in French the song she'd been rehearsing to herself in the dressing room ("Quand l'amour meurt")—now in that unique sound of hers, like a speaking voice trying to be a singing one, taking what flight it can on pure and infectious enthusiasm. It wins the audience and there is a smattering of applause. Then a pause—with the music vamping she accepts a glass of champagne from one of the ritz tables. "A votre santé," she says, in the high fluting voice she mostly speaks in here, raising her glass to the swells and drinking it.

She turns to go back to her song. She still has her music backup and the crowd's attention—when she hesitates, and looks again at one of the women (the prettier one), who looks around at the others and giggles nervously: it's all in fun—but still . . . The impersonator approaches and touches the flower in the young woman's hair. A beat. Then: "May I have this?" "Of course," says the woman. And Dietrich bends, cupping the woman's chin in her hand and kissing her on the mouth. To silence, then an outburst of laughing applause—as she saunters off with the flower. Stopping only to throw it to Legionnaire Brown—who catches it in midair.

You want to applaud the kiss, too (and if you're in a movie house audience, in my experience, you do)—to respond out loud to this bold and witty final gesture. Or so it seems to be—until it's even sort of topped by her throwing the flower to Cooper on the way out. Who grins and puts it behind his ear, accepting the challenge.

She has been evoking male power, of course (it's not the costume of a newsboy—or even a Legionnaire), but more casually than willfully, even dreamily, as if she'd just woken up in possession of it and thought she might walk it around for the rest of us. It's the same feeling her love affair with the Legionnaire will have. They are both of them brave and fabulous creatures, with secrets never to be disclosed—to us, or (as you suppose) to each other—circling each other warily. Their love play will have the same suspense, scene by scene, even line by line, that her drag act does.

His impassivity in the movie matches even hers. But it's *her* performing style that holds your attention—it's the more stylized one. Her words are generally brief and to the point. And if there are more than a few of them, they are timed to intermittent pauses and movements in the long takes that Sternberg favors, and they are uttered by her almost without inflection. "There's a foreign legion of women, too," she tells Cooper at her apartment, rising from her place beside him and stepping through the Malacca curtains onto her balcony, throwing her cigarette over the railing and turning to face him again, folding her arms—"but we have no uniform, no flags"—she leans toward him, touching the medals on his chest—"and no medals"—she straightens up and puts her hand on her hip, smiling slightly, then in a falling voice (after a pause)—"when we are brave"—she leans against the archway and touches his face with her hand, then withdraws it and, going onto the balcony again, turns and looks at him—"no wound stripes when we are hurt." And she turns her back again. "Look here," says Cooper, "is there anything I can do for you?"

If that question seems almost inconsequent (her answer, of course, is no, thanks), it's because this speech, less from its meanings than from the way she delivers it, makes clear how little she seems to be asking for sympathy, either his or ours. The peculiarity of Sternberg's staging here makes an important point—or remakes it: that this heroine will always surprise us. These pauses and turns, as we watch and listen to her, keep us always a little off balance. Even in the most banal situations (as with that flop-sweating boss earlier on), she will always be a little bit ahead of us. Someone to be watched closely—just as these two lovers watch each other (we are hardly more secure with the Cooper character).

Even at this early stage, the Dietrich-Sternberg collaboration was unique: never before in big studio filmmaking had a single director been given such exclusive—and eccentric—personal control over the creation of a star image. And Dietrich was as gratefully compliant as he was controlling. He described himself (in his autobiography, *Fun in a Chinese Laundry*) as being "a cold-eyed mechanic" whenever he was directing her, giving her the most precise instructions: "Turn your shoulder away and straighten out . . . Drop your voice an octave . . . Count to six and look at that lamp as if you could no longer live without it . . ."—and so on. She was his puppet, he said in interviews (in their personal lives, that relation seems to have been reversed)—and Dietrich never denied it. Not that the idea could have much surprised anyone who'd been watching their movies. What's curious—and interesting—is how much Sternberg clearly wanted that control to show on the screen. As it increasingly does, from *Morocco* onward.

She had made such an impact in that latter film that she was nominated for a Best Actress Academy Award—almost the last time that anyone would accuse her of "acting." But even then—with Sternberg's help—she was doing something else. More like Being a Movie Star. Acting, she thought—so her daughter and biographer Maria Riva tells us—was something you did in the theater, not the movies: a movie performance was created by your director—first on his set and then at his editing table.

And yet she was not only his "puppet" but his eager student, eventually learning almost as much from him about making a Dietrich movie as even he knew. After their fifth film together—*Blonde Venus*,

Morocco: with Gary Cooper

a flop—both he and Paramount decided he needed a break from her, and Dietrich was required—over her vehement resistance—to make a picture with another director: *Song of Songs* (1933) with Rouben Mamoulian (just before he would go to Metro for *Queen Christina*). Experienced as Mamoulian was, nothing had quite prepared him for the arrival on his set (according to Maria Riva again) of what was known as "Miss Dietrich's mirror," a full-length prodigy on wheels with its own lights and trolley, junction box and cables, from which the star could see herself at all times exactly as she appeared on camera. She would go from there to instruct both the crew and the director on how to light and photograph her à la Sternberg.

Her X-27 in *Dishonored*, their third collaboration, had already been a more heightened fabrication than Lola-Lola or Amy Jolly. And Shanghai Lily in their next one, *Shanghai Express* (1932), would be even more so. His visualization of her is now nearly delirious—the black gloves, a black feathered cloche hat with a black net veil shadowing her eyes above cheekbones that seem molded in light. Unveiled, the eyes—in the evolution of the Dietrich face—have a new prominence, are larger and more lustrous than before. And their movements—whether up or down, or side to side, or gently rolling— seem as carefully choreographed as all the other motions in the film. Which tend to be slow and ambiguous—especially if they are hers. So does the talk—at least between the principals (the comic supporting players talk normally). Clive Brock is the granite-faced hero, a British army doctor, and Anna May Wong is Dietrich's companion exotic, the movie's other high-class prostitute, and they must all "talk like trains," Sternberg instructed them, according to Clive Brook's account—"this is the Shanghai Express!" And so the hypnotic monotone of the dialogue is underscored by the unceasing "real" train sounds: the steady low clickety-clack of wheels on rails, sounding along with the flow of chat or filling the portentous silences.

In lots of ways the movie is as much about the romance of trains of that time as it is about the one between the two leads. Sternberg's care with his train ambience is part of what makes the movie, with all its dreamy languor, so compelling (it was a hit—their last one). Especially in the traveling-through-the-night scenes. As when Lily and Doc find themselves alone together on the open-air rear platform of the observation car, parrying with each other like the lovers of *Morocco* (except that these two have an offscreen past between them) and then finally coming together: he extends his arm and she falls back against it, all but disappearing into her huge and looming fur collar, its hairs stirring gently in the wind, as he holds her and as she reaches up and with one gracefully splayed hand on the back of his head and draws his face down onto hers.

But he's a hard case. Much later on, once he thinks she had been willing to sell herself to the villainous Chinese warlord (that is, if her chum Anna May Wong hadn't killed him first), his priggishness comes between them—even when she is in her black negligee, leaning against his compartment door and looking at him. She asks for a light to her cigarette, he gives it, and she returns alone to her own compartment, switching the lights off, standing against the wall and into the chiaroscuro that falls on her from the night light above, throwing her face into relief,

Shanghai Express: two man-eaters on the train—Anna May
Wong is the other one.

foregrounding the cheekbones and hollows beneath and the moisture
gathering at the base of her upturned eyes. Her cigarette (the smoke
giving the image an added diffusion) hangs from the center of her
mouth. She takes it out. And the sinuously curved upturned hand that
now holds it next to her face is trembling, you notice, to the soft
clackety-clack of the moving train. Or is it rather because Doc has just
touched her (lighting her cigarette), as she has said to him just before
this? Mockingly, it seemed then. But maybe not. Are you meant here
to be looking at the image of a woman so pierced by heartache that she

becomes a vision of it—or at a fashion shoot? What you are not looking at is a person who is doing something (Garbo reclaiming her flowers in *A Woman of Affairs*) or being something (Garbo in her box at the theater in *Camille*) but at someone who is very definitely *looking* something.

Something beautiful, of course (there is at least no ambiguity about that), on the level of the breathtaking. But breathtaking here trumps inward—and you are mainly conscious of a pose. Even as you're enjoying it you're aware of both what it's alluding to and what it's avoiding at the same time—namely, a Garbo-like inner life. And Sternberg's sumptuousness (he also gives her a solitary praying scene—equally sumptuous) only underlines the absence. He seems more and more—in this film and the two that follow—to be turning into a kind of Ziegfeld to her showgirl, presenting and decorating her with ever increasing elaboration. *Shanghai Express* itself is like an extended, small-scale, infinitely detailed production number in which ravishing figures (don't forget Anna May Wong) move raptly and gorgeously to indeterminate purposes. But there is no music—except for the train sounds, and the occasional blasts of hot jazz from Lily's Sadie Thompson–style gramophone.

In *Blonde Venus* (1933), there is. The first musical numbers he's given her to perform since *Morocco*. The storyline had been her own "inspiration," it was said, but by the time the movie got going, having been vetted by studio and censors, neither she nor Sternberg had much zest for it—except, it would appear, for those numbers. Helen (Dietrich) is a young wife and mother (of a son) whose adultery with rich playboy Nick (Cary Grant)—for impeccably noble reasons, but never mind—compels her to flee with her child, setting her off on the usual course: from megastardom in Paris to prostitution in New Orleans before a final reunion in New York with her husband (Herbert Marshall). A scenario that offered her a maximum number of picturesque guises (from nightclub chanteuse to skid row boozer) and backgrounds—all of them artfully cluttered, claustrophobic, and ravishingly lit in the Sternberg manner.

Her first song here is "Hot Voodoo"—a now famous number that was more or less ignored in the reviews at the time (it was almost too peculiar to be noticed), in which she slowly emerges from a gorilla suit while ranks of brown-stained Afro-haired chorines brandishing spears and shields shag and shuffle in rows behind her to the jungle jazz

Blonde Venus: The gorilla (passing among the tables
on a chain) gets a look at Cary Grant.
Then *we* get a look at *her* . . .

beat—the same chorines who have just led her (in full gorilla garb) on a chain through the tables to frighten the customers a little (the gorilla takes a second look at customer Cary Grant) as a warm-up to her transformation (into a sequin-studded costume with feathers at the hips and a blond Afro wig) and to her song. Which is all about how this jungle rhythm is driving the singer wild. Though it's hard to imagine anything much wilder than what we've been seeing. But she can handle it all, it appears—and still sing, still roll her eyes to the music, still flatten and slur her vowels in that wonderfully suggestive way ("I'd follow a cave man / Right into his ca-aa-ave . . ."), and make this strange sound, this mocking growl, with its controlled loss of control, reverberate in your head like some inspired dirty joke.

Her second, much later song—"You Little So-and-So"—is more sedate. It's at a swank Paris club where she goes among the tables undisguised—though once again in drag. Once again preceded by a troupe of girls—harem ones this time, wearing mouth veils and below-the-navel skirts, sauntering hands on hips in and out of mosquelike arches. She strolls onto the stage behind them—she is all in white (the only black is her long cigarette holder), in top hat, white tie, and tails with diamanté lapels—to applause over the music. She is smiling, flirting with one of the chorines who passes her (they are going offstage), then turning her attention to the applauding crowd—with a sudden look of passionate mischief, still smiling, smoking, widening and flashing her eyes, mock-threatening, mock-inviting—her *just wait* look. This, too, is the essential Dietrich—not the laid-back, unexpectedly moving one of *Morocco*, but the full-wattage, full-frontal star. Forget moving—this is dazzling. And for the moment anyway—and in the spirit of her mischief—it's more than enough.

She saunters forward and begins to sing a second song—this one in French, very jaunty and up-tempo, more slurred vowels and flashing eyes—walking along a runway that winds among crowded tables and private boxes. In one of the latter, next to a large gilt torso of a female nude, sits Cary Grant—once again among her audience (they've already had the affair that caused all her travels). It's the *early* Cary Grant, still billed below the title, and visibly uncomfortable in the movie's limp romantic scenes—but looking here at least like the star he soon would be, full of coiled intelligence.

She doesn't see him right away—as she sings in close-up and then backs into the shot that includes him. As she does so she finishes the song's verse, nods to the applause, and as her orchestra vamps, turns and acknowledges him—looking off and smiling her ironic smile. "Well," she says drawlingly, "if it isn't old Nick himself." Is she pleased, or what? And her next words make that seem even more indeterminable. "I expected you to pop up someday," she adds—with a seemingly derisive emphasis on the plosives of "pop up." She is keeping her counsel, as she always does. Not so "Nick"—"If this is a dream, Helen, I hope I never wake up," he says ardently. Then: "Let me come backstage tonight, will you?" The irony for her seems to grow. "I seem to remember," she answers, "you came backstage once before"—with her killing half smile. At which she moves past him—her band still vamping, her audience still clapping. She turns to them, enjoying it all—then steps back to him, putting him in the frame again.

Then comes one of those gestures that can make movies like this one—the hieratic trash kind—seem magical. Looking off, not at him, she puts her hand on his shoulder—the band still vamping—while he, also looking ahead, not at her, puts his hand over hers; and on the same interchange of movement she withdraws her hand and raises it, palm

"Well . . . if it isn't old Nick himself."

upward, to signal the orchestra to resume its normal volume as she starts to sing again. This time in English, "I Couldn't Be Annoyed" (it's about eating crackers in bed: "What *have* I got to lose?" cries the defiant singer). They are old lovers, and in this silent exchange of hands and averted gazes, the ambiguities of their talk are suddenly resolved—at least for the moment. And the relation between them seems unexpectedly (if temporarily) large, redolent of time and experience, of common memories and understandings. They don't have to look at each other— she doesn't even have to pause in her song for more than a moment.

It's the inspired choreography behind all this that she owes to Sternberg, of course—but he owes to *her* the power and depth of her presence and performing style. As he surely understood. But it's also that she's enacting here what is clearly for this filmmaker ("Miss Dietrich is me," he once said) a central magical thing—in her character's easy and glamorous mastery not only of her act and her shifting gender, but of the whole human space around her, the chorus girls, the audience, the orchestra, and the man who is still in love with her. And the excitement of this control comes off the screen—powerfully.

And who knows?—maybe *too* powerfully for her mentor. In any case it was in their next (and final) two films (after the interruption of the Mamoulian film) that he would consolidate *his* control: "completely subjugating my bird of paradise," as he put it, "to my peculiar tendency to prove that a film might be an art medium." Whatever—*The Scarlet Empress* (1934), the film he's talking about here, has Dietrich playing Catherine the Great as she rises from a guileless young princess to a corrupt and lascivious monarch, against and within settings of rococo delirium—every detail, Sternberg assured us, personally designed and supervised by him. And the result is certainly something to see, turgid and hermetic as it is (it would be an influence for a turgid and hermetic masterpiece to come—Eisenstein's *Ivan the Terrible, Part One*). The kitsch afflatus becomes compulsively watchable, even jaw-dropping. But the whole thing has a small, sour spirit to it—and leaves a bad taste. "Subjugated" she certainly is.

As she is again, even more decisively, in *The Devil Is a Woman* (1935). Again she is a man-eater, though on a smaller scale—Concha Perez, a Spanish street singer. And given that profession, you might think the life Dietrich comes to when she sings would be back for her—but no. The single song she does in the film ("Three Sweethearts

Have I") is performed in a strange piping little voice and in the painfully arch manner of her whole performance here. Concha is the femme fatale as space cadet, more Lucy Ricardo than Amy Jolly—the sort of siren who puts her lover in the hospital (character actor Lionel Atwill, a Sternberg look-alike) and then blames him for spoiling her day by being there. It's Dietrich as never before—an ersatz Latin spitfire, pouting and pettish and foot-stamping, prattling and flouncing and batting eyes now huger than ever, with eyebrows fixed in arches halfway up her forehead. And Dietrich—ever complicit with her Svengali—thought she looked more beautiful than ever (those eyebrows were her idea) and called *The Devil Is a Woman* her favorite film up to then.

This look of fixed surprise, wide-eyed and wondering, on the face of a woman so obviously wised-up as Dietrich would always seem, had a comic potential that seems to have escaped Sternberg, but that would be fully realized by her next film at Paramount (they had let Sternberg go). *Desire* (1936)—reuniting her with Gary Cooper—is a Lubitsch comedy, in all but the director's credit. Frank Borzage directed it, but Lubitsch prepared the script with the writers and oversaw the shooting—the most he could do once he had become (very briefly) the studio's production head, too occupied to direct a single film. Here the Dietrich heroine's faked innocence (she is really a professional jewel thief) is the central joke in her romantic collision with Cooper's naïve Capraesque hero. And Dietrich (no surprise) gives a richly inflected and very funny comic performance.

But by the midthirties, when *Desire* was released, that was not enough—and not different enough in the public view—to redeem the ossified image those last Sternberg flops had stuck her with. All she can do is pose, people said—and the fact that the posing had become in *Desire* an elegant joke that she was fully in control of wasn't enough to take the curse off it. Far less so would her next two pictures, both for independent producers (*Garden of Allah* for Selznick and *Knight Without Armor* for Alexander Korda)—in both of which she really *was* supposed to be an innocent, all Sternberg and Lubitsch ironies left far behind her. So, it seemed, were her audiences.

She returned to Paramount—and to a picture actually directed by Lubitsch (no longer a studio boss). They didn't get along in their new and greater proximity, and *Angel* (1937) was a major bomb—a classy comedy about *very* classy types (she is a British lord's wife), cleverness without laughs. Paramount dropped her. Lubitsch, too, had to look for work outside the Paramount gates. Those were the heyday years of the screwball comedy—not a good time at first for either of them. But after two and a half years off the screen and nobody much missing her, it seemed, Dietrich said yes to an improbable offer from the Universal producer Joe Pasternak (another European émigré) to do a Western there.

And *Destry Rides Again* (1939), with James Stewart opposite her, was a very big hit. "The greatest single comeback in movie history," according to her biographer Steven Bach—and maybe so. It certainly began a new phase in her movie career. As well as an astonishing transformation. Even before *Destry* was released, the "new" Dietrich was being heralded. Publicity stills showed a heavily rouged floozie in corkscrew curls and cowboy vest. The remote unflappable icon of glamour, it was promised, was going to knock around like one of the girls. Going to *be* knocked around, too—kicked and pummeled and even drenched to the skin. Her all-out saloon brawl with supporting player Una Merkel was famous to people well before they could see it on the screen, filmed and reported by *Life* magazine and other journals, with on-set photos of Stewart pouring buckets of water over the two entangled women on the floor.

This was a new Dietrich all right. But still the same, if not more so in some ways. The same ironic, elegant, haunting presence no matter what her surroundings or the filmmaking style—no matter how loud and raucous the performance or the singing, as she whoops and hollers through numbers like "See What the Boys in the Back Room Will Have" while firing pistols into the air on top of a bar.

It was a comeback, sure—but a comeback at Universal, not Paramount, in the near-programmers that Universal specialized in. *Destry* was a B movie in A-movie disguise—a compendium of tested and surefire stuff: brawls and stunts and sentiment, jokes and songs and running gags with stock clowns like Mischa Auer and Billy Gilbert and the undiscourageable Charles Winninger. Without too much concern about how it all fitted together: just keep it moving. It was aimed at the action house crowd, at Saturday matinees and blue-collar tastes. What was surprising to everyone was how well all this seemed to suit her. Whereas bringing Garbo down to earth (in her last film) had seemed to destroy her, it or something like it seemed to fulfill Dietrich,

Americanizing and all—bringing her to new life, even. Lola-Lola rediviva—though a bit cleaned up for the American market.

"Destry Dietrich Does It Again," proclaimed the Coming Attraction for her next one. "Fighting, Playing, Laughing, Loving," said the words unscrolling over a scene of her being knocked around again, this time by a man ("I've been hit before, and harder," she says to him). But *Seven Sinners* (1940) is closer to the earlier Sternberg Dietrich than *Destry* had been: she plays a sexy chanteuse named Bijou, rides in a rickshaw, sings a draggy, haunting "I Can't Give You Anything but Love, Baby," even does a song in drag ("He's in the Navy") among clamoring sailors at her saloon in the tropics. And *Seven Sinners* pairs her—for the first of their three movies together—with rising star John Wayne (he'd just done *Stagecoach*). He's visibly uneasy around her here—looking as if he doesn't quite get the point of her. Not that she seems to notice.

Until *The Spoilers* (1942), their next movie—in which he not only gets it but takes the movie away from her, with what looks like her happy complicity. She's noticed him this time, and more than that, so that there really seems to be something at stake in their scenes together. They are at another saloon, this time in Gold Rush Alaska— and there's another (as in *Sinners*) epic male brawl at the end. But by their third Universal film together, *Pittsburgh* (1942), he is the center attraction, in one of those two-men-and-a-woman star vehicles that were popular in the forties: Wayne is Clark Gable (or Tyrone Power) and Randolph Scott is Spencer Tracy (or Don Ameche) and Dietrich (still top-billed) fills the Myrna Loy (or Alice Faye) role as Josie, the steadfast loving heroine who still can't rein in the selfish reckless charmer played by Wayne. Josie is a "hunky from coal town," and Dietrich is surprisingly convincing—as she had been the year before in Raoul Walsh's *Manpower* at Warners—as a vaguely ethnic working-class type (the Hollywood idea of it, anyway, à la Ann Sheridan or Ida Lupino), struggling to get away from the old slum or even the old prison sentence (*Manpower*).

But in the end she was just too odd a bird (and getting older) to thrive for long in forties Hollywood, with its blander, overexplicit, more literal-minded kind of moviemaking. She was still too much the ironist goddess. She could only be sold, if at all, in action films—and she would soon have to give up that singing of hers altogether (her single song in *Manpower* was cut for the final release). Soon—as in

Costarring with John Wayne, as he goes from below-the-title leading man (in *Seven Sinners*) to central player (in *Pittsburgh*, with Randolph Scott at left)

MGM's *Kismet* (1944)—she would be doing the kind of publicity stunt role ("dancing" for the Grand Vizier, slithering across a black mirror floor wearing gold paint) that got her in the news more than she was in the movie itself.

At the same time, however, she was beginning to do in earnest something her former costar Wayne would only be acting in the movies—going to war. Entertaining Allied troops, putting herself at genuine risk and through real hardships near the front lines at or near almost every major battleground in the Africa and Europe campaigns (she was particularly at risk from German armies, of course). Is it true she slept with Eisenhower? she was once supposedly asked—"Darling, Ike wasn't *at* the front," she replied, supposedly. What she certainly did say, and more than once, was that her war service was "the only important thing" she'd ever done. It was partly, of course, the star's idea of importance—being worshipped by hundreds of men or more wherever she turned up (Dietrich had certainly never wanted to be alone). But her courage and even her heroism for those men was beyond questioning.

There were still a few movies for her after the war, hit and miss affairs, and sometimes they even let her be terrific again. She again sang thrillingly in Billy Wilder's *A Foreign Affair* (1948), as a Nazi-tainted nightclub chanteuse making do in the ruins of postwar Berlin, and with her personal composer (since *The Blue Angel*) Friedrich Hollander playing his songs on the piano behind her. That was a leading role (she was second-billed to Jean Arthur but stole the movie from her) in a highly successful film. But her next and even more memorable job was a brief "guest star" appearance in a movie that almost nobody saw at the time: Orson Welles's *Touch of Evil* (1958).

She is in it for hardly more than seven minutes—in two sequences, one at the middle, the other at the end. And the whole thing was an afterthought, a sudden idea that came to Welles in the middle of the shoot, then filmed in a single night. And yet—as she said about it later—"I've never been as good as I was in that little teensy part."

She is Tanya, in a black wig and a gypsy costume, keeping a one-woman brothel (as it seems) at the Mexico-Texas border, and remembering—once prompted by his sudden reappearance—the at first quite unrecognizable Hank Quinlan (Welles), a corrupt local cop who was once apparently an old fling, or at least a customer, and who has now ballooned near retirement age into a monstrous obesity ("You should lay off those candy bars," she says to him). He is surprised ("Tanya's still . . . open for business?") and glad to see her again, but he's in the midst of hunting a killer and leaves.

He comes back much later when he himself is the killer being hunted (by Charlton Heston) and demands from her (she reads cards) to know his future. And she tells him that "it's all used up." She pronounces his epitaph later, too—while his dead body floats grotesquely atop a pool of oil-slimed water—saying the now famous line "He was some kind of man," then walking off into the night and ending the movie. Which she has tied together and invested with a richness that it would never have had without her—as Welles knew. As he later said to Peter Bogdanovich: "I think all that Dietrich part of it is as good as anything I've ever done in movies . . . Really, Marlene was extraordinary in that. She really was the Super-Marlene. Everything she has ever been was in that little house for about four minutes there."

Everything she has ever been . . . yes. Her glamour, her wit, her toughness and refusal of self-pity, her combination of unflinching realism with utter improbability, her "steady routine"—in Robert Garis's words—of the "theatrical impersonation of sexual authority," and so on. All there. And by this time she was only two more major roles away (*Witness for the Prosecution*, 1958, and *Judgment at Nuremburg*, 1961) from the end of her movie career. And the people who had complained that she was always the same weren't wrong about that even now. What they were wrong about was *her* always-the-same. For "the Super-Marlene," that condition didn't foreclose deepening—as those "teensy" scenes Welles had so brilliantly written and staged for her reveal. Her Tanya's relation to the terrible Quinlan ("Her great unwavering eyes see everything and know everything"—Garis) is as moving as it is precisely because it feels both deep and finally impersonal. The femme fatale as earth mother.

She had yet another career to come—what are called her "international concert years" during the late sixties and early seventies, in the one-woman show that she'd been developing for years on stages and in clubs and recording studios from London to Paris to Las Vegas and that she would bring to Broadway in 1967, billed by her producer Alexander Cohen—not inappropriately—as "Queen of the World." It was a

huge success, and she returned with it in 1968 to the Lunt-Fontanne Theatre. That's when and where I saw it.

For me, at least (and with the exception of her Tanya), she had never been more moving or more mysterious than she was that night standing alone and mostly immobile on that stage (the orchestra was in the pit—you don't want to crowd the queen of the world), under her careful light and before her stand-up mike, in her sequin-spackled illusion of a topless gown, with a sumptuous white cape and train made of (so we had been told) swans' feathers, and singing as wittily as ever the numbers you mostly expected ("Falling in Love Again") and some of the ones you hadn't ("Honeysuckle Rose").

It was all fine, really, but it only became something much more than that when she got to the songs about war (our Vietnam one, which she had publicly denounced, was at its height)—when she rose up, as it were, on the show's accumulation of her and our memories, of her movies, of her careers, of even the knowing, skeptically inflected kitsch she had been purveying that night, finally to sing, to a throbbing accompaniment, and like the warrior she partly was, Pete Seeger's "Where Have All the Flowers Gone?"—and to blow the theater apart. By this time it could also freeze your blood. Her Mother Courage side.

She had gone to war once, and she'd come back, and now she was protesting the ongoing war with the rest of us. And with far stronger credentials than most of us behind her. And yet . . . was she ever more outlandish? More surreal even—with her "nude dress" and her swan coat and her ageless death's head beauty? But she was also inadvertently testifying to something else that night—to one of the mysteries of art, the way the extremest artifice can sometimes touch and sound the most urgent kinds of truth. It was a culmination, in a way, of what she and Sternberg had so long ago begun together.

OPPOSITE PAGE: *Touch of Evil*: the femme fatale as earth mother

3

Bergman and Selznick

THAT INGRID BERGMAN would be compared to Garbo—being beautiful and Swedish and praised for her acting—was probably inevitable. "The Garbo of the Forties," U.S. newspapers called her, even before her Hollywood career had properly begun. And once it had, the comparison became even more insisted upon. "There has been nothing like it," wrote James Agee in *Time* about her performance in *For Whom the Bell Tolls*, "since her great compatriot Greta Garbo enchanted half the world."

But Bergman represented as much a reaction *against* Garbo as Dietrich did—although in ways that made her just as much a contrast to both women. Bergman was not mysterious: her glamour lay in her being unglamorous—at least in all the ways that people had been used to. That they were ready for a change in all that by the time of the forties was something that David O. Selznick had intuited when he signed her to a Hollywood contract.

She was natural and blooming and unaffected, guileless and seemingly transparent. She offered her onscreen radiance, her purity even (a word she often evoked from reviewers), to the world without reserve or disguise. And audiences gave their adoration back—to a degree and on a scale that even Garbo may never have known (much less Dietrich). What Bergman offered made no problems for anyone—highbrow or lowbrow or in between.

For one thing, she cheered us up. It could make you happy just to look at her. For her, unlike Garbo, there were no "haggard equine renunciations." When Bergman at movie's end loses her lover—to his wife in *Intermezzo*, to the enemy army in *For Whom the Bell Tolls*, and so on—she does it with full-hearted grief. *Her* unhappy endings felt as shocking and arbitrary as Garbo's felt inevitable. "You are too happy for tragedy," observes the heroine's doting elderly voice teacher at the beginning of *Gaslight*, conceding his pupil's failure at managing a tragic aria. But then, he adds—almost as if speaking for her fans—"happiness is better than art."

From the beginning she appeared—as it seemed—without makeup. It was the other leading woman in *Intermezzo* (1939), the straying hero's loyal wife (Edna Best), who had the requisite pencil-line eyebrows and the lacquered look that went with them in those days, while Bergman, eyebrows notably unplucked, looked as if fresh from a shower. *Not* the way she appears in the same role in the Swedish original (1936), in which she wears noticeable amounts of lip rouge and eye shadow, the sort of minimal cosmetic intervention that her bland youthful prettiness would seem to have required. She had starred in nine Swedish movies looking more or less like that: it was only in Hollywood, of all places, that she came clean—under Selznick's obsessive supervision. Because, as he explained, he wanted American audiences to see "the fresh and pure personality" that had caused him to sign her to a contract. And though he was massively involved with his *Gone With the Wind* when she arrived from Europe, he would remain deeply invested in his bet on her. Which was seen by *tout* Hollywood as a long-odds one. Especially once they met her—at a party thrown by the Selznicks. Where the veteran star Joan Bennett was heard (by Irene Selznick) to inquire whether they were now importing the kitchen maids.

Selznick decided against an advance buildup for her. He wanted the public to "discover" her in *Intermezzo* the way they'd discovered Hedy Lamarr in *her* first U.S. movie, *Algiers* (1938). "But Miss Lamarr," said the Selznick memo to his staff, "is comparatively easy to photograph and is a much more obvious type of beauty"; nevertheless, even Lamarr had been "made" by her photography (by James Wong Howe), and so would Bergman be, he claimed, if they got it right—because unlike almost anyone else on the screen he could think of, Bergman could look either beautiful or totally ordinary. "Nothing is more important to the picture than the way she is photographed" (by Gregg Toland, as it would turn out).

Selznick fussed endlessly about Bergman's entrance into the movie—her introduction to the American audience. And he shot it (the in-name-only director was the ungifted but compliant Gregory Ratoff) more than thirty times, Bergman later said: "And would you believe it, we'd finished the movie and we were still doing retakes of that first scene!"

The final version could hardly seem more casual. In a dark cloth coat and hat, Bergman enters the house unnoticed, just as Leslie Howard is playing his violin for his adoring little daughter and her attentive little dog, all three of whom get more glamour close-ups in the sequence than Bergman does—who gets only two, both of them nice but far from glamorous. You see a big shy pretty girl, entranced by the overheard music, in a hallway taking off her coat and hat, listening intently. More shots of the others, then back to her. She steps out into a shadow that darkens her forehead and highlights her earnest shining eyes. The music stops and she enters the room, sheet music under her arm, coming to meet her piano pupil's father, the famous violinist.

Selznick's memos worried also about her "size." She was even taller than Garbo (neither of them was ever filmed wearing high heels) and with an equivalent breadth of shoulder. But Bergman seems apologetically big: she enters the room in this scene with the prissy, rather grudging little steps she would take through the rest of her career. Unlike Garbo, she would never stride. And Selznick on this point could not have been a help: his memos to Ratoff are full of instructions like "keeping her head down as much as possible." Which she does—in a full-length traveling shot.

But this underwhelming first entrance turns out to be shrewdly calculated. What then happens over the course of *Intermezzo* is that she grows steadily more beautiful—under the influence of love and music, and Toland's photography. The fresh-faced prettiness is gradually modulated into something you can recognize as conventional movie star glamour. Especially in the love scenes, of course. In which Howard has a glow of his own (no confusing him with the "ordinary") and Toland doesn't neglect it. It's Bergman, however, who grows into an iconic vision right before your eyes. The sense that almost everyone would eventually and somehow get about her that her beauty

Intermezzo: the piano teacher (with Ann Todd)

came "from the inside"—what one critic called "her very real inner goodness"—gets its start with Selznick's *Intermezzo*.

But "inner goodness" on the screen has its limits—as Selznick well knew. But that's still how he wanted to see her—and persisted in seeing her, to her growing impatience. He kept her off the screen for more than a year after her debut. And when she appeared next—as a wonder-working governess in *Adam Had Four Sons* at Columbia, and as a war refugee married to a psychopath in *Rage in Heaven* at MGM (both 1941)—both films were turkeys, and close to B's as well. But she kept her goodness in both of them. Which was precisely how her boss thought she should continue to be promoted and sold: "our being quoted" (by an interviewer, presumably) "as thinking she is sexy," he wrote, was not only untrue but made him look "silly."

But she was sexy enough in person to persuade Victor Fleming, director of *Dr. Jekyll and Mr. Hyde* (1941) at MGM, that she should play the tart instead of the nice girl she was originally assigned to (as the story goes), switching roles with costar Lana Turner as a result. And she is sexy indeed: her scene of attempted seduction of Spencer Tracy's Dr. Jekyll has an emotional nakedness under the toughness (she's a bar girl) that makes it feel almost embarrassing—and memorable (two things it was unlikely to have been if Turner had played it).

After this she went back to the stage (she'd played *Liliom* on Broadway the year before, opposite Burgess Meredith), this time rather tentatively, in a local Selznick-sponsored production of *Anna Christie*, directed by John Houseman and opening in Santa Barbara—where the audience howled with laughter (as she writes in her autobiography) when she pronounced the opening lines the Garbo movie had made so famous: "Gimme a whiskey, with a ginger ale on the side, and don't be stingy, baby." She wasn't that tough—nor would she ever be.

Selznick didn't want her to be a bad girl, but he did want her to be in a bad girl's kind of movie—like *Algiers*, say, the movie that keeps coming up, however irrelevantly, in his memos concerning her. So that when Julius Epstein, the screenwriter, could tell him ahead of time (practically all he knew at the time) about *Casablanca* that it would be full of "that *Algiers* schmaltz—lots of atmosphere, cigarette smoke, guitar music," Selznick agreed to it for his star. And it would be *Casablanca* (1942) that would turn her into the kind of star who could seize people's imagination. Her Ilsa is ambiguous from her first appearance—a woman of mystery—and remains so (even to Bergman herself, she claimed) through most of the movie. And that her mystery should be the focus of Bogart's terrible and beautiful sorrow made her seem all the more starlike. That, and the "cigarette smoke" (never her own of course).

The star role she'd really coveted, however (who knew then what the seeming disarray of the *Casablanca* shoot would finally amount to?), was Hemingway's Maria in the screen version of *For Whom the*

OPPOSITE PAGE: *Dr. Jekyll and Mr. Hyde*: the bar girl

Bell Tolls (1943)—and once Vera Zorina, who was originally cast in it, was dropped, she got it. She had been Hemingway's choice for the role all along, as *Life* magazine had revealed—and she was the only thing about the final movie that he would turn out to approve of. But it was big box office, and in Technicolor, and in her carefully coiffed, much publicized, close-cropped haircut (meant to represent one of her character's pre-movie humiliations by men), she glowed like a peach, more beautiful than ever. It was a role reminiscent of *Intermezzo*'s: she is all open-faced ardor and impending heartbreak, even more powerfully.

For Whom the Bell Tolls: the guerrilla (Cooper at her left; Arturo de Cordova and Akim Tamiroff in foreground)

And though the movie itself was limp and muddled, it was a great triumph for her.

So was her next one, *Gaslight* (1944). As an innocent young wife driven close to mad in a Victorian London town house by a furtively criminal husband (Charles Boyer), she won her first Academy Award. Being victimized at feature length was a help to that, of course. But Bergman—under George Cukor's direction—avoids both monotony and bathos, if only by finding in the role so many nuances of suffering and humiliation at the hands of the peerless Boyer—who is genuinely chilling as the awful husband.

It's a highly theatrical piece, based on a play by Patrick Hamilton, successful in both London and New York. It ends—the penultimate scene in the movie—in a Big Moment for the wife, the worm-turns scene. Not only are we ready for it but we know that it's coming when she asks the inspector (Joseph Cotton) to let her see her husband—who has been tied to a chair after an escape attempt—alone. She enters the attic where he is tied up: Get a knife and cut me free, he says, without noticing that her composure now is a form of seething. She brandishes the knife under his nose and then flings it aside: she's lost it, she says, and if only she were not a madwoman she might find it. Then with rising excitement: "If I were not mad I could have helped you—whatever you had done I could have pitied and protected you. Because I am mad I hate you—because I am mad I am rejoicing in my heart without a shred of pity—watching you go with glory in my heart!" And she calls to the inspector: "Mr. Campbell! Take this man away!"

Bergman brings all her skill and energy to making the scene work ("glory in my heart" is hard), and it nearly does. It's not that you're resisting it—it's on the same melodramatic level you've been submitting to and enjoying all along. But what's interesting is how it just misses in her hands the synthetic high it promises. It's a diva scene and Bergman is not a diva. (Think of Bette Davis—or Crawford!) That negative capability is part of what made her seem so "natural" on the screen—her absence of temperament. So notable that she hardly seems like an actress at all—let alone an Actress. (There are no drag queen Ingrid Bergmans—nor is one even imaginable.) The trap for her in performance is not mannerism, not overemphasis or overacting, but the way "naturalness" can shade into blandness.

Her own awareness of that may be one reason she wanted to do

Saratoga Trunk (1945), after *For Whom the Bell Tolls* (and before the filming of *Gaslight*). Also, she and costar Gary Cooper were still enjoying the affair they had begun during the Hemingway movie—an event that shows even more happily in the second film than it did in the first. Cooper is again top-billed, of course (he has almost a separate plot to himself in the film, about a railroad war with lots of brawling), but *Saratoga* is her movie this time, and her story, from an Edna Ferber bestseller. She is Clio Dulaine, an adventuress, who sets out for 1890s New Orleans with a plan to outrage her upper-class relations there (in revenge for their expulsion of her late mother, also an "adventuress"). And then with the money they give her to get out of town, she entrains to Saratoga, where she passes herself off as the widowed La Comtesse "de Choo-choo"—as an acerbic onlooker (the fabulous Florence Bates— of *many* movies) pronounces it—to catch a rich husband there. Which she surely would have done if she hadn't had such a lech for cowboy Cooper all along. Who is mostly in this movie as a bemused observer of *her*.

It was of course another role that Selznick wanted her *not* to do: audiences would never accept her in such an "unsympathetic" part, he said. (And he was right: they didn't—though the movie made money.) As Bergman wrote about Selznick to a friend: "He just didn't understand how the Warner people could see me in that Vivien Leigh part." (Leigh, another Selznick contractee, was their original idea for the role.) "He was going to save me from disaster by not letting me do it . . . He asked me to consider what it would do to my reputation to play Cleo [*sic*] after Maria!" She could never be "wicked," he told her, let alone conniving and domineering and affected, all three of which the part would require her to be. She replied that she would never play the role the way Vivien Leigh would do—and wondered why *he* was being "such a coward" about it. After all, "wasn't it going to be fun and interesting to watch me to find out what I was going to do?"

He gave in. And fun and interesting is exactly what it is—and then some. In a movie that is sometimes draggy and overlong (it was directed, like her Hemingway film, by Sam Wood). She's never looked like this before: she wears a becoming black wig, fancy corseted dresses with bustles and ruffles, and a lot of lip rouge. And if it's true that she just misses the glory-in-my-heart high in *Gaslight*, never mind—she's on a steady one here, and riding on it to the end. Promenading through

town with her parasol and her small but exotic retinue, a dwarf foot-
man and a fussing censorious nanny—flicking her fan, smelling the
flowers in the stalls, tasting the street seller's jambalaya as the onlookers on the street wait in suspense for her verdict. Then sweeping into
the posh restaurant, claiming the relatives' family table (won't they
be surprised when they arrive), accepting a waiter's withdrawn chair
as if it were an overdue apology, eating pieces of cake hummingbird

Saratoga Trunk: the adventuress

style off the tips of her arching fingers as she compliments the dissolv-ing maître d' and ogles the cowboy hunk across the room (Cooper—who else). She is not only funny and free and happily preposterous but . . . beautiful. "I mean . . . *beautiful*," says the bedazzled family lawyer (Curt Bois) in a later scene. "Yes," she replies, with a smile, without skipping a beat, "isn't it lucky?" And the self-delight, the wouldn't-it-be-fun-to-watch-me style of this, leaves the little man even more dazed. As it does us.

Miscast she may be (so the reviews said), but part of the fun is the way she seems to invent the character before your eyes. Especially in the Saratoga scenes. Not only is she a Comtesse, flourishing her bra-vado and her imperious command of French among the American yo-kels, but she is also masquerading as a recently bereft widow still in deep mourning—for "the Comte," of course. And hardly welcoming under such circumstances the hotel manager's intrusive and suspicious inquiries—nor the sudden intervention into the resulting awkwardness of the very formidable Mrs. Bellup (Bates), the spa's unofficial hostess. Who then surprises us all. "I want to welcome you to Saratoga," says Mrs. Bellup very sweetly, "and to tell you that I had the pleasure of knowing your late husband, dear dear Pepi." "Is it possible?" says the "Comtesse," startled but still haughty, towering over her. "Well, *isn't* it?" says the shrewd little lady below her, with a killing little smile. She has sized it all up and joined the "Comtesse's" game—as a fellow con artist. "I may look like a washwoman," as she says later, "but I have family and influence." And she and Bergman will make almost as warily magical a pair as Bergman and Cooper do.

And as for *them* . . . Sitting with him on a piano bench, playing and singing a jaunty Creole folk song, teasing and laughing, looking away from him as much as at him, savoring her power over him—and her happiness at being beside him. *His* feelings about all her plotting and scheming, about her "la-di-da-ing around," as he calls it, are decidedly mixed, even disapproving. Though he will sometimes try to disapprove *less*, to put a better face on what he's seeing in her: "You're just a little girl, dressed up in your ma's long skirts" is one such try. A feeble one. And yet it might sound even feebler if it didn't also have a ring of truth to it. Because Bergman here manages to "be" a roaring phony—someone who is always "on," as Clio is—without ever quite feeling like a *real* one. And just because she doesn't, she keeps your interest and sympathy in a way that a more actressy type (a Vivien Leigh?)—in this consummate and marathon diva role—probably never could have.

But she is "herself" again—wholesome again, that is—in the great Leo McCarey's hokey but cannily conceived and directed *The Bells of St. Mary's* (1945)—as a spunky saintly nun, one whose artless shining sexiness offers a foil to the unflappable celibate cool of Bing Crosby's parish priest. This role for her (it's for Loretta Young, isn't it?) could have been a disaster (again, Selznick opposed it—again, she got her way), with all the archness in performance it might seem to invite. But she turned it into another personal triumph. Making it not only tolerable most of the time (Crosby was a help—they have real on-screen rapport) but authentically sweet and touching. Amazing. Maybe it *was* "inner goodness" after all—if she can even redeem a Leo McCarey nun.

But the fact still remains that she was always more interesting in those halcyon Hollywood days of hers—when it seemed as if she couldn't *not* make a hit, whatever she appeared in—when she was playing some kind of phony, when she was working against her own transparency. Just as she does in what is probably her greatest movie of this period, Hitchcock's romantic thriller *Notorious* (1946)—where you watch her (she's an American spy) trying to fool her besotted Nazi husband-of-convenience Claude Rains, and even more perilously his dragonish mother with her terrifying little eyes (the ineffable Madam Konstantin, as she was called)—and succeeding, for the most part (except for the mother-in-law)—when all along it's Cary Grant's cold and suspicious spy-boss that she longs for—hungrily even, even after he's ditched her. Another act to put over, strangling the yearning and playing it tough—radiantly again, and with an intuition for the nuance in close-ups that marks the greatest stars. She is both sexy and moving in *Notorious,* never more so either before or after it. And it was another hit for her, following on the three she'd had in the single year (1945) before: *Bells, Saratoga Trunk,* and Hitchcock's *Spellbound.*

But by the end, of her eleven Hollywood movies up to now, only two, *Intermezzo* and *Spellbound,* would be made by the man who had brought her to Hollywood and who had controlled her so obsessively from the beginning. She got away from him finally—not only by winning so many arguments, but by her stardom at a time in the business when stars were seizing the power from the moguls. And hers was at its peak when her Selznick contract expired. The choices she makes after that with her new liberty are the story of chapter 11.

4

Wayne and Ford

I.

GOD KNOWS John Wayne was no hero—at least by the standards of the wartime forties, when other male stars—Stewart and Fonda and Gable, Robert Taylor and Tyrone Power and Robert Montgomery, et al., even his lifelong friend and mentor John Ford—went off to the Second World War, and felt themselves profoundly changed by it ever after (especially Ford and Stewart), while Wayne remained in Hollywood. Where he played the war hero again and again (almost always the war against "the Japs") in movies like *The Flying Tigers* and *The Fighting Seabees* and *Back to Bataan* in the early forties, and later in John Ford's *They Were Expendable* in 1945. While doing so he wrote letters to his buddy Ford, serving in the Pacific at the time, about meaning to enlist any day now; he even wrote to the War Department, but he never made the final move. Instead, he let his Poverty Row studio Republic (he'd become their single profit-making big star) go on getting him draft deferments. Ford, a famous hater, would never really forgive him for this—humiliating him later on in front of the military personnel who populated both the crew and the cast of *They Were Expendable*, in which Wayne was playing not only a real-life naval hero but one whom Ford had personally known and admired.

But Wayne's fans never held this dereliction—if they even saw it as that—against him. And his patriotic militance during the Cold War, when he became an icon of the Red-baiting right, obscured the record even more. As did his ongoing career as a movie warrior—which never seemed to falter even in spite of age and increasing girth. At fifty-seven he was Davy Crockett defending *The Alamo* (1960)—directing himself in his own production. At sixty-one he was leading *The Green Berets* (1968)—again producing and directing.

Well, it worked for us—sort of. If not those last two movies, dreadful and tendentious as they were, there were all those others, some of them among the greatest American films ever. And at his death in 1979 (just six years after Ford's) he was universally and genuinely mourned, even by those he had regarded as being on the Other Side—i.e., Democrats. "In an age of few heroes," said the Democratic president Jimmy Carter in his eulogy, "he was the genuine article." But John Wayne was specifically *not* the genuine article—he was the illusion of it. And that illusion had clearly taken.

He was, of course, a genuine movie star—the most genuine of them all by a measure like popularity. His has endured even beyond his death, and before that through thirty-five years of box office dominance and international stardom. Not just an icon but *the* American icon. Which was largely the doing of John Ford.

Begin—as they did—with two of the star's most famous entrances. The first was in *Stagecoach* (1939), the movie that rescued Wayne from Poverty Row. It's almost twenty minutes under way before he even appears—after we've met all the other characters, the passengers in the coach, which is now en route across Ford's beloved Monument Valley, coming over a ridge and down a dirt road. A rifle report rings out, the coach slows—so does the cavalry escort behind—and comes to a halt. The rifleman (Wayne as "the Ringo Kid") looms in full-length close shot against a rear-projected desert (Wayne's shots here were done on a studio set), in a white hat and black shirt, saddle and blanket under one arm, the other outstretched and gripping the rifle by the trigger guard: "Hold it!" he commands—twirling the rifle in his hand, looking straight ahead as the camera moves swiftly in on him until his close-up fills the screen, his neckerchief lifting in the wind.

This sudden camera move (very un-Fordian) is like a nudge in the ribs: Look at *this*, will you? It not only rhymes with and takes up the stopped movement of the stagecoach, it seems meant to be star-making. And Wayne of course carries it off: with his size, his personal authority, his vibrant good looks, the iconic cowboy in short—it's all

With Claire Trevor in *Stagecoach*

there. But so are other things, less expected: a certain unease, a hint of shyness, a distressed look that seems elicited by his own "hold it" command—almost as if it pained him to give it at all. This is not the Gary Cooper or Randolph Scott face—chiseled, impassive, resolute— but the face of someone who *feels* what he's doing in his stomach, enough to show some strain about it in his furrowed brow, though no less determined to do it.

But then—famously by now—there is a slight balls-up in the track- ing shot: on the way to the close-up that it ends with, the focus slips a little, softening and diffusing, then regains itself, still moving. And just as it does so, Wayne's expression changes, too, the determination behind the command replaced by something like wonder, the face boyish and unguarded, the eyes widened, the forehead uncreased. It's meant to be—as we learn from the dialogue that follows—a look of surprised recognition (Ringo turns out to know the coach's driver), and by that measure the actor's "take" is clumsy and overdone. But the fact that it seems to come out of nowhere when we first see it only enhances the effect: the glimpse of ingenuousness under the authority. It's no wonder the shot is so renowned; it may have been a screwed-up one by studio standards, but Ford knew better than to redo it.

Just as he knew, twenty years later, how to present his by then indispensable star in the opening shots of *The Searchers* (1957). No happy accidents here—megastar Wayne's appearance is as carefully composed as a musical number. As in part it is, of course: the score by Max Steiner, in full throttle from the start, segueing from the country-western twang of the cowboy song over the opening credits ("What makes a man to wander?") to a grand full-orchestra launch into the sight of a door opening in the center of widescreen blackness; the camera going through it following close upon the shoulders and head of a woman walking out onto a porch into a dazzle of sun and space, of brown earth and blue sky stretching endlessly away toward mesas at the horizon, and at screen right in the far distance, something moving. That's what she's looking toward—a delicately beautiful woman of middle age with wide eloquent eyes and brown hair—as she puts her hand on the porch post, the other shading her eyes with fingers curled, the wind blowing gently in her hair, as she strains to see into the distance. And then we see it, too, in the next shot: rider and horse approaching. At the house a man comes from inside to stand on the porch next to her—he, too, is looking into the distance. She turns and looks at him. He looks at her. "Ethan?" he says softly. No reply.

But the question—like the music under it—has a surprising resonance. Not only from the biblical ring of the name but also from the way it gets said, sounding both incredulous and inevitable. And from the way the woman reacts to it—just looking mutely at the man, then turning back to the distance again. As if such a question were too big (on the scale of the scenery, and the swelling music) to be answered. The man comes down the steps into the foreground and the sunlight. He has a weak chin.

Now their children appear on the porch, too, one by one: a teenage girl, a boy carrying firewood, a little girl with her doll, and then her dog. Who barks. At the man riding toward us now. We can see clearly now that it's Big John Wayne, under the shadow cast by his big black hat with its outsize brim fluttering in the wind, as he gets off his horse and comes slowly forward, in a long gray many-layered army coat, a red flannel shirt, and blue denim pants, his hand on the saber at his belt, his gaze unwavering and unreadable. "It's your uncle Ethan!" says the teenage girl to the boy, who breaks into a happy grin.

A somber wordless handshake between the men—after which the husband looks back at the wife on the porch. She comes down the porch steps—to the music. Wayne removes his hat and goes to her. "Welcome home, Ethan," she says, her hand touching his upper arm, her eyes closing, almost reverently, as he bends down to kiss her forehead. She turns then and goes up the little flight of steps again—but facing him as she does, as if backing onto a stage (or an altar). The music underscores this movement with a pause, a downbeat, and then a launching into melody again as she ascends with hands on the billowing apron that lifts softly on the wind in front of her, and backs wordlessly, welcomingly, into the house ahead of him. And the others follow, in a concluding long shot of the porch.

And yet we hardly see Wayne's face through all of this. In the shifting arrangements of the figures he is the towering gray-coated one. But we've seen his tenderness—in that leaning from his great height to kiss the wife on her brow. In this sequence, her face has been the focal point. But at the end, as she moves back, leading him through the door into her home, his monumentality effaces her, both in the door frame and the one on the screen. Not ominously—gently, even sweetly. Like that kiss. That engulfing monumentality is a sign of what Ford by the end of the fifties has made of Wayne both as his actor and as his star. And *The Searchers* is its richest expression.

Her name is Martha (Dorothy Jordan), and she will soon (in the following sequence) be saying goodbye to this man she has welcomed to her home, her husband's brother. And by that time we will have gathered—mainly through Ford's subtle orchestration of the pair's looks-and-looks-away in the middle of the clamoring family scene—that there is or has been Something Between Them, however unfulfilled.

The local preacher and lawman, the Reverend Samuel Clayton (Ward Bond), has come to visit the family by way of recruiting Ethan

"Welcome home, Ethan": the kiss—then leading the way

and the other men for a scouting party, to check out an Indian danger alert. Waiting for the men to assemble, the Reverend stands alone in the kitchen, by the enormous family table, drinking coffee from a mug and looking off. But then he sees (as do we) Martha, by herself in the next room, getting the men's coats ready—and caressing and kissing Ethan's . . . The Reverend looks away—he's eating a doughnut, too. Behind him Ethan enters. And then Martha, too, from the opposite room, bringing him his hat and coat. Silently. There is another grave forehead kiss, another resigned and lowered gaze, another touching of his arm (at the elbow this time, and more urgent), all of which is very pointedly *not* observed by the Reverend, who stands in the foreground holding his coffee, raising the cup to his lips, chewing thoughtfully on his doughnut, and looking off abstractedly—as the couple behind him draw heartbreakingly apart . . .

There is hardly a movie scene anywhere, it seems to me—at least when I watch this one—that moves you so much and so powerfully by its delicacy, its mixture of tact and tenderness, as this one does. Ford at such moments (not untypical for him) makes those other classical masters, justly famous for their "touches," their civilized elegances (Lubitsch, Ophuls, Stroheim, et al.), look almost ham-fisted.

Delicacy is not something you normally associate with Wayne, either. But in a way, it was his secret weapon—just as it was Ford's. This was apparent in their collaboration from its beginnings—not only in *Stagecoach*, but in the movie they made shortly after that, *The Long Voyage Home* (1940), an intensely arty low-budget film made in the expressionist style of Ford's *The Informer* (1935), based on Eugene O'Neill's one-act plays about unhappy men at sea, and photographed by Gregg Toland.

Wayne was top-billed but turns out to be mostly on the fringes or in the background of the major scenes, where the strenuous acting is done by a cast of the sort of whimsical character actors Ford specially liked (Frank Qualen, Barry Fitzgerald, his brother Arthur Shields, Thomas Mitchell). And when those scenes turn ugly (as in the persecution of the mysterious Ian Hunter character) in the ship's claustrophobic belowdecks quarters, Wayne is nowhere to be seen. As the gentle giant named Ole Olsen, he seems often used for decoration (the cast is not handsome) and for mood-enhancing close-ups. He is the boy in the gang of men, the one the other crewmen watch out for.

Ethan with Debbie the child (Lana Wood), as Martha (Dorothy Jordan)
and family look on

He talks—in a faint but distinct Scandinavian accent—about leaving
the sea and going back to the family farm in Sweden. They all talk
about something like that, but Ole is the single one, as they all recognize, for whom his dream might come true. If he isn't too trusting and
dumb, that is—as he threatens to be in a saloon encounter with a
Cockney whore (Mildred Natwick) who is reluctantly—at the orders
of a sinister pimp—setting him up to be drugged and shanghaied back
to sea.

The episode is filmed mostly in an intimate two-shot at a table in
the saloon, and Natwick's sad little tart—she tells Ole that what do
you know, she comes from Sweden, too ("There's no place like home,

is there?"), but had to leave before mastering the language—is both funny and touching. But Wayne's Ole is something much more. It's a remarkable early demonstration of how many levels he could give to even ordinary exchanges onscreen. But even more remarkable here is the way he seems to *glow* (the Toland treatment—à la Bergman). He was a little old for the role (in his thirties, having used up his first youth in quickie westerns), but the broad face-changing smile is distinctly boyish. So is the respectful attention he gives to this strange older woman (Natwick was actually a year younger than he), whose questions about his Swedish home and family are not always easy for Ole in his unsettled situation to answer. Does he have a sweetheart back home? "I don't know, Miss Frieda," he replies, "I think so." And the wistful gravity, the care and gallantry of his responses to this friendly inquiring lady—all amount to something you have to call sheer niceness, ordinary enough to be sure, but here in its purest human form. The *star* size.

And it is a good thing to have access to if you are going to spend the rest of a long career—as he would—playing roles (unlike Ole Olsen) that require you to run things, giving orders to other people: teaching the greenhorn how to shoot, the drunk how to get sober, the recruit how to be a marine, the modern woman how to be a real one, and so on, ad infinitum. Through nearly two hundred movies, and for almost a half century, as a Top Ten major star.

In 1930, when he was a total unknown doing his first starring role, even then he was cast as the boss—of a cross-country pioneer wagon team, in Raoul Walsh's *The Big Trail*. It's a shock to see that performance now. The cliché feels inescapable: he looks hardly old enough to shave (he was twenty-two). A face untouched by lines or loss or experience. Modest in manner, almost demure, with thick curly hair, an errant curl now and then falling on the forehead, dressed in form-hugging deerskin. He looks bigger than his horse when he gets on it—even bigger than that when he throws his leg over its head to get off again. But he had an athlete-dancer's grace even then. And the ballsy, rolling, slightly pigeon-toed walk is already there. And in spite of his callowness you never have trouble believing in his leadership of a crowd of pioneers who appear much older (Did only elderly people go west? one review asked).

How did Walsh find him? (He wanted Gary Cooper, but Cooper

was unavailable.) Wayne—then called "Duke" (as opposed to Marion) Morrison—was around the Fox studio as part of the Ford gang. He had been an extra and occasional walk-on in Ford's late silents and early talkies, and a prop man, too. Director Walsh saw him moving furniture on a set. "Dammit, the son of a bitch looked like a *man!*" he said later. And *The Big Trail* was a major undertaking, shot on outdoor locations in a mass trek across five states and over two thousand miles.

It was also filmed in a "revolutionary" new widescreen process called Grandeur (it would later be called Cinemascope—and called new again). But movie houses had to be remodeled to accommodate this new process and screen width at a time in the Depression when they felt lucky to stay open at all—and *The Big Trail* was a flop. Virtually all that the young Wayne got out of it (so few audiences even saw it) was his new professional name (courtesy of Walsh) and his cowboy persona (not the one he would have chosen—he didn't like horses), which he then took into the seemingly endless succession of serials and six-day westerns he would do for Poverty Row studios like Mascot and Monogram and Republic, the kind of movies that were hardly shown outside the rural small towns they were made for. You didn't graduate from being a star in such films, as Wayne soon was, into stardom in the mainstream ones (though you could take the reverse path, like George O'Brien and Tim Holt). And it seems likely he would never have made it into another A-picture lead if Ford hadn't cast him in *Stagecoach* when he did—after drinking and hanging out with him through the nine years the actor toiled at Republic.

Although it was still Republic that owned him after that, from then on they lent him out for bigger and better things—to Universal for his three films with Dietrich, to Paramount for a second male lead (Ray Milland was the first) in DeMille's *Reap the Wild Wind* (1942), where he fights a giant octopus underwater. As well as being an action star, he was a reliable leading man, much in demand during the romantic actor scarcity of the war years, when he partnered some of the queens of Hollywood, uneasily—and except for Dietrich, in only one picture apiece: Joan Crawford (*Reunion in France*, 1942), Jean Arthur (*A Lady Takes a Chance*, 1943), and Claudette Colbert (*Without Reservations*, 1946)—his career burgeoning as each of theirs seemed fading.

Nobody thought much about his acting—least of all John Ford— any more than they thought about Errol Flynn's. As with Flynn, the charm and masculinity were more than enough. But that perception of Wayne began to change when Howard Hawks's *Red River* appeared in 1948 with Wayne as a tyrannical boss of a growingly mutinous cattle drive—for the first time playing older (rather than younger) than he was, with graying temples and a crick in his back and no big love interest. Even his buddy Ford was impressed. Not to be outdone, he cast him the next year in a *real* geezer role—as a cavalry officer entering his retirement and getting a gold watch from his men in the first reel—in *She Wore a Yellow Ribbon* (1949), another hit. But even before that, thanks not only to *Red River* but to Ford's *Fort Apache* earlier the same year (1948), Wayne had become the hottest star in postwar Hollywood.

And in the thirty years he had to go yet, he seemed almost never to be off the screen. The movies were mostly junk (just before *The Searchers*, he appeared as Genghis Khan in *The Conqueror*). But there were still more major ones with Ford—like *Rio Grande* (1950), the last of the so-called Cavalry Trilogy (after *Fort Apache* and *Yellow Ribbon*), followed by *The Quiet Man* (1952), filmed on location in Ford's beloved Ireland, and finally *The Man Who Shot Liberty Valance* (1962), filmed on studio sets, as in the old days. And there were two more wonderful westerns with Hawks: *Rio Bravo* (1959) and *El Dorado* (1967). Henry Hathaway's (not the Coen brothers') *True Grit* in 1969—with Wayne doing a witty sendup of his own image, playing a choleric, past-it, one-eyed bounty hunter, fat and drunk and still giving the orders ("*Here*," he says blearily, sprawled on the ground where he's just fallen off his horse, "we'll camp *here* . . .")—got him his first and only Academy Award. And Don Siegel's elegant and elegiac *The Shootist* in 1976 was the star's moving final appearance, as a gunfighter dying of cancer. As he himself was by that time. He died three years later—years filled with appropriate tributes and outpourings of acclaim and love.

One of the movies that best shows why he meant so much to us is *The Man Who Shot Liberty Valance*, his penultimate film with Ford (*Donovan's Reef* a year later was their last). A strange movie, to put it mildly, though audiences hardly seemed to notice or to mind at the time—probably because they were too much at home with the two iconic figures, Wayne and Jimmy Stewart, who center it all, to feel the absence in this western of scenery or action or even horses. True, there's the usual frontier town, with saloons and stores and hitching posts lining the single street, but it's like a theme park version of it, reduced and cramped and more than usually synthetic-looking. And then there is the fact that almost everyone in the cast, except the heroine (Vera Miles) and the villain (Lee Marvin), looks too old for their role (Did only elderly people go west?)—especially the two stars, who seem to be (at fifty-five and fifty-six respectively) reenacting the roles of their youth: Stewart the green gawky kid and Wayne the big brother who protects him—the fancy pants from the East meeting "the fastest draw west of the Picketwire."

But though for Wayne it's a standard role, like that studio set town, it seems curiously reduced. Certainly secondary to Stewart's. Who is—as Wayne later described him—"the shitkicker hero." It's true that Tom Doniphon (Wayne) gets to save the "shitkicker" in the climax, but he does it not by an O.K. Corral showdown (as in *Stagecoach* and countless others) but sneakily, by firing a rifle out of the shadows, then letting the unwitting Stewart take the credit and become the (seeming) hero of the title. Wayne complained mildly about all this in a later interview with Dan Ford (the director's grandson). Stewart had the hero part, he said, and Lee Marvin had the villain, and Andy Devine (the cowardly sheriff) and Edmond O'Brien (the bloviating newspaper editor) had all the humor—"And shit, I've got to walk through the goddamn movie."

But that walk, as we knew by then, was impressive enough. As the gunfighter Tom Doniphon, he is no longer unsettled by his own power but relaxing into it, like a comfortable coat. With all his outdoor ease in the low-ceilinged space of the town café, lounging against a wall or rocking on his heels away from it, pivoting on his leg and planting a boot heel on the wood plank floor, he seems both too big for the space and inhabiting it more naturally than anyone else in the frame, with his genial skeptical attention, his comic-looking open-mouth grin, his glow of humorous appreciation as he watches the stressed-out waitress Vera Miles tending to Stewart, the new arrival in town, who has just been wounded in a holdup. "He's a lawyer, y'know," offers Wayne—and makes that information sound risible. He's just an amused onlooker here, and yet somehow in command of this space where he's being technically ignored (Stewart's become its center)—especially by her. Except when he irritates her—and she responds by knocking the drink out of his hand (one too many). "Mind if I *smoke*?" he asks—

amused again. And even a passing exchange like this seems to illustrate Wayne's famous answer to an interviewer who asked him about how he worked: "Ordinarily they just stand me there and run everybody up against me," he explained.

One of his functions in this haunting Ford movie—this "wintry remembrance of springtime," as Gilberto Perez calls it—not only in these early scenes but thereafter, is to make you feel the force of presence itself, in this film about loss, about the passing of time. Presence not only in the person of Wayne but even in the contrast he inevitably makes with Stewart—who generally has to work a little harder (or as it seems, "act" a little bit more) to make his effect. Doniphon is dead when the movie begins (Stewart and Miles have returned for the

James Stewart on the floor between Lee Marvin and Wayne in
The Man Who Shot Liberty Valance

funeral), and the main story is one long flashback. Then back to the movie's "present," and the coffin, and the cactus rose, freighted with memory, that Hallie (Miles) leaves on top of it—before she and her husband entrain back to the East again. And these are the strongest scenes in the film, in a way—no wonder Wayne complained later—the ones where Doniphon is definitively gone, and where we and those others on the screen are invited to register the loss—where we get to *miss* John Wayne.

II.

YOU DON'T HAVE to be Irish to hate *The Quiet Man* (1952), but it certainly helps. With its relentless tweeness, its parade of stock Irish types seemingly meant to be adorable, especially when they drink a lot, and if they are furtive and cute about it, like Barry Fitzgerald, even more so. It was heavy going when I first saw it, just as I feared it would be. But I loved Wayne—if only because he loved Maureen O'Hara. And because—as the movie demonstrated—she was a match for him, even physically, it seemed. They both looked bigger on the screen than the usual romantic pair—and that was part of what made them feel so sexy. Homerically so, to cite a word used by the village matchmaker (Fitzgerald) the morning after their wedding night, when he first sees their vacant but collapsed wedding bed.

But as we know by then, it wasn't lovemaking that had collapsed their bed, but instead one of the movie's frequent furious preludes to it (she had bolted the bedroom door on him, he broke it down, then threw her on the bed and left her). As in the film's single most memorable image: of O'Hara, cracked like a whip at the end of Wayne's powerful right arm as he pulls her back from an open doorway and into a tempestlike wind, spreading her across the screen like a flying pennon, her body arching, her red hair streaming and skirt billowing, her free arm outflung—as he leaves her out there for an instant, then pulls her back against his chest and into a back-bending kiss. At once putting her down and turning her on, it seems. Until she hauls off and socks him. Something she's often trying to do and not always succeeding at. As later on when she misses, spins around, and loses her balance—giving him his chance to kick her on the behind. (Understandably: he's right in the middle of fistfighting with her brother.) Fordian foreplay.

Never mind: she's John Wayne's ideal woman—onscreen at least. Whereas Crawford had made him look preadolescent (anyway, she went to the hand-kissing Continental guy at the end), Colbert made him look grouchy, and Arthur made him seem bemused, with O'Hara he looks fated—home at last. And in *The Quiet Man* it helps that the issue between them is relatively clear: married they now may be, but she won't come to his bed until he gets for her the dowry money that her legal guardian, her brutish elder brother (Victor McLaglen), has been withholding.

Ford thought that *The Quiet Man* was his sexiest movie. The competition wasn't keen, but sexy it is. Even to its final surprise at the end. The story has been building not only to the delayed fuck but to O'Hara's finally getting her cash dowry (Wayne having bested her brother in their public fistfight). And then, before the whole shocked community, she throws all that money into the fire in a grate. It's one of those Ford moments that opens up levels you've been noticing without quite noticing that you had—until now, when you take the full measure finally of this heroine's abandon and recklessness. Sexy indeed. It almost redeems the movie-long cock-tease.

Ford had first teamed Wayne and O'Hara two years before this: in his *Rio Grande* (1950), as a more mature couple, married but apart for fifteen years, coming together again on a cavalry post over the issue of their underage son (Claude Jarman, Jr.), who had run away to join his long-absent father's troop but who now needs his mother's consent to stay in it. She's been withholding it and has turned up on the post solely to get her boy back home. She gives the idea up after a while, it seems. It gets subsumed, like almost everything else in this less-than-coherent movie, into the tension and attraction between her and Wayne.

They are having a charged dinner in his tent, by candlelight—with O'Hara growing more and more uneasy and with Wayne smoldering across the table at her. So it's almost a relief when his regimental singers (the Sons of the Pioneers, Ford's favorite group) appear outside and request permission to serenade the colonel's lady. The couple rise and go outside the tent to receive this tribute. But they are both somewhat

discomfited when the song of choice turns out to be "I'll Take You
Home Again, Kathleen." We can see that it must have been Their
Song at one time—and of course her name is Kathleen. And in an
unmoving close-up two-shot we watch the two of them respond.
O'Hara goes from initial embarrassment to sadness and then to a
giving in to fond recall as the song goes on. She is touching, but it is
Wayne in the same extended reaction shot who is truly moving—with
his startled heartsick look above the bristling military mustache. A
guilty boy's face at first—then a man's, struck to the heart, registering
a sudden shattering consciousness of irretrievable loss.

The fact is that no one does this sort of thing much better than
Wayne. ("I don't act," he once said, "I react.") And Ford's Wayne does
it even better than that. It's what Ford more than anyone else does

Rio Grande: with Maureen O'Hara

with Wayne—connecting him over and over again to images of loss and longing, of yearning toward the distant, the far-off, the unrecoverable: toward life on shore in *The Long Voyage Home*, toward the departing ships or the crippled returning ones in *They Were Expendable*, over his lost command and the grave of his wife in *She Wore a Yellow Ribbon*, against images of fallen comrades at the end of *Fort Apache*. And most hopelessly of all, toward his brother's wife in those early scenes of *The Searchers*. A little later in that film he will have to stagger into the burning wreckage of her home after Scar the destroyer has left it and call out her name in anguish—offscreen. Open and undisguised anguish is not much in Wayne's line. He's more at home with desolation, with the settling in of loss, with the view into the empty distance.

It's the other meaning of Monument Valley, of his at-home-ness there. Could any other star seem so in harmony with that space on the screen—Ford's space—as he does? The Wayne hero belongs to distances—and distances even beyond. It's one reason the famous ending of *The Searchers*—with Ethan walking away from the camera and into the desert and the final fadeout, after he's watched the others walk into the house and toward us, the audience—never prompts you to wonder where he's going. It's too appropriate—that he goes off merely. Wherever. Like Garbo—though in an utterly different register—Ford's Wayne belongs to the cinema of memory.

Wayne had more power on the screen than anyone else in movies, Howard Hawks said of him. But it's often a troubled power—as his first great close-up in *Stagecoach* already suggests. Even at his most implacable he can look somehow stricken. And with reason. The Wayne hero is not someone who learns new things readily, if at all. He knows too much already. "You talk too much, you think too much," he tells Stewart in *Liberty Valance*. Of course he's against all that. But his ignorance is never simply proud or smirking—stubborn, God knows, but usually tinged with regret. Even when he's telling someone off—as he does Donna Reed and her navy nurses in *They Were Expendable*—he looks sort of sorry about it. Sometimes it's less his slit-eyed stare you may remember from his movies than the abashed look that follows it.

But still . . . "Won't you change your mind for just once in your life?" Coleen Gray as his soon-to-be-lost love (the Indians again) challenges him in *Red River*. But he never does. Not until the last reel, and

The final image of *The Searchers*

then just barely. He is the decider—like the erstwhile U.S. president he almost certainly would have admired. And so he has the *job* of being right, even when he's not sure that he is. And watching that unease grow in his character is one of the chief interests of Hawks's movie. "You'd'a shot him through the eyes!" accuses his surrogate son Montgomery Clift, after a nearly fatal confrontation with a disobedient cowhand. Replies Wayne's Matt Dunson, slitting his eyes, no regret: "Just as sure as you're standin' there." But then just after this, when he's alone with his comic sidekick—the admirable Walter Brennan—"Go ahead, say it," he growls. "You was wrong, Mr. Dunson," the other replies. As we know Dunson already knows.

But where Hawks glamorizes his fallibly intransigent hero—as when he shows him walking to the climactic gunfight in town, striding through that herd of cattle everywhere in his way, his big hand parting them like a curtain—Ford goes even further: he mythologizes him in *The Searchers*. Ethan is neither another Dunson nor another Captain Bligh (whom the *Red River* screenwriter Borden Chase once likened the Dunson character to) but another Ahab, whose white whale is Scar (Henry Brandon), the Comanche warrior who has slaughtered Martha and her husband and their young son and abducted the two daughters, Lucy (Pippa Scott) and little Debbie (Lana Wood). But "We'll find 'em," says Ethan, "as sure as the turnin' o' the earth"—one of the movie's most famous lines. Another one, also Ethan's, is this: "Injun'll chase a thing 'til he thinks he's chased it enough and quits," he says to his young two-man posse as they ride along beside him. "Same when he runs. Seems like he never learned there's a critter'll just keep comin' on."

And "comin' on" Ethan does—for fifteen years and with his "posse" down to one, Martin Pawley (Jeffrey Hunter), himself with Indian blood, adopted into Martha's (and Ethan's) family. But in the end it's this multiracial kid who does the job, not only rescuing Debbie but killing Scar—while Ethan, late to the scene, has to be content with taking the dead man's scalp.

The movie characteristically underplays the irony of this, but there's no question that it lends a complicating touch of futility to Ethan's general awesomeness—something less Melville than Samuel Beckett, for whom even "the turnin' o' the earth" could feel comically pointless. Ahab at least gets to have a climactic showdown with his whale—all Ethan gets is that scalp.

And his fierceness has none of that ameliorating unease about it that Dunson's had. He is the Wayne hero at his most implacable. What's more, he displays the racism that is only implied in a figure like Dunson (or like John Wayne). Young Martin had been taken in as a baby by Martha's family after an Indian raid had killed his own. But Ethan with his unfailing eye spots Martin's Indian blood (one-eighth Cherokee) on their first meeting. "Fella could mistake you for a half-breed," he growls—*not* friendly.

He is not just a parlor racist but a proactive one: shooting retreating braves in their backs after a skirmish, decimating their buffalo herds so as to starve them, shooting out the eyes of a dead warrior so that he will have to "wander forever between the winds," as he knows the Comanches believe. But worst of all, from young Martin's point of view, is that he's also a little nuts—as "a critter who'll just keep comin' on" is likely to be.

"He's a man that can go crazy wild," Martin tells his sweetheart, Laurie (Vera Miles), a man who has become a threat to his own lost niece. That's why Martin can't leave the search or Ethan's side while the older man persists in it. Debbie, Ethan declares, is no longer any kin of his—"she's a Comanch." When they started their search, she was a little girl, so that if she has survived till now, it can only have been by one means: (Ethan again) by being raised "as one of their own, until . . . until she's an age tuh—" Well, you know . . .

But what Ethan can't bring himself to name here, Laurie, Martin's frustrated fiancée (she just wants him to stay home and marry her), does—and memorably. He *has* to "fetch Debbie home," Martin insists. "Fetch *what* home?" she exclaims, "—the leavings of a savage buck, sold time after time to the highest bidder, with savage brats of her own . . . You know what Ethan will do if he has the chance? He'll put a bullet through her brain. And I tell you Martha would *want* him to!"

Ethan may be nuts, but nobody could suppose that Laurie is meant to be, in spite of the wickedness of this speech. "Savage brats of her own" makes you wince—but then (as usual in Ford) it vividly evokes the problem. Laurie is voicing attitudes that anyone in her embattled frontier community would recognize and most would share. Because Ethan, outsider though he may be—a mercenary and a wanderer and probably an outlaw, welcomed home like a hero, then left to sit on the porch and pet the dog while the woman he loves goes to bed with his brother inside—is still deeply in touch with these folks at home. His clear authority in their world—like his authority in our own—comes as much from his deep connection to them (and us) as from the glamour of his disconnections.

He's also their delegate, in a way, to the worst of the horrors around them. Partly because of expertise beyond theirs: he is the one who knows the good of shooting out the dead brave's eyes, who can spot the slightest tinge of Indian blood, who can even identify a white woman's scalp hanging among the others in Scar's tent (it's Martin's long-dead mother's). And he knows enough to knock Martin unconscious before the boy can rush into the smoldering house to see the carnage of his second family—the sight that Ethan has just returned from seeing. "Don't let him go in there, Mose," he instructs his holy fool sidekick (Hank Worden). "Won't do him any good."

And later, after he has found—as we later learn—the despoiled body of Lucy and buried her in his army greatcoat, he comes riding back to his two-man posse, nearly falling off his horse, not seeming to hear the young men's questions: Where's he been? What's wrong? Where's his coat? "I'm not going back there," is all he answers, then remounts his horse and leaves them.

But later when Lucy's sweetheart, Brad (Harry Carey, Jr.), returns to their camp to report that he has just seen Lucy alive among the Indians, even walking around—he's sure it was her—Ethan tells him that she is dead: "What you saw was a *buck*, wearing Lucy's dress." But why hadn't he told them this before? "I thought it best t' keep it from yuh," he says—and that's that. But Brad is distraught and stammering: "Did they—? Was she—?" And Ethan explodes: "Whata you want me to *do*! Draw you a picture? Spell it out?" Then the deep gravelly voice breaks: "Don't ever ask me—long as you live, don't ever ask me more." At that he turns away from them, rolling over on his side and onto his stomach—as if taking the evil into his gut. Like his Sergeant Stryker in *Sands of Iwo Jima* (1949), falling on the grenade to save his men.

In the wake of a U.S. cavalry massacre of a Comanche settlement, Ethan and Martin cross paths with the women and children who survived the slaughter being herded into a stockade by the troops. Are any white women among them? Martin asks—and he and Ethan are brought into a shed with a soldier standing guard at the door. Sitting on the dirt floor, a woman in rags, held by the arms of a woman on a bench behind her, screams in terror when the two men enter. The guard rushes over to her with a bracelet of tiny bells and shakes it in front of her face—which seems to calm her.

Neither of these women is young. The crazed one is played—with a clear pointedness—by Mae Marsh, the Little Sister of Griffith's *Birth of a Nation* (who jumps from a cliff to escape an aroused black, thus bringing about in that film the beginning of the Ku Klux Klan). But nearby are two girls who would be just about Debbie's age. They are holding on to each other and staring silently at the strangers, one seeming to cower in fear, the other grinning up at the men with wild eyes, an Indian sign inscribed on her brow. It's the lascivious-looking one whom Martin seems to take hope in: "Debbie?" he says tentatively, and shows her the rag doll that once belonged to his sister. But the girl takes no notice of it, only grinning back at him, even more lewdly.

At this point the madwoman in the dirt comes to life again, leaping up and grabbing the doll away from Martin, sitting again and clutching it to her breast, rocking with it and crooning over it. This is hopeless— and the two men turn to go. "It's hard to believe they're white," says the soldier guard to Ethan. "They ain't white," replies Ethan, "—any*more*. They're Comanch."

But then as he reaches the door—the woman in the dirt continuing to rock and croon over the doll—he turns and looks back. And Ford's camera rushes up and onto Wayne's face in close-up (the Ringo Kid has come a long terrible way)—the fierce laser eyes under the shadow of his hat brim gleaming through the dark. It's a look not just of revulsion but of hatred. Back to the woman and her doll—then back to Ethan again, to that fixed blood-chilling stare. Then, as if pulling himself away by an effort, he turns and goes out the door.

"Hard to believe they're white" is one of the film's richest lines (the screenplay is by Ford's son-in-law and former *Times* movie critic Frank S. Nugent). Since it's hard to conceive how the women could *be* much whiter—they are all of them some degree of blond. As if nonwhite meant rolling-eyed and crazy. What it means to Ethan, you recognize here, is less about a "redskin" than about someone who's had her brains fucked out by one, by more than one even—someone who's been lost to uncontrol and who is not coming back from it, who's become "the leavings of a savage buck." And as we also know, Ethan has his own temptation to un-control—the other side of his I-thought-it-best-not-to-tell-you authority.

And soon the big endlessly foreshadowed moment arrives. Ethan, astride his horse and with Scar's scalp dangling from his hand, comes upon Debbie, alone and on foot after the federal raid on her tribe's camp. He had encountered this Comancheized Debbie once before, earlier on, and raised his rifle on her then, but Martin had come between them to save her, and she had escaped back to "her people." And now seeing Ethan alone she tries to escape him again, running across the sands. He rides after her. Now Martin reappears—panicked but also on foot and soon far behind Debbie and her pursuer. As Ethan rides her down, he catches up when she stumbles and falls against a rockface. He jumps from his horse. "No!" cries Martin, running but still too far away.

Then a close shot of the girl on the ground as Ethan looms above her. He reaches down, grasps her under the arms, and lifts her in one swift and sweeping movement—which Ford's camera follows and even imitates, swooping downward to frame her on the ground, then following her upward in the thrust and lift of Ethan's arms, showing her raised and held in his hands against the sky, with small and impotent fists clutched in front of her—as she is brought suddenly downward again to lie across his arms looking into his face, still terrified, fists still clenched. A pause—then the great rumble of a voice says (almost casually), "Let's go home, Debbie." The girl takes this in slowly at first, then puts her arms around his neck as he cradles her and turns with her to go back to his horse.

What makes this scene so powerful? It's become one of the most famous in American film. More to the point, perhaps, what makes it convincing—as most people, if not all, seem to find it? The whole movie has been building to this moment, promising—and not just in Ethan's scene with the captive women—some kind of tragic outcome. Which now doesn't happen—and the movie (as if to say "Take it or leave it") more or less ends. It's true that Hollywood by this time had made us used to arbitrary happy endings, even to happy endings we weren't seriously meant to believe (think Douglas Sirk, or Nicholas Ray's *Bigger than Life*). But what is it about this one—more seemingly arbitrary, less "explained" than most—that makes it feel revelatory? Explanations for Ethan's turnabout can be found, of course; the definitive Ford biographer, Joseph McBride, attributes the sudden reversal to Ethan's conscious recall of his lifting Debbie in just this same way when she was a little girl with a doll ("the spontaneous reaction to a long buried memory"); the late novelist (and Ford critic) Thomas Flanagan ascribes it to a postorgasmic calm, Ethan having been released from his hard-on for vengeance by just having scalped his nemesis, Scar, in the previous scene—and so on. But however much such observations may help to account for what Ethan feels and does in this scene, they hardly touch what you may feel watching it.

It's one of those great movie epiphanies that feels convincing to you

Debbie found—and unclenching her fists

not because it feels explainable but because it doesn't, not finally—a moment that both surprises and persuades you at once, and that persuades you partly *because* it surprises you. Reminding you as it does of how feelings of tenderness and love—like Ethan's—can invade you, inexplicably even. Of how suddenly, even mysteriously, we can rise above our own worst characters and impulses. It's what you've hoped for from Ethan all along, of course (and what Ford, one imagines, hoped for from himself). The sort of interior event that Simone Weil finds so powerfully present in the violence of the *Iliad* as she reads it: one of "those brief, celestial moments when man possesses his soul."

And even if such moments, as she concedes, don't always last, for her it's enough—and sort of hopeful—that they exist at all. And their all too frequent brevity is the sobering reality that Ford prompts us to remember by what he does next in *The Searchers*—dropping us from the arguably sublime into the unquestionably vulgar and low-comic: dissolving from Ethan with Debbie to Ward Bond's Reverend, who is somewhere nearby after the battle. He is in the mooning position, baring his wounded tush (victim of a clumsy recruit's sword) for some painful first aid. And this jarring cut, with all the hard-headedness it implies, seems to me almost as moving in its way as the scene that precedes it.

Because of course in the end we know that Ethan—after his "moment"—is not going to be a liberal humanist. Someone like us, that is. But we also know that—and *unlike* us perhaps—he's not going to congratulate himself, either. Being John Wayne.

5

Davis and Wyler

I.

SOME IMAGES ARE indelible. When Bette Davis, at the very start of William Wyler's *The Letter* (1940), sweeps out onto the porch of a tropical bungalow and empties her handgun into the back of the faceless departing man below, she reaches a kind of iconic apogee, becoming virtually a meta–Bette Davis—as well as a precursor to Lisbeth Salender and countless other angry heroines to come. Bette Davis doesn't moon around the faithless man like Garbo or Dietrich, or suck around him like Bergman. She takes her gun and fucking *fires* it! As if to say, *so let's begin . . .*

When I was small, before I was allowed to see "grown-up" movies like hers, I remember that the grown-ups in the family when they mentioned her (there almost always seemed to be one of her movies in town) would always call her "Beet" Davis. It was a deliberate mispronunciation, meant to express—as I understood even then—not only a certain amusement with its object but even a kind of fondness. And why not? She was—after all—something.

It was William Wyler, among her many directors, who seems to have understood how much more than that she could be, and it was for him that she made her three best movies. *The Letter*, based on the well-known and shrewdly written Somerset Maugham play (also filmed with Jeanne Eagels in 1929), was the second one. (*Jezebel* and *The Little Foxes* were the others.)

She is Leslie Crosbie, the wife of Robert (Herbert Marshall), a rubber plantation owner. Hammond, the man she has killed (whom we never see), was a neighbor, all of them part of the Singapore British colony, who draw uniformly around her once they hear her story of what happened: that Hammond had tried to attack her and that she shot him in self-defense.

She sends for her husband (who's away at the forest camp). The police come, of course; so does an "officer of the court," Leslie and Robert's lawyer and "family friend," Howard Joyce—played by the much-undervalued James Stephenson, a relatively obscure Warner contract player until he did this film and was then nominated for an Academy Award (he died only two years later): his aquiline pukka-sahib handsomeness is almost a rebuke in itself to Davis's corrupt round-eyed prettiness.

She calls him Howard, of course—he calls her Leslie. She asks after his wife, and whether her sister has arrived from England yet (she has), before turning to the painful account of all that happened leading to the body on the ground outside. But even her story of that—before she gets to the attack and her defense—has its homely details, such as her annoyance that Hammond, when coming on to her, should compliment her on her hands, which she knows are not her best feature; at this, the men exchange just-like-a-woman little smiles.

But they seem to have no doubts about her story. Except perhaps Howard, a bit later, when they are alone and he says to her, apologetically as usual, that it *does* seem, even from a cursory early inspection of the body, and judging from the angle of the wounds, that she was pumping bullets into her assailant even after he had fallen to the ground. "Oh, Howard," she says, in her distressed confiding way, pausing in midgesture (she was just putting something in her purse), "I was so terrified I hardly knew what I was doing." Of course.

They are taking her that same night into the city for her arraignment, so she prepares a light meal for everybody before they go—not knowing, as she says, "whether to call it a late supper or an early breakfast." Anyway, it won't do to be hungry on the way. Howard is sitting at her elbow at the table. "Will I be arrested?" she asks him, almost shyly. He is afraid, he replies, that she is "by way of being arrested now." Oh . . . Will she be in jail long, does he think? "Well, my dear," he says, "it depends on what the charge is." Yes? And he supposes, he goes on, that "only one charge is possible, really . . . Murder . . ." And on this word they look directly at each other—something she never does here with the others, least of all her doting, credulous husband.

There is that link, then, between her and Howard—beneath the banal bantering talk. It first shows approximately here, and expands and deepens through the movie. It doesn't stop the bantering or the falsity. It's at the underside of all the banality where they truly meet, even come together in a way. It's not only that Leslie offers to be innocent, which she may or may not be from his point of view, but that she offers to be ordinary, which he knows she is not—just as she knows that he does. It's no wonder that he can't take his eyes off her. Nor can we.

Just look at her walk from her jail cell, with her matron alongside, to meet him in the visitors' room—her striding gait (very different from Davis's more usual staggered, foot-planting one), preceded by her shadow (as she often is in this movie), down the prison hallway, in skirt and blouse and heels, shooting her cuffs, adjusting her belt, smoothing her hair, crumpling a kerchief in her other hand, going implacably forward—the self-possession is acute enough to seem glamorous. The disturbance underneath only gives it an added edge. And once she enters the room to meet him, he can't seem to get past his opening observation of how well she looks. "Considering," he adds. "Oh, Howard, don't feel sorry for *me*," she says—everyone here has been so nice to her. And now he has brought her this lovely flower from her very own garden—and so on and on as she occupies herself with pinning and adjusting the flower on her blouse, offering to his steady gaze those quick sidelong glances that betray her uneasiness.

It's a movie about watching—as so many movies importantly are. But in *The Letter* the exchange of looks—of gazes, stares, glances—is something like the movie's central action, if only because the faces here are so guarded. Even comically so—as when Wyler sets up and extends a competition in respective poker faces between Howard and his unctuous and devious native secretary Ong (Sen Yung). "A face like a mask!" exclaims Leslie with a shudder, describing to the lawyer Hammond's Dragon Lady wife (Gale Sondergaard, with slit eyes and lots of beads and bangles). But as we've realized by now, the real masks in the film, the hard-to-read, successfully concealing ones (Mrs. Hammond's, glowing with Mysterious East malevolence, is all too legible), belong to the British colonizers. And most of all to Leslie herself.

The Letter: the "light meal" before the arraignment, Herbert Marshall at far left, Bruce Lester, Bette Davis, and James Stephenson

So you and Robert had stopped seeing Hammond once you found out about his Eurasian wife? Howard now asks her in the visitors' room. She is settled into the couch beside him as they talk. Yes, they stopped inviting him, she says. Not that they ever *had*—that much. Then: "He was very popular," she explains—sitting forward now and turning to look at him (or in his direction), straightening her back, rising on her spine, rather grandly—as if summoning herself to attend to the recollection. Howard waits. "There were," she continues—now lowering her eyes, still sitting erect—"lots of calls on his time." A pause: So there hardly seemed any point, she adds, "in showering him with invitations." *So*, having made it through *that*, she offers the lawyer a bright smile, as if to say: There . . . and waits serenely for the next question.

But he has brought her something besides the flower from her garden: a copy (thanks to Ong and his connections) of the letter she had written to Hammond the day before she killed him, a passionate personal appeal demanding to see him that night. Leslie is flustered, defensive, making up a story—and Howard now loses patience with her lying. All he wants to know from her now, he says angrily, is whatever he needs to know to save her neck. At this, her extraordinary will seems to lock in place, like a grinding of gears—bulging her eyes and disjointing her jaw—and she faints, falling to the floor off the couch.

In the next scene she awakens in the nurse's station, prone on a gurney alongside the wall, the camera below and behind the back of her head, looking over it at Howard and the matron both standing at her feet, in the ubiquitous slatted-blind shadows thrown by the moonlight across the white wall and ceiling above them. It's a long stationary take: all we see of Leslie at first, after the matron departs, is the back of her hair and her upraised forearm resting against the wall at left, with Howard standing beside her as they talk—saying that his having distrusted her from the "beginning" (as she has just accused him of doing) is "neither here nor there" now. The camera's focus is on him, but it's hard to take your eyes off that shadowed, serpentine forearm in the soft-focus foreground, and the hand folding and unfolding on top of it as they talk.

She wants him to buy the letter (she guesses that it's for sale)—more for his close friend Robert's sake (her concern for the doting deceived husband always seems genuine) than for her own. And when Howard refuses—indignantly—and she is sitting up now against the wall, she accuses him of despising her. "I don't despise you!" he says angrily, coming toward her—"it isn't important what I feel about you, do you understand!" As he looms over her.

And the look she gives him now—in silence and in a high-angle close shot—taking the full force of his judgment, of his height and his anger, and still managing to suggest—back to the wall, tipped to one side on her elbow, wide eyes looking up—what *else* he might feel for her if he cared to—is one of the high points in the film. And it has its effect within it: "I'm going to do what I can," he says at last. And her hand goes to his shoulder in relief, her head dropping onto his chest—

making him stagger back a little. And for good reason: what he's offering to do for her, as he's said, is "no better than suborning perjury."

But now at last there are no more lies between them. For him at least, her mask has dropped. Leaving the mystery. Her hypocrisy is so achieved, so steady and unruffled. Like that lacework she's always doing, behind big unflattering spectacles, eyes cast down and hands incessantly working while the others around her chat and plan and have their tea. What is she making? another woman asks her—"it's too fine for a tablecloth." "A coverlet for our bed," she replies, then looks up to meet, as she knows she will, Howard's obsessive stare. But it's a clue, that lacework.

As he says to her later, "It must take enormous concentration—and patience." They are alone again, about to go to an arranged and clandestine meeting with Hammond's widow to get the letter's original and to pay the blackmail. They are seated at opposite ends of a couch on his veranda, and she is growing a little uneasy over her lacework under his gaze. She accuses him of doing "*what?*—trying to read my thoughts?" "I'm trying to understand you," he says. "Why?" she asks. "Because I'm so"—now sitting straight up and forward, turning away from him—"so *evil?*" Wyler cuts to a reverse angle, her profile in the foreground, with Howard, slumped in the background, looking up at her. "That's it, isn't it?" she adds. He doesn't answer. It seems such a melodramatic word—for such a man to endorse, or for such a woman to speculate over. She says it as if trying it out—on both of them. And it's the sort of moment, at the tipping point of painful self-knowledge, that Davis does with unique power.

But then it comes time, inevitably, that they have to tell her husband about the letter—to show it to him (he's the one, unknowingly, who paid the blackmail). And after he reads it, of course she must "explain" it, before both men. And so she does, making no effort to palliate the story of her consuming obsessive passion, and of her rage and jealousy when Hammond resolved to end their affair. "I was like a person who was sick with some loathsome disease and doesn't want to get well. Even my agony was a kind of joy." She is now addressing Robert's back, where he has slumped forward on the couch, with a moan, his head in his hands. And by the end of the confession she no longer seems to be talking to anyone but herself: "There's no excuse for me," she says. "I don't deserve to live." Robert rises and staggers from the room. She stands in profile behind the couch, holding on to its back, frozen in her familiar pelvic slouch watching him go. Howard, still there, at left foreground and seated, his arms on his knees, his eyes on the floor: "He's going to forgive you," he says softly, without looking up at her. In a close shot now, she looks at him, their unhappy intimacy taken for granted by both. "Yes," she says—then, lowering her eyes, "he's going to forgive me." And she is going to be acquitted, too—thanks to Howard's suppression of the evidence.

So it's back to the normal hypocrisy—at the big festive do laid on for her by Howard's swanning and chattering wife (Frieda Inescourt) to celebrate the acquittal. And then, alone in the lawyer's guest bedroom, she and Robert try to carry on—they are going back to their plantation in the morning. They have to get an early start, she says, as she makes as if to begin packing for them. But Robert is withdrawn and not responsive, and the uselessness of her effort overcomes her, too. We can't go on, can we? she asks him. He's not sure. But if you love someone, he says, you can forgive anything. It gives her hope: she will do anything to make him happy again, she says, she'll really try. And when he asks her if she loves him, she says yes. But then they kiss—and she pulls away. He pulls her back and lifts her face to his. "With all my heart," she says, looking at him with tear-filled eyes, "I still love the man I killed"—the play's (and the earlier movie's) famously hokey curtain line.

Davis did not want to look at Marshall when she said this line. She insisted that her character would be too ashamed to look at her husband when confessing such a thing. But Wyler prevailed—and what we finally see from Davis as a result of his insistence is someone who is too ashamed *not* to look at her husband—who has not only to wield the blow but to confirm her own shame by watching it land—an *utter* sort of self-abasement. "I don't deserve to live."

And principally because of Wyler (in collaboration with the screenwriter, Howard Koch) and his understanding of his star, there is quite another sort of looks-and-looks-away strategy at play in the movie. One that begins at the beginning when Leslie has emptied her gun into her lover's back and the moon emerges from the clouds to illumine her from above, standing over him, turning her enormous angry eyes upward, as if to say: What the hell is this now? It's only the moon. But what feels remarkable about that startled look of hers is how truly challenging it seems.

After the crime—confronting the moon

This same moon—full and radiant at the center of a turbulent cloud-strewn sky (and with its own signature sound: Max Steiner's restless descending three-note theme)—is the unifying image of the film, shown first under the opening credits and then throughout— alone with Leslie, and each time with her gaze at it seeming more longing than challenging. As when Robert, early on, comes into their bedroom and finds her outside in their garden—it's as if he's interrupted a tryst. Hearing him, she steps back into the room (she has to pack for her jail stay), turning and closing the slatted doors behind her—slowly. Then—slowly, reluctantly—closing the louvers, shutting out the light, slowly again, then finally. Has she been a good wife to him? she then asks Robert. The best wife a man ever had, he replies— unhesitatingly, and meaning it.

In the final sequence, and after the movie's final spoken line (the curtain one: "With all my heart . . .") Leslie goes to her death in another garden (the Joyces'), seeming as much impelled by the moon as by her intuition that her would-be killers (Mrs. Hammond and a native confederate) are waiting there to strike at her. It's a beautifully filmed and staged sequence, in the high-Wylerian style, even though its central event (Leslie pays for her crime with her life instead of with a continued marriage to Herbert Marshall) was strictly censor-imposed. But for the woman that Davis and Wyler have characterized, the retribution seems inevitable: a succumbing not just to death but to the final self-destroying honesty that she has been tempted by—alone with the moon—through the movie. Much in the way that John Wayne belongs to Ford's Monument Valley, Bette Davis at her best belongs to Wyler's witnessing moon.

II.

SHE HAD A surprising sort of face for a supposed great actress at the time, let alone a movie star. Not unattractive but overemphatic (those popping eyes)—there seemed something mongrelish and underbred about it. (Davis was so far from *her* idea of a movie star that Dietrich, reportedly, refused to say her name aloud.) Bette Davis at first simply

OPPOSITE PAGE: After the acquittal—and the moon again

looked like hard times, poor nutrition, city streets, very much in the proletarian mode of Warner Bros., her home studio. (In fact she came from New England small-town gentility.)

But it had been Universal that first brought her to Hollywood, after her few Broadway theater appearances, and then decided they'd made a mistake (her looks, partly). But she had something, no question—even if it wasn't "sex appeal" (Universal's head, Carl Laemmle, having famously compared her in that respect to Slim Summerville)—and that "something" was more than vivid on the movie screen. George Arliss, then a major international star, saw it there and asked for her for the female lead in his next movie at Warners, *The Man Who Played God* (1932). And at Warners she would stay—for fifty-four films and sixteen years—so successfully and dominantly that she came to be called "the fourth Warner brother."

Warner stars in her early years there were not glamorous—the camera didn't linger over them (the Warner cameras didn't linger over anything) the way they did at Paramount or Metro. The women (Stanwyck, Blondell, Dvorak) were dames rather than glamour girls, and the men (Cagney, Muni, Robinson—Dick Powell for romantic leads) were like a collection of gargoyles. The studio famously favored their male stars. And though Davis outdid them all—even the fractious superstar Cagney—in her struggles against the studio tyranny, it's hard to imagine her being quite as much at home anywhere else. Warners was a no-frills, hard-driving operation—just like her own. Where a Garbo or a Bergman in her career might appear in one or two (carefully prepared) films a year, Davis even at her most celebrated would do four or five. It was almost a different kind of female stardom—no less grand but more insistent, in a way more exposed.

"The film star," says the great critic André Bazin, "is not just an actor but a hero of legend or tragedy, embodying a destiny with which scenarists and directors must comply, albeit unwittingly." But then what kind of heroine of legend do we make of a film star who appeared convincingly in the same few years (from the late thirties to midforties) as a Manhattan call girl, Queen Elizabeth I, a Welsh schoolmistress, a gangster's moll, Empress Carlotta of Mexico, a Southern belle, a celebrated New York beauty, and several versions of the homely spinster figure—and others? In Bazin's formulation, that sort of shape-shifting belongs to the destiny of the actress-star (as Davis regarded herself) rather than the movie legend. But Davis was both: it was these transformations (sometimes within the film, as in *The Old Maid* and *Now, Voyager*) that made her a legend—that and the fact that she remained unmistakable and the same through all of them.

And she was hugely popular in those years. Especially for women. As Pauline Kael remembered, Davis always seemed smarter than a woman was supposed to be then. (Part of her troublesomeness.) And for men, her pictures promised at least a ride for their money—more than a Norma Shearer one or a Joan Crawford, say. The fact is, whatever the reasons, moviegoers' tastes never quite recoiled on her the way they would on other great female stars. She never had the dismaying ups and downs in box office favor (at her peak, all her movies made money) that marked the careers of Garbo, Dietrich, Katharine Hepburn. She was in some ways a more comfortable presence. Her "legend" (in Bazin's term)—her heroism—belonged to the will. Something closer to ordinary experience than the sort of mystery that Garbo could evoke. Davis, too, could inspire awe in her audiences—but they knew better where they were, feet on the ground, so to speak, inside their familiar skins, when they felt it. In the early forties, the columnist Ed Sullivan took a poll of his readers and declared Bette Davis "the Queen of Hollywood." Never mind that "the King" was Mickey Rooney (there was no ceremony).

From her beginnings at Warners they had been trying to turn her into a standard leading lady for their assembly line product—she was even a platinum blonde in a musical (*Fashions of 1934*). But then in the same year she got them to loan her out (the first—and next to last—time they would) to RKO to play Mildred, the cockney waitress in the film of Somerset Maugham's novel *Of Human Bondage* (1934), with Leslie Howard as the sensitive clubfoot hero. And she was a sensation—giving the performance that would be her career's first big turning point. For audiences the novelty was in her boldness—as if some heretofore agreed upon limits were being violated by the performance itself. Certainly any notion of "underacting," of adjusting your level to the intimacy of the camera. Nor was she "theatrical," the way stage stars like the Barrymores or the Lunts could be on film. What she was, the reviewers seemed to agree, was shockingly "real." What she did was not so much like recognizable true behavior as flesh and blood charged with awful life, all but leaping off the movie screen. A termagant sexpot.

But no one then seems to have openly remarked how sensual her Mildred was (as if that would be almost too frightening). There is a scene in *Bondage* that opens with her standing before a mirror trying on a clinging silk frock—a close-up of her hands on her buttocks pushing downward, then going up her sides and resting splayed on her hips as she turns around, the camera traveling slowly upward over her breasts to her not displeased face as she looks at herself. Satisfied, she turns to thank the onlooking Philip (Leslie Howard), crossing the room to him with her slouching hip-sprung walk. Not even Harlow in ambulation leads so insistently with her pelvis as Davis's Mildred does. For Mildred, however, the movement is less provocative than grudging—like an ambulatory pout.

And it's that grudgingness, and the unease behind it, that holds your attention, however nervously—it's like waiting for someone in a movie fight to jostle the nitro. "Oh, Phil, I love yuh so," she says in a much later scene, sitting on the arm of the chair where he's reading, pressing her mouth into his hair, encircling his shoulders with her arms, "I can't live without 'chuh." But she's been unfaithful with his best friend and he's caught her at it and it's too late for this, for sure. He pulls away from her, accusing her of making a fool of herself, and of him. This leaves her standing alone in a full-length shot that's almost too squirm-inducing to look at: in her frowsy negligee, head tilted to one side, arms folded in front of her, one hand moving up her arm inside the sleeve, eyes wide and aggrieved, staring at him, as she ponders her next move. But she plunges ahead (she's always out of her depth with him, and she always plunges ahead) and he rejects her brutally—it's Philip's payback moment. "You disgust me!" he says—thus provoking the speech that became one of Davis's most famous, now appearing as it does without fail in the documentary surveys of her career. "I disgust you!" she begins. And then continues—into legend—berating him, with a ferocity almost never seen in a female star before this: "It made me sick when I had to let you kiss me . . . And after you kissed me I used to wipe my mouth! Wipe my *mouth*!"—which she demonstrates by a slow swipe of her forearm that looks violent enough to take the mouth with it—and concludes by calling him a cripple, "a gimpylegged monster!" (this is the movies: he gets totally cured in the next scene).

Warners responded to this triumph of hers not by giving her better pictures but by now top-billing her in the usual four or five bad ones. But they gave her a compensation of sorts with *Dangerous* (1935), equally bad but more ambitious, a star vehicle clearly designed to cap- italize on her Mildred performance. She plays a Great Actress now on the skids, "modeled" (as it was given out by the studio) on the tragic Jeanne Eagels. Franchot Tone—on loan from Metro and playing here with his usual deftness and unflappable sanity—is the artist who remembers her past greatness when he comes upon her wandering the streets in an alcoholic daze. He sets out to save her and to return her once again to The Stage. The first step (of course) is to take her to the country, to his posh gentleman-farmer place. Where, having finally gotten sober, she sets about seducing him in his barn—with an amus- ing mixture of guile and good humor—in the movie's best scene. It's her masochist cow-eyed husband (John Eldredge) who makes her go bad-humored, Mildred-style: "Every time I think that those soft sticky hands ever touched me, it makes me sick—*sick*, do you hear!" Well, maybe (you suppose they thought) the magic or whatever it was would work *again*.

And so it did—in a way. Though nobody much liked it, *Dangerous* won her her first Academy Award as Best Actress—widely understood to be a consolation prize for her not winning it for Mildred the year before, when Capra's *It Happened One Night* had swept all the major awards. But *Dangerous* shows something not remarked on at the time: how appealing Davis could be in quiet moments—like that attempt on Tone's virtue. And as she was again in her next picture, *The Petrified Forest* (1936), where she is a dreamy young girl in a hair ribbon, her life stalled on a desert truck stop, who falls in love with vagrant poet Leslie Howard's fancy talk and big thoughts (from Robert Sherwood's Broad- way hit). What's striking, even unexpected, is how readily Davis makes you believe in the girl's innocence, her yearning openness, her eager- ness to escape her own limits. But then without such likability—or at least the potential for it—Davis almost certainly couldn't have become the great popular star she was.

It's the same story with Michael Curtiz's *Kid Galahad* (1937)— where she is memorably named Fluff (another version of the hair ribbon), the moll to Edward G. Robinson's crooked but good-hearted fight promoter. This is the movie where she presides with Myrna Loy–like amiability over the riotous and drunken marathon party her boy-friend is throwing for all his pals—and then assures him when they're alone again that she is "happy," no matter what he gets up to next. He is lucky to have her, he tells her, and you think he's right. His bad luck—and hers—is her falling for the young fighter he takes on next (Wayne Morris). But Fluff manages even that difficulty equably, sympathetically—though she ends up alone at the end. It's one of her best pre-legend performances.

And it was the second of the four 1937 vehicles that were meant to mollify her after she had so famously defied the studio and its lawyers the year before by embarking to England, threatening to do a movie there, until the British courts decided against her and sent her home. But by that time, Warners had begun to learn how valuable to them she could be and set about trying a bit more to please her, with hope-fully better films like *Kid Galahad*—and before that with *Marked*

Marked Woman: with Jack Norton and Mayo Methot

Woman (1937), in which she was the sole above-the-title star (her leading man, Humphrey Bogart, hadn't yet reached above-the-title status)
and in an iconic sort of role (at least at Warner Bros.): a nightclub hostess (read prostitute—as audiences at that Production Code–ridden
time could easily do) in the stable of a big-time pimp-racketeer (Edu-
ardo Cianelli), whom she rats out for D.A. Bogart after her young sister
is killed by a john. It was a role that set her squarely and promisingly in
the studio's trademark cycle of successful gangster films, as an authentic don't-mess-with-me tough girl. And in her bangs and slouching
walk and bugle bead gowns, she is pretty memorable. But her over-the-
top performance is finally monotonous, played once it gets going on a
single note of unmodulated anger. It's more convincing when she is
playing the character's exhaustion, after a hard night with the johns,
trudging her way home at dawn with her almost as memorable sisters
in sin, including Lola Lane and Mayo Methot (Bogart's wife at the
time), as definitive a bunch of bad-luck broads as even Warners could
assemble.

III.

BUT NOTHING IN her record by then of thirty-six films (twenty-nine
of them for Warners) could have prepared people at the time for the
thirty-seventh: as a willful Southern belle in antebellum New Orleans
in William Wyler's *Jezebel* (1938), her first great film with her first (and
arguably her last) great director.

And ever after, it seemed Davis would give Wyler full credit for the
success that it was, all but saying—as Laurence Olivier did say about
his work with Wyler in *Wuthering Heights*—that he taught her how to
act for the movies. But if she didn't say it, others did: never before had
this by now familiar and almost veteran young star shown such depth.
"Popeye the Magnificent," *Time* magazine called her in a cover story at
the time. And magnificent she is—from the movie's very start.

She rides her unruly horse clattering over the cobblestones into the
courtyard behind the mansion, where a little slave boy grabs the reins
as she jumps down. She goes toward the back door, toward the party
inside where everyone (as we have already seen) is waiting for her. She
raps on the door with her riding crop, then steps back to address the

boy, who is having trouble with the fractious horse. "T-Bat!" she says brightly, "don't stand there with your eyes *bulgin'* out—he *knows* you're afraid." "But Miss Julie, he bite," says the boy—a cutie, as always in such roles at the time (when the white kids were usually insufferable, the black ones were nearly always the opposite)—as he struggles with the horse. "Well, you just plain bite him *back*," says Julie laughingly, gesturing at T-Bat with the crop, then using it to hike up the train of her long dress and flip it over her shoulder as the door opens for her and she goes in.

Wyler had her do that tricky gesture with the riding crop and the train again and again—practicing it at home, then doing it on the set for more than thirty-five takes. It was worth it: it's like one long effusion of delighted control, and you laugh at it in appreciation. Julie is so good-humored in this opening, not just a riveting presence but a vibrant, spontaneous one. And the scene inside takes the cue and continues on the same note—light and funny and infectious. In the hallway she hands her riding crop to the elderly butler, Cato, while looking toward the big room with all the people—it's her engagement party, a formal event, and she is late. "But Miss Julie—horse clothes?" says Cato when she tells him she won't bother to change (after all, she's *late*) and strides past him into the great room, suddenly looking small and delicate in her long heavy riding dress, pausing in the archway to greet all her guests: "I'm terribly sorry to be late, I had trouble with the colt," she says—and the camera shows her from behind so that we get a look at the amazed faces in front of her. Especially her guardian Aunt Belle's (Fay Bainter)—who comes quickly forward, addressing her in a mortified whisper, to try to stop her from entering. But Julie sweeps on through the crowd, with her airy regrets. "So sorry," she says, pausing before a couple of especially wide-eyed old biddies, "but y'know when a colt gets high-handed it's best to teach him his manners right now or ruin him." "Yes, that's so important, isn't it," says the lady, nastily—Julie both notices this and decides not to at the same time, pressing onward. ("I hope I'm broad-minded," says the other lady, "but I declare . . .")

She was late, but her fiancé, Pres (Henry Fonda), hadn't shown up at all. He couldn't—as everyone understood. His business at the bank (man's business) as one of the board of directors is too important. So in the next sequence Julie challenges decorum again by charging into the bank—an unattended woman in a men's place—and very nearly into the boardroom itself, until Pres comes out from the meeting inside and intercepts her. She wants him to leave so he can help her choose her dress for the Olympus Ball. He can't, he says—and she gives him her little routine of feminine grievance (he cares more about the bank than he does about her, and so on), both mocking it by her baby-dollish style (plucking at her purse, batting her eyes, talking breathlessly in a little voice) and using it for all it's worth. Not much this time, as it turns out: Pres stays put and sends her away. Still smarting from this in the next scene—in the dressmaker's fitting room—Julie rejects the conventional white ball gown, obligatory for the unmarried young woman, for the red one she was never even meant to lay eyes on. But it's vulgar, says the dressmaker. "Isn't it!" says Julie. Think of *Pres*, Aunt Belle warns. "That's just who I am thinkin' of," says Julie.

The tone of all this is securely lightweight and comic. In fact it's more or less Clio Dulaine—and Scarlett O'Hara as well (though predating both films). In *Saratoga Trunk*, when the pissy-ass hotel manager tells Bergman that absolutely no one is allowed to talk to that important rich man surrounded by his flunkies on the veranda, she merely laughs and sails onward onto the veranda to talk with him. It's the usual way with these spunky courageous heroines of popular fiction up against their convention-bound societies—they get away with it. Just as Scarlett gets away with *her* red dress at the ball—if only because of Melanie taking her side.

But you never suppose that Julie *will* get away with it. Partly because everyone in the movie tells her she won't—even her rascally backup boyfriend Buck Cantrell (George Brent), who declines to take her to the ball in Pres's stead ("That dress'll cause no end of trouble, Miss Julie")—but even more so because she is Bette Davis. This is not Ingrid Bergman's "Comtesse" having her fun, nor Vivien Leigh's Scarlett having her way—this is someone courting real danger.

Buck had come to pick her up for the ball but hadn't seen the dress until he got there. But Pres—who had seen it and had forbidden her to wear it—is still on his way. And when he arrives, she steps out before him in her full, low-cut, bare-shouldered red (as we're told) splendor. He orders her to change, of course, and she refuses, accusing him of being afraid (her characteristic challenge to the menfolk: *she's* not afraid), of fearing that he might have to defend her honor against some other man's insult. Whereupon he takes her by the arm and off they go—along with Aunt Belle and a distinguished-looking male relation—an appalled group of four.

And they walk into the Olympus Ball, full of formal gents and their white-gowned ladies, in motion and in conversation all around. Which more or less stops when they get a look at *her*, on her escort's arm, stepping together through the slowly parting groups, as Pres pauses to glare at any young beau who even *looks* as though he might want to make a remark. None of them does, of course. And Julie has now become the slightly shrinking appendage of *his* will and bravado—taking each step in sync with his, but with that emphatic foot-planting shoulder-swinging walk that was already recognizable as a Davis mannerism—modified here, enough so as to show not only her characteristic ballsiness but her loss of nerve, too.

And they haven't even danced yet. Pres insists on it, even though Julie wants to leave. But he sweeps her onto the crowded floor—which soon clears, as the wonderfully ominous Max Steiner waltz clangs and thrums on the soundtrack, as they spin and twirl, Julie rigid in Pres's arms, circling the growing great space of the floor, ringed by the crowd of now onlooking nondancers. The orchestra on the podium tries to stop, but Pres makes them—and her—go on. It's a big and thrilling movie moment, and no one forgets it. And yet it's fully earned.

If only because it's so complicated. Fonda's Pres seems to you almost as perverse as she's been—just as self-willed and much less sympathetic. He is, after all, solidly on the side of the conventional, the stately boat she's been intent on rocking. And the tight smugness Fonda brings to his clashes with her is not so very unlike the quality he will later bring to his comic brushes with Barbara Stanwyck in *The Lady Eve*—except that *there* the movie is pretty simply on the boat-rocker's side. Whereas *Jezebel* seems directing you to feel—as Julie herself will come to do—that Pres is mostly in the right. That you don't actually resist feeling this more than you do (the movie is arguably more reactionary even than *Gone With the Wind*) has to do with the way that Davis and Wyler keep us focused on another far more interesting subject: the divided character of Julie herself.

OPPOSITE PAGE: *Jezebel*: but the band plays on—after Pres (Henry Fonda) orders them to

There is then a dissolve from the high overhead shot of that embattled waltz across the empty floor to the enclosure of Julie's front door, where Pres has brought the two women home. "Good night, Aunt Belle," he says to Fay Bainter, who preserves a speaking silence as she precedes Julie through the door and into the house. "Good night, Julie," he says. "Is that all you've got to say to me?" she demands. "There's nothing more *to* say," he replies—their profiles turned to each other in the doorway. Followed by a close-up of her, with face shadowed but angled into the light, eyes moistened by anger and hurt, a single earring glinting against her hair and rhyming the glistening eyes. As usual in a Wyler close-up of her (the cinematographer was Ernest Haller), there's a lot to look at—and in this one there is also that frown of alarm, behind the defiance, that crosses her brow as she looks up at him. Davis at such moments is like a cynosure of the tortured will, fierce and suffering and very powerful, harrowed by her own bravado, showing not just the willfulness but the cost of it. At her best she never left that out.

Pres breaks their engagement in this scene, announcing that he is taking a job in the North (he gets slapped in response). And in the sequence that follows—"A Year Later," says an overtitle—we see and hear what Julie has become in that year. A virtual recluse, neither receiving people nor going out. Except for a single (offscreen) visit to the theater. To see, as we are told, *Camille*. "I hated it!" (not a surprise).

So that when Aunt Belle springs the news on her that Pres is coming home, Julie is stopped in her tracks. She turns her head to show a plain-brown-wren sort of profile in a close shot, her tightly drawn hair gathered in ringlets behind her ears, her gaze at Aunt Belle both hopeful and humbled at once—it's her glowing homely-beautiful look: "We'll be married," she says, once she takes it in, almost brimming with the thought in all its enormity. What's more, she's going to admit her own fault, going to tell him that she was "vicious and mean and selfish, and ah'm gonna tell him ah hated myself for bein' like that even then." She is going to "beg his forgiveness."

And so she does when he arrives. But Julie's self-abasement (as her preview of it has already suggested) has the same recklessness and over-determination as her self-assertion had had. She doesn't know, however, nor does anyone else, it seems, that Pres is bringing with him his new bride from New York (Margaret Lindsay). And when he arrives with her, Aunt Belle is downstairs meeting them—and reeling a little from the surprise—while Julie is upstairs preparing *her* surprise, putting on that once rejected white ball gown for him. And as the others go upstairs to their rooms, she comes downstairs in order to find Pres alone there.

You have no trouble understanding why he is struck dumb at the sight of her. Her hair covered in white lace, her hands resting on the huge billowing white skirt, she seems like an embodied flood of light, commanded by those extraordinary eyes. Which she fixes on him now—imploringly. But coquettishly, too—does he remember, she asks, when she wouldn't wear white? But all he can say in reply is her name—and then, "Julie, you're lovely—lovelier than ever . . ." But then (and you want him to stop her) she sinks below the frame, descending in next downward-looking shot into the middle of the dress's ballooning whiteness: "Pres, ah'm kneelin' to you—" "Julie, don't," he says from offscreen. But she goes on: "T' ask y' to forgive and t' love me as I love you." Enter the new wife—as Pres quickly pulls Julie to her feet.

At first she can't believe it—struggling for control, having to welcome the newcomer. But that night, once she has rallied from the shock and the humiliation, she follows Pres into the garden—as Aunt Belle plays Chopin for the guests inside—and comes on to him again. She is rebuffed again, even more decisively.

At the big formal supper that follows this scene, Julie, before the assembled guests, at her archest and most mischievous, commences to do her Southern belle shtick, exerting her power over the clueless Buck to provoke a clash between him and Pres. But when Pres is suddenly called away to an emergency (plague in New Orleans), it's his younger brother Ted (Richard Cromwell) who steps up to answer Buck's "insolence" by formally insulting him, thus incurring (as everyone at the table understands) a pistol duel at dawn. While Julie, now in a panic about what she may have just brought about, tries to intervene. Uselessly.

As Aunt Belle says to her: "We women can start the men quarrelin' often enough. We can't ever stop 'em." Julie's socially sanctioned power over these men—as an upper-class woman, as the mistress of the home they're guests in—has suddenly failed. The masculine stupidity she has been playing to and manipulating—appealing to Buck's anti-Yankee bigotry to incite him against Pres and his New York wife—is now in control. What has happened has now become something that is no business of "the womenfolk." "Buck, I forbid you!" she cries, detaining him at the foot of the hall stairs, "—as a guest in my house!" "Forbid me what, ma'am?" he replies innocently. And even she hesitates to name it: "To do what 'cher plannin'," she says. "What do you mean, Miss Julie?" "Stop play-actin'!" she cries—he looks at her blankly. Then, risking everything: "Your stupid code—it's for *fools!*" An outburst that puts him farther than ever beyond her reach. He goes up the stairs and leaves her.

But Buck *is* stupid, that's quite clear (Brent's performance is a witty one)—and we hardly need to be told that Julie would know this about him. But it's a major moment when she betrays—at the foot of that staircase—that she does. It's a moment when you take the full measure of the mischief she's just been making—manipulating attitudes that she herself sees through easily, "play-acting" just as she accuses him of doing but even more dangerously, even more willfully.

Maybe only in retrospect do you register how much outside the movie's other characters you always are—like Fonda's unbending hero.

With George Brent: "Your stupid code—it's for *fools*!"

What you care about is her—never mind whether (a great concern to the studio at the time) Julie is "likable" or not. When the earth opens at her feet, as it does here, when she recognizes what she has done and then tries to undo it, rushing in panic from Buck to Ted to Aunt Belle, you're moved, even surprised to be moved, in spite of all the mechanics of the melodrama. It's because Julie's rebellion, notwithstanding the movie's pro forma censure of it, has been its most satisfying element—and now it's turned ugly, putting these nice thick people around her at genuine risk (poor Buck, as it turns out, is the one who gets killed). And you know she is going to have to live with the outcome—and you feel her knowing it. Never will Davis seem deeper or more agonizingly alive on the screen than she does in this moment of appalled recognition. (It's an event with some precedent—a felt one to me—in Jane Austen's Emma Woodhouse, another heroine whose self-will turns to bitterness and remorse. If the movie's writing, much of it by the young John Huston, is far from that league, the performing and filmmaking are at least closer.)

Like Davis's, Julie's bravado is what makes her appealing—and it's inseparable from her anger, from her impatience with conventional limits, with the moderate and the lukewarm (even as she finds it in herself, you suppose). If Ingrid Bergman's persona risks blandness, even complacency, Davis's runs very different sorts of risk: not just recklessness and overemphasis, but self-doubt—self-dislike even. It's what we "like" her for, in fact—at her deepest.

IV.

EDMUND GOULDING'S *Dark Victory* (1939) was one of her biggest hits. It's about a high-living rich girl who learns she has a brain tumor and only a short time to live and who is transformed before the end by love (with her doctor, conveniently). The play was a 1934 Broadway flop starring Tallulah Bankhead. But Selznick, then at Metro still, thought it would make a swell project for Garbo after *Queen Christina* and he bought it for her. But Garbo turned it down (if she hadn't, there might have been no Garbo *Camille*), and Warners then bought it shortly afterward—for *their* reigning dramatic actress at that time, Kay Francis. But by the time Davis had eclipsed Francis and every other woman at the studio before her, the property was earmarked for her.

But it gave her the jitters—according to her most astute biographer, Barbara Leaming. And the studio's advance publicity may not have helped. Here at last, said a studio release, is her ideal role, the one she has "longed" to play: not a "character" part, but "a natural, normal woman who faces all that fate can offer," and so on. "Natural," at last— even "normal." What next? But the fact was that Davis had, even before *Jezebel*, successfully played more "normal" women, as Hollywood conceived of them, than any other kind. But it was the malignant loonies, like the bad girl in *Bordertown* (1935) (who goes insane on the witness stand), or the viragos like Mildred, or the "maenad" heroine (the hero's word for her) of *Dangerous*, that people associated her with. She could play sexy—as she had done so notably in *Cabin in the Cotton* (1932). She could even play beautiful—something that she was noted, often enough at her own insistence, for not being. But when she means us to see her that way, as in *Jezebel*, or even the otherwise misguided *Mr. Skeffington* (1944—as "the most beautiful woman in New

York"), we have no trouble doing so. But *Dark Victory*'s Judith Traherne was meant to be *noble* by the end—and meant to be lovable long before that. *These* were hard.

"Here is this gallant little figure all alone," Barbara Leaming reports the director, Edmund Goulding, saying to his star, "who can't tell anybody what the problem is and won't let anyone feel sorry for her." Anybody, that is, but us—and we are meant to feel powerfully sorry for "this gallant little figure," more and more so the "littler" she gets. As in the preoperation scene at the hospital: "I've never given in a fraction to anyone before," she says to her doctor (and future husband), who is showing her how the hand crank on her hospital bed works, "and here I am letting you bounce me up and bounce me down." Adorable—right? (She and Brent—who were having an offscreen fling—had a hard time getting through this scene without breaking up.) And she has brought with her, she tells him, some lovely new "nighties" to wear instead of the hospital gown they have put her in. And that she must stay in, he says gently, draping one of the nighties around her shoulders, daddy-style, as she looks up at him dotingly.

She was more at home playing the character's early willfulness: the spirited glamour-girl socialite who all the men except him are afraid of, according to her studly Irish stablehand (Humphrey Bogart—no kidding). What she was most dreading, Leaming tells you, was the noble stuff at the end: the self-transcender who dies all by herself (she even sends the dog away) so as to make her husband feel better about the whole thing . . . Again, don't ask. But Davis pulls it off (you really *don't* ask—hardly) by a consummate Wyler-style stillness: with Judith climbing her stairway (slowly), lying down on top of her bed, looking blindly (the end sign) into the final close-up as it lets her go slowly, slowly out of focus. A Hollywood death to be sure—but her concentration makes it feel momentous somehow, and certainly touching.

But over her next few films, that concentration seems to give way to something much more effortful, less fully imagined. And though she would go on playing different degrees of nobility (such were the requirements of the "woman's picture"), she would do so more and more mechanically. So that when you first see her in something like *All This and Heaven Too* (1940) you feel you've seen enough—her character is already so rigid with gallant littleness, and with her Terrible Life So Far (setting up the feature-long flashback). As the new teacher at a nineteenth-century girls' seminary confronting her cruel and gossiping class (re her "scandalous" past), she talks in that prissy consonant-biting broad-*a* enunciation that she would more and more affect in her movies, especially when playing a suffering woman of culture.

And such mannerisms (which Wyler's discipline in *Jezebel* had reined in) were growing. In each of her two movies before this, *The Old Maid* and *The Private Lives of Elizabeth and Essex* (both 1939), she assumes (with makeup man Perc Westmore's help) a new and startling appearance. In the former, as a withered and bitter maiden aunt (after appearing as an attractive young heroine in the earlier scenes), she is almost unrecognizable—that is, until she starts to act. And her Queen Elizabeth—half bald in a red half-wig (in Technicolor) and a calcimined face—is all twitches and tics and hearty self-parody.

All these films were hits. But *The Letter* was another unqualified *personal* triumph for her (just as *Jezebel* had been). And even before they had finished shooting it (and before their disagreement about Leslie's final line, presumably) the director and star were planning their next collaboration. Davis began pleading with Jack Warner to be loaned out to Goldwyn for *The Little Foxes*, if only to work with Wyler again. Warner reluctantly agreed (in exchange for Gary Cooper in Howard Hawks's *Sergeant York*). In the meantime she would do two lightweight Warner vehicles. *The Great Lie* (1941) is a woman's picture of a familiar kind—like *The Old Maid*, two women contending over a missing man (George Brent again) through his child—with Mary Astor in "the Davis role" (i.e., the bitch) and taking over the movie in her bluff funny performance as a famous concert artist, who plays her piano as though she's punishing it ("I'm sweating like a stoker," she says backstage after a particularly exalted performance), with Davis as her nice-girl rival. Then a screwball comedy—a real departure—with James Cagney, *The Bride Came C.O.D.* (1941): the runaway heiress story, with both stars looking too old and too short for their roles, which were themselves too old by the forties. Even at the screwball genre's peak, Warners had never had the knack—and they displayed that incapacity once again with this late-to-the-party misfire. It made money, like all her movies then, but it was a widely conceded mistake for both stars.

V.

THE FIGHTS BEGAN almost as soon as production on *The Little Foxes* (1941) did. Davis walked off the set again and again, even threatening to walk off the film—until she was placated and appeased by everyone except the equally determined Wyler. He had objected even before they began filming to her makeup (she had brought Perc Westmore with her from Warners): a clown-white powdered look, nowhere so outré as her Queen Elizabeth face but still fairly startling (she said she wanted to look older: Lillian Hellman's Regina was forty-one, while Davis was thirty-three). And he also did not like the way she was playing the role: he wanted a "sexier" Regina with less villainy and more shadings of temperament than he thought Davis was giving her. And once again they quarreled over her mannerisms. But *this* time—as the reports had it—she won most of the battles.

And yet Davis—whose growing disinclination to take either advice or direction would eventually do her career in—seems in this instance, on the evidence of the final movie, to have been, if not right, at least not that wrong. We can never know, of course, what the performance Wyler would have ostensibly preferred from her might have been like, but the one he got is fairly magnificent.

Take that makeup job that he so objected to: her Kabuki mask face with its chalk-white skin and rosebud mouth, above all its hooded eyes (thanks partly to the weight of her false eyelashes). It's less a real sort of beauty than a triumphant flaunting artifice, which both cites a then current fashion—the casually regal Gibson Girl—and characterizes the woman herself—in her achieved toughness, both inviting and forbidding at once. And Regina enjoys her own show—why not? With her abundant hair looming in soft waves above her broad forehead and folded in wings above and around her ears, with her ample bosom, offered like a gift, couched in a bed of black feathers, and with her hourglass figure, she is a grand and imposing hostess, good at giving dinners, at welcoming and presiding and saying good night. Especially saying good night (she tires easily—or is it you?).

Here, the fulcrum of Davis's body movement is no longer at her hips but at her spine and shoulders—balancing the big hair like a Follies girl's headdress when she walks. Or sitting on a sofa, spreading her arms wide across its back, lifting and extending her leg under the heavy skirt, turning her foot in the air in front of her, studying her shoe thoughtfully. She's a woman who enjoys, even savors, all these extensions, all this *reach* into the world around her. Where others seem to crouch—all these people clinging to the small nowhere town she only wants to get out of and take her adolescent daughter, Alexandra (Teresa Wright), away from. Her two brothers may have the power and the money, but she has the style—and that gives her, often enough, the edge.

The jovially sinister Ben (Charles Dingle) is the one she parries and jokes with—about his coarse manners and the way he looks in his nightdress and his sharp business practices. Ben is her apparent ally—the one she tells to tell their other brother, the slow-witted Oscar (Carl Benton Reid), to be quiet or to go home or just to stop interrupting her. They are *all* going to be rich, it seems, with this new investment scheme they are celebrating in her parlor.

But then Regina begins to suggest that her banker husband, Horace (Herbert Marshall again)—who is ill with heart trouble at a sanitarium out of town—might just want more than a third of a return on his investment of a third (which they absolutely need) in their business deal. Oscar doesn't understand: If you put in a third, you get back a third, don't you? (Oscar never fails her.) "Well, I don't know," she says, rising and walking to the fireplace, turning to face them, speaking almost plaintively: "I don't know about these things . . . It would *seem*"—a beat—"if you put up a third, you'd *get* a third—and yet there's no law about it, is there?" At this she touches her hair and laughs, enjoying herself and looking at Ben, who laughs with her. She goes on: "I should think if you knew your money was badly needed"—she comes forward, like someone about to introduce a guest—"you might just *say*"—again a beat, taking another step, pivoting on her hip and addressing Ben more directly—"'I want more, I want a larger share' . . ." Her sweetly reasonable sound, sort of crooning. Then more matter-of-factly: "You boys have done that—I've heard you say so." And almost before you know it she has turned and seated herself in a nearby chair, landing with her hands on her hips, looking up at them. As she waits for the response.

The Little Foxes: from right to left, Regina, her dim brother Oscar (Carl Benton Reid), Oscar's wife, Birdie (Patricia Collinge), and Regina's shrewd brother Ben (Charles Dingle)

Although a quiet one, this is just the sort of diva moment that Hellman had built her very entertaining and surefire play around, as well as its wonderfully theatrical leading role. This scene is in the first act, and Regina will be routed in the second one, and then triumphant again in the third. But this is a "serious" surefire play, and so it will all turn to ashes in her mouth by the end. Wyler, of course, was on the side of such orthodox seriousness (his next two Hollywood films, before and after his war service, were *Mrs. Miniver* and *The Best Years of Our Lives*). His issue with his star, you presume, was his way of making sure that she was, too. That she was not reducing it to her familiar star turns.

But her Regina is specifically a triumph of the Davis manner—and even of our own familiarity with it. The role is suitably grand for this point in her career, and she brings to it the kind of size and power that not only enlarge the character but deepen her. Regina's "character" *is* her manner—and the lurking despair behind it. Something Davis both captures and understands, with a performance that even touches a sort of perverse sublimity at times.

"You must hate me very much," she says resignedly to her husband, Horace, settling on her couch, her arms stretched along its back. (She has just learned from him that he really means to stand in the way of her making all that money she and her brothers were planning on.) "No," he says. "Oh, I think you do," she says. They are both looking off into space, each in profile, Horace in his wheelchair in the foreground. He doesn't hate her, he says, if only because he still remembers how much in love with her he used to be. She responds by talking, slowly and reflectively, about how *she* felt about that love—more or less talking him into a heart attack as the scene goes on.

You may not know, the first time you see it, that that's where the scene is going. That's mostly due here to the subtlety of Davis's playing. It's true, we've seen Regina tell Horace earlier on that she hopes he will die soon. And since that exchange, they have been occupying different parts of the house. But his recent discovery of her brothers' theft of his bonds has brought him downstairs again to her parlor. And to these shared reflections on their married past. "I thought you'd get the world for me!" she says, with a thrilling alto lilt that evokes all the longing, all the bitterness of her disappointment. Instead, he became what he is still—"just a small-town clerk." "That wasn't what you wanted?" "No," she says, "that *wasn't* what I wanted"—lifting herself from the chair on the "*wasn't*," looking at him as she does so: he still doesn't understand what it is to want the world the way that she once did. It's not hatred in her look, but impatience, both towering and despairing.

She goes behind him to the big bay window, the rain streaking its glass. She stands beside the lamp, looking out, her back now turned to him and to us—just as he is now turned to hers. But it's Horace who is in the shot foreground (Gregg Toland's photography), his eye and face half turned away dominating the frame at left. She is in equally sharp focus in the right background—talking about the disgust he filled her with even then. The old refrain: "I couldn't bear to have you touch me" and so on. But her tone is so weary, so matter-of-fact, that the brutality creeps up on you—just as it seems to do upon her as she talks. "Why didn't you leave me?" he asks, now struggling for his breath. Because she had no money and nowhere to go, she answers, turning away from the window. "I didn't think about it much, but if I had, I'd have known you'd die before I did. But I couldn't have guessed"—she is behind him now and she walks offscreen—"you'd get heart trouble so early, so bad . . ." Horace clutches his chest and struggles forward in his chair, toward the medicine bottle and spoon on the nearby table, the camera following and reframing him. As it does so we see her now in the background sitting and relaxing into that unyielding couch for two. "I'm lucky, Horace, and I'll be lucky again," she says, assuming an indolent pose, crossing her legs, dangling her hands over the front of the armrests, not looking at him as he struggles—as he strains for the life-saving bottle, and turns it over, spilling it on the carpet . . .

Now she *is* looking at him, in a close-up—startled, frozen-faced, pressing herself against the couch's back, as if she'll burst, encased in her tight stiff bodice and throat-enclosing lace collar, restraining herself from speaking or moving, or from looking away from him now—as he looks back at her and understands, to his horror. He turns away from her and tries to call a servant but he has no voice. He staggers up and out of his chair—to make for the stairway behind them. But once he's on his way, Wyler's camera focuses on her.

And she achieves in these close-ups a frightening ugliness that has nothing to do with makeup. As Horace's shadow passes over it, as his hand from offscreen grasps her chair and rocks it, the face stays averted in its lair, as the fierce eyes get bigger and the rosebud mouth gets littler. As he passes she strains upward, following him without looking, rising slowly on her stiff and lengthening spine, stretching her neck, turning her head, not to see but to follow his sounds on the stairway—where we see him struggling to climb in distant soft focus behind her. It's a face—like the Japanese demon's in Brecht's poem—that shows "what a strain it is to be evil," rising up out of this plush and homey parlor like a snake charmer's cobra. Until she hears him collapse, and resumes her human shape, as it were, rushing to the stairs and calling for help.

In the movie's last scenes, Regina—abandoned by her daughter at

OPPOSITE PAGE: "What a strain it is to be evil." The dying Horace (Herbert Marshall again) is just offscreen.

the end—shows that exhaustion of the will that the heroine of the Davis legend has arguably been tending toward all along. Regina's will has won out, and it has left her (in a final close-up at her window) haunted and desolate and alone. Not to mention awfully tired. And Davis herself will rely more and more in her films that follow on a kind of triumphant weariness—carrying all before her, ending all discussion. The extraordinary and resonant divided self that she had once embodied so movingly (her Regina was already past all that) was put more or less to rest for good.

And after getting through this third film with Wyler (their *Jezebel* affair was long over—and *he* had broken it off), she seemed more able than ever to put what she'd learned from him behind her. And more and more unable to learn from anyone else. There was at least one more great performance, a luminous and controlled one in *Now, Voyager* (1942, a big hit). There were other good performances—a light comic one in *Old Acquaintance* (1943), a high theatrical one in *The Corn Is Green* (1945, in the Ethel Barrymore role). But the disastrous (yet still moneymaking) *Mr. Skeffington* (1944) was the real harbinger, as it turned out. Director Vincent Sherman, who had decided (we didn't ask, but he tells us in his autobiography) to sleep with her during their previous film together (*Old Acquaintance*) in hopes of gaining more control over her, tried the same thing again. But this time nothing worked. Whenever he tried on the set to moderate her in a *Skeffington* scene (it couldn't have helped that she was playing an invincibly stupid woman) or to invoke plausibility (no one could talk her out of the voice she had decided to use—an affected full octave higher than her own well-known one), she rejoined that such excesses were what her fans both expected and wanted from her. She may well have been right about that—but it would not be a good strategy to be going forward with.

And her Warner vehicles and performances grew cruder, climaxing with the famously ludicrous heroine of *Beyond the Forest* (a Mexican sexpot) in 1949. After that, the studio dumped her, declining to renew her contract. But at Fox, just one year later, for producer-director-screenwriter Joe Mankiewicz, she has one last great incarnation—as the aging Broadway star Margo Channing in *All About Eve* (1950).

In this film she turns the growing weariness and mannerism into a brilliant comic turn, showing a critical self-awareness that had seemed to be deserting her altogether. But no—here she was again, more than ever, sharp and sad and triumphant, with a new sort of warmth even, playing the joke in her own outsizeness and flamboyance. And movie audiences loved it.

It had been a gift—both from the gods (first choice Claudette Colbert had been unavailable) and from Mankiewicz, as writer as well as director. Almost equal to the ones that Wyler had given her—if only for a single picture. And in her next one—*Another Man's Poison* (1952), a lurid British melodrama—and thereafter, she was back to her old self-indulgences. She was in her early forties and she would go on, and on, but with alcohol and bad judgment and the shambles of her personal life taking their toll. She would make more than twenty-five more appearances in movies, nearly all of them unhappy, some of them worse than that.

6

Charles Laughton

I.

DIRECTING THE STAGE production of *The Caine Mutiny Court-Martial* in 1954, Charles Laughton was having severe problems with his star, Henry Fonda—as Simon Callow recounts in his biography of Laughton. Until one day Fonda, who was unhappy with both the play and his role (as Barney Greenwald, the prosecuting attorney), made a remark in anger that Laughton never forgave (he never spoke to Fonda again, not even ten years later when they were in a film together). Laughton, during the rehearsals, made some comment about military behavior, when Fonda turned on him and said: "What do you know about men, you fat, ugly faggot!" It's one of those stories his biographer tells (there are many) that put the reader profoundly on Laughton's side. Throughout his life Laughton had a propensity, it seemed, for provoking in others the stupidest, most self-exposing kinds of brutality. As a child, too: "He was the kind of boy," said one of his contemporaries in later years, "one longed to take a good kick at." It was almost like a gift. And it became the substance of his art.

The Fonda story stands out not only because of its stupid cruelty but also because it reminds you how much Laughton's art, in his most deeply imagined performances, from Captain Bligh to Quasimodo, stood against such cruelty, and especially those forms it took in "the world of men." Laughton's passionate opposition to systems of masculine authority—to militarism, command, patriarchy—is one of the things that make him seem most sympathetic now.

He grew up at the beginning of the last century in his parents' Scarborough hotel, raised mostly by servants, until he was old enough to be sent to a series of strict Catholic boarding schools. His ambitious mother's Catholicism was as fierce as her business instincts (the hotel was a great success), and he grew to hate the Church. Just as he hated the army later on, when he served an appalling year in the trenches during World War I. He was near to a breakdown when he came home from the slaughter, and Callow tells you, quite plausibly, that he was never to lose "the darkness he brought back with him." His first great successes on the London stage in the late 1920s—Solyony in *The Three Sisters*, the gangster chief Perelli in *On the Spot*, the murderous Mr. Marble in *Payment Deferred*, and so on—were as characters who embodied the darkest human impulses. These were the impulses of his audiences, too, he wrote to an actor who was about to play one of these roles on tour—adding that "they naturally want to crucify me for telling them so." But the audiences were also making him celebrated, and he was soon crossing the Atlantic to play Mr. Marble on Broadway, with his wife, Elsa Lanchester, in the cast as his daughter, as she had been in London.

From Broadway—though briefly—to Hollywood. He was in fact a born movie star, if an unlikely one. There were a couple of false starts in his first Hollywood year: *The Devil and the Deep* (1932) at Paramount, opposite Tallulah Bankhead (he was her mad submarine captain husband), and *Payment Deferred* (1932) at MGM, his great theatrical coup turned into a lackluster film. But the great movie roles soon followed. He played the emperor Nero as "a monstrous perverse baby" (Callow) in Cecil B. DeMille's *Sign of the Cross* the same year— and then did a marvelous nonspeaking vignette for Lubitsch in the omnibus film *If I Had a Million*, as an oppressed clerk who gives his boss the raspberry.

He went back to England then to do Alexander Korda's *The Private Life of Henry VIII* (1933). The movie was hugely popular, and his Holbein-inspired performance seemed so definitive and vivid (and amusing) that it got him his first (and only) Academy Award. He returned to Hollywood in triumph, an international movie star, and his

Charles Laughton as the emperor Nero in *The Sign of the Cross*

next three films there stamped his image on the public mind: the tyrannical and incestuous Mr. Barrett in *The Barretts of Wimpole Street* (1934); the implacable Inspector Javert in *Les Miserables* (1935); and finally and most famously Captain Bligh in *Mutiny on the Bounty* (1935), defying both his crew and the sea itself. A patriarchal horror show: three figures of repressive and repellent masculine authority.

In the same year he also appeared as the gentle butler hero of Leo McCarey's *Ruggles of Red Gap* (1935), one of the decade's most popular comedies. And his *Rembrandt* (1936)—for Korda again—was a powerful and moving creation, arguably the most convincing portrait of a great artist the movies had yet recorded. And like *Ruggles* it was one of the few famous Laughton roles that didn't require him to exploit some repugnant aspect of himself. These triumphs culminated in *The Hunchback of Notre Dame* (1939)—which is about physical repugnance (Laughton insisted on a particularly hideous and painful makeup, outdoing even Lon Chaney's) joined in the deformed Quasimodo to a baffled and inchoate tenderness. And clearly for Laughton—and in spite of the mediocrity of the film that surrounded it—this extraordinary performance was some kind of apotheosis, drawn from his lifelong obsession with his own ugliness. They wanted to crucify him—and now he let them. The burden of Quasimodo was his final challenge to the world of power and authority: the ultimate "fat-ugly-faggot" role, a Christ without the heavenly connections.

He felt at home in the movies from the start. The camera, for one thing, suited his performing style ("Feel it in your guts, and then let it dribble through your eyes," he advised the actor Marius Goring). And big studio production methods, sometimes allowing for nearly endless retakes, suited his perfectionism. Then, too, there was that enormous popular audience to be reached. (When Brecht asked him why he acted, he said, "Because people don't know what they are like and I think I can show them.") Besides, he had never entirely mastered the disciplines of the stage; he was too dependent on his own inspiration. A theater audience could hardly wait for this to happen, but a production crew could, however reluctantly.

And in Hollywood he got along best, of course, with fellow artists who were literate or aspiring to be—like Irving Thalberg, his great supporter at MGM, and directors like *Hunchback*'s William Dieterle (formerly of the Max Reinhardt company) or *Les Miserables*' Richard Boleslavski (formerly of the Moscow Art Theatre), people who could be impressed by his aims and ambitions and even by his travails. Where he had trouble was with the "professionals," the hard-nosed, "down to earth," and incurious ones, to whom acting and filmmaking were mostly a job and no big deal otherwise. The sort of problem he had during the filming at RKO of *They Knew What They Wanted* (1940), with Garson Kanin directing and with Carole Lombard— whom Laughton detested for her loud and profane mouth (he had worked with her seven years before on something called *White Woman*, and they hadn't gotten along)—costarring. Everyone else in Hollywood adored her, of course: she was so famously a "regular gal." (He detested Gertrude Lawrence, too, his costar in *Rembrandt*, who exchanged dirty jokes on the set with director Alex Korda and then shrieked with laughter—Laughton had screens put up around his soundstage to block them both out.)

Although it had been filmed twice before (once as a silent, both times under other titles), *They Knew What They Wanted* was still an "important" production: a Pulitzer Prize play by a famous Broadway playwright, Sidney Howard. And Kanin, at twenty-seven, also from Broadway, was the new RKO studio wunderkind, having just directed two hit comedies for them, *Bachelor Mother* (1939) and *My Favorite Wife* (1940)—as well as two sentimental "sleepers," both about heroes who were lovable losers (*A Man to Remember*, 1938, and *The Great Man Votes*, 1939). And that is exactly what Laughton was meant to be as "Tony Patucci" in this one—a prosperous but simple immigrant California grape grower who gets a mail-order bride (Lombard) by sending her his handsome foreman's photograph. It was another role turning on his physical unattractiveness—this time with a heavy infusion of Italianate broken English, or at least Sidney Howard's idea of it.

What are you going to do about the accent? Kanin wanted to know (the star's early tries weren't encouraging). Laughton replied that he was going to read Dante aloud in the original. He was also going to study the paintings of Michelangelo and listen to Vivaldi. None of this worked, apparently; they finally had to call in the dialect coach. And when Laughton himself felt that a major scene was not working, he asked Kanin to drive him to the vineyards in the Valley, where in a peach orchard after midnight he played the scene until he got it—and then lost it again the next day on the set—so back to the orchard again—and so on. But nothing, it seemed, could save Laughton's performance.

Callow makes sure when you read all this in his biography that you identify so much with Laughton's ambitions—his desire to focus "some kind of world-pain" in any character he played, his stated commitment to revealing "the god in man"—that it's the others, with their common-sense objections to Laughton's behavior (when you die, Kanin told him, it will be "of acting"), who seem foolish. In Callow's book, the joke is on the jokers. Why not Vivaldi?—Laughton had made things like that work for him before, mostly by looking at paintings.

But not this time. He is very bad—flamboyant and one-dimensional—in the finished film. Callow blames this mostly on Kanin, who failed to give the actor the kind of understanding he always needed from his director. But surely some of the blame must have attached to the role (much more persuasive when musicalized and sung in the Frank Loesser stage version), with its lovable humanity and simple earthy wisdom—hard to take seriously, even with the help of Dante.

After this failure—"he never again tried so hard," says Callow—Laughton set out in a new direction, it seems: "he came down from the cross . . ." "Thanks to Charles," said Deanna Durbin in 1941, just after doing a film with him (*It Started with Eve*), "I discovered that making pictures could be fun." (Thanks to *whom*? Could be *what*?) Now *he* was showing those others that it was no big deal. He was tired of suffering and inspiring revulsion. "What's so terribly, terribly sad about all of this," he said to Kanin at the wrap-up party for their movie, "is that some day you'll come to know what a damned nice fella I really am." As if all along, inside the aloof and tormented Englishman, there was a friendly American, a "fella" who just wanted to be liked.

He continued to act in movies—usually (as in two Deanna Durbin movies) in gruff but amiable character parts. But he had still at least two major screen performances to give in this period (maybe trying not so hard was a help): in 1943 as a Vichy France coward turned hero in Jean Renoir's *This Land Is Mine*, one of his beauty-and-the-beast variations, opposite Maureen O'Hara again. And in Robert Siodmak's *The Suspect* (1944), as a sympathetic wife killer (the beauty here—the always interesting Ella Raines—returns his love), he is compelling and moving in one of his most understated performances.

In the fifties he began a celebrated new theatrical career as an avuncular reader-storyteller, traveling across America and becoming a kind of unofficial spokesman for culture and beauty, offering selections from Shakespeare, the Bible, Thomas Wolfe. And with his staged readings of *Don Juan in Hell* (from Shaw's *Man and Superman*) in 1951 and then *John Brown's Body* in 1953, he had become a "hot" new Broadway director, an "innovator" of middlebrow theater. His biggest success was his production of Herman Wouk's *The Caine Mutiny Court-Martial* (he even helped the novelist Wouk to write it), with its notorious final act paean to militarism and blind obedience to authority. (Eric Bentley called the show "Captain Bligh's revenge.") Where the iconic Laughton had been associated with the excessive and outré, this new public version seemed almost obliging to a fault, as reassuring as he had once been unsettling. Reading the Bible on *The Ed Sullivan*

With Ella Raines in *The Suspect*—one of his finest performances,
for one of his favorite directors, Robert Siodmak

Show—then coming back to introduce newcomer Elvis Presley (as if
to reassure us about *him*).

But even in those more compliant years, he managed some daring
and remarkable achievements: his three-year collaboration with Bertolt
Brecht over the text and stage production in 1947 of *Galileo* (he played
the leading role), one of the central events of modern theater; *The
Night of the Hunter* in 1955, his astonishing late-career debut as a film
director; and his even later attempts in 1959 at Stratford-upon-Avon,
in spite of age and illness, to play *King Lear*, a lifelong ambition, and by
some accounts at the time a movingly realized one.

Earlier on, when at the peak of his movie stardom, the monstrous-ness he showed his audiences, he said, in figures like Bligh and Javert had been something he found in himself, in the terror of his own depths. That's how he could make such monsters nearly as moving as they were repellent, drawing you in through his own intensity and pain. Where other actors, like Olivier, seemed almost to hide behind their roles (his Richard III, for example), Laughton found a way, in even the most improbable and impenetrable guises (Quasimodo's, for example), to seem to be revealing himself. And he had no interest in verisimilitude, in acting that was merely realistic, in the timid compro-mises of a naturalist style. A true artist, he believed, creates rather than mimics. The demonic life that he drew upon in himself required a demonic outer one—a kind of superrealism, involving the behavioral exaggerations which became at the time a kind of gift to imperson-ators everywhere. It was this demonstrative, larger-than-life style that endeared him to Brecht, of course—who took it for a confirmation (yet one more) of his own antinaturalist theatricalism. It's less likely, how-ever, that Brecht the materialist would have approved of Laughton the artist's almost Arnoldian idealism, his "high seriousness" and moral ambition. An idealism that was inseparable from his relation to Amer-ica, his adopted land.

II.

COMMITTED FROM THE beginning of his career to an art of painful self-exposure, it's no wonder that Laughton felt at odds with the En-glish theater of his time, with its stifling professionalism (he liked to boast that he was an "amateur"), its decorum and caution—and that he was drawn to America, where he could find recklessness answering to his own. A place where people were much less sure of what acting was or could be. It might even be what he did—why not? (Garson Kanin finally did, after all, drive him to that orchard—and twice.) Americans were more tolerant of intense self-absorption. They were even capable of being impressed by it: after all, if "truth" isn't inside you, if it isn't a matter of "honesty" and "sincerity," what could it be?—if it isn't *personal*? In his particular way Laughton prefigured the Method, the most profoundly American acting style of our time. Marlon

Brando was his descendant. So were the boy-man stars of the 1950s and 1960s, from James Dean to Steve McQueen—movie stars who promoted a more narcissist conception not only of leading men but of men in general, of who and what they are.

And he felt at home here almost from the day he arrived. In America he imagined he could have an impact beyond anything he might have dreamed of in England. First in the movies, with their great popular audience—later on by his public reading tours. The wide-open spaces, whether in the landscapes or on the faces of the Americans he read aloud to, were a sign to him of something to be filled ("Charles believed," wrote Elsa, "that in America people never stopped wanting to learn") by the great thoughts and beautiful words he offered with such passion and earnestness. He became a teacher and a prophet. But—as with many of us—the America he experienced most reliably was the one in his head.

Nothing makes this clearer, or in a more alarming way, than *The Night of the Hunter,* the one film he directed (its box office failure precluded any others), which Callow, like many others, regards as a masterpiece. It is certainly a very personal work: Laughton not only directed but controlled every aspect of it, even to writing the screenplay (James Agee, who gets the credit on the screen, was too far gone in drink and illness to earn it), adapting it from a bestselling novel by Davis Grubb. Set in a remote riverbank town in a timeless rural America derived from (and in tribute to) the films of D. W. Griffith, it's about two children (Billy Chapin and Sally Ann Brice) whose widowed mother (Shelley Winters) marries an evil preacher (Robert Mitchum), who is trying to get some stolen money their dead father has left with the boy. After murdering their mother, he pursues the children in their flight downriver—where they are at last taken in and saved by the good-hearted Widow Rachel (Lillian Gish). The story is told mostly from the children's point of view, and the two of them are onscreen more than anyone else in the movie. What seems curious, even bizarre at times, is how little genuine interest the movie appears to take in them.

Callow tells us (and Mitchum told similar stories in interviews) that Laughton had difficulty on the set even being around the two child actors. He loathed the little girl from the start, it seems—especially after her grandparents got her to perform her "little French song" for

With Robert Mitchum on the set of *The Night of the Hunter*

him ("*Dites-moi*" from *South Pacific*). And once the little boy started citing the acting awards he'd won ("Get that child away from me!" cried Laughton), Mitchum had to take over the direction of both the children for the rest of the filming. And the problem shows in the movie itself: the girl is coy, the boy mechanical.

But this—as it tirelessly insists—is a movie in praise of children.

"Lord save little children, they abide and they endure," intones Lillian Gish, as the benevolent widow who fills her house with waifs of all ages. "It's a hard world for little things," she says, likening modern times to the "plague time" of the Bible ("them olden days, the hard, hard times"). "My soul is humble when I see the way little ones accept their lot," she says at another point, to the camera and to us. "The wind blows and the rains are cold, yet they abide." But this emphasis on the resilience of children is repeated so often that it begins to feel suspect. The pseudo-biblical rhetoric (much of it drawn from the novel) seems as empty of the concern it lays claim to as the movie itself finally does. The clearest feeling it conveys, in fact, is something quite different: a persisting undercurrent of sexual hysteria.

And you're almost sure something has gone out of control when a townswoman at the church picnic (Evelyn Varden in a shrill one-note performance) proceeds to talk about her apparent frigidity over forty years of marriage ("I jus' lie there thinkin' about my canning") as loudly and ringingly as if she were announcing a run for public office. The film alternates between such clunky theatricalism and conventional movie naturalism—just as the town and the river are both real (location shots of water and sky) and fake (a studio tank, a Plasticene "riverbank," a cyclorama—Laughton even uses semitransparent scrims for the walls of Gish's small house). It's like the way the characters talk: a regional sound with a rhapsodic overlay. "I feel clean now," exults Shelley Winters at the same picnic. "My whole body's just a-quivering with cleanness!"

Which means, of course, that she is pretty much not getting any from her new husband, the preacher. Whose potency is figured by a switchblade splitting through his trousers, whose fulfillment is in murder. But since the movie's imagery throughout feels so unmoored and disconnected (the spectacle of a church meeting, for example, being as hollow and unconvincing as the earlier one of a burlesque show), the result seems both inchoate and tendentious, its nightmare effects feeling strangely out of proportion to the familiar and banal attitudes they are meant to convey: the therapeutic-sentimental notions of health

OPPOSITE PAGE: *The Night of the Hunter*'s theatrical-expressionist style: Lillian Gish guards her ward and her home, while Mitchum, beyond the scrim, menaces them.

and sanity ("You were lookin' for *love*, Ruby," says Gish to her oldest, most troubled young ward), the reduction of human evil to pathology and repression. It's like D. W. Griffith crossed with William Inge. And all of it cast in the grandiloquent folksy-arty mode that Laughton was so often drawn to (his stage production of *John Brown's Body* by Stephen Vincent Benét, his readings of Thomas Wolfe) when he set out to evoke this country. In a way, the most American things about Laughton's film are what it gets wrong—above all, its powerful will to innocence, by which a real-life antipathy to those children gets translated into a self-congratulating benevolence, a fantasy of loving kindness. America had taught him something, it seemed, about how to handle his horrors.

III.

THE NIGHT OF THE HUNTER was really an art film (hence its dismal box office at the time)—far indeed from the kind of lowbrow vitality

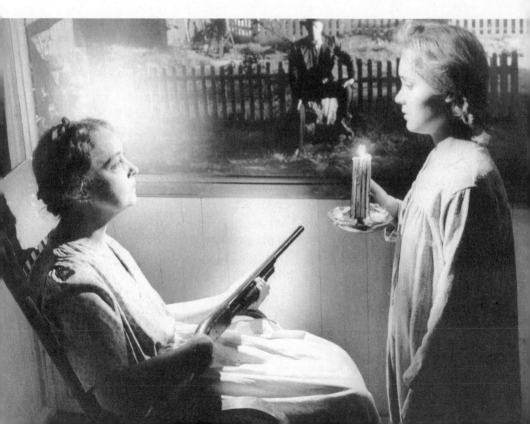

that Laughton had admired in Hollywood when he first arrived there. He had "a passion for slapstick," as Callow says, and a craving to be involved in "a genuinely Popular Art." When he received his 1933 Best Actor Academy Award (for *Henry VIII*), he made the startling announcement that it should have gone to Walt Disney. "There's your great man," he said, pointing at Disney, "great because he is simple and unaffected." That's also how he understood common American life—where the smart-ass talk from their cabdriver made Elsa and him, fresh off their boat from England, laugh out loud with delight ("We laughed because we knew we were free to say the same kind of thing too," he said). At a stuffy London dinner given in his honor, when the American next to him made an inappropriate joke sotto voce, Laughton found himself wanting "to get back to New York so bad I could taste it." American irreverence delighted him, and next to it the English versions—Noël Coward's, say (or Gertrude Lawrence's)—seemed pale and trifling. By comparison to Walt Disney—or to Leo McCarey, the man who had directed the first great Laurel and Hardy comedies, and whom Laughton described in the midthirties as "the greatest comedy mind now living." Laughton was the one who insisted that McCarey should direct *Ruggles of Red Gap*.

Ruggles the butler was his favorite role. And yet he is not good at slapstick—or even at comedy: he seems somehow to get it wrong again and again while everyone else on the screen—an ensemble of some of Hollywood's most gifted comic players (Charles Ruggles, Mary Boland, ZaSu Pitts, Maud Eburne)—is getting it exactly right. No question he is ponderous—even worse, he is plaintive, giving the role a misplaced emotional intensity. That intensity is certainly understandable: Ruggles is not only a man in "service" (as Laughton had felt himself to be at his family's hotel) but an Englishman who learns to love America and who finally chooses it over his native land. Laughton even manages to recite the Gettysburg Address (entirely his idea) in what became the movie's most famous scene. But his ardency is nearly fatal to the poise of the film. It's not just that he can't do slapstick, or that he draws your attention "to complexities which are irrelevant" (Callow again). It's that he doesn't have the impersonality of comedy, with the result that his Ruggles gives almost the same feeling of tendentiousness, of an intrusive personal reference, as *The Night of the Hunter* does.

That tendentiousness made him seem out of place not only in comedy but in Hollywood itself in those days—where the dominant tone and style often put him at a disadvantage. There is a single movie that shows this happening—so clearly that you could almost think the demonstration was intentional. It's Twentieth Century–Fox's *Tales of Manhattan* (1942), directed by Julien Duvivier, the first big "all-star" omnibus movie since Paramount's *If I Had a Million* ten years earlier—in which Laughton also appeared. That film connected its separate stories by a millionaire's bequest; this one does it by a tailcoat, which the movie follows as it passes in a downwardly mobile direction from owner to owner, going from Charles Boyer in the first story, making love to Rita Hayworth in a Long Island mansion (where he gets shot by her husband, Thomas Mitchell), to Paul Robeson at the end, singing and praying with Ethel Waters in a Catfish Row–style shantytown. There are five stories altogether; Laughton stars in the middle episode. But the first two are the most assured and stylish.

The first one—with Boyer's doomed romanticism and Hayworth's lush beauty, with its looming shadows and perverse love triangle—looks back to the Expressionist-style thrillers of the thirties and ahead to film noir. The second episode—with Ginger Rogers and Henry Fonda meeting at her fiancé Cesar Romero's apartment, and falling thoughtfully in love over a letter meant for Romero, while he is out of the room—belongs to screwball comedy. In themselves these episodes are hardly more than sketches. Partly their function is to remind you, in happy general ways, of other movies: they are like trailers for their genres (noir, as it came to be called, was just beginning its vogue in 1942, and screwball, though still around, was running down). And they demonstrate how much power and glamour those genres could evoke even in vignettes when done with conviction and intelligence. The Laughton episode (another "genre" altogether) follows.

He is a poor and struggling composer making a living by playing honky-tonk piano in a saloon. Until the maestro of a major orchestra (Victor Francen) offers him the chance to conduct his own music. The sequence is vintage Laughton, involving as it does a public humiliation:

Laughton does comedy in *Ruggles of Red Gap*—Mary Boland
and Charlie Ruggles at left

while he is conducting, the tailcoat, which is too small for him (having
been made for the Boyer character), splits up his back, and the fancy-
dress audience laughs and jeers at him until he drops his baton. But
the maestro saves him and the concert by standing and removing his
own coat, and in the end Laughton triumphs.

'When this unlikely episode begins, Laughton is at his piano in
the empty saloon—looking reproachful and suffering over the boiler-
plate barrelhouse music the bartender (Dewey Robinson) is forcing
him to play. Then in close-up, doing his great befuddled eye-blinks,
he sneaks in some phrases of the "longhair stuff." No use—the bartender yells at him. He resumes the honky-tonk sound and grimaces

into the camera—startlingly. It's one of those go-ahead-and-kick-me faces—defiant and ingratiating, winsome and self-loathing all at once—and it's a familiar Laughton effect, like the eye-blinks. What makes it so jarring here is the way it intrudes self-pity into the middle of the film—at the same time reminding you that self-pity is what the stylized modes of the best Hollywood movies of the time kept firmly at bay. Those tough thrillers and screwball comedies were about the glamour of growing up; Laughton's performances were not.

That self-pity is disabling, I think. Davis at her best drew on her self-rejection but not her self-pity. And though Laughton sometimes transcends his, it still reverberates somewhere in too many of his performances. Other stars (including Davis) privately may have been just as sorry for themselves, just as painfully self-absorbed or even more so—but that was not something they were supposed to show to us. And Laughton does. He breaks a compact that movies of his time with their circumscribed realities made with their audiences: not always that the stars and leading players should be beautiful or even dignified, much less serene and imperturbable—but that they should preserve in what they did and revealed to us a certain impersonality, a kind of detachment not only from us but from themselves. As Boyer and Paul Robeson do in this film.

Robeson and Boyer, of course, are iconic stars by almost any measure. Probably Edward G. Robinson is not—but he appears in the episode following Laughton's and, remarkably, almost rights the balance in the movie that Laughton has upset. This is all the more surprising because the episode itself is not notably less mawkish than Laughton's was. It's another humiliation scenario—about a down-and-outer who goes to the reunion of his Ivy League graduation class and tries unavailingly to pass himself off (in the traveling tailcoat) as a worldly success—with another last-minute turnaround in his reception at the end.

Robinson was neither a genius nor a hero of acting; he was cautious and unadventurous by comparison to Laughton (most actors were). But where Laughton is moist, as it were, Robinson is dry—bringing a sharp, almost acerbic edge to everything he played, as he does in this film. He, too, was "physically unattractive"—short, round, and sour-faced—so that he often played Laughton's kind of role, including the lovelorn ugly man that the heroine shudders away from. But in Robinson's version of this role you were likelier to feel, as you were meant to, that the loss of the woman weighed more than the pain of being ugly—whereas with Laughton it was almost the reverse. Robinson had—effortlessly, it seemed—a kind of human authority on the screen that Laughton had perceptibly to work for and often failed to reach. Not always (certainly not, for example, in his Siodmak and Renoir films, where he seems quite at ease), but often.

There is often something wheedling about Laughton on the screen (as Pauline Kael once remarked about Jack Lemmon: What does he want from us?). Even his seriousness as an actor was often compromised by that self-abasement—and by his obsession with his own ugliness, an unending and lifelong concern, as Simon Callow tells us. That concern, as it turns out, is one of the things that make him seem most contemporary, but it limits him fatally.

It's worth remembering that men at Laughton's time were not *supposed* to be concerned in a crucial way with their own looks. *That* indignity, in all its permutations, was reserved to women—more or less. Laughton was an exception to this pattern, or so it seemed. His fatness, for example, was something he suffered on the screen, one of those degradations he acted out of and offered to the rest of us. How different he seemed—and seems now—from the "fat men" in the movies around him, the Edward Arnolds, the Charles Coburns, the Eugene Pallettes, et al., those Prosperos and benign patriarchs of the great romantic comedies. The rounder they were, the more bodiless they seemed. Their fatness, far from being a defeat of the flesh, was a kind of triumph over it—a refusal of narcissism. But it was exactly Laughton's narcissism that made a problem, for example, when George Cukor cast him as Micawber in MGM's *David Copperfield* (1934): Laughton couldn't quite convey the geniality toward the children, and especially toward Freddie Bartholomew's David, that the part required. It's extraordinary to think that he was replaced (and triumphantly) by W. C. Fields—who *truly* hated children. But then it wasn't, we may assume, that Fields offered a "warmer" sort of father than Laughton might have done—only a less self-involved one. One of the advantages of being, or of imagining yourself to be, a successful father, of course—in the ideal, if not always in the event—is that you stop hoping to be, even stop despairing of being, the beautiful son. Laughton never could, it seems—Callow calls him "a disappointed narcissist." But it is the pain of this disappointment that Laughton the performer too often asks us to look at, in those moist and pleading eyes. The humiliation, as it turns out, is contagious.

PART TWO

REALISTS

7

Robert De Niro

I.

BETTE DAVIS DIDN'T believe that acting should be like real life: you can see that anywhere, she said in interviews, as well as to directors trying to restrain her exaggerations. And probably she wasn't far from the point that the distinguished drama critic Stark Young once made about a Garbo performance (in *As You Desire Me*): it was like real life but different, and that difference, he claimed, was what you call *acting*. And it's true you don't normally see a Garbo inhabiting ordinary life. No more do you see a Brando. His Terry Malloy in *On the Waterfront* is about as improbable a Jersey longshoreman as Garbo's Grusinskaya is a Russian ballerina. But they are *both*, in their different ways, deeply believable. "There is no realism in American films," Jean Renoir once said, "but something much better—great truth."

But Robert De Niro, unlike Laughton and Davis, and like Brando before him and all the other Method people who revolutionized Hollywood acting, was committed to the "real" as a way to truth. Even overcommitted, some might say ("Bobby only exists when he's in someone else's skin," said the *Taxi Driver* screenwriter, Paul Schrader). Famously, he didn't *act* Jake La Motta's disfiguring weight gain—as Laughton did Quasimodo's disfigurement, with prosthetic help—he gained the weight himself, closing the *Raging Bull* shoot down for three months to do it, to eat his way from his original 145 pounds to the middle-aged La Motta's 215. (Long before the virtuoso weight-

transformers in our current movies: Christian Bale, Matthew Mc-
Conaughey, et al.)

Watching De Niro then was not so much like watching other movie
stars—not exactly anyway. Not like watching Garbo as Marguerite or
Bogart as Rick. More like not watching De Niro but rather Jake La
Motta or Travis Bickle—or just as startling, Rupert Pupkin, in Scorsese's brilliant but underrated *The King of Comedy* (1983). An actor
like the "invisible" author or artist who disappears into his own creation. The invisible star.

Far from invisible, however, De Niro was—from the seventies to the
mideighties—the biggest actor-star in movies, the closest thing we'd
seen at that time to another Brando—whom he'd actually played as the
youthful Don Corleone in Coppola's *The Godfather: Part II* (1974). Like
the young Brando, the young De Niro was sexy and magnetic, but he was
a less romantic, less overwhelming presence than Brando had been—
lighter, somehow, and more antic, less personal, more hidden. If Brando,
rising as he did during the breakdown of the old studio star system, was
the great postclassical star, De Niro was the postmodern one, distanced
and ironic. Two of his finest performances are as reconsidered figures
out of old movie genres, the heroes of the backstage musical (*New York,
New York*) and of the gangster film (*Once Upon a Time in America*).

Scorsese's remarkable *New York, New York* (1977) is about a musical couple in the big band era: it's the she-goes-up-while-he-goes-down
formula plot. It's mid-movie and Jimmy (De Niro) has been reduced to
playing in a band instead of leading one. He's now working at a Harlem club, where his pregnant wife, Francine (Liza Minnelli), comes to
meet her agent with the record producer who wants to sign her to a
singing contract—she only wants to be sure that the contract terms
are okay with her husband, Jimmy, who sits at the table with them on
his break. Francine seems not to notice his discomfort, even his hostil-
ity to the other two men. So he excuses himself, crosses the crowded
dance floor, and goes to a wall phone next to the bandstand, in a doorway at the foot of a flight of purple stairs narrowly enclosed by yellow
walls (the movie's public spaces, by production designer Boris Leven,
look more like Oz than the fifties America they nonetheless succeed in
evoking). When down the stairs comes this tall beautiful brown-skinned
woman (Diahne Abbott) all in black and white: a cascade of black hair to
one side of her face, swaths of white fabric cutting across her black shoul-

derless gown from shoulder to hip. She is adjusting her left-wrist bracelet as she comes. "Family night?" she says, side-of-the-mouth style, as she passes him at the phone. "Come 'ere," he says lecherously, reaching for her and missing as she goes past him and up onto the bandstand to sing. He makes his phone connection and commences to talk (we don't hear him). Then in a long shot, the camera (on a crane) tracks in over the heads of the couples on the dance floor to this mesmerizing lady at the mike above them—beginning to sing the vocal, jauntily, insouciantly, in a breathy, rather small voice, to Razaf and Waller's "Honeysuckle Rose."

And the sequence cuts back and forth between him and her—though it's her rather than him that we listen to. You don't know what he's saying into the phone or what it's about, but you never think you want or need to. For him, it's enough that it took him away from his wife and her new enablers. For us, we're glad that Abbott's terrific song isn't overridden and interrupted by someone else's dialogue (as it would most likely have been in the old movies that this one is modeled on). Also, you're pleased just to watch him talk—it's interesting in the special way that people talking can be when you don't at all know what they're saying. So he talks, then listens, intermittently looking toward the singer, then across the room toward his wife at her table, who is now giving kissy goodbyes to her important friends. Cut to Abbott again, in a tracking shot moving to a close-up, schmoozing the mike as she sings, revolving her shoulders sexily to the beat. And so on.

And he hangs up—in a close shot—sighing lightly but visibly, leaning on the wall, thinking now, his eyes down, his mouth tightened. And Scorsese's camera circles him slowly, an imitation of his own abstraction. He stays like that. Then he shifts his weight, slowly, disconsolately. End of song—end of sequence.

What's also interesting about this is its daring—in a late-seventies American movie made for a mainstream audience (who didn't show up anyway)—the way it invites us to look at thinking, to contemplate contemplating, not the content of it but the outwardness. De Niro is never truly "invisible," of course (despite his aspirations in that direction), not even as Jake La Motta. But in moments like this one he reaches something akin to that: a sort of egolessness, the act of not-acting made visible and moving.

Scorsese tries a parallel sequence—cut from the film's first release but later restored—with his other star, Liza Minnelli: an extended

wordless scene of the pregnant Francine, alone in their first apartment, doing her nails, accompanied on her phonograph by a ravishing
Django Reinhardt recording, ending with a widescreen close-up of her
eyes looking into a mirror. It's a lovely scene; and you don't have to be
a Minnelli fan—I'm not, mostly—to appreciate how marvelous she is
in this film. But she can't achieve the inwardness that De Niro can,
the *privacy* even, that a moment like this depends on.

Brando at his height plugs right into your feelings—where De Niro
leaves you to deal with them, and good luck. It's almost as if Scorsese
and he had set out to illustrate that contrast at the end of *Raging Bull*
(1980)—when the out-of-shape La Motta, now a nightclub act, check-
ing his lines before going on, recites Brando's famously heartbreaking
I-coulda-been-a-contender speech into his dressing room mirror, without affect, without inflection, before shadowboxing and puffing into
the movie's final fadeout.

He's not a leading man, David Lean told Elia Kazan after a screening of Kazan's *The Last Tycoon* (1976), starring De Niro. It's true that
the movie roles that had first made him known—the dying baseball
player in *Bang the Drum Slowly* and especially the triumphantly de-
ranged Johnny Boy in Scorsese's *Mean Streets* (both 1973)—were supporting ones. As was the young Don Corleone (for which he got the
Supporting Actor Academy Award in 1974). Scorsese's *Taxi Driver*
(1976) was the first time De Niro got to dominate a whole picture instead of stealing it. And once people saw this film, as well as the *Mean
Streets* and *Godfather* ones before it, they thought that he could do
almost anything—even *Tycoon*'s Monroe Stahr, the hero (modeled on
Irving Thalberg) of Fitzgerald's unfinished novel, and of what came to
be Harold Pinter's screenplay for the producer Sam Spiegel.

Kazan in particular had wanted De Niro for the role—"Bobby" was
like Marlon, he said in his autobiography: "a tough kid . . . capable of
extraordinary sensitivity." And one of the hardest-working actors he'd
ever known, even wanting to rehearse on Sundays. And this time he
would *lose* weight for the film, going from 170 to 128 pounds, according to Kazan. "He actually looked frail."

The film was a bomb (only the French liked it, and not even that
until much later), and De Niro himself seemed curiously squelched in
it, muted and dim. Kazan later blamed the Pinter screenplay, which
the playwright had adamantly refused to alter. And Spiegel (who was

in awe of Pinter, Kazan said) blamed De Niro, who was "nothing but an East Side punk," he said to Kazan, without any of the dignity or the complexity that the role called for.

But if Monroe Stahr had been a stretch for him—as even Kazan conceded—his next role, in Bertolucci's massive Marxist epic *1900* (1976), was even more so: playing a weak-willed Italian aristocrat, opposite Gérard Depardieu as his peasant buddy and historically inevitable final nemesis. The film—six hours long, shown in two parts in Europe, reduced to a single four hours for America—was another bomb (even in France). And alongside Depardieu (the French Brando,

Robert De Niro with costar Gérard Depardieu in Bertolucci's *1900*

he was sometimes called), with all his cheerful vitality, De Niro seems once again dim. It can't have helped that his dialogue in this international coproduction had to be dubbed by another actor for the Italian-language version and postsynched by himself for the English one.

Sam Spiegel says that "Bobby has no nobility," Kazan writes in his diary of *The Last Tycoon*, and that "he has a 'petty larceny' look, particularly when he smiles." Kazan assured the producer that he would not let their star "smile often" (a promise he seems to have kept). But it was letting him *grin*—as he does at the beginning of *Taxi Driver*, or in the last shot and freeze-frame of *Once Upon a Time in America*—that they really had to watch out for.

You first see Travis Bickle from behind, a tracking shot of the back of his head, as he enters the cab company's hiring office. The boss behind the desk is a little uneasy about him—as are we (Bernard Herrmann's ominous opening score is a clue). Partly because his manner is so vacant. Until the hiring guy asks him about his driving record. "It's clean," he replies in a close shot, "real clean—like my conscience." And he breaks into a crooked grin that transfigures his face, almost shockingly, making you wonder where *that* came from—and why. "Don't break my chops!" says the other, feeling challenged and unnerved. And the smile is promptly tucked away: "Sorry, sir. I didn't mean that," says Travis, a good boy again. And Scorsese's camera draws in closer to catch the unmistakable flicker of contempt in the now penitent eyes.

That grin is so transforming that it seems almost crazy: the opaque lean high-boned face with the small close-set eyes imploding into this spasm of jollity (or is it?), slitting the eyes, sending the mouth up into suddenly appearing folds of flesh like concentric ripples in a pond. Pauline Kael called his smile in this movie "cretinous"—resenting its effect on an actor who could sometimes look to her "as handsome as Robert Taylor." And it's true—when the De Niro smile begins, at least, you can almost think you'll see blacked-out teeth in the center of it. But when it turns into a grin it looks more menacing than dull-witted. At whatever stage, however, between smile and grin, it works against "nobility"—as Sam Spiegel would later claim.

His first Scorsese film was *Mean Streets*, where he plays Johnny Boy, the unhinged sidekick of the hero Charlie (Harvey Keitel), a buttoned-down, straight-arrow (by Mafia neighborhood standards, anyway) main-chancer who is both trying to control Johnny Boy and save him, but who is also getting high on the kick of his uncontrol—until the maniac in the end finally sinks them both.

Earlier on there's a frenetic but dreamlike montage, to a percussive rock beat on the soundtrack, of Johnny Boy, after one of his royal screwups, careering on foot through the nighttime Village streets, bumping into another guy going by, punching and mauling him almost in passing, then rocking on and appearing on a tenement rooftop next, raising his arms against the New York skyline first in a victory gesture, then a fuck-you one—before jumping down and leaving the frame. To the extent you're invested in his movie by this time, you think Omigod! as you watch this—you're like his appalled friend Charlie. And like Charlie, you feel the kick, too—the elation, even.

And that obsessive self-destructiveness is in all the Scorsese–De Niro characters. Even in the ones, like Rupert Pupkin and Travis Bickle, that it pays off for in the end (they both become celebrities). But their obduracy before that is so great, so unreasoning, it gets thrilling: they should *stop*, after all, they should let up, *anyone* would . . . Not Jake in his living room as he fiddles uselessly with a malfunctioning TV, suddenly (and groundlessly) accusing his visiting brother Joey (Joe Pesci) of shtupping his wife—or in the ring, as he pounds to a bloody pulp the face of a boxer the same wife had once remarked was "a good-looking kid" (not anymore). This sort of thing is more than ordinary perversity, even ordinary craziness—it's epic even: your objections, if that's what they were, collapse before it. And you *can't* look away.

And that's the creepy fascination of *The King of Comedy*, of nerdy aspiring comic Rupert Pupkin's mad movielong pursuit of his idol, the legendary TV host and stand-up comic Jerry Langford (Jerry Lewis), and of all Rupert's attempts to get past the gracious, super-reasonable agents of rebuff whose job it is to guard the star. Like the knockout young blonde (Shelley Hack) who emerges from the inner offices to greet him—in the *outer* office. Politely, of course—no need to alienate a fan—she is a pro at all this. And to watch Rupert, with his little mustache, his wiglike roof of hair, and his prissy little mouth, refuse with equal politeness to be put off, is close to excruciating—if it weren't so fascinating. The young woman is chic, articulate, almost helplessly would-be-helpful, but also effortlessly in charge—her personal authority alone should be enough to shut Rupert up, but he is, unlike the rest of us, unalive to such embarrassments. He wants Jerry (as they both call him here) to listen to the tape he's brought of his own stand-up routine, and he wants to deliver it in person. And though she would like to be nice to him (what's the *point* of feeling disgust—or even superiority?), she can't get rid of him—can't stop him from countering every put-off, from remaining planted in that outer office (if Jerry is out, as she claims, then he'll wait, he says, for him to come in) or from invading the inner ones (security in pursuit).

She prevails in the end, of course (security catches him). But obsession has its own authority, its own power—an extension of that flicker of contempt in Travis's eye. The Scorsese De Niro is beyond humiliation. And so he is beyond the reach of the rest of us—the wusses who feel embarrassed even to watch him, and who go on watching nonetheless. How could we not? He's achieved the ultimate fuck-you state—being superior even to his own lost dignity. And he wins in the end—he actually becomes a TV star.

II.

JIMMY DOYLE IN *New York, New York* (1977)—the movie that Scorsese and De Niro made following their success with *Taxi Driver* (and the failure of De Niro's Kazan and Bertolucci films)—is a smaller-scale version of the same De Niro. He has the same doggedness, but it's more in touch with mundane obstacles, like career and marriage problems. And "Jimmy" is also in a traditionally comic mode—screwball comic, in fact, for the half or more of the movie that feels like the old romantic comedies. But the film as a whole is, as I said above, a riff on a less buoyant, more soap-operatic genre, the backstage musical one. Where the union of the lead couple, both on- and offstage, is threatened by his ego and arrogance and by her answering reasonableness and in the end by her greater success, when the Big Producer asks her but not him to play the Palace—it's Alice Faye with Tyrone Power, Betty Grable with Dan Dailey, Judy Garland with Gene Kelly or James Mason. Finally everything hinges (in the nonmusical variants, too: Myrna Loy with Clark Gable, Bette Davis with Errol Flynn, et al.) on the challenge that she becomes to his male ego.

It was never a great genre, but Scorsese and his stars turn it into something clear-eyed and extraordinary. And into the sort of movie that makes a world of its own—a movie you can live in, and visit again. That has in part to do not only with the great standard songs (Youmans, Gershwin, et al.) and big band arrangements, but with Boris Leven's stylized production design (he had also designed one of the movie's most famous early archetypes, 1938's *Alexander's Ragtime Band* with Faye and Power), in the witty self-declaring artifice of his sets: a night-club that's all red neon lights (if nothing else, we can get a nice tan here, says a customer); a motel room with purple furniture and an ominous-looking *Mona Lisa* knockoff on a green wall; an outdoor snowscape that's all black tree silhouettes against a sky-blue backdrop like a modern greeting card, and so on.

In every way, the movie was a calculated experiment—almost as if Scorsese had set out to verify Renoir's remark about "great truth" in the Hollywood fakery by heightening both the fakery and the truth. Against stylized backgrounds, he shows what he called "the documentary," the naturalistic behavior of the dramatic scenes (a scarifying quarrel scene), which were usually and largely improvised—and a greater frankness, a more painful honesty (Jimmy's serial infidelity) about the familiar characters and situations. But the shoot itself was an unhappy one, Scorsese later said, much of the time feeling out of control (not just over budget and over schedule, but marked by drugs, more than usual, and by Scorsese's ill-starred romance with Minnelli). If the movie's good, he said later (he wasn't so sure), it's mainly because it's truthful. (It was a huge flop.)

You first see Jimmy (De Niro) in the middle of New York's V-J Day festivities on the street, then inside a vast and breathtaking penthouse ballroom, with throngs on the dance floor and "Tommy Dorsey and His Band" playing from a vertiginous platform (the camera circling them) high above the crowd, against the New York skyline outside. Jimmy looks like the only one among the male dancers on the floor who's not in uniform (he threw it out once he was discharged) but in a Hawaiian shirt and chinos—a costume that both sets him apart from the others and connects him (for us) to the movie past (Bing Crosby's *Road* pictures, Montgomery Clift's *From Here to Eternity*). He's trying to pick up a girl, any girl ("It's V-J Day and I wanna get laid, man")—even to the point of pulling her away from her partner on the dance floor while talking fast (about his mother and sister "just over there").

While Francine (Liza Minnelli) in contrast, in her WAC uniform, is sitting by herself at a ringside table, rather showily, even defensively, enjoying the music, waiting for her friends to rejoin her any minute now, she says, and that's why Jimmy can't sit down there. Not that that stops him. Soon he's not only sitting down but playing at falling against her, at kissing her hand, at being undiscourageable—in spite of all her resistance. "We could avoid all this," he says, if she'd give him her phone number. And if he were a gentleman, he'd leave, she says. "Do I *look* like a gentleman?—in this shirt and these pants?—to *you*?" That stumps her. "So give me your phone number." No no. "What am I gonna do with it?" "*Call* it!" she nearly shouts. Okay then—he decides, as he puts it, "to take a rain check." And seems at last to have gone away. Until the WAC friend that Francine has been waiting for shows up with Jimmy's soldier buddy—who is on the point of scoring with the WAC, and who was going to fix Jimmy up with the now anathema-to-him Francine. Who walks out and leaves him.

It's love, of course. And it doesn't at all hurt him with her that he is so funny. Or even that he is such an operator—managing to live on the town while eluding all the bills, especially the hotel ones. His technique generally is more to overwhelm than to dupe, not so much taking people in as putting them on ("my mother and sister just over there")—less like a con artist than a deadpan comic, turning his victims into hapless straight men—or women.

Like the dignified young stiff in the morning coat behind the posh hotel's front desk, talking to Francine (she's looking for her girlfriend again) the next day. And they both see Jimmy at the same time, as he tries now limping off, as if crippled, to slip by them. No use. The desk clerk wants to know when he is going to pay his bill for all the hotel stuff he's been signing for—and not only at *this* hotel: "Would you mind telling me where you were before this?" the clerk asks. "Where was *I*!"—Jimmy can't believe it. "Would you mind telling me where *you* were! Because you know where *I* was? I was in *Anzio*!"—shouting the name for everyone in the lobby to hear—"I remember now!" Then displaying for the disbelieving clerk his lifeless right arm, the way it just flops down between them when he tries to hold it up: "I might have it amputated tomorrow and you tell me I signed those bills!" But that's his signature, isn't it?—and the clerk appeals to Francine (whom Jimmy has identified as his sister). Yes, she says promptly, yes, it is: "*That's* his signature." Jimmy lunges as if to throttle her but then tells her in her ear that her girlfriend and his buddy are upstairs in the room together and that she must go and warn them and above all retrieve his saxophone and his suitcase from under the bed so that he can go to his audition this afternoon. There's a short struggle, but she goes. In the meantime, he has hoisted his leg up onto the counter between him and the clerk: "You see—it's all wood, you can knock it anywhere"— doing so. "You can drive nails through it . . . It's the best kind of wood but still it's a wooden leg. You have a cushy job and I lost this leg so that you can accuse me of not paying bills in a hotel, I can't believe this!" Then, parenthetically: "Will you push it off please? Push it off. I can't even control it." Next—before Francine can come down to the street with his saxophone—he is doing a Groucho-style dash through the big public lobby pursued by the clerk, who puts his neck in an armlock and frog-marches him back to the desk. He breaks away and joins Francine and his sax outside in the cab.

She's a conventional nice girl, of course—but she is his match. ("Enough small talk," he says. "Can it *get* any smaller?" she says. And so on.) And when he gets to his audition at a Brooklyn night spot (she goes along, of course—under protest, as always), she takes him aside to give him some advice (you're glad someone does) about how he might get along better (it's already getting worse) with a prospective if cornball employer—and that's *not* by deploring the guy's taste in music, as Jimmy, a jazzman, has just done. He tells her to sit down and shut up. Then relents, sort of: "Sometimes I just put my foot in my mouth." "How about *my* foot in your mouth," she answers. And when the club boss calls him over and asks him to play something more like Maurice Chevalier, like "You Brought a New Kind of Love," say, Jimmy cannot believe how square this guy is. And just before he gets to tell him so again, Francine steps out—with a rhythmically staggered walk, to a jaunty finger-snapping beat—and starts to sing:

> If the nightingales could sing like you
> They'd sing much sweeter than they do,
> 'Cause you brought a new kind of love to me . . .

And he starts to play his tenor sax. He's still in his Hawaiian shirt, and she is in her dressy echt-forties outfit—high heels and padded shoulders, black suit and white gloves, with a clarion call of a hat that's like a riposte in itself to his wailing sax—as they turn their music into a witty and elating collaboration.

The boss is delighted—he'd wanted an act "with a girl." "Can you dance?" he calls out—and Jimmy does a couple of steps while playing. "Not *you*—you crazy?" She dances a little, next to the sax. The boss wants to see her legs. She almost starts to show him, things are going so well, but then she thinks again and starts to circle Jimmy as she dances, framing him with showy hand gestures and telegraphed looks. And they end up, as she starts to sing the chorus again, facing each other, bending to each other at opposite sides of the wide screen, singing and tootling and carried away with mutual delight, in the music and each other. It's beyond anything we ever saw from Alice Faye and Tyrone Power—or even from Garland and Kelly. It's closer in a way to Astaire and Rogers—making love to music. But it alludes richly to them all.

A mutual delight—with Liza Minnelli in Scorsese's *New York, New York*

The pattern of their comic byplay is familiar, too, from the great old comedies: he orders her around, she resists, cracks wise, and submits. It's *His Girl Friday* again—with Cary Grant's Walter Burns and Rosalind Russell's Hildy. Like the Grant hero, Jimmy is all but defined by being overbearing. And if, unlike Grant's Walter Burns, he sometimes shows a fonder side, that, too, tends to be overwhelming. As when—after a New York night of celebrating their new job together (a classic night-on-the-town montage: club names in lights, cocktail shakers in motion, over images of the two lovers dancing and drinking and nuzzling)—he can't, when they reach her modest hotel, quite let her get out of the taxicab, continuing to hold and kiss her while she is vainly trying to back her way out the open car door. We see her tight-skirted behind, which has escaped onto the street, wriggling in the rain (shades of Martha Raye), her feet in high heels sliding and dancing in and out of the curbside puddle, as the unseen (except for the Hawaiian shirt) Jimmy inside holds on and smooches her again and again—and again.

And once she extricates herself, saying "Call me at noon," he follows her into her hotel lobby, threatening at the desk to register there, too (another unpaid bill). Until she talks him out of that. But before he leaves he grabs her again, one hand holding his suitcase, the other holding her, bending her back over the hotel desk behind her while he gives her a deep and lingering soul kiss as she flails for balance with her free arm, knocking noisy objects to the floor, while the mild-mannered silver-haired desk clerk, his back filling the shot's right foreground, stands and looks impassively on at them (the small hotel is not an exclusive one). Jimmy departs, leaving her sort of upright at last—facing the clerk and looking bleary-eyed at him, still balancing herself against his desk on her elbow, as they look at each other. What is there to say? . . . Then: "That's a *great* suit," she says. "Why, *thank* you, Miss Evans," says the man, pleased and surprised. Until she remembers that Jimmy has got her suitcase and runs out in the rain again. Too late.

So she is making her own sort of progress beyond embarrassment—thanks to him. But not beyond a certain wistful relation to conventional sentiment. She makes it clear later on that she would rather not have been proposed marriage to by having him say "Get your shoes on and come on"—as he does. She's in her nightgown on a winter night in

Jimmy's good-night kiss

their motel room (they are on a band tour in the sticks—she's the singer, he's the tenor sax). "Uh, I don't know what we're doing now?" she says, plaintively almost, as he hustles her out the door to the car. What they're doing, as it turns out, is waking the justice of the peace in the middle of the night to get married. And when she complains tearfully about the style of all this, he gets on his knees to her in the snow, with the J.P. and his wife looking on from their porch, and tells her he loves her—proposing to her properly, even movingly. "Oh," she says, "I love you, too," sniffling—pausing to wipe her nose before bending down and kissing him. Then he flips her over into the snow and jumps on top of her, as she screams and—in a far-off overhead shot—laughs.

Soon she is pregnant—just as she is beginning to outshine him on the bandstand, where he's become the band's leader—and so she gives up the rigors of their tour for recording work in New York. On the road he has a covert affair with the new and awful girl singer, and finally loses the band. When Francine gets her first big-time recording contract, he is playing that Harlem club and snorting coke in the bathroom with the band. She is needy, he is withholding. They quarrel a lot. And by the time the baby arrives, the marriage is more or less wrecked. And in the scene that confirms that, De Niro is extraordinary.

She is sitting up in her hospital bed—postdelivery, puffy-faced and haggard-looking—when he comes in to the new-mothers' ward to see her, in his orange-brown suit, his bounce-and-strut walk, clearly nervous. She stares at him with her now-what's-next? look, as he sits uneasily by the head of her bed, one hand spread out on the bedside, the other planted and spread on his knee. "Did you see him?" she asks. "Who?" "The baby." "Oh, the baby. It's a him?" He looks around the room. "I named him Jimmy," she says tonelessly. He looks at her, then to the side at the nurse going out the door, then at the woman in the bed behind him—there are enemies everywhere now—adjusts his jacket with a shoulder roll, leans forward toward Francine, plants his hand on his knee again, bobbing his head: "You named him Jimmy?" he says—she shouldn't have done that, he says, without asking him. He's *trying* now to talk in a whisper, at her side, while she looks straight ahead, implacably. "And maybe I don't want to see the kid for that reason—" *That's* a new thought—and he's having trouble with it. He breaks off.

"He never stops fussing with props," Kazan observed about his star in his *Last Tycoon* journal—and it was one of the De Niro things, like the De Niro smile, that he wanted to minimize. But until I read that (in Kazan's autobiography, *A Life*), I had never noticed how much "fussing" De Niro actually does (the broken TV in *Raging Bull*, the candy counter selection at the porn theater in *Taxi Driver*, and so on)—his total effects seem so unfussy, so true (as Kazan also observed). And one of those effects that manages to be all that and brilliant as well happens here—in the middle of this speech, when Jimmy seems, in his discomfort with her and with himself, to have turned his own right hand into a prop: discovering it as he leans closer just below his chin, holding it up (what is this?), turning it distractedly around under his nose, then putting it down and away with his left hand, all done in one quick seamless motion, before looking back at her and going on—the mounting panic checked. "What do you think—you're gonna make me feel guilty about it? Give that name to that kid running around?—with all that's happened with us?—you had to give the kid the name Jimmy? No way." The improvisatory life of these speeches—of the dialogue in general—is remarkable ("that kid running around" couldn't have been improved on if it'd been scripted—or maybe it was). He whispers now: "I don't wanna see the kid 'cuz if I see the kid I'm gonna break up . . . What am I gonna say to him? Hi, I'm your father, I'm going away?" And then he does break up. "I'm sorry, I can't say anything." He rests his head on her breast, his arm across her waist. She holds his head, kisses his hair. "I'm sorry, too," she says softly. He starts to go and she calls him back. He comes back, they kiss—"Goodbye, baby!"—he tells her he loves her, and goes. And she's left sitting up in her bed, with roughly the same comically dazed what-hit-me? look she ended up with on V-J Day when he first came on to her—except that now she looks tearful and wasted.

Minnelli's tenderness with him is very touching. And she's sustained it throughout the movie, even through those moments when Francine is angriest and weariest—and it keeps the quarrel scenes (long and painful) from seeming merely squalid or dumb. And even here where the marriage ends, as it seems, you really feel that something importantly sad is happening. De Niro and Minnelli give you the clear sense—as great movie couples will do—that Jimmy and Francine make each other larger, richer, deeper, just by being together. And that's what they are giving up on now. Sensibly enough.

He is too difficult—and she is too loud. As the next scene—hers, a few years later, in a recording studio—prompts you to remember. It's the "Ol' Man River" interlude, about things just rolling along—only it's Kander and Ebb instead of Jerome Kern, and it's called "But the World

"I'm sorry, too," she says.

Goes Round," one of those anthems of impending breakdown the
team had been writing for Minnelli since her triumph with their *Caba-
ret*, given force and almost dignity this time by the desolation that hospital scene has just left us feeling. And Jimmy Jr., the little boy, now
preschool size, is sleeping behind her on a couch.

And they roll on. She quickly becomes a big movie star (too inevitable a development in these movies to be lingered over in this one).
And Jimmy, we learn (in a montage of photos and news clips), becomes
a jazz name, with his own club and sextet and reviewers' raves, his
recording of "New York, New York" a bestseller. It's not a success on
her level, of course, but at least (and you're relieved) it's not the gutter
(as it sometimes was for him in these movies). And so he goes one
night to see her new hit movie, called *Happy Endings*. We see it, too
(though we didn't in the film's first U.S. release, when it was cut)—an
imitation movie (within *this* imitation one) that's an extended production number (twelve minutes that feel more like twenty) with Kander

and Ebb songs again, the total effect more like Vegas than Vincente Minnelli (an object of the homage).

And the next scene is at a big blowout for her in that V-J Day penthouse space. And instead of "Tommy Dorsey" and his band on that sky-high platform, there is Francine, about to sing "New York, New York," the song she and Jimmy had once composed together (his music, her words). And so she does—in a style that's like a drum majorette on uppers, and to a Nuremberg Rally–size audience and their plaudits. The hysteria makes you squirm a little, but it works "in a way," as Jimmy will later say. And now you see that he is there, that now he is the one sitting alone at his table—and that he is, like us, reluctantly impressed. He even smiles (he didn't after seeing her movie by himself—he just left).

They meet at the party afterward. Uneasy but pleased, even fond. She wouldn't mind being reassured about what she just did with their song. "It works well," he says, and she is glad. But he can't stop: "It's another way of doing it," he adds, "but it works well." Then: "I saw *Sappy Endings* the other night." *Happy Endings*, she corrects him, half-smiling. "Yeah, *Happy Endings*," he repeats, his eyes going up and around, his face turning aside. "You liked it?" she persists teasingly. "Yeah, I loved it." But seriously, he says, he's very proud of her—"in a way." They talk a bit about their kid, how talented he is and so on. But it never stops being awkward. "Well, I guess I better go," he says, and starts, and stops, and looks at her with a smile, with narrowed glinting eyes, and a you-really-are-something expression, looks away, then looks at her again—like: I-look-at-you-again-and-you're-*still*-something. No wonder she thinks again. No wonder he does. "How do I get outa here?" he says next—but he phones her from the corner. Does she want to blow that party and meet him? Sure she does, she says. But she doesn't. Neither does he. At the elevator she presses the down button, but then goes up instead. At the phone booth, he lingers for a bit, then walks away—into the night and the end title.

Of course. Why go through it all again? This downer of an ending didn't help the movie's box office (if anything could), but it suited the sort of honesty Scorsese and his improvising actors were committed to. And it suits De Niro's Jimmy, who is too fundamentally disabused a presence for the harmless agreed-upon lie of the earlier films, the happy reconciliation at the fadeout.

New York, New York, among his films with Scorsese, is in a way the most undiluted De Niro experience of them all. He is the one who centers the movie—whose presence and character give almost everything else in it, even Francine and her story, its feeling of real consequence. De Niro's Jimmy is less the subject of his movie—as Travis and Rupert and Jake are of theirs—than he is its controlling sensibility.

III.

DE NIRO HAS the same centrality, even more so, in another and even more magical movie, Sergio Leone's last and greatest film, *Once Upon a Time in America* (1984)—another riff on classic Hollywood, on the movies of the thirties and forties that the director grew up with in Mussolini's Italy and never got over. Leone (who died in 1989) made his first great success, of course, by reinventing the western in the 1960s, in his *Dollars* trilogy with Clint Eastwood. *America* is some version of the old gangster movie, at least on the surface—closer to a film noir below that. And it's as monumental, as Wagnerian even, as Scorsese's retro musical is playful and light. True, there are more jokes than in Wagner—but like his, they tend to be a little heavy, a little brutal, derived as they are from the unappetizing activities of a gang of bullies, both as kids (rolling drunks, intimidating storekeepers, setting fire to a newsstand) and as grown-ups, four thugs and killers for hire, bonded from boyhood. De Niro's character, Noodles, is the sort of sensitive one—the one with romantic longings. But he is also the one who rapes the heroine, Elizabeth McGovern's Deborah—and twice (in the European version), in the same backseat of a limo and on the same morning.

Not that there *is* a heroine, exactly. Deborah is the woman who both embodies and defeats Noodles's dream of romance—the movie's female lead, and she's convincingly unforgettable. But its central love story is between two straight men, between Noodles and the gang's top honcho, Max—brilliantly played by James Woods over a chronology that extends from Prohibition in the twenties to New York in the late sixties. An *epic* movie, and epic, Leone said, is a masculine genre. It was a project he had been gestating for some fifteen years, and preparing with teams of writers for six. The shoot itself took two full years. And though the action is mostly confined to New York, the filming took place, it seemed, almost everywhere else as well: Venice, Hoboken, Paris, Rome, and so on. Everywhere except Hollywood, where the money, or a crucial part of it, came from. Without De Niro's participation, it probably never could have been made, at least on the scale that it was. Leone's last two pictures, the epiphanic *Once Upon a Time in the West* (1968) and the misbegotten (even to its English title) *Duck, You Sucker* (1971), had both flopped in the United States.

Here the gangsters, as in the original pulp novel Leone was adapting, *The Hoods* by Harry Gray, are meant to be Jewish instead of the usual Italians; but not a lot of effort is given to convincing us of this (not even by casting Jewish actors). Anyway—once upon a time etcetera—it's all sort of a fairy tale. But much less of one, as Leone conceded, than it would have been without De Niro—along with the sort of New York actors the star could feel comfortable with (Woods, Weld, Danny Aiello, Joe Pesci, Treat Williams—McGovern, from Evanston, Illinois, was the exception). Leone had always favored the kind of poker-faced iconic star that Eastwood was in these films (as the director had made of him), or that Charles Bronson was in *Once Upon a Time in the West*, his "frozen archetypes," as Umberto Eco called them. He directed them much in the way that Sternberg had directed Dietrich, it seems—just the way, according to McGovern, that Leone directed *her*: look here, look there, turn your head now, and so on. This time, he felt, as he told Woods (who reported it to Leone's exemplary English biographer, Christopher Frayling), less like a *metteur en scène* than a documentarian, filming these actors, real actors, at work. Especially De Niro.

But the powers in Hollywood would soon remind themselves that De Niro hadn't had a profitable movie for almost a decade, not since *The Deer Hunter* in 1978. And this one, when it was finally turned over to them, was nearly four hours long. Though it was released at that length in England and Europe, the American backers (the Ladd Company and Warner Bros.) insisted on cutting it (even *The Deer Hunter* had been an hour shorter). But how? Since the four hours they'd got were already fairly murky, given Leone's deliberately scram-

The epic scale and style of Leone's Proustian gangster film (Noodles
and his boyhood gang after a successful heist)

bled chronology, in which he mixes three widely separated years (1923,
1933, and 1968) and the events within them, how could they cut it and
still have it make any sense at all?

The solution, of course, was to begin at the start of things and simply straighten it all out, cutting an hour and a half (even shorter than
The Deer Hunter!). This made what was left intelligible (sort of) but
finally pointless, except as a sort of badly out-of-date genre piece, a
feebler, less authentic *Godfather*—as the universally hostile American
reviews noted. Leone wanted his name taken off it: "It was never my
intention," he said, "to make a gangster film." (Had he told them that
before? you wonder.) "But the American version looks like one now
because they have left only the squalid episodes, one after the other."
It became his third-in-a-row American flop. But after the initial release, the full version got shown that same year at the New York Film
Festival, and that's the version we see now, of course—thankfully.

So it begins—with a dim, distant, barely audible playing of Kate
Smith's "God Bless America" recording over the opening titles (white
letters on black). Then a succession of unexplained, seemingly disconnected scenes: a beautiful young woman is blown away by gunsels in
her bedroom; a bartender in his saloon is beaten and tortured. Then
De Niro is shown in what seems to be an opium den. As he puts the
pipe to his mouth, a phone starts ringing. And ringing and ringing,

over a nighttime crime scene with flashbulbs popping around some covered bodies in the rain. Then we're in the middle of a speakeasy jamboree, celebrating the end of Prohibition, with charged-up-looking people exchanging significant looks across the room and over the heads of the revelers. And the incessant phone, still ringing on the soundtrack, finally stops, as a cop in a police station somewhere picks it up to answer, waking (it seems) De Niro in the opium den, just in time, as it turns out, for him to escape the young woman's killers, who have tracked him there.

The woman is his mistress, Eve (a radiant Darlanne Fleugel); the bartender is his friend Fat Moe (an almost equally radiant nonactor named Larry Rapp). You find all this out fairly soon, but it takes nearly three hours to learn about that phone call, who made it, and why it was important. But the deliberate disorientation, apart from being a fairly usual film noir procedure, gets you to focus on the question of where you are in time at almost any given moment. Just so—as Leone later said, his movie, his magnum opus, is all about time, and about memory and "about cinema itself." "That's why you can't see it in chronological order," he also said.

The cinema itself—yes. Because you feel the power of old movies, of movieness itself, in every foot of this film, from its very first images onward—of Leone's childhood movies and your own. That time when movie houses were not only like palaces (not by accident) and movie screens like towers of light, but when even the spaces outside were bigger. Like the ones in Leone's film: an opium den like a cathedral, a run-down East Side saloon with so many large connecting rooms that it could pass for a decaying mansion, with a storeroom in back (where the young Deborah dances) the size and shape of a department store atrium, illuminated from on high by an equivalently scaled skylight. Even on a TV screen, Leone's imagery looks grandiloquent.

Though not the bus station Noodles uses to get out of town and away from those killers. That space is fairly modest, though no less rich in detail. Like the station's improbable but striking wall-size collage of Coney Island posters (Reginald Marsh style) with a magical-looking mirror in the center. Noodles doesn't look in that mirror just yet (it's 1933), not until the next scene (1968), when he returns to the same station (from his exile in Buffalo—"the asshole of the world," as he later calls it) thirty-five years after. A sequence that begins with a close-up of his face in the same mirror, an old man now, dressed warmly and adjusting his red wool scarf inside his overcoat, gazing at himself in the glass, not so much at his reflection as into and past it, before turning to go. Back to the old neighborhood.

Ennio Morricone's remarkable music score was so important to Leone that its completion preceded even the screenplay's by some six years, so essential did it become to the director's imagination of his movie. And later on he had it played on his sets (as in silent movie days) nearly every day before and sometimes even during the shoot, virtually choreographing his movie to it, so that it became integral to the actors' experience of the film, too, and the cameraman's and crew's as well.

It's meditative music, mostly, and it's only during the violence (and the brutish sex) that it's quiet altogether. "It should come," as Leone said, "from a long way away." The main recurring theme is a sound of stately, settled melancholy: a slow, descending five-note phrase in the strings, a couple of beats, then repeated in a key change that makes it feel more urgent, then extended and elaborated—embellished by a piano roulade, or sometimes by a wordless soprano vocalise—in a way that makes it sound almost ecstatic over its own soaring beauty, though no less sad, no less bereft, until it resolves itself and dies out.

It accompanies, for example, the elder Noodles's homecoming to the neighborhood—the nighttime part—which begins with a close shot of Fat Moe's red neon window sign and Moe himself inside the bar turning it off. The camera then tracks slowly and lengthily alongside the saloon's windows as it follows Moe's movements within, right and then left and then right again: his answering the phone at the end of the bar, then going to the door to see out the night's last customers, then returning to the phone as the last one exits onto the street. Then the camera rises on the music, pulling slowly back and lifting up and up, above the saloon and over the street, finally descending in place until a glassed-in phone booth with De Niro inside talking (soundlessly again) fills the right foreground of the big screen. Noodles talking to Moe—gravely, intently—reclaiming the past. And that music swelling on the soundtrack, you realize, is the sound of memory—of nostalgia and loss.

And this is where De Niro becomes crucial: his gravity and inwardness, his concentration even. And that all the rising and lifting and
floating of both camerawork and music here should finally come to rest
(it's a single take, like a phrase of music) on *his* gravity, on the concern
in his intent face—that his presence should bring the dazzling camera
flight to ground—is something both moving and pointed. Because it's
De Niro whose personal authority finally grounds the whole movie—a
film that often threatens, in all its empyrean, quasireligious yearnings,
to take off altogether—well over the line between enchantment and
inflation. That line is part of what makes it so exciting; it's De Niro
who makes it feel powerful and true.

He comes to Moe's back door (through the movie, Noodles favors
back or side entrances). "Noodles!" Moe exclaims softly, and moves to
embrace him. But Noodles, in his fedora and overcoat (nattier than the
one he left in thirty-five years ago), his suitcase in one hand, doesn't
respond. "Lock the doors," he says—and then: "I brought back the key
to your clock." Moe takes it—this sweet-faced man never gets the other's
full attention, it seems, but is still the picture of goony happiness here,
standing in the background of his old friend's return. He crosses the
room and winds the grandfather clock with the key. With Noodles back
again, time can start again—after all these years. But why has he come
back? "They" sent for him, Noodles replies—the same mysterious "they"
whose hired thugs he'd once fled from, it appears. So here he is again—
out of curiosity mostly, he says. About all the unanswered questions.

And he moves about this time-saturated place with his now slow,
measured, slightly myopic walk, leading with his face (like Lear's
Gloucester—"let him smell his way to Dover"), his arms limp at the
sides, instead of the weightlifter's angle they'd swung at when he was
young. He looks at the old photographs of himself and his friends—
Moe's walls are covered with them (the first time we see McGovern's
Deborah, "a famous actress now," is in a photograph). Moe shows him
to his room and stands in the doorway as Noodles goes to the coat
hooks on the nearby wall, removing his hat (he is half bald) and hanging it, then lowering his head, unbuttoning his coat and hanging that,
his hands resting on it for a moment—like a priest at the altar. He has
that ecclesiastical look that old men sometimes have, going through
their lifetime motions, bowing to the inevitability of things, like coat

hooks in the right place. "G'night, Moe—thanks," he says, removing his scarf and hanging it. Moe can't resist: "What you been doing all these years?" he says, from the doorway in the background. Noodles's hands rest on the coat hooks, he looks at the wall, turns his head but not his face toward Moe, then looks forward again. "Been going to bed early," he says, lowering his eyes—as if thinking that over. Something to think about. His life is gone . . . That can happen.

Noodles is probably the most thoughtful ex-hood the movies have ever given us. Thinking both before and after he speaks. Which suits Leone's characteristic tempo, dragged out and pause-laden, his slow hieratic pacing of both dialogue and movement (often "choreo-graphed" to that elegiac music). Both the music and the tempo mark Noodles's next move—as he wanders back through the barroom, coming to a luminous white door in the wall. He opens it and goes through it and down a darkened passage to a backstairs john. He puts the toilet seat down and climbs on top of it. He removes a piece of wood from the wall that had blocked a horizontal opening. Light from the opening floods the outline of his face (a left profile close-up), drawing him slowly forward into it, as the camera with equal slowness moves into him, his eyes fixed on the sight beyond. Like some visionary—or like a movie projectionist in his booth, peering through the viewing aperture.

Then a reverse shot—looking into his eyes from the other side of the aperture, which frames them, tracking slowly toward them—as the familiar main theme (with a choral vocalise added) fades slowly into its resolving chord, softly, almost inaudibly. As if out of deference to what we're seeing more and more closely now—the elderly man's red-rimmed eyes, the pain, and the gathering tears. ("The eyes are everything," Morricone said to an interviewer, talking about the inspiration of his music here.)

Another musical theme now: the tinny sound of an old phonograph playing a languid, insinuating rendition of "Amapola," performed on horns and banjo. And then we, too, see the vision—it's not an anticlimax. A beautiful child-woman in long shot, in toe shoes and a Giselle-length white skirt, practicing her ballet steps to the record. In the center of a sepia-tinged light-filled storeroom with a vast skylight above her, stacks of burlap bags all around her, she seems to be floating just above a framing haze of dust and flour—yet looking sardonically from time to time through the curve of her careful port de bras in the direction of Noodles's spying post (the same direction as ours). This is the Young Deborah, of course (the amazing—even then—Jennifer Connolly), and the Young Noodles (Scott Tiler). It's the beginning of the movie's boyhood chapter (1923), close to an hour of straight chronological narrative. The time when Noodles and his buddies first encounter Young Max (Rusty Jacobs), who soon becomes their leader—being the wittiest and most daring one of them all. Noodles is his number one man—and is also, as it turns out, the one who takes the rap for the whole gang when they are all arrested for a killing. He goes to prison for ten years. They watch him walk into prison, the gates closing behind him. And they are there, now grown-up men, when he gets out (as Robert De Niro).

This early romance-of-boyhood episode—though including plenty of violence and squalor—is like the movie's pastoral, a remembered innocence *within* the violence and squalor. Above all, a remembered loyalty—the intense bond between the two leaders, Max and Noodles, and the just as intense one between their followers (like Fat Moe) and them, forged in craziness and danger and lawbreaking—especially lawbreaking—all of it a communal, even ecstatic thing. There is a trope for this in the movie's recurring events around deep water ("Let's go swimming," says Noodles) and their plunging into it together, first as boys (from a boat) and then as men (from a semisubmerged car), risking separation and drowning (as Young Max, staying under the longest, pretends to do—convincingly), and then coming up laughing, still together. We never see their families—the adult figures who were cut out or never filmed at all. But families could never be *this* much fun—as this made-up family, on its own and on the loose.

Young Max—like the adult one—keeps an eye on Deborah. "That ball-buster," as he calls her. But only from concern for her effect on his buddy. It's true she's a tease—she even lets Noodles see her undress through his peephole. And she *is* a ball-buster—calling him "roach" for crawling up walls to spy on her, and accusing him of never bathing. But she's also irresistible—sexy and flirtatious and glamorous, from another world of beauty that's partly his only through her. And in her way she's even encouraging—holding him off but coming on to him at the same time. And in a scene in the storeroom where she reads to him from the Song of Solomon ("My love is white and ruddy . . . His eyes are as the eyes of doves"), interpolating her own deflating remarks about his hygiene and dirty clothes. "He is altogether lovable," she concludes, "but he'll always be a two-bit punk. So he'll never be my beloved. What a shame," she adds, seeming to mean it. But he is so besotted with looking into her eyes that he almost doesn't seem to register the discouragement in this. And they kiss, very tenderly. Until Max calls him from outside. "Go on, *run*," she says bitterly "—your mother's calling you."

She repeats the same challenge, though more resignedly, when they first see each other again as grown-ups (as her brother Fat Moe has the band play "Amapola") at the big party celebrating Noodles's getting out of prison. How many years was it—how many days? She lost count. "That wasn't my choice," he says. Yes it was, she replies. Anyway, she's dancing in a Broadway show now and has to go to it. It's a painful and conflicted meeting, leaving him free once again to go to Max (who's been watching them this time, too). The trap of boyhood. That romance, at any rate, is simpler than the one with her. With Max at least he knows where he is. (He turns out to be wrong about that.)

Leone thought that Jews knew more about guilt than Italians did; and if other markers of Jewishness are missing here, that one is pervasive. Not only in Noodles—though it never turns into remorse—but even in Max, by the end. When Leone first signed De Niro he offered him a choice of either Max or Noodles—almost like a choice between *Mean Streets*'s Johnny Boy and Charlie, either the wild man or the observer. That De Niro made the choice he did (if he'd played Max, it would have been a very different movie) shows how far he'd traveled by this time from the manic inspiration of those earlier roles.

Noodles is the contemplative role, the consciousness through whom the whole movie is refracted (there's barely a moment he isn't in). It's Max who feels like a star, even as a boy (the young actor who plays him is nearly as compelling a presence as Young Deborah). "You can tell the winners at the starting gate," the elderly Noodles says to Moe, about Deborah's later success in the theater. But Max (James Woods is brilliant) is not the star of the movie. Which is really about the star's shadow—who is also his patsy (as we later learn). In a way, Noodles's chief distinction is that both of the stars-in-life, Max and Deborah, love him—for a while. He is the big might-have-been they both finally give up on, the he-had-such-promise case. "I'd 'a bet everything I had on you," the elderly Moe says to him, in his moony, doting way. "You'd 'a lost," says Noodles. One thing that accounts for all the keening music we've been hearing: this epic is about a loser.

But he and the gang got very rich in 1933. So rich that Noodles decides, Gatsby-like, to give Deborah the kind of after-theater night that's like the ultimate romantic dream (before this we'd just seen one of the "squalid episodes," as Leone called them, Tuesday Weld's nympho turning pro at their whorehouse)—taking her to Long Island (it was really Venice, and its Excelsior hotel), to a glittering ballroom with orchestra and waitstaff for just the two of them, to dine and dance (to "Amapola"), to lie on the beach under the stars, where he tells her how he dreamed of her in prison, how he read the Song of Solomon every night. And she tells him—not quite able to look at him—that she's leaving for Hollywood tomorrow, on the early train: "I wanted to see you tonight to tell you." Oh . . . Then it's daylight and they are back in the limo, both of them silent and grim and motionless. Until she reaches up and kisses him consolingly on the cheek. So—he rapes her, violently, and at some length: Leone makes the scene as ugly and punishing to watch as possible (it turned people against the movie at Cannes)—leaving her, by its end, in torn clothes and undergarments, hysterical and sobbing, him abject and pleading with her as the chauffeur (suddenly fearless) stops the car and pulls him out, leaving him stranded on a desolate oceanside road, at land's end.

Next morning: the old Penn Station, presumably (really the Gare de Nord in Paris), Deborah at a gateside newsstand buying a paper and proceeding to her train. It's almost touching to see how pulled-together she looks now (after the way we last saw her), even elegant—as the camera and the music, discreet but mournful, rise to show the train on its track and the arches of the glass shed above, as she walks among crowds on the platform to her car. Then at her compartment window, pulling the shade half down, opening the newspaper. Another trackside shot from the gate, redcaps and people coming through clouds of steam, and a conductor calls all aboard.

And then Noodles walking from out of the steam into a medium close-up. Not to say goodbye, obviously, but to watch her train go— hatless, his hair, as always, parted in the center (a fashionable men's style then) but mussed, his white shirt open and rumpled, his face unshaven and haggard, his hands plunged into the pockets of his shapeless black overcoat. He enters the screen at left, stops, and leans slightly but perceptibly to the right, looking down the track of the departing train.

It's De Niro's Garbo moment—this shot. Partly because of that lean. It's one of those movie star close-ups that imprint themselves on your brain, that live there even beyond the movie itself. Like Garbo's at the end of *Queen Christina*, it's not the face you exactly expect to see at such a classically climactic moment. It's stricken, as you do expect, even harrowed, but it's also ambiguous, not easily readable. What's moving—even startling—is how innocently quizzical it seems, alert, even inquiring. Like someone who has seen something he can't quite explain and so has to look again. Noodles has become the onlooker at his own wreckage—just as perplexed by it as any stranger might be. (It's always hard to believe it at first—when hopelessness really lands.)

Elizabeth McGovern, as the grown-up Deborah in *Once Upon a Time in America*, leaving on a train

In her window shot again now, Deborah—her face like a mask—looks up and out, toward us, and with a slow, lovely finality, as the train whistles and starts to chug along, she pulls her shade all the way down. In his next close shot, De Niro is settling into grimness, straightening up, lifting his jaw, frowning again—looking more like a western hero now, surveying the carnage after the battle, unable to move just yet but thinking about riding away in a minute, then turning to walk off, back through the steam. The tears he sheds will come later (not for us, though—because of the film's scrambled chronology we've already seen them).

He's lost the Deborah dream but not the pastoral one: his loyalty to Max and the gang remains intact. Even to his doing something covert—at the urging of Carol, who has become Max's masochist mistress—enacting a plan meant to ensure Max's safety but that leads instead to his death in a shoot-out (those covered bodies in the rain). Or so the elderly Noodles remembers and believes.

But none of this—as we learn—turns out to be exactly true. Max, the master planner of his own apparent if unintended death, is alive, although now turned (with dreamlike improbability) into someone else altogether: State Secretary Bailey, a wealthy and important public figure. Who is living with Deborah, now a famous stage actress. The two winners. (Carol is in an elder home.) With a son of Max's named David, named after Noodles (whose real name is David Aronson), and played by the kid who had been Young Max. And it's Max, or rather Secretary Bailey, who has summoned Noodles back to New York City. Knowing that he's about to be done in by the Mob—or the government, or both, it's unclear—he now wants to offer Noodles the contract instead, as a reparation of sorts for all the betrayals of him he's committed in the past. I took your money, your girl, your life, he says. Accurately.

It's all pretty implausible (the disastrous shortened version of the film in the U.S. just eliminated a lot of it, like everything to do with the connection of "Bailey" to Deborah and their replicant Young Max son). But you believe it, in just the way that this movie about time and memory and cinema asks you to believe it. Because that's what you're told here at the end—that such betrayal was really what Max was up to back then, and so forth. But that story is not what you've seen and actually gone through in the movie before this—what you've seen is

Noodles watching the departing train

what Noodles remembers. So that for him and for us, memory trumps reality, just as movies do. (It's no use later revisiting that enormous room you knew as a kid and seeing that it's tiny—it's the big room that you have now, and had then.) Noodles refuses the contract, just as he does the offer of reparation. For him the story will always be a different one, as he tells "Secretary Bailey" now. Sorry, somebody else will have to kill him. Noodles's revenge—whether he means it or not—is not only in returning Bailey's loaded pistol but even more so in refusing his scenario of the past. His triumph over his ultimate betrayer—whatever shred of that there may be—is his inaccessibility, his privacy even—maybe even those recent early bedtimes.

More time tricks now: the old man goes down the long walkway from the Bailey mansion; some soprano at the party inside is singing "Summertime"—as if "from a long way away," says the screenplay. He sees a couple of strange things and hears them, too ("God Bless America" again), before he's back in 1933, at the end of Prohibition, in the opium den again, taking a humongous pull on that pipe—and it's not working! Wait—there it is . . . And he relaxes, on his back now, in extreme close-up, sensuously, luxuriantly, his face breaking into that startling implosive grin of his, at least as unnerving now as it was in *Taxi Driver* almost ten years ago. But this time it's not, as it was then, for some other figure on the screen—but for us. Even more unnerving—and still ambiguous. But a moment of happiness here, surely—the film's concluding image, frozen on the screen. Why not? But the final wrench in this infinitely sad movie is that even this moment was a drug-induced delusion. Noodles, like America itself (the larger meaning that Leone clearly intends), has chosen the pastoral—for whatever good or ill it does him.

Noodles's final close-up

IV.

DE NIRO ALL but holds this massive movie together not only by his acting but by his presence and intensity—almost as if he were holding it all in his head (which Noodles himself may be doing, in one of the film's many possible readings). His achievement should have been a widely acknowledged triumph—instead it was hardly noticed at the time. It was certainly jinxed by the butchery done to the American version (Pauline Kael: "I don't believe I've ever seen a worse case of mutilation")—which was the one that most people saw then. But it couldn't have helped that he himself seemed to dismiss it, refusing to do any promotion for it, either here or in Europe, after the scandal and animus it provoked (in its original version) at Cannes.

But it was (up to now, at least) his last great performance. He would go on to make more and more movies—two or three a year and still going—most of them junk. And in even those that weren't (like Michael Mann's *Heat* or Scorsese's *Casino*), the ones that were more ambitious, he would often seem almost creepily blank and expressionless. A star who was known for his power, for his banked rage, for his danger, now seemed almost to disappear on the screen in front of us without actually going away. What had registered in the Leone film as a kind of contemplative strength now looked and felt like withdrawal. But in *Jackie Brown*—thirteen years and twenty-eight films later—he at least gets to *act* that withdrawal, entertainingly and even wittily.

8

Altman's Nashville

I.

NASHVILLE IS A great American movie. It seemed like that when it first came out in 1975 (some compared its impact then to *Citizen Kane's*) and feels the same for many of us even now, more than thirty-five years later. Our national life has changed a lot since then, God knows, but Robert Altman's masterpiece goes on seeming revelatory. As do Ronee Blakley and Lily Tomlin, who play two of its many characters. They are the two that I mostly want to talk about here. They are extraordinary. And it doesn't at all hurt, of course, that their film (the first for both) is, too.

Altman called it "a metaphor for America." But the large public meaning that claim implies depends, as it turns out, on the small ones the movie accumulates, stunningly, even thrillingly, as it travels through its congeries of people and songs and interlocking dramatic vignettes. Where Sergio Leone seems to ponder his characters, Altman immerses you in them, and in the excitement and commotion they inhabit. He warns you with his opening credits—a jumble of credits and twanging country music "hits" along with a blaring-voiced announcer's pitch for us all to be sure and buy "the record" of the movie even before we've seen it, while the images and names of its "twenty-four stars" (like Blakley, mostly unknowns at the time) unroll on the screen before us. It's already sort of fun—or the promise of it. And it will be fun as it goes on in just the ways that climates of general disorder can be—as Preston Sturges once knew, and knew about American life in particular. *Nashville* is one of the last great films in the Sturges tradition of seeing America as full of eccentric aliveness on all sides.

Though without Sturges's verbal brilliance, of course. *Nashville* was nearly as much improvised by its performers as Sturges's movies were written ahead of time for his. For a start, anyway, there was a screenplay (credited) by Joan Tewkesbury, but it would finally serve mostly as a game plan for the actors (in collaboration with Altman) to base their own roles on, even to write their own songs. They needed a blueprint, appearing as they do in the final film in multiple overlapping story lines, taking place over five days of a Grand Ole Opry music festival.

We are all involved in politics whether we know it or like it or not, says a countrified male voice coming from the bullhorns on a truck that is just pulling out of a garage and going slowly down a deserted city block on the morning of the movie's first day (Friday). It's the voice of Hal Phillip Walker (the one important character we never see), whose offbeat campaign for president (he's against tax-free churches, lawyers in Congress, the current national anthem, and so on) will go on at the same time and often in the same places as the festival does.

Cut to a deeply shadowed recording studio, where an angry-looking little man is singing into a mike about America—to a martial drumbeat. About Paul Revere and Bunker Hill, about his daddy who "lost his leg in France," his brother who'd "fought with Patton," and himself "who saw action in Algiers"—launching into the song's defiant refrain: "We must be doin' something right / To last two hundred years!"—the mean little eyes (*Wanna fight about it?*) glinting and shifting in the dimness as the backup quartet huddled in the brightly lit glass booth behind him echo his words in a reassuring croon.

This is the beloved country star Haven Hamilton (Henry Gibson), as we soon learn. But here, in embroidered ranchhouse shirt and white neckerchief, wearing enormous earphones on top of a ratty toupee, he looks like a cowboy poltergeist. Not wanting his sons to go to war, as he sings now, but "if they must they must," and "in God I place my trust," and so on.

Cut to an adjoining studio, where a youthful black choir wearing black robes and white surplices is in full exultant cry recording a spiritual ("I Believe in Jesus"), with a single white, Lily Tomlin, among them, as they whoop it up all together, robes flapping, hands in air clapping to the beat, to the making of a joyful noise. Cut back to Haven Hamilton—and the sound of self-pity, thrumming, lugubrious, unstoppable: "I've lived through two depressions," he sings, "And seven dust bowl droughts / Floods, locusts, and tornadoes / But I don't have any doubts" (you knew he wouldn't). Then once again, "We must be doin' something right," before he breaks off to scold one of the band for a mistake. And for his long hair, too ("This isn't Woodstock").

Intercuttings like this are an essential part of the way the movie works. And you learn to resist "reading" them too quickly. They come too thick and fast, for one thing. And it's not so much that the juxtapositions make any particular point, you come to feel, as that they almost do—and then don't (as here, say, about religion and patriotism). That hovering possibility is a pattern characterizing the whole movie—evoking a stereotype or a platitudinous meaning and then resisting it.

There is one character among the "twenty-four" who never does resist such meanings—Geraldine Chaplin's Opal, the supposed reporter from the BBC, who goes about eagerly missing the point of everything in favor of the clichés she shares with her tape machine—like her comments here about the gospel choir and their rhythm "come down in their genes" from "darkest Africa." Fair warning—if you need one.

The next sequence is the commotion at the Nashville airport. The country megastar Barbara Jean is arriving in her private plane. But so, it seems, is everyone else involved with the festival, music acts and their hangers-on, their promoters and fans. It's here that we get introduced to at least half of the "stars"—mostly in passing. Like the spooky guy on the *Easy Rider* cycle (Jeff Goldblum), who reappears throughout the movie without uttering a sound, and who now does magic tricks with the table salt for the pretty waitress at the airport luncheonette, Sueleen (Gwen Welles), while Wade (Robert Doqui), her black cook protector, looks on suspiciously; Mr. Green (Keenan Wynn), the elderly gent meeting his niece from L.A. (Shelley Duvall) without being quite prepared for her bizarre new persona (she now calls herself L.A. Joan) or her assortment of wigs and hot pants; Del (Ned Beatty), the local legal hotshot assigned to meet and greet Hal Phillip Walker's campaign director, John Triplette (Michael Murphy); the shy soldier who is a Barbara Jean fan (Scott Glenn) standing next to the hip leather-vested folk-rocker (Keith Carradine). "How yuh doin', Sarge?" says the latter, "yuh kill anybody this week?" while the "Sarge"—a private in fact—ignores him. They are pressed together in the midst of a crowd at the big airport windows, looking out (airport security in charge) onto the celebration on the field.

"We are waiting here," says the TV announcer, "for the arrival of Barbara Jean—who as you know has been away for special treatment at the Baltimore Burn Center"—*we* didn't know that, of course, and almost before we can take it in (*burn* center? *special* treatment?), the commotion on the field begins: the high school band playing, the drum majorettes parading, the Tennessee Twirlers (as they're called) twirling, the little girls in formation drilling with fake rifles, and Barbara Jean's plane now taxiing down the runway. There is Haven again, being driven across the field in a jeep on his way to take charge of things as the high school band launches into the national anthem. With him—we've seen her before at his recording session—are his manager and mistress (his wife is in Paris), the serenely alcoholic Lady Pearl (Barbara Baxley), and his golden-boy son Buddy (David Peel), who has just graduated from Harvard Law. "Did you ever see such pretty little girls in your life?" asks Haven now at the mike. Lady Pearl avows that she never has. And shy Buddy (still single, his father points out) stands up to say hello. But she is coming now, says the TV man—"*our* Barbara Jean!"

Her plane has stopped and Barbara Jean (Ronee Blakley) is appearing at its door and waving. But like the crowd inside the terminal we are still at a distance from her—even as she comes down the stairs in her trademark chaste long white gown and crosses the field with her entourage trailing her, the TV announcer narrating their progress. She arrives at the speakers' stand, stepping into the medium close shot that she now shares with a chuckling and fawning Haven.

She seems both ardently present and not quite there, bright-eyed and dazzled, darkly pretty, with her head thrown back and her mouth half open, raven-black hair drawn into an inverted widow's peak above her broad high forehead. "It's hot as a firecracker," she says—at which Haven alone laughs and applauds ("What's so funny about that?" says a low offscreen voice—her husband's, as it turns out). But everybody loves Barbara Jean. They can forgive her for being a little embarrassing.

Barbara Jean (Ronee Blakley) greets her fans, with Haven Hamilton (Henry Gibson) beside her and Lady Pearl (Barbara Baxley in dark glasses) below.

Just as her husband has to do—the surly Barnett (Allen Garfield), president of Barnett Enterprises (all hers, of course) and always at her side.

But her frailty makes you uneasy. And so does her big toothy grin—the way she thrusts it up into the air for us while the deep-set eyes above it go suddenly hooded, almost closing. And the way it can vanish, too. As now—she is frowning darkly in the direction of the glass windows of the terminal: "Barnett, who are those people?" she says in her tiniest voice—"did they come to see me?" Yes? Well then she wants to go see *them*.

And so she takes off, like a ship setting sail, skirts billowing, down the broad walkway, the band launching into one of her familiar tunes,

the entourage hastily following and regrouping around her, her long
sleeves swelling and fluttering, the young woman always at her elbow
scurrying and bending to lift up the trailing gown as the star goes on
her way serenely forward. And collapses on the tarmac—with people
crying out and surrounding her. And so it's back to the hospital . . .

Now there is a massive traffic pileup on the road outside the
airport—and more characters, more scenes of the ones we've already
met. Then a commotion at the hospital, with Barbara Jean holding
court from her bed at its center, and Barnett trying to control the disarray around her. And that night, a jamboree at Deemen's Den, Lady
Pearl's self-styled "Old Time Picking Parlor"—and a phone call to
there by Del the lawyer (Ned Beatty). Who is at home conferring with
Tripette, the Hal Phillip Walker flack. And whose wife, Linnea (Lily
Tomlin), is in the dining room—having just set the table for their eve-
ning's guest, standing beside it now and under the low-hanging chandelier, with a wineglass in her hand, absently wiping it with a cloth, as
she watches and listens to their twelve-year-old son, Jimmy (James
Dan Calvert)—who is deaf—as he tells her about the day's swimming
class. His younger sister, standing next to her mother, is also part of
the audience. Where Del, the father, now also in the room among
them, seems comparatively excluded. Not just by a lesser interest but
by a certain incomprehension.

Now the numinous thing happens—as it will more than once in
this movie, when in the midst of its enlivening and seeming random-
ness you are suddenly prompted to register something quite different:
here it's Tomlin's gleaming-eyed fixity of attention, her wholeness of
response, and the boy's answering absorption in it as he relates, signing with his hands and with steady excitement, how he swam the
length of the pool underwater today, and how the coach in response
had named him—a pause—"Goldfish!" And he says the word fully
and aloud—and the smile that comes with it is purely beautiful.

Tomlin, of course, has her own great smile—horsey and long-
toothed (think of *Laugh-In*'s Ernestine). And her eyes can smile even
when her mouth does not—the sort of thing that can make the attention she gives someone seem as dangerous as it is serious. But
here—Linnea with Jimmy—it is purely serious: not a mother kvelling
over her kid with my-son proprietariness, but contemplating him,
without flourish or emphasis, gravely and deeply, so that the circuit

Linnea (Lily Tomlin) watches her son, Jimmy (James Dan Calvert),
sign about his swim class that day, with her daughter
(Donna Denton) and husband, Delbert (Ned Beatty), at center.

between them here, around the waiting table under the low-hanging chandelier, looks and feels nearly magical. And the effect is the way it can happen in life sometimes—when you see some stranger or strangers, on a street or in a park or across a train aisle, being marvelous unawares—seeming deeply thoughtful or spontaneously generous or just brilliantly *there*—and it feels like a parting of the veil.

II.

SATURDAY, THE FOLLOWING day, begins with Barbara Jean still in hospital and with PFC Kelly, the soldier from the airport, who has kept vigil over her sleep all night, being flushed from her room by the morning nurse; with Albuquerque (Barbara Harris), a fugitive wife from the trailer camp (intermittently pursued by her husband) who has run away to become another Barbara Jean, waking up after sleeping the night in someone's open car (and causing two others to crash behind her when she strolls onto the highway in her miniskirt, fussing through the belongings in her bag); with Kenny (David Hayward), a haunted-looking, bespectacled, polo-shirted young man clutching a violin case and approaching the house of Keenan Wynn's Mr. Green, renting a room there and being introduced on the spot to L.A. Joan, the niece. While the ever-prowling Hal Phillip Walker truck, out and about elsewhere, goes blaring past the house of Del and Linnea. With Linnea sitting around the parlor table with the two kids, signing and singing a song with them, while Del alone in the kitchen hovers indecisively at the stove. "Del, yuh sure you don't want me to come in there and fry yuh an egg?" she calls out. "No, honey, I'm gonna hardboil me a couple," he replies, in one of those wonderful, ringingly prosaic exchanges the movie abounds in.

When the phone rings at this point, husband and wife in their separate rooms both pick up, but it's Linnea who speaks first. The one on the other end is Keith Carradine's Tom, the lead singer in the folk-rock trio known as Tom, Bill and Mary—a languid male beauty with a serious resemblance to stained-glass images of Christ (as one of Altman's jokier cuts points out) and a compulsive womanizer, who is just at this moment waking up with the BBC's Opal in bed beside him, with one of his own recorded songs (as always when he's been making love, it seems) playing on the nearby tape machine (the song is "It Don't Worry Me"). This is the second time he has phoned Linnea—to remind her that they had met before at recording sessions and to tell her that he found her "very attractive"—both times without getting anywhere. "Tom who?" she says now. "Oh, come on, you know you want to see me," he says. "I never said any sucha thing," she says with rising voice, "and I'm not foolin' and dontcha ever call here again!"—and hangs up on him. "Who was that, babe?" calls out Del from the kitchen—who has been listening in since she picked up. "Jus' some crazy person been callin' here," she answers him, "and the next time he calls, I want yuh t' get on the phone and tell him you're gonna get the police on him." And she resumes the signing and singing lesson.

She has your special attention by now, amid all those others, and she turns up next at Haven's big barbecue bash on his wooded estate that same afternoon—where you find her talking with another woman, desultory accident-and-illness talk, about the dangers of those low-slung bikes you see everywhere now (Jeff Goldblum has just ridden by on his), and those tiny new cars they make now and how a friend hit her head on the door getting into one, about how "the blood begun to drain into behind the eyeball, y'know, and the pressure caused her eye jus' t' *boolge* out"—all the while looking absently around at the party in progress. Reminding you that Linnea is not that far from the sort of women Lily Tomlin often sends up.

But then Tom phones her again—two days after this. And this time she is home alone—and she doesn't hang up. He offers to meet her

Tom (Keith Carradine) of Tom, Bill and Mary in bed
with Mary (Cristina Raines)

that night at the Exit Inn, where he'll be performing. He hopes she'll
be there—that's all.

And in the next scene she is. Slipping in at the rear of the crowded
club. Some comic hillbilly singers are holding the stage just then and
Tom is lounging at a table in front of it, alone and beside an empty
chair. Linnea starts for the chair but L.A. Joan, out of nowhere, gets
there first. Linnea turns and goes to an empty booth at the back wall.
She is joined there by a mildly drunken stranger—the diner cook
Wade, Sueleen's friend—who introduces himself and settles in beside
her, offering to pay for her drink. She refuses—coldly polite. As the
next number begins (it's Tom, Bill and Mary now), she sits far forward
from him on her elbow, chin in hand. And when the number is over,
Wade excuses himself for the john, Linnea following his exit with a
coldly assessing stare—which she turns to the stage, chin still in hand,
as Tom appropriates the mike for a solo and his two partners step down.

It's a song he's just written, he says—to the clearly adoring crowd. And he is dedicating it "to someone kinda special who just might be here tonight." And he begins—the song is called "I'm Easy," he says—bending over the guitar in his lap cradled in his arms, his longish hair falling over one eye, talk-singing in a reedy baritone with a faint vibrato throb to it a plaintive, winding, meditative appeal to a woman he fears may be toying with his feelings. Still he won't resist—still he's available:

> *Take my hand and pull me down,*
> *I won't put up any fight,*
> *Because I'm easy . . .*
> *Yes I'm easy . . .*

It's a seducer's song, of course—in the tradition of Dietrich's "Falling in Love Again," but without Dietrich's wit or self-knowledge—self-serious in a way that she could never be. But Tom's sexy, moody narcissism has its own kind of power—almost as real to us as it is to his audience onscreen. But also for us, and not for them, there is the wonderful irony of his seeing himself, if only by imagining, as the casualty of a lover who simply can't feel as deeply as he does.

In fact, three of his current conquests are in the place right now—as well as Linnea, the critically impending one. His two most recent lays are there—L.A. Joan and Opal, each of whom is imagining (as we see in their close-ups) that he is singing to her. The third and more serious one is his partner in the trio and the wife of his other partner, Bill, the transfixingly beautiful Mary (Cristina Raines), with her almond-eyed chagrin, who is seriously smitten with him (and whom we've also seen in bed with him, with the familiar tape playing) and who knows at this moment that he is *not* singing for her.

Just a moment ago she was on the stage with him and her husband, where she had been taking the lead in one of the movie's most galvanizing song numbers, singing about disappointed love ("Since you've gone . . . My heart is broken / One more time") with a startling and moving ferocity. To much applause. Now she is back at their table in the audience, next to the awful Opal and alongside Bill (Allan Nicholls), her feckless husband, turned away from the two of them and leaning on her elbow into the hand covering her mouth as she listens to her lover's song to another woman.

And during that song the film cuts back and forth between Tom's performance and these four women watching it—chiefly Linnea. And yet, where it's easy enough to "read" the close-up faces of the others— the star-fucker's rush (L.A. Joan), the sentimentalist's self-delusion (Opal), and the betrayed lover's bitterness, respectively—Linnea is (as you expect) not so clearly legible. Her conflicted yearning is more complex, her close-ups more enigmatic.

Alone during the song in her booth at the back wall (Wade never returns from the john), she is surrounded in the widescreen frame by darkened out-of-focus heads in the foreground, her eyes shadowed by the corner of light falling on her from above, her black poodle-cut hair resting on her brow like a proscenium arch, and her stunned look below at the center of the image. She is nearly motionless each time Altman cuts to her—each time more riveted, each time more disturbed. First with her forearm lying on the table, then with her hand resting on her scarf, then inside it resting on her throat, then slack-jawed with her mouth fallen faintly open. Then a tight close-up of him, as he sings, gazing burningly through the forelock that's fallen over his eye, into the camera—that is, in her direction. Followed as he sings by a slow, slow zoom shot into her, past and between the darkened heads around her, moving in on her, as if mimicking the descent into herself that we seem to be looking at on her face, the falling away behind the eyes. And the song finally ends and there she is again, sitting tilted to one side, pressed against the wall as if she'd been pinned to it. And as the crowd's applause rises around her, still fixed in place, she heaves a just barely visible sigh.

What's moving about this is Tomlin's gravity, the sense she gives you that something serious is taking place in spite of the crummy situation— and in spite of your certainty (supported by the movie) that her Linnea is seeing the same Tom that you are seeing—not the one those variously besotted others are looking at—and being overwhelmed by him in spite of that as well as because of it. The Hopperesque image of Tomlin in that space of light became the most famous single still from the movie. Deservedly. It's she more than anyone else who gives the film its occasional feeling (somewhat misleading) of novelistic depth.

Next, the postcoitus scene. In Tom's by now familiar bed, the familiar tape playing. What's different this time is the feeling of mutual tenderness, though it seems oddly skewed at the beginning of the

Linnea at the Exit Inn, as Tom sings to her

scene. Tom is recumbent, his smooth brown chest uncovered. Linnea beside him is propped up on her elbow, in her slip, looking down at him—almost maternally. He turns the light up. She offers to teach him how to say something by signing it. What about "I love you"? he says—and you register her flicker of hesitation. Oh, *many* ways to say that, she replies, quickly and brightly, and she shows a couple of them—then adds an "I'm glad to have met you," too . . . He lights a cigarette. She is a nonsmoker and playfully waves the smoke away—but then asks to take a drag herself. Okay, he says—but now he is the parental one—she doesn't even look good smoking, he says. Silence—she looks at him fondly. But she has to leave now, she says. Stay—another hour? he asks. No, no, she says as she turns to get out of bed—but the touch of his hand on her back makes her sit up shiveringly. She still has to go.

He looks bereft now, sitting alone in the bedclothes. He picks up the phone on the night table and calls a girlfriend in Chicago—who sounds delighted to hear from him. They chat, he drawls and she giggles (you can hear her neediness almost painfully), while it's Linnea who is holding the screen, at the bathroom mirror getting ready to leave, donning her blouse, buttoning her jacket, adjusting her scarf. Then turning around—almost whipping around—to gaze at Tom on his phone as she tucks her blouse into her skirt. All set now (he's still talking), she smiles at him, bends to retrieve the nearly forgotten panties between the sheets, puts them in her purse, blows him a kiss, and goes out the door—her exit shown at the side of the screen reflected in the mirror beside his bed—while Tom himself is center-screened, still on the phone, still pretending for its sake to be alone (Oh, that was the maid I was talking to).

In that last skirt-tucking gaze of hers at Tom on the phone—steady but impassive—she seems more hidden than ever. What it stands for, you suppose, is some private and final refusal of judgment. And *that* is moving enough, it seems to me. (Like the Marschallin's final words of rueful recognition, her softly uttered "Jah, jah . . ." at the end of *Rosenka-valier*.) There is, after all, something momentous—not too strong a word for it, I think—about Tomlin's presence in this film, about Linnea's privacy in a movie that is so much and so relentlessly about public performance, even public exposure. (Tomlin, too, had a solo singing spot at one point in the film's planning, but Altman finally decided against it.)

III.

BUT IT'S ALSO a movie—through and through—about the pure zinging elation of popular music, about the excitement of making it, of even just being around it, and around the people who do it. There are plenty of mediocre (or worse) song numbers in the film—mostly by

people who play and sing and then disappear—one of the chief things
the contemporary reviews faulted it for. But it's the *atmosphere* of music
making more than the artistic high points that the movie celebrates—
and the communality. Performers (apart from Tom and Barbara Jean)
are rarely by themselves on the stage, and their audiences are generally
as brightly illumined as they are. Besides, there are other ways to be
remarkable than by being good.

As Haven Hamilton shows us when he sings for a capacity crowd
on Saturday night's Grand Ole Opry broadcast—when he sings a song
so richly false that it's almost moving. (His own authorship, of course—
and in reality the actor's, Henry Gibson's.)

At center stage with mike in hand he gives the downbeat signal to
the band behind him, and as the strings begin plucking anticipatorily,
he commences his footlights stroll. With chin held high (he is *very*
short) he looks benignly over and around at the audience in the seats
below—and begins. And as he does they applaud—signaling their
recognition of the song:

> *Unpack your bags*
> *And try not to cry—*
> *I can't leave my wife.*
> *There's three reasons why . . .*

Then, in an overhead long shot looking down on him onstage and on
the front rows, he continues:

> *There's Jimmy—*
> *And Kathy—*
> *And sweet Loralie . . .*

as the same shot begins a slow upward pullback lengthening our distance from him, taking in more of his audience. Then the refrain:

> *For the sake of the children*
> *We must say goodbye . . .*

—the words repeated in a croon by the quartet behind him, the fawning doo-woppers from his recording session.

That slowly ascending pullback—beginning at just the moment that the song's mawkishness begins to climb ("There's Jimmy—"), and then to climb yet again ("sweet Loralie" is beyond praise)—is both stealthy and thrilling, giving a visual trope to the way that the movie itself seems to enlarge at just this moment, to expand just as our view on the screen is doing, becoming not just about this singer and this place or even this specific subculture, but about America, about its propensity for the comforting cliché and the false retrospect, its penchant for turning squalor into self-congratulation. Haven's song—with its mournful tone, its restless rockabye rhythm—is of course a parody. And ludicrous, if only a shade more so than the real thing might be. But Altman doesn't play the number for laughs (as he more or less did Haven's earlier song)—that stately camera pullback alone would have prevented that—but rather for a kind of sour grandeur. Gibson makes the song's dreadful appeal so palpable that instead of our feeling mired in the familiar smarminess, we seem to take off with it, to ascend with the camera into something closer to a tragic view (to hear America singing!). *Nashville* is not only fun, not only a comic epic, but a heart-sore one as well.

IV.

OF COURSE MOST classic pop songs—and not just the country-and-western kind—get a power of sorts from their own genre limitation, from the gap between the major emotions they talk about and the minor mode they can't escape. And it's just that gap that Altman's *Nashville* inhabits and makes poignant, most especially in Ronee Blakley's Barbara Jean. Of all the in-and-out figures in the film, she is the most finally important, the one most connected to the "metaphor for America" Altman claimed his movie was. She is the aching wound at the movie's center.

She is, of course, too sweet to be true. We are not surprised to see how bad-tempered she is when out of the spotlight and alone with Barnett—in the dimly lit hospital room, where she sits morose and crosslegged on top of the bed painting her toenails with her head down, surrounded in the movie frame by stands of red flowers from well-wishers and with Barnett sitting in a darkened corner nearby, feeding on some takeout under his handlebar mustache. The Grand Ole Opry is on the radio. And they have just heard Haven tell the audience how "Barbara Jean cried real tears because she couldn't be with you tonight." He then announces that she is being replaced by Connie White (Karen Black) and Barbara Jean tells Barnett to turn the radio off. She certainly doesn't want to hear Connie White (a detested rival) while she herself is stuck in the goddamn hospital with no friends anywhere and everybody saying that she's gone crazy again. And now *he* wants to go off and leave her and go "hobnobbing" at the King of the Road club after the Opry. Take Connie White some flowers, why doesn't he! she yells, throwing a funereal-looking wreath at him and then collapsing on the floor. Barnett stays calm. He only wants to know if she is going "nutsy" on him again, if she is gonna have one of her "nervous breakdowns" on him again. And soon she is promising not to, on the floor at his knees, whimpering. He is not easily appeased, and he makes her repeat after him what he says to her now: how he is going to the King of the Road tonight on *her* business because he loves her and because he's been managing her life pretty good up to now—as he backs away toward the door and as she, still on the floor, echoes his words in a spooky baby voice that now comes to us from below the frame line—ending with "Bye . . . Bye-bye" (creepy stuff) as Barnett closes the door and departs.

It's standard stuff, too—the tortured star and her Svengali—but the hysteria feels genuine. And the whole episode makes the next time we see her all the more powerful: she appears next at the climax of a virtuoso montage of the various characters at their various churches on Sunday morning (the third day) with their various rousing chorales. From a Catholic mass with a hymn-singing congregation, to a Baptist choir singing—and signing (Linnea's boy, Jimmy)—"Amazing Grace," on to a full-immersion baptism at a black church with an exultant choir (Linnea in the front row) singing "Free Grace, Sinner" to welcome the newcomer. These are ceremonies all three—as Altman shows them to us—of great dignity, even joy, and of an untroubled commonality (also it's interesting to see in the close-ups which characters belong to which churches—Lady Pearl to the Catholic one, Haven to the upscale Protestant one, and so on). But it's all instantly—almost

Barbara Jean sitting on her hospital bed

shockingly—followed by another sort of voice and worship—alone and pained and personal: Barbara Jean (in medium close-up) singing for the first time in the movie, in her small contralto voice, in a wheelchair and a white lace gown, in front of a small bare altar (the hospital chapel's), her elbows on the chair arms, her hands clasped on her lap—as she closes her eyes and sings to a harmonium accompaniment, and with a piercing sort of intimacy, a familiar hymn ("In the Garden," with its gloss on the Magdalen first meeting the risen Jesus):

> *Oh, He walks with me,*
> *And He talks with me,*
> *And He tells me I am His own . . .*

her head moving raptly from side to side, drifting and rocking, not only to the slow lilting melody but to her own intensity, to this imagining of the God who comforts . . .

> And the joy we share
> As we tarry there . . .

lifting her head slightly on "joy," then "tarrying" herself on the next line, before declining, slowly and gently, into the blessedness that's waiting—

> No other . . .
> Has ever . . .
> Known.

And as she goes on to a second chorus, the camera tracks slowly, reverently, back over the sparse and scattered congregation in the pews (including Mr. Green, and Barbara Jean's soldier fan PFC Kelly, and Barnett, as always, on the watch).

Comes Monday, the fourth (next-to-last) day—the one with the most sustained dramatic episodes (Linnea and Tom's tryst, Sueleen's humiliating strip, and other incidents). But it begins with the usual collage of disconnected scenes. First, Opal in long shot, wandering through a school bus parking lot, talking into her tape recorder, trying (and failing) to derive an aperçu from the predominance around her of the color yellow. Barbara Jean is at last getting out of the hospital this morning—riding down the hallway in her wheelchair, clucking and smiling and saying goodbye and surrounded by her ever-present fans. "Okay—let's get her in there," says the impatient Barnett, pushing her chair through the crowd and toward the waiting elevator. But not before she asks Mr. Green whether his wife (the patient in the room next to hers) has been taking her vitamin E and is assured that she has. "You take care, darlin'," she cries out, to whomever, and gets backed by Barnett into the elevator, singing as she goes and the door closes on her.

But Mrs. Green has just died, as the nurse now informs her overwhelmed husband. While Opal, back from her bus yard tour and chatting with Triplette, offers her theory that it's all the guns in America that make all the assassins. Then we revisit Kenny—and his ominous violin case—back at Mr. Green's rooming house. He is telephoning his mother from his room—with the ever flirtatious L.A. Joan (who never did manage to visit her dying aunt in the hospital) entering and hovering in the background as he talks.

When he can get a word in. The querulous feminine voice on the other end is a generic one: the sickly, controlling, passive-aggressive mother—familiar from fiction if not from life—enumerating her genteel alarms and grotesquely misplaced anxieties (all the unseen voices in this film feel powerfully "visible"). "A girl lives in that rooming house? . . . Who owns that rooming house? . . . A *man* owns that rooming house? . . . I bet the sheets aren't very clean . . . You can get this parasite fungus in the South, you know, and it's very difficult to get rid of . . . You left your blue suit hanging in the closet . . . I really would like you to get home as soon as you can . . . Kenny! Don't you talk to me in that tone of voice—"

At which point Kenny covertly cuts her off and then says into the dead phone, "I love you, too, Mother, I really do" (because L.A. Joan is listening?) over a close shot of his finger pressing down on the phone button. And then, here at the end of one of this frenetic movie's quietest scenes, comes one of its most thrilling shock cuts (almost lifting you out of your seat if you're seeing it on a big theater screen)—flipping you over onto a burst of sunlight and music at the *Opry Belle*: with male and female dancers on the showboat balcony in blue-fringed yellow outfits pumping and jumping and butt-bumping to a crashing propulsive musical beat as the Olympian-view camera slow-zooms backward over the heads of the crowd in the onshore bleachers (Barbara Jean has been promised to appear).

But there is something about this jolting cut that feels deeply recognizable: it's not only the connection it suggests between Kenny's mother's world and the *Opry Belle*'s—between two familiar kinds of inanity—but the one it makes in your stomach—the one that's been growing there through the movie—between omen and ersatz joy.

Now Barbara Jean comes wafting out of her trailer—once again prompting confusion, which she responds to in all directions: "I wish you didn't rush me this way," she says to someone at her left, and "Did you get that shot?" to a camera at her right, as she goes chattering and sauntering on with Barnett at her side, in her billowing whites, pink ribbons pinned to the back of her ebony hair, the customary smile pinned to her face. "I'm a little excited, y'know," she says to her husband as he takes her arm on the way to the stage. "I feel a little rough," she adds. "How do you feel?" he replies—less a question than an instruction. "I feel great," she says brightly. Of course it's all great—isn't it? Or is it? As we know by now, she generally has to ask.

The band strikes up (one of her tunes) as a chorus boy leads her ceremonially down the ramp to center stage in front of the band. She takes up her hand mike with its cord and begins to sing—a number that natters along like a rushing brook, the band racing after, about a putative "cowboy" who rides a tractor, listening both (or alternately) to his radio (for fishing tips) and to his tape deck, and who we learn in the song's refrain is also good in the sack: "No there's nothin' like the lovin' of a hard-drivin' cowboy man." Which she belts out, head thrown back and mike in the air, Broadway-diva style. Except for the tremolo—country-style—she inflects it with.

Applause—and the band launches zestfully into her next number, almost as if it were going to be cheerful: "I won't take no more, baby," she sings, "It hurts so bad / It gets me down, down, down," and so forth—in a kind of moan, over the ravishment of those country fiddles (close-up of a benign-looking fiddler) and plangent plucked strings (close-up of the pluckers), which seem both to confirm the singer's pessimism and to argue with it:

> I wanna walk away
> From this battleground.
> This hurtin' match,
> It ain't no good . . .

Cross-cutting between her and her audience: teenagers and young families with their kids and portly Shriners in their fezzes and so on. And as always, some familiar faces. Opal's, for one—as she slips in late and takes a seat on the steps next to Barbara Jean's soldier fan. The mysterious Kenny is sitting in the row below them. Opal asks the soldier if he was in Vietnam. But he is too involved in Barbara Jean's song to answer. So Opal answers herself: "Yes, you have"—then adding (inevitably), "I can tell by your face." Back to Barbara Jean. Back to Opal. "Was it awful?" she asks, still studying him. Replies the private, affectlessly: "It was kinda hot and wet." Cut to Kenny, in close shot below, overhearing this and looking up at them, looking troubled, then turning back to look (on "battleground") at Barbara Jean, frowningly.

As she sings the last hopeless words about "this hurtin' match," then lapses into a wordless humming diminuendo, swaying and almost sinking, then rising, sculpting the keening sound in the air with her free hand, she brings her song to a mournful close. She raises her head, smiles, and nods to the applause. Which is understandably more restrained this time.

Foreground, left to right: Kenny (David Hayward), PFC Kelly (Scott Glenn), and Opal (Geraldine Chaplin) listen to Barbara Jean at the Showboat.

Where Tomlin's Linnea suggests a strong private self attending closely to the outside world, Barbara Jean attends to nothing but private voices and is all public self. Even her breakdowns become public events—like the one that follows here, in Blakley's almost-too-painful-to-watch enactment. Barbara Jean, smiling and cheerful as she always is in public, is suddenly confused, distracted, offering to start her next song and then stopping in favor of a rambling monologue about Munchkins and chipmunks and even imitating the way a chicken sounds (she thinks it's comic)—while the band stirs behind her. She starts again—so do they. But then she spots a cloud that looks like rain, and she is soon off and onto memories of her grandmother, who used to clack her false teeth to the music on the radio, and so on. Clearly, this is "nutsy"—and Barnett is soon at her side trying to usher her offstage (she doesn't want to go), but not before he chastises the restive audience for their rudeness and promises them that she will be appearing and singing tomorrow afternoon at the Hal Phillip Walker political rally at the Parthenon. The fifth and final day . . .

From the start, the feeling of gathering excitement is nearly overwhelming. So is the feeling of gathering omen. But so far the excitement dominates. There is a blimp in the morning sky with a Hal Phillip Walker sign blinking on and off, and on television, Howard K. Smith (the real one) is talking about the candidate himself, and a folk singer on the loudspeakers at the Parthenon (a plaster replica of the original, as Del tells Triplette—Nashville being called "the Athens of the South") is singing about "Trouble in the U.S.A." (Vietnam and Watergate are both named) as a long black limo in the distance slowly travels with its police escort ("You're going the wrong way!" a voice shouts at them) toward the great lawn behind the building's broad pillared open-air stage where the crowds are now milling and gathering. The far-off limo stops and disgorges a man as Triplette crosses the lawn to meet him (we hear their voices)—it's Hal Phillip Walker, it seems. But the excitement is on and around that stage, where the music is now in progress.

V.

THERE IS NO big entrance this time for Barbara Jean. Altman's wandering camera finds her already onstage, in a happy duet with Haven.

One of those buddy songs, about always being able to rely on each other (even "when I feel my life vanishin' / Like waves upon a shore")—and it's the first time you get the sense in the movie that Haven's affection for Barbara Jean is at least partly the real thing.

And then there are all those others, from the rest of the movie, the "twenty-four stars" and more. This is the sequence when you see almost everybody again; it has a curtain-call feeling to it even from the beginning, and it's oddly touching. You see the familiar faces either among the crowd or on the stage waiting to go on (it seems) or just waiting—Lady Pearl in her customary chair with Buddy beside her,

Sueleen leaning against a pillar and singing along (we've heard her singing—if that's the word for it—this same song earlier on), Linnea and her choir in their black robes, Tom and Mary (Bill of Tom, Bill and Mary is among the crowd now—with L.A. Joan), Albuquerque sprawled on the lip of the stage, head in hand, a big hole in the knee of her stocking—and many others. And it's a beautiful day (with occasional passing clouds)—an expansive day. Like the crane shots that rise over the happy crowd, the crowded stage, the two happy singers, who have now finished their song—the one handing off the other (kissing her hand and stepping back) to her real destiny: aloneness before a crowd.

And now she really takes off. No hurting matches or fishy (and fishing) cowboy lovers this time. This song is about her Idaho home, the one that we all remember somehow, and all the better for ourselves never having been there: the Great Depression hardship, the close loving family on the farm weathering it all together, the up-by-your-bootstraps American idyll. All of it here not generalized or idealized as it had been by Haven, but offered plainly, in a kind of Whitmanesque detail, on a cascading uptempo:

> My daddy grew up on his own more or less.
> His mama died when he was just eleven.
> He had seven sisters to raise him—
> But he dreamed of his mama in heaven . . .

And so on, and at length, with a kind of rapture that grows with the excitement of Blakley's performance. "We were young then," she sings, the strings plucking excitedly, "we were together"—and Altman cuts (movingly) to a full wide-screen close-up of the enormous American flag, strung across the pillars, as it lifts and billows hugely and softly behind her: "We could bear floods and fire / And bad weather," she sings. And her iteration of defeats and joys ascends at the end of each verse into the anthemlike refrain in her belting range, her faithful fiddles rollicking along, into a thrilling rising invocation of distance and space and ongoingness—we would sing together in the car, she tells us, and "our laughter would *ring*,"

OPPOSITE PAGE: Singing "My Idaho Home"

Down the highways . . .
On the beaches . . .
Just as fa-ar
As mem'ry reaches . . .

evoking those (pre-expressway) country highways that really did seem to wind and stretch to the horizon and far beyond. But "reaching" to where in this song? Only to a kind of anticlimax: I'm grown up now, she says, dropping into a *sprechstimme* mode, but "I still love Mama and Daddy best / And my Idaho home." And then in her speaking voice, and with a demure smile, she adds: "To Mama and Daddy," as Haven steps up and takes her hand and raises it to the applause that follows.

And in the next moment he will be throwing his body over hers—to shield her from the gunshots that have suddenly rung out and slammed her to the floor of the stage. It's Kenny, of course (there goes *his* mama)—we've been seeing his growing distress during this last song, seen him take the pistol stealthily from the violin case. Only from a distance do we see him firing it from out of the crowd, where we then see the ensuing shock and grief. Our shock, too. In spite of all the movie's foreboding, you're probably not ready for *this*.

In the confusion and panic, Haven tries to take charge—though wounded in the shoulder and having lost his toupee. "This isn't Dallas—this is *Nashville!*" he shouts, over the panicked milling crowd. "You show 'em what we're made of! They can't do this to us in Nashville!" Linnea is standing in a daze, her hand held limply up before her as if to ward off the next minute, the next horror. Nearby, Sueleen is weeping. Triplette is stunned, wandering briskly back and forth behind the pillars, as if he still had some business to do. Del is looking now for his wife—who is still with her young choir. "Sing," commands Haven, still trying to calm the crowd, holding on to his bloody left shoulder—and hands his mike blindly to the nearby Albuquerque, coming out of nowhere, as she always seems to do. And so she sings—one of Tom's songs (we've heard fragments before this)—tentatively at first, and then rousingly, in her infectious, bluesy, big-ranging voice. Then with the young black choir, still onstage (Linnea having departed with Del), backing her up. And then at last the crowd, joining in, singing along—

You may say
That I ain't free
But it don't worry me

in defiance of their grief and fear. And so the long movie ends—in this stirring display of communal courage. And yet not entirely that, either. The final image is of the camera rising slowly above them as they sing, the triumphal voices fading out into the endless, soundless sky.

Although you are rocked by Barbara Jean's sudden death, you may also feel that it's at this moment that the whole movie comes finally—and shatteringly—together. For me it begins to do that even before, in her final song, about the same time that Kenny in the crowd fully registers for himself the connection between the sick woman at home and the one on the stage. *Nashville* is, among other things, about just this connection—between public and private madness.

Like the madness of the American belief in our national innocence. A belief that's reflected here in different ways in most of the movie's songs—but nowhere else so movingly as in Barbara Jean's final one. Haven performs the hypocrisy of that belief—Barbara Jean its painful ambivalence. In Ronee Blakley's enactment of her, she is both heartbreaking and appalling at the same time. You want to save her (Altman's single general instruction to his cast: *everyone* loves Barbara Jean) and you want to kill her. That's the unresolvable final pain at the heart of the movie—the thing it leaves us with, as Altman's camera rises at the end into the sky and the silence.

So what is that thrilling defiant anthem at the end about? And it really is thrilling—and moving (Altman's great film simply keeps topping itself). Especially when it's combined—as it is near its fading out—with the faces of the children in the crowd. Is the defiance the song expresses (earlier on, it's the song we hear on Tom's bedroom tape) a warranted one—or is it the familiar American problem, a defiance of reality? The song of a populace that makes their history by ignoring it?—and then feels left with no choice but to ignore it again? The invaders of Vietnam—and Iraq. Haven was wrong—this *is* Dallas, which tends to repeat itself.

"We are the most illusioned people on earth," said the historian Daniel Boorstin. "We risk being the first people in history to have been able to make their illusions so vivid, so persuasive, so 'realistic' that they can live in them." *Nashville* is partly about that illusionary condition—and if the movie feels even more trenchant now than it did decades ago, that's not, I think, because the tyranny of illusion over our public life has necessarily grown, but because it now includes (as it did not so clearly in 1975) our resistance to both the evidence and the urgency of the planet's decline. The final—as it may turn out to be—"livable" illusion.

9

Jackie Brown and Others

ROBERT DE NIRO is one of the stars in Quentin Tarantino's *Jackie Brown* (1997), a labyrinthine multicharacter cops-and-robbers film derived from the Elmore Leonard novel *Rum Punch*. He plays Louis Gara, a dim and hapless ex-con just sprung from prison. His opposite number in the film's action is Bridget Fonda's Melanie. They are the two bottom-feeders in the criminal circle around Samuel L. Jackson's character, Ordell Robbie, a hipster thug and international gun runner. Melanie is his putative girlfriend, one of them anyway, the beach bunny that he keeps in his fanciest apartment.

Ordell, an American success story in himself (as well as being a vehicle for Tarantino's compulsive "nigga"-studded blackspeak), appears to have several apartments (even a house) with a different woman friend—a wigged-out druggie, a teenager from the backwoods, and a middle-aged lip-synching lap dancer—waiting for him in each one. Melanie is in the beachfront one, and she is as lazy as she is surly. We first see her lounging in front of a TV in her stringy bra top and cutoff jeans, taking hits from a bong while Ordell, disapproving, watches her from the kitchen: "That shit robs you of your ambition," he says. "Not if your ambition is to get high and watch TV," she answers.

And Louis, their guest—who is waiting for his own turn on the bong—laughs sheepishly. But as he will later warn Ordell: "You can't trust her." Ordell knows that, of course. So then why does he keep her around? "I told you, man," he replies, with a wide grin (the triumphant consumerist), "she my fine little surfer gal." Louis had taken the fall for the bank that he and Ordell had robbed together, and now that he is free, Ordell is taking care of him. And although Louis (unlike Melanie) is grateful and loyal, he is never easy around his boss's triumphant ongoing self-performance. Ordell needs to be the center of attention wherever he goes, while Louis just wants to wait in the car, or be ignored altogether.

He has a habit of responding ambiguously when put on the spot or asked for an assent: doing a faint steady bobbing of his head, up and down, in what looks like agreement, then suddenly thrusting his arms out and folding them across his chest, in what looks like thoughtfulness—but who could be sure? Ordell isn't—when he shows Louis the body in the trunk of his Mercedes (a stoolie he's just killed) that now needs to be disposed of. Is Louis cool with that? Louis takes the sight in, then looks off and away—bobbingly. "So we on the same page?" persists Ordell. "I follow," says Louis. "My nigger!" says Ordell, beaming at him. And they do a fist-bump in the air—but with a slight double-take by Louis: Is he meant to do it again, then? Oh, no—he got it right, and lowers his arm. "My nigger" indeed.

In fact he rarely looks directly at anyone—unless they're on television. Not even at Melanie when he's fucking her (standing up and from behind). But as far as Melanie is concerned, both guys are fundamentally losers. She will conceal that opinion from Louis, however, as long as she imagines he may help her to double-cross Ordell. But when it turns out that he won't—and when they are both on a carefully timed assignment from Ordell to do a big shopping bag money switch at the mall—she's a total pain. Making them late, kvetching at him in the car all the way there, taunting him when they get there for getting them lost inside the mall ("the world's largest"—at the time), then outside in the parking lot when they can't find their car again. They wander around—and she never shuts up.

It's not that what she says to him is apt at all (Melanie is not too bright herself)—it's just incessant. It's his name mockingly pronounced, the same idiot jeering sound, over and over again: "*Loo*-iss," both syllables prolonged, both the croon and the hiss, repeated relentlessy, over and over again, with no way to stop it. Except by taking his gun and shooting her. Which he does. After a clear warning: "Don't say

Robert De Niro with Bridget Fonda: "Don't say anything else, okay?"

anything else, okay?" he says. "I mean it, don't say *one* fuckin' word . . ." A pause. "Okay," she says—subsiding. And then . . . "*Loo*-iss." And that does it. And he still never quite looks at her.

Ordell can't believe what he's hearing when Louis drives up to meet him: "You *shot* Melanie?" Really? He couldn't have just talked to her? Or just hit her? "*You* know how she is," says Louis, eyes on the road as he drives. So he had to *shoot* her? *Twice*? Ordell still can't believe it . . . "Is she dead?" he says. "I . . . I . . ." replies Louis—then: "Pretty much." But what kind of answer is that? Louis concedes that she is dead. (Very soon he will be, too—once Ordell discovers that the shopping bag is full not of money but of shredded newspaper.) That "pretty much" is not only a brilliant De Niro line (improvised?—it's neither in the Tarantino screenplay nor in the Elmore Leonard novel), an inspired verbal extension of the bobbing head and averted eye. Not only a reflection of Louis's relation to the world of the film but something of De Niro's relation to his own career by then: immersed (more movies than ever) but all the more averted.

Tarantino said that you had to see this movie at least three or four times just to figure out the convoluted plot. But once you had, once you knew what was coming and no longer had to wait to find out, you could get into the real point of the movie—which was hanging out with the characters. "It's my *Rio Bravo*—my hangout movie." And it's the "hangout scenes," not the story, that you really want to see it for—to be around the people—and then to see it again. And he recalled the fifteenth or so time (a conservative estimate, I'd bet) he'd seen *Rio Bravo*—and it was better than ever. His first two movies, *Reservoir Dogs* (1991) and *Pulp Fiction* (1994), the latter a worldwide success, were meant to "blow your mind," he said—but not *Jackie Brown*. This was his "mature" movie—coming between the mind-blowers (the epically inane *Kill Bill* ones would come after it). A movie that focused on character, that would "dig deeper," that would "go underneath."

But *Jackie Brown* only resembles such a movie. "Hanging out with" is not always the same as delving or probing. And Tarantino's film is not (unlike *Jezebel* or *The Searchers*, say) much more about "character" than it is about its other nearly ostensible subjects: crime, race, drugs, American consumerism. What it is about—for him and for us alike (and it's his best movie so far I think)—is the excitement of some rich and vivid human presences. Not Louis's or Melanie's, to be sure—nor even Ordell's.

Pam Grier as the eponymous heroine appears to us even before the opening credits—and even if an audience doesn't "know" her, they can't but know that she is meant here to be the star. As she moves, unmoving and in profile, onto the right edge of the widescreen frame, which then begins to follow along beside her (the credits, after her name alone above the title, coming and going at the left) as she is standing (statuesque) on an airport people-mover taking her slowly past and along an unending blue tile wall, to the soundtrack accompaniment of a seventies soul song about striving to escape the ghetto ("Across 110th Street"). Clearly, as Robert Garis has written about another star and movie (Dietrich in *Touch of Evil*), "the ceremony of glamour is being celebrated."

But this time it's not about some timeless legendary exotic but a familiar (at first glance at least) kind of contemporary middle-aged woman. She is black, with even a suggestion of Native American. She is tall and zaftig, a stewardess in a rather ill-fitting blue uniform, and she looks formidable, especially in her face's aquiline profile: slanting downward from her brow to the tip of her nose, the unyielding line reinforced here in the set of her mouth, the gravity of her steady forward gaze, but softened by her long bounteous-looking brown hair, pulled back and tied behind to cascade down her uniformed back.

Credits ending at last, she steps off the transit belt with her shoulder bag and starts to hurry in a long-legged, loose-limbed stride, in her high heels and miniskirt ("Yuh have to be *strong* if yuh wanna survive," growls the singer on the soundtrack, ending with a piercing squeal). But now she looks elated—as you now feel just looking at her—as she goes through the terminal and the people, the camera still watching her from the side, then from the front, from the floor even, tracking along before her, looking up at her height, her grace, her zest and energy. Her expression is humorous, her cheekbones high and prominent, her skin copper brown, one eyebrow slightly arched.

She begins to rush, picking up her stride. At the gate, the other stewardess, also black but much younger, is already announcing their flight over the public address system before a small group of waiting passengers. This second stewardess with her soft big-eyed prettiness offers a sharp contrast to the other's warrior queen beauty. And the sense the latter has already given us of powers precisely deployed—the easy lope into a loose-gaited run, the quick adjusting of skirt and scarf, the long red fingernail tucking in the errant strand of hair, all on the run, all briskly accomplished, until she reaches her plane, stows her flight bag inside, and takes her post, where she turns with her sensible smile to greet the boarding passengers filing past her. "*Buenos días,*" she says in a close shot now, "welcome aboard . . ." The conventional sort of greeting that still conveys as she offers it what you wouldn't have doubted but may not yet have thought of—that in spite of her imperial presence and the at-her-feet camera angles, how simply uncomplicatedly *nice* she probably is.

No other special point gets made about her by this extended introduction—except for the vague uneasinesses you might feel about her uniform and her job respectively; but if she seems slightly too big for the one and slightly too old for the other, it's also clear that she is managing fine—if a bit edgily (being almost late), the way smart people in dead-end jobs often do. And Jackie has been at *this* one, and at various airlines—as we later learn—for twenty years. And because she has also acquired a police record, falsely incriminated by a drug pushing ex-husband, it's nearly the best she can hope for.

That was almost the same amount of time that Pam Grier's onetime career as a cult film star had seemed to be in storage. Her youthful celebrity, although widespread and genuine, had been fleeting—depending principally on the hit status of two blaxploitation pictures, *Coffy* (1973) and *Foxy Brown* (1974), among others. But unlike other blaxploitation hits of the time, the male-centered *Superfly* (1972) and *The Mack* (1973), with their pimping and dealing high-living heroes, hers were moralistic: she was the action heroine who fought drugs in the hood and women's degradation and outwitted the pols and the big-time pushers, both black and white, no matter how often or how completely she had to undress for them to do it before gunning them down at the climax. She was in her midtwenties in those days, sporting an enormous Angela Davis Afro. And whether or not anyone else in the casts and crews of these shrewd, funky, C-budget movies took them seriously, Grier certainly did. And her performances in them have—along with her beauty and brains—the sort of earnest amateur charm that can be hard to resist. "I thought I was doing *Gone With the Wind*," she later said. She even read Stanislavsky's *An Actor Prepares* to get up to speed (something more, you imagine, than Vivien Leigh did).

But blaxploitation flamed out even before the seventies were over, and there wasn't a whole lot for her after that. Though she went on working, it was in small parts in movies and TV that sometimes obliquely alluded to her cult eminence. That at least persisted, in spite of the marginal jobs she was having to rely on. Until two decades passed—and suddenly there was *Jackie Brown*! The biggest, longest (two and a half hours), most ambitious movie she'd ever done (*Gone With the Wind* at last!) by the hottest filmmaker going, thanks to his *Pulp Fiction* three years before. This was his first film since then. What was he going to do?—to match that success? And the answer, it seemed, would be a movie for Pam Grier . . . wow! Not only "bringing her back," as Tarantino had just done for John Travolta (whose renewed career, not being that of a middle-aged black woman, fared much better afterward)—but also reaffirming the sort of extra-mainstream movie taste that had singled her out in the first place.

She is not only the single above-the-title star but the one who would outwit all the others in a scam they're all involved in, all of them at cross purposes. But it's Jackie who pulls off the final bait-and-switch (that shopping bag) and in the end gets away with both her freedom and the loot. Even Max the bail bondsman (Robert Forster), her smitten coscammer, isn't on to her until the movie's end. Not that he minds even then.

On her flights into LAX she has been regularly smuggling the cash payments owed to Ordell by his Mexican clients. But now Jackie finds

Jackie (Pam Grier) argues with her sometime boss, Ordell (Samuel L. Jackson), on his oceanfront balcony.

herself being met at LAX when she lands by two cops, one local and the other federal (a Treasury agent), who find in her luggage not only the money but a stash of coke she hadn't even known was there (a gift from the Mexicans). It's the local cop, Dargus (Michael Bowen), who tells her exactly, once they are all sitting down together in the exam room, why she should now cooperate with them: because she is "a forty-four-year-old black woman" with a record (Grier was forty-eight) who is "desperately clinging to the one shitty job" she has "been fortunate enough to get"—even if it's only for the (in virtuoso Tarantino-speak) "shittiest little shuttle fucking piece of shit Mexican airline that there is." And for only "thirteen thousand a year." "Sixteen thousand with benefits," she replies—hopelessly.

So she will eventually agree to help the feds get Ordell—who is a whole different story, of course—with the advice and steady collusion of Max Cherry, the bail bondsman (talk about shitty jobs), who is also the movie's leading man and who is played by another figure from our and Tarantino's movie past.

Robert Forster was a Stanley Kowalski type then (he came to notice playing the role onstage)—a handsomer Charles Bronson with a similar simian sexiness. And like Grier, he sometimes appeared on screen in the buff (*Reflections in a Golden Eye*, 1967; *Medium Cool*, 1969). No more of that: he is fifty-six now, just as Max reports himself to be in the movie, where we see him for the first time talking on the phone at his office desk to a young client's mother while signaling to Ordell, who has just walked in (Louis stays in the outer office), to sit down. They've not met before—Ordell is there to arrange bail for Beaumont, the fink he plans on killing once he's been sprung.

Whereas Ordell in this scene is all attitude and veiled menace—with his long thick ponytail and little Fu Manchu goatee—Max is all open (so to speak) wariness. "How can I help you?" he asks at the end of the phone call, as Ordell crosses his legs and leans back in his chair, looking down at the lighted cigarette (close-up of cigarette) that he holds in the hand resting on his upraised knee. "Where would you like me to put my ash?" he says. Max looks at him silently before looking away. He has seen too many Ordells. "Use that cup right there if y' like," he says—neutrally. He's used to these sullen hoods with their pissy-ass games. Used to ignoring them, too—that's part of being the pro that he is.

A weary one—a face rutted and seamed by sad intelligence, a look of ruined handsomeness. Thick black hair, a furrowed forehead, a deep crease between the eyebrows, a five o'clock shadow, and a settled mild puzzlement in the deep-set blue eyes. He is doing the requisite paperwork on Beaumont now—then finishing: "If I have to go to Key West to bring him back," he says to Ordell as a final thing, "you pay the expenses." "You can do that?" says Ordell, impressed in spite of himself. "Done it," says Max, without looking up, snapping his ballpoint pen shut. That click of his pen is very nice: Max has authority. While Ordell only has its facsimile: he seems noisy and hectic even just sitting near the other and listening to him.

Later the movie shows us another contrast in styles of masculine ballsiness—it's between the two cops who meet and detain Jackie at the airport. In the exam room scene that follows, it's Dargus, the cop, with his thick brown mustache, his striped shirt and suspenders, who leads the questioning, leaning casually back in his chair with a familiar sort of cop's complacent insolence.

But federal cop Ray Nicolet, who is played by Michael Keaton (one of the movie's six above-the-title stars), remains quiet at first, leaning forward, staring at her across the table. Crew-cut and clean-shaven, in T-shirt and leather jacket, coffee-drinking, shaking a sugar packet in the air before tearing it open—never not looking at her here, he seems almost bursting with . . . what? If only with his own interiority—a familiar Michael Keaton effect. He's the sort of actor, as one reviewer said, who seems always to work on the balls of his feet—and here, even his silent concentration seems to come up from there. And Ray is attracted to her—which doesn't hurt.

He is her natural ally, of course—just as Dargus with his programmed incuriosity is her natural opponent. And very soon she and Ray together will be planning a trap for the dangerous Ordell (that shopping bag exchange at the mall), who is the one that the feds are really after. But Jackie makes quite another plan (unknown to Ray) with Max—which involves (among its details) her stopping to buy a suit at that shop in the mall where everything seems to go wrong for the cops. And it's that suit (she looks great in it) as well as the missing money that make Ray fairly certain afterward that he's been played.

So now she is back again in his examining room, sitting and waiting for him (in her cool new suit) and smoking nervously. "You didn't

Jackie with Ray the Fed (Michael Keaton)—who'd like to think he can trust her

tell me you were going shopping," he says, as he appears in the doorway behind her. "I thought I did," she answers weakly, without turning
around.

He comes into the room, in his customary jeans, whipping off his
denim outer shirt and planting himself in a chair with the table between them, his ID tag dangling outside his T-shirt. Keaton is the
movie's sole mannerist performer. Take the elaborate gestural way he
inflects his first sarcastic speech to her. "Y' know," he begins, mock-
wondering, staring at her, "if it was *me*"—lifting his arms and spreading his hands above his head—"and I got all this shit hangin' over *my*
head"—fingers pointing down to his head—"like you got hangin' over
yours"—hands down again—"*I* don't know . . ."—cupping his jaw in
his hand, offering a wide-eyed gaze across the table, as if speculating
again—"I'd go shopping *later* . . ."

And the rest of his questioning is even more animated: rising and strutting, leaning against the wall, pushing himself off, tugging at his crotch, jumping and perching on his chair back, returning to the wall, then to the chair back again, then sitting and planting his forearms squarely, challengingly, on the table in front of her, and so on—all as a way of acting out, however inadequately, the sheer unbelievability of what she has been telling him. Which reminds us, too, that he'd thought he could trust her. "I hope you haven't done anything foolish, Jackie," he says finally—meaning it. He also hopes, as she does, that they find Ordell, who is still on the loose, before Ordell finds her. (They do, finally.)

Keaton goes near the limit and yet never seems a show-off or phony. His baroque playing in this scene seems as natural and spontaneous as the surge of clarity (and disappointment) with which he fills that exam room, confronting Jackie's deceptions. Ray is not preening or even particularly self-conscious—he's absorbed. And even having fun in his way. As Max says about him when Jackie asks what he's like: "he's a young man who enjoys being a cop." And Tarantino—with his love of actors on the screen—makes sure that we enjoy it, too. Ray is "playing" the cop—as cops, like other authority figures, will tend to do. But where his colleague Dargus, with his sneering complacency, is playing the role dully, lazily, and stereotypically, Ray is playing the excitement, and even (as in that "dance" off the walls of the exam room) the poetry. You feel let down when his scenes end.

But he doesn't get the close-ups—for the most part anyway—in spite of his appeal and the empathy the movie shows for him. (Nor do the less appealing figures of Ordell and Melanie and Louis.) Those go to the movie's two leads predominantly, as you'd expect. And Tarantino, in full and ecstatic hangout mode, has a lot more of them to show us.

Notably that first meeting between Jackie and Max. She's been in jail and Ordell has hired Max to bail her out. Max—part of his service—goes to the jailhouse that night to pick her up upon release. He's never seen her before. "Max, here she comes," says the policewoman in the guardhouse. And Max gets up from his bench under a streetlamp where he's been waiting and reading a paperback, turns, and stands facing the prison gates. As the camera, looking past and over his shoulder, refocuses through the gate's bars to show Jackie in the distance, in darkened outline. She is just turning in at the far end of the empty courtyard alongside the jail. Then coming toward us, down the long broad walkway, passing in and out of pools of light thrown from the jailhouse windows, her heels in the silence softly clip-clopping on the pavement as she approaches. And then suddenly the enraptured beat of a soul song (Bloodstone's "Natural High") kicks in on the soundtrack—as she comes slowly forward, in a collapsed, hip-sprung, almost spraddle-legged walk, one carryall bag over her shoulder, another trailing in her hand, like a Valkyrie dragging her shield after a hard night on the battlements. This is not the head-on, clear-sighted view of her that we had in the movie's earlier scenes, at the airport or police station. It's the apparitional Jackie—alone with herself, and far from us, in those shadows. And somehow, with that slow staggered walk toward us, even more impressive than before. "Why do I feel this way?" cries the singer on the soundtrack—and then, on a high-pitched yowl: "—and I don't even *know* you!"

And then there's Max. It's this scene with the two of them that most people remember from the movie more than any other. And they usually remember it as mostly showing *her* (as even Tarantino seems to do in interviews), when in fact we see Jackie here less than we do *Max* seeing her, in the classic shot-countershot edit. We see him in a slowly tightening close-up that moves (almost imperceptibly) up to and in on his face, as she in turn comes in her long shot nearer and nearer. And as she does, and as his close-up gets closer, you see the shrewd skepti-cal eyes fill with wonder, the brimming look that begins in them take over the whole face. And so Max's face becomes heroic: the lines and creases like marks of muscular solidity, the cords in the neck like col-umns of force rising into the straight firm jawline, the strong square chin—as she comes closer (offscreen now) and as his bedazzlement grows . . . *Here she comes, Max* is right.

And then here she is. Coming through the gate, slumped and dispirited-looking, her copper-colored hair loose and undone falling over her shoulders, the uniform she was arrested in rumpled, her white shirtwaist falling out below the buttons. She looks at him—she is *not* in a good mood. "I'm your bail bondsman," he says, and shows her his card. She takes it and looks at it, still without speaking. She gives it back to him. He offers to give her a lift. "Thanks," she says—without affect. And they get into his car.

Here she comes, Max (Robert Forster as Max)

And now we see her closely again—mainly from his point of view at the wheel beside her. She is cross, worn-down, disheveled—and so fiercely beautiful that you—like him—can scarcely believe it. Her close-ups here are as unsparing in respect to wear and tear as his have been, showing the lines around her mouth, the shadows under her eyes, the pores of weathered skin. And again it's the self-possession, the eagle-sharp eyes (different from his soft canine ones), the regal curve of the cheekbones that fix your attention. And her sullenness here, unhappily for Max, only enhances her glamour: outside it, he looks canceled.

Until she riles him a little by asking to see his ID before they start. "You serious?" he says—since he's just shown her his card at the gate. She looks at him without speaking—seriously (she never knows who Ordell might send her). So he shows her—lighting up the photo ID fixed to his dashboard. "Who paid my bond?" she says softly, her eyes still on the dashboard—"Ordell?" "In cash," Max replies, without looking at her. She gives him a sardonic glance, then turns away, facing front again. He shifts the car into drive (the second close shot of his dashboard here) and off they go.

She looks for some cigarettes: close-up of his glove compartment—finds nothing there but his gun. He suggests stopping at a cop bar he knows to buy some. She suggests a 7-Eleven instead. "I thought you might like to have a drink," he says, eyes on the road. "I'd love to have a drink," she says, out of the side of her mouth, "but not there." She lowers her window (close shot: red-nailed finger on window button). "What about the Hilton near the airport?" "Is it dark?" "It's sort of a sports bar," he replies. "It doesn't *sound* dark," she says drawlingly, looking out her window. "Why does it have to be dark?" "'Cause it looks like I just got out of jail, that's why," she says, looking in his direction now but not quite at him. And she suggests a bar she knows that's near her place. And Max at the wheel smiles to himself (so do you). And in the next scene they are sitting across from each other in a booth, with drinks, bathed in red saloon light.

But she also steals his handgun. And he is sort of pissed when he has to come to her house for it the next morning. "I'm sorry, Max," she tells him then, "but I knew you'd have to say no if I asked you for it." So would he like some coffee? She has a lot to tell him about—how Ordell (as we've seen) had been there the night before, how she'd made a deal with him to hold him off, and to disguise the deal she will make with the cops to set him up—and to disguise from them in turn the one she will later make with Max himself, and so forth. But then as Tarantino says, you're not there for the plot.

She is barefoot when he arrives, unmade-up, wearing a white chenille robe (she just washed her hair, she says, it looks nice, he says), then standing and smoking and chatting in the kitchen doorway, holding her elbow propped in the other hand, cigarette aloft, until the coffee is ready. Does he like it black? Oh—it's *very* black, she says in warning (close shot of coffee, then of pouring into a mug). And she sits down across from him at her breakfast table, the two of them framed in a stationary medium shot. She wonders, how does *he* feel about getting older? Fine, he guesses—except for losing some hair. He bets that she hasn't changed that much. "My ass has," she says. "Bigger?" "Yeah." "Ain't nothin' wrong with that," he says with a grin. And so on. "I just feel like I'm always starting over," she says finally, and if she loses her job now, at her age, she'll have to start all over again with whatever she can get. "And that scares me more than Ordell."

Not only does the plot come from Elmore Leonard (who also coproduced the movie), so does much or even most of the dialogue. But the leisureliness of the movie—the "slowness" reviewers complained about at the time—is all Tarantino's. So is the insistent literalism—all

Together at Jackie's place

those close shots of objects, dashboards and window buttons and coffee mugs and ashtrays and so on, following the gazes of the characters, mostly. But to what point?

But then there's her—standing in the kitchen or in the sunlight through the living room curtains or bending at her knees to pick out a favorite old record to play for them (it's the Delfonics) or just sitting and leaning back against the breakfast nook wall, her head turned toward him as she talks in her quiet voice, a girlish contralto with very knowing, very grown-up inflections. "Ain't nothin' wrong with that," he'd said. Yeah, she'd said back, as in *yeah, sure*—and you know what she means: getting older and wider *still* sucks. It's like the nearly constant message of that Elvis-style curled-upper-lip smile of hers, one of her strongest enchantments, signaling that however reassured she may consent to be, she is still not fooled. Pam Grier is *ordinarily* likable. Which doesn't make her any less powerfully so. But it separates her from the icons.

When I first saw *Jackie Brown* two decades ago, this was the place—this sequence at the house—where I first felt unexpectedly moved. And what did it for me (as I recall) was the scene's uninflectedness, its simple uneventful attention to the two people—the absorption in them that gets reflected in the rest of the movie in the leisureliness, and even by those close-up details, where if they look at something, we do, too—whether it makes a point or not.

In the novel, almost everything seems more pointed—and finally more conventional. Jackie there, though still forty-four, is blond and white. She and Max sleep together, inevitably—and the whole experience is hot. Not here, though—where Tarantino seems to have toned everything down—less violence, less sex. Between Max and Jackie, none at all. Except for their kiss at the end, before she leaves him to take off to Spain. These are two people—much more than they are in the novel—who *know* about limits, even after they've pulled off a triumphant daydream sort of scam together. "Are you scared of me, Max?" she says. He smiles: "A little bit," he says, holding up two fingers close together. "Come over here," she says. And the kiss is long and tender. "I'll send you a postcard, partner," she says as she climbs back into her new car (the deceased Ordell's), and that sounds tender, too.

This accomplished and diverting movie has many rewards (even

"Are you scared of me, Max?"

including that plot), but nothing deeper and richer than the performances of these two together and apart. If "performances" are what they were, however: Tarantino seems to have believed that his two leads, with their long and varied experiences both on and off the screen, only had to show up in front of his camera to be great. So he said, anyway. "They don't have to do anything," he said—it's all "right there." In their presence on the screen.

But this minimalist approach to characterization (especially in the screenplays—Tarantino writes his movies, too) is what critic Daniel Mendelsohn, in a characteristically astute and mostly adversarial take on Tarantino's films (the first *Kill Bill* one had just come out), took particular exception to: "For Tarantino, the movie fan who knows everything about the actors he loves, it's unnecessary to write psychology or motivation into the movies."* The filmmaker is assuming, says Mendelsohn, that you, like him, can supply all that:

> In the *New Yorker* profile the director asserted that what fills in the blanks of his cartoonish characters, what provides the "backstory," is what the audiences already know, as movie audiences, of the actors themselves. "Robert Forster's face is backstory," Tarantino said . . .

* "It's Only a Movie," *The New York Review of Books*, December 18, 2003.

But what, Mendelsohn asks, if you don't know who Robert Forster *is* (as most audiences probably would not)?

As Mendelsohn surely knows—as Tarantino, too, must do, in spite of his characteristic bloviations to *The New Yorker*—is that not knowing about Robert Forster can hardly much impoverish your reaction to Max's face on the screen. But he seems to think that more written characterization, more and clearer "psychology or motivation," would enhance it—which I doubt. Faces in the movies, whether familiar to you or not, *are* backstory, among other things. And the enforced intimacy you have with them there subsumes almost everything else going on as well. Even motivation—if it's too much insisted upon—can feel like an intrusion, a distraction from the central thing.

10

Godard's Close-ups

FILM IS "RULED" by the close-up shot, said the mid-twentieth-century theoretician Bela Balazs—by the "language of the face" and its inevitable "spiritual dimension." So, too, Jean-Luc Godard, a bit later on: "To photograph the face," he said, "is to photograph the soul behind it." And his *Masculine Feminine* (1966) is the movie from his early New Wave career that seems most invested in such close-ups.

Like the memorable one it begins with—of a twenty-year-old Jean-Pierre Léaud (as a Godard stand-in named Paul), sitting in a café and writing a poem (it's about loneliness—what else?) and looking so young and vulnerably serious that it almost hurts to look at him. He reads each gnomic word or phrase aloud as he composes, writing as he talks, between pauses for thought and long gazes off. Willy Kurant's remarkable black-and-white photography (the kind that reminds you how unreal movie color can seem) with its crisp, gleaming, almost wintry sheen makes even the strands of Léaud's hair and the sleekness of his skin seem vivid. As he now reaches into his tweed jacket (traffic sounds offscreen throughout) for a cigarette, then flips it into his mouth, looks warily to his right, and lights it—a touch of bravado in the midst of isolation . . .

And Godard's Léaud on the screen here—it's immediately apparent—is something quite different from Tarantino's conventional movie close-ups of Forster and Grier, say. Those are the close-ups of two pros. Pros at being photographic subjects, that is. And being such a pro means that you no longer offer to the camera the sort of privacy that the intimacy of a close shot can threaten. (A consideration, as Gilberto Perez points out, that might have given Griffith pause before he shot the historic first close-ups of his beloved star Lillian Gish.) And the young Léaud in this film yields himself to the camera with an especially touching openness. Godard would rightly describe him as both "a very good actor" (he was the only real one in the cast) and "at the same time . . . a complete non-professional."

Enter the girl (a *real* non-professional)—Chantal Goya as Madeleine. And she seats herself at a table across the way from him and opens a glossy magazine, taking out a little pad to make notes. He asks her if she knows a friend of his and he talks about looking for a job. She says she will inquire about it for him at the magazine she lately worked at— and goes back to reading the one in her hands. He keeps talking, about having just been in the army and now working in a factory—and she keeps sort of listening, going back and forth to her magazine, then leaning on her elbow to look at him, touching and smoothing her long lustrous black hair, fussing absently at the bangs that cover her forehead (this is largely a movie about hair). She is not exactly discouraging— half interested, at least. And she is breathtakingly pretty.

So how's it going? she asks him a couple of scenes later. He has gotten the magazine job, and she is back to visit for some reason, and they are both outside the ladies' john area, where she is standing at a sink washing her hands in front of a mirror. He has been waiting for her to come out and stands nearby against the wall, hands crossed at his waist, looking quelled and miserable. As she runs the tap he comes forward and fills a drinking glass, returns to his wall and sips from the water, wiping his lower lip with his finger, regarding her turned-away head at the mirror gravely and steadily. Does she know, he wonders, what date it is today? And does she remember she had promised to go out with him tonight? No, no, I never said that, she replies, turning to look at him, smiling and tossing her head.

It's the first of two boy-girl question-and-answer scenes, a sort of set piece each time, with the boy coming on to the girl, exchanging the usual inquiries about feelings and sex and dating life, banal but urgent on his part, casual on hers. What's said is less interesting than their evasions in front of the camera, in alternating close-ups, with Paul at the

At work: Madeleine and Paul (Chantal Goya and Jean-Pierre Léaud)

wall and Madeleine at the mirror, where her principal defensive strategy becomes her slow endless by-fits-and-starts making up: rouging her lips in the mirror (three times), powdering her face with her compact (twice), most of all and throughout combing and touching and primping her hair—by way of deflecting the mostly somber attention from behind that he is directing at her. She repeats her denial that she promised him a date. He says that she is lying. Until she finally admits it: "That was a lie," she says, turning and lifting her face at him, with a smile that's like a showgirl's big entrance. But Madeleine's narcissism feels unaffected, as natural and spontaneous as her youthfulness. What you mainly register about her in this early sequence is how simply and flatly adorable she is.

When she can't think what to say next, confronted by his gravity, she seems to withdraw into herself, even when she seems to be listening closely—then to come back, startled into delight when one of his questions makes her laugh: asking her if she thinks his nose is too big or telling her he likes her breasts very much ("Listen, that's important").

But it's Paul's discomfort that we mostly look at here: as he looks at her with head tipped back against the wall, eyebrows twitching faintly; or as he gazes at her levelly, jaw muscles flexing; or stares at her laser-like as if he could will her to turn around and face him, then making a bad-boy face at her again when she turns away. He tries his cigarette flip again and just misses. Another face: bugging his eyes and thrusting out his chin to register his incredulity at her—at what he's just heard her say or at what she's just asked him. When he says (to her question) that yes, he would like to sleep with her, he is offscreen—but when he tells her (her question again) that he is hoping for "*tendresse*" from her, he's in full and melancholy possession of the frame. Would you be happy if I told you I might love you someday? she asks from off the screen. Of course, he says (but what does she *mean?*). And so the sequence ends—at what feels like an impasse.

The second such scene, much later on, is between another couple, Madeleine's roommate Catherine (Catherine-Isabelle Duport) and Paul's working-class buddy Robert (Michel Debord)—an even more problematic pair, the girl more discouraging and the boy more bluntly insistent. Here the pacing is brisker, the close-ups less extended, the thrust-and-parry sharper—and so the awkward pauses are fewer. But in both these interview scenes it's the girl who has and keeps the control—the best *he* can do is to rattle her a little. And both interviews, despite the differences, provoke in you the same sort of uneasiness—something like embarrassment, something like your own awkward pause. Although you've seen this clumsy courtship scene in countless movies before, this one makes you feel you never really have. Once again, as if you're intruding on a privacy.

And to a degree you are. "I ask the actors to be themselves in structures that are not their own," as Godard summed up his general method. "I don't direct them much," he also said; "I leave them rather in the dark." And in scenes like these, even if you don't consciously register it, you feel not only the characters' unease but the inexperienced actors'. "Every film is a documentary of the actors," he said. And here he allows his performers to show us both the documentary and the fiction at once, both the personal coping and the alien "structure"—and as a result both intensifies and complicates the intimacy of the close-up itself.

Because of course he's not doing narrative realism, here or

elsewhere—he's riffing on it. Inviting you to follow the mixtures of tones, styles, and perspectives. These characters even look at the camera occasionally—Catherine and especially Paul—to share some joke or some insight with us. And even a single sequence may pass through quite different "realities." Like the movie house episode, in which Paul and the three girls he's with watch and respond, each in their separate close-ups, to the serious erotic movie that we see them seeing. Whereas the film that *we* see is a joke parody of Ingmar Bergman (*The Silence*, presumably) with two Swedish players (Godard's film was a Swedish coproduction, as was Bresson's *Balthazar* the same year) grunting and rutting in a laborious softcore simulation while Paul offscreen in a voice-over speaks of seeing still a third sort of movie: one in which "Marilyn Monroe had aged terribly . . . it made us sad." The discontinuities—like unfolding perspectives on the same event—feel less surprising by this time than enlivening. Cubism at the movies.

And absurdism, too. And Brechtian alienation effects. Like the ricochet of rifle fire that accompanies the number and beginning of each episode ("Fifteen Precise Facts" in all)—paralleling the random acts of public violence that everyone in the movie seems to take for granted as they happen. A woman with a gun rushes from the café to shoot her husband outside, and Paul calls out for her to shut the door (it's cold out there). A man in the arcade threatens Paul with a knife, then instead stabs himself in the breast—and Paul (one of the movie's nicest details) catches him in his arms as he falls. "Let this poor Christ pass," says the man with a gasoline can as he passes before Paul and Catherine standing together in front of a concrete wall. The man returns then to ask Paul for a light and then walks off with the matches. "My box of matches!" cries Paul. Offscreen, as we learn, the man sets himself on fire, as Paul and Catherine each runs offscreen and then reports back again to the other, first that the man is on fire, and then that he has died, leaving a "Peace in Vietnam" sign behind (in front of "the American hospital"). And Paul's reaction to this is less distress or horror than irritation. "Oh, the bastard!" he exclaims—twice. Understandably, however: first the man takes his matches—then, even worse, becomes a *real* sort of "poor Christ." "Oh, the bastard" is right.

Elsewhere it's like a Chekhov play, with five principals. Paul is in love with Madeleine, a rising pop star (two hit records), who is mostly in love with herself. But then with him, too, after a while. Though she

At the arcade: a guy with a knife

also appears to have had a thing going (or is it?) with her more so-
phisticated roommate Elisabeth (Marlène Jobert)—who clearly has
a thing for her still, and is more than a little grouchy about Paul. Especially after he's lost his rented room and moves into their apartment
with them—and with their other roommate, Catherine. Who turns
out to be in love with Paul. When it is really his buddy Robert, a factory worker and political activist, who's in love with her. Unavailingly,
it seems.

But this story is told obliquely, in fragments and scattered clues,
becoming something like a narrative subtext to the absurdist-style essay film that proceeds by fits and starts on top of it. And yet this sub-
ordination of the story really seems to enlarge it, bringing it closer to
your sense of lived experience—as that important thing that happens
to you mostly in the midst of distractions. And though *Masculine
Feminine* offers to be sort of comic in the usual Godardian ways, it is
mostly without the hectoring facetiousness he sometimes indulges. It's
playful, but it's grounded in the gravity of those close-ups—and in
Léaud's Paul, the filmmaker's onscreen surrogate. Who is "a kind of
Werther," Godard told *Le Monde*, "in the midst of the Rolling Stones."

He wanted to study contemporary youth, he had also said, those whom one of his intertitles calls "the children of Marx and Coca-Cola"—the generation just after his own (at thirty-six he was almost twice the age of his young cast members). But then later he would say it was less an essay film, or a sociological one, than "a piece of music"—call it "a concerto on youth." He wasn't kidding—the movie does have a kind of musical afflatus to it. More than any movie I know it captures that special liberated feeling of being young and at home in the freedom of a great modern city—making your world with your friends in the privacy of public places. And in semipublic acts of defiance—like showing your buddy at the café how to cop a feel from a stranger by reaching for her table salt; or calling "U.S. Go Home!" at a strolling U.S. Army officer with a cute young girl on his arm, or chatting up his uniformed chauffeur ("Things are going good in Vietnam, right?") while your buddy paints a peace slogan on his limo, or phoning to commandeer a French Army car for a joke with the girls—and then having it actually arrive! Or improvising a love poem out loud ("The stars are falling, Madeleine, and here we are in the city") in an arcade recording booth—or finding just the right table at a café (away from two old farts reading aloud to each other from a porno novel) to propose to your girl at, and then ending up in the doorway together, and she's in a hurry. Or you and your friend putting up posters for the Left "all over Paris" and then running in long shot and jumping over benches with the girls laughing and chasing after. (As with the kids in the Leone film, there are no parents or families around.)

Not that these two guys aren't depressed. How could they not be? Robert is sleeping in his car—and being turned down by Catherine. But they know how to make comic capital out of that, too. A pair of grave clowns—joking unsmilingly about turns of language (the meaning of "putting yourself in his place") or daily routines ("I decided to say I'm terrible until ten o'clock." "It's five after ten." "Okay, I'm fine."). About brassiere ads and Bob Dylan and Mitterrand and James Bond—and about a Pinteresque encounter with ominous strangers that Paul describes to Robert at the Laundromat. And as they sit together before the drying clothes, Paul tells him a Camille joke (her cough as a sex aid) that makes them both laugh. But then— "I wonder why I'm enjoying myself so much," says Paul, "because actually I feel strangely sad." "Because of Madeleine?" asks Robert. Of course.

She is a yé-yé singer who despises Mozart (unless she is being interviewed about her music tastes). She is also a shopper: we even glimpse her in the act in a department store montage (when we see Paul in a big store, he is stealing a book). She and her friends are carriers of the American plague and its culture of consumption. Even her diaphragm, as Catherine tells Paul, is "a thing that comes from America." ("A guy from Air France brought some for Elisabeth.") "You're in the Pepsi generation, aren't you?" says the interviewer who's been waiting for Madeleine outside her recording studio (a shot rings out—no one reacts). He has seen the phrase, he says, on "enormous American billboards." "Oh, yes," she replies, laughing. "I *adore* Pepsi-Cola!"

But by the middle of the movie Paul has become an interviewer himself (better money, he says) for a French government opinion poll. And in the longest single take in the movie (six minutes), the ninth "Precise Fact" or chapter (entitled "Dialogue with a Consumer Product"), Paul, offscreen throughout, interrogates the newest lucky winner of the "Miss Nineteen" title, bestowed by a magazine of the same name. This is all real—the magazine, the contest—and the young woman is not acting, you can tell as soon as you see her: she is Elsa, a doll-like blonde with a stunned look and a fixed half smile, posed in a medium close shot against a window, one hip leaning against the sill. She has long straight hair curling up at the ends. She wears a sweater and skirt, both hands in the pockets, and is half turned toward her unseen questioner, Paul, who establishes first off that she is "a friend of Madeleine's" ("Yes, I know her well"). So the questions begin—to which she responds, sitting-duck-like (she would be very angry about all this later), with unflagging vacuity and a growing unease. Questions about her baccalaureate degree, and how did she get her magazine title (luck), does she fall in love often (no), does she think that socialism has a future (duh), can she say what socialism is (no), and so on. Does she prefer "the American way of life"? And what is that to her? But in fact she's lucky enough to have been to America. And what was it like? Oh, terrific—"everything is different from France . . . they work very hard, but everything is very fast, you have the impression of—of running nonstop, of being very important, of having lots of things to do . . ." And what about birth control—what different methods can she name? Now she's embarrassed—she doesn't care to answer. Oh, but she has to—this is a survey, and everybody is answering these questions. So of course she relents and continues. Until he asks her if there is a war going on anywhere now, and can she tell him where? No, still smiling. No? She could but she won't. But then she really doesn't know—as she finally says, laughing. And cut to black—as a pinball machine bell rings out on the soundtrack, a punctuating sound we hear almost as often as those rifle shots.

In the Laundromat sequence earlier on, Robert observes to Paul that in the word *masculine* there are actually two other words as well, *mask* and *ass*. And in the word *feminine*? asks Paul, with eyes cast down, and in extreme close-up—and waits for the answer. "There's nothing," replies Robert, offscreen. And Paul looks up and straight into the camera—at us, unmistakably—with a face both startled and stricken.

At the Laundromat: Paul and Robert (Michel Debord)

One of the problems he had when making the film, Godard told the novelist and journalist Marcel Vianey at the time, was his feeling about the girls. "They're very good," he hastened to add, "they're perfect, and yet they don't really interest me." But they certainly interest us—if we are with the film at all. Have they escaped in that way some part of the filmmaker himself? That can-it-be-true? look into the camera that Paul gives us seems partly a joke—Paul's joke as well as Godard's. But it is also partly—for this film is about the gulf between the sexes—a genuine question. To which Miss Nineteen might seem to provide one sort of answer. But if she displays a familiar sort of banality, those other girls display an equally familiar ambiguity. Which in this film is no joke at all.

"We are not the girls for you," says Elisabeth to Paul, "we'll only make you unhappy." But why "we"?—when it's only Madeleine he cares about? But he doesn't really object to Elisabeth's formulation of his dilemma. It's not just that Elisabeth may or may not be having or have had a fling with Madeleine: it's just that she is so implacably *there*— with Catherine tagging along. There is an eloquent but silent early shot—under Paul's voice-over—that shows him first meeting Elisabeth on the street, both faces in profile showing instant mistrust, with Catherine in the near background between them looking gravely on.

They are after all "girl friends," with their own understandings and feelings and lines of alliance, and therefore an ill-boding presence to an uncertain young man in love with one of them. Even when he moves into their crowded flat with them, and when he has come to bed for the night with Madeleine, joking with her about body part names while groping her under the covers, Elisabeth is on the other side of them both, reading a book, to be sure, but still there. No matter that Madeleine otherwise regularly makes love with him, lets him touch her breast in public (the three of them are in a restaurant together), has even become pregnant by him (Elisabeth doesn't believe this when Paul tells her—but Paul's Madeleine has secrets even from her), she still belongs in some irremediable part of herself to that closed world of young women where Paul remains at best a baffled visitor.

Madeleine's record is climbing in the charts (number six in Japan), while Paul listens to Mozart. He has a vinyl record of the Clarinet Concerto, which he plays one night after supper for a seemingly appreciative Catherine. "If you're going to listen to that barbaric music,

I'm leaving you," says Madeleine—and does so. As the music fills the room, Catherine sits with chin in hand by the record player, and Paul paces and hums, still carrying his dinner plate, "conducting" with his fork, waving it in the air to signal an approaching special beauty in the orchestra: "It's coming, it's coming!" And then subsiding when it arrives—with "*Fantastic!*" But soon he is distracted by another sound (laughter and talking) and sight (nakedness behind frosted glass) of Madeleine and Elisabeth in the shower together.

When Madeleine, coming from a recording session, finally arrives at the restaurant where they are waiting for her, she gives Elisabeth and Paul each a copy of the latest Sylvie Vartan record (autographed). Paul—sitting across from Madeleine and next to Elisabeth, saying "I prefer Bach, the Concerto in D"—puts the record gift aside and begins to whistle the Bach, closing his eyes and keeping time with his forefinger. While he is thus absorbed, Elisabeth, leaning forward on her elbow into her hand covering her mouth, reaches with the other hand to Madeleine's face across the table and in time to Paul's "music" traces its outline in the air, as Madeleine smiles and leans into it like a sculptor's model into a mold. Until Paul stops whistling and looks up again and they all sit back again, exchanging a round of quick glances: Elisabeth's is sly and knowing, Madeleine's innocent, and Paul's is what-just-happened? He looks at Elisabeth, who looks at Madeleine, who looks at Paul, who looks back at her. And then all around again. Then they resume—in silence—their eating.

Elegant and witty, it's the closest to a laugh-out-loud scene in the whole movie. The joke, of course, is on Paul, and it has a kind of brilliance that makes him (for the first time almost) look plodding. And for us it somewhat complicates Madeleine, uniting her with Elisabeth in a deeper kind of mischief than we've seen in her before.

Elisabeth is the chic one, of course—with her dry manner, her freckles obscured by makeup, her stylishly cropped helmet of blond hair. The most authoritative of the girls and the most sexually knowing. At the erotic film, where the others in close-up look either disturbed (Madeleine, touching her hair) or turned on (Catherine, touching her lips), Elisabeth, who has put on her glasses to watch it, looks unimpressed. And in the restaurant scene, she even tells (or reminds) Paul about the man who took Madeleine and her to the country last weekend and who wants to bring his wife along the next time. Whatever

At the restaurant: Elisabeth (Marlène Jobert) at center,
with Madeleine and Paul

that's about, it cannot be comforting to Paul, nor is it meant to be. "I'm interested in Madeleine," says Paul to Catherine earlier on, "but all the same it's a shame." "You said that, I didn't," replies Catherine.

Where Madeleine is playful and teasing, Catherine is direct and no-nonsense—even in her yearning after Paul. And she is open to both the young men, even if she gives Robert a hard time—open to their seriousness, that is, to Robert's political radicalism, to Paul's intellectualism, as the other girls are not. Her occasional ability to look into the camera at us (Madeleine is too "nice" to do that—Elisabeth couldn't be bothered) is one sign of this. So is her bared forehead (she's the only one of the girls without thick bangs). But her vaunted openness—her outspokenness and "sincerity"—Paul tells her, is really what she hides behind—and you think he's right. She is finally the most enigmatic of the three.

As Madeleine is the most mysterious. In spite of her Miss Nineteen side—which hardly affects her considerable charm and even makes her in some ways more seriously touching. And Paul's relation to this "consumer product" side of her, though generally both mocking and disapproving, is more ambivalent than it first appears (he, too, after all, is partly a "child" of Coca-Cola*). In the movie's penultimate "Precise Fact" (number fourteen) he visits her recording session—Catherine, with her percipient gaze, going along, of course. After a bit, Paul beckons to Madeleine from behind the window of the control booth, where her voice is being mixed with the prerecorded band. He goes into the live recording space, where she stands before a hanging mike, looking alone and vulnerable, wearing the big earphones, and singing, as it seems, to herself. The purity of her unaccompanied sound, without orchestral support or backup, is poignant, her tiny piping voice bleating away in the reverberant silence. It reminds you of an earlier vision of her in the movie, in bed with Paul and nestled in his arms (Elisabeth just offscreen, of course), her face turned into her close-up and framed in darkness, as she recites—in another fracturing of the realist surface—some poetic lines about the solitude at the heart of love ("And here we are against death . . ."). Even she, it seems, knows something about the darkness.

Our last direct encounter with Paul is back at the café table we first saw him at and in the same close-up framing, smoking and pondering, as we hear him in a voice-over to random scenes of busy Paris life (ending with a nighttime boulevard in the rain), where he reflects on his interviews, coming to the conclusion that the questions and the answers are not only unimportant but misleading—that what is important is not asking but seeing, being open to the world and watching, concluding that real "wisdom would be if one could see life, really see."

And the movie's final sequence, as I take it, is offered as an instance of that conclusion—however tentatively. It consists of two sustained

---

* Godard himself was a big admirer of the Rolling Stones.

close-ups. And the second of these, for me at least, is the film's single most powerful event.

But first Catherine, in her turned-up vinyl coat collar, sitting in front of a white wall, looking around, her face slightly turned toward the sound of an offscreen typewriter—and toward a question: "So what happened?" says a man's voice. It's a police station interview, as you quickly suppose. And Catherine gives her answer: Paul got an unexpected inheritance and used the money to buy an apartment for himself and Madeleine in a high-rise still under construction. They were visiting it together and they had a quarrel—Madeleine wanted Elisabeth to live with them and Paul was against it. He also wanted to take some pictures, Catherine says—"and then he slowly stepped back too far and he fell . . ." She pauses, looks off to her left and then back at the policeman. She cannot believe it was a suicide: "It's not possible." She looks down. "It was really a stupid accident . . ."

"Next," says the cop. A glimpse of his back at the typewriter—over the offscreen sound of a chair moving and scraping the floor. "Your turn," says Catherine's voice, and now Madeleine's face fills the screen, her throat covered by her striped scarf. She is looking demurely downward, waiting her turn, "You are Madeleine Zimmer?" And she looks up, yes, she says, smiling slightly, almost with satisfaction: she is there when her name is called and she is on time . . . It's her catnip smile. The typewriter taps again and she looks down again.

It's a jolt to have gone so suddenly from Catherine's perfectly clear opaqueness to Madeleine's drifting innerness—particularly under this dramatic new circumstance. It's the same close shot, more or less—but now it's closer, tighter, more intrusive, more assaultive even. But you know as soon as it begins—and if not by then, by the time of that slight smile—that she will weather it, even triumph over it if she has to. It's not a documentary-style close-up (as Catherine's has just been) but a movie star one—with its subject retaining her privacy.

"What happened?" he begins. She looks in his direction, a sort of aggrieved look—like a good girl who feels unjustly reproached. "It happened like Catherine said," she replies (after all, what could she add?). "It happened like that . . ." Revolving her head, preoccupied, looking up and around, touching her hair.

The cop's next question (unmistakably in fact the filmmaker's) is this: "Your friend Mademoiselle Elisabeth Choquet said that you were

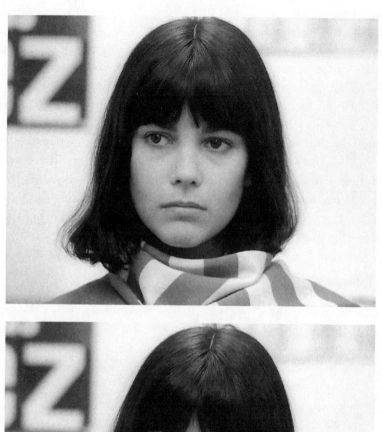

At the police station. Will she smile? She begins to . . .

pregnant. What are you going to do?" The words seem to reach her from far away at first. There is a fleeting little frown, more head turning. She really seems to be pondering now—but is it about his question? "Well, I don't know," she answers, fingering her hair as she speaks. "I don't know . . ."—looking up, then down. "I'm not sure . . . Elisabeth suggested using a curtain rod . . ." Another little frown. She looks at him, looks off, then touches her scarf, pulling at it a little, then returns her hand to her hair. She straightens, raises her head, pushes her chin forward, with the beginning of a little pout, then looks off again. You're watching ambiguity in motion, it seems—and it feels both terrible and moving. Someone in distress but at the same time out of touch with her own feeling. And then it feels chilling sort of. Not only the "curtain rod" image but the way she repeats "I'm not sure" (the movie's final spoken words). But is she really going to smile at him now—again? Yes, she is—you see her just beginning to just before the screen goes black, and the word *"Feminin"* in white letters turns into *"Fin."*

You have recognized her now. If only from other movies (Godard has not yet entirely revoked his ties to classic Hollywood). She is the noir heroine—Jane Greer in *Out of the Past*, Kim Novak in *Vertigo*, or Jean Seberg in *Breathless*, even Karina in *Pierrot le fou*, and so on. Who is fatally unknowable—even to herself.

PART THREE
TRANSCENDERS

11

Bergman and Rossellini

I.

"THAT CLOAK BECOMES you," says the Dauphin to Joan of Arc. "You look radiant." The dialogue in this movie was like that. Reminiscent of something more like Mel Brooks's Two-Thousand-Year-Old Man (telling interviewer Carl Reiner that yes, he knew Joan very well: "How did you feel when she was burned at the stake?" "Just *ter*-rible," Brooks replies). And the movie itself, *Joan of Arc* (1948)—one of the most expensive in Hollywood history up to then, coproduced by superstar Bergman herself and directed by *Gone With the Wind*'s Victor Fleming, an old lover and a tired one—was a disaster. Bergman plays the role with relentless close-up piety, a prim but distressed Joan, leading an army but not wanting to be obtrusive about it—a simple girl who "really wanted to stay at home and watch her sheep and do her spinning and weaving," as she later, she said, told George Bernard Shaw himself (he still wanted her to come again). She never wanted to do *his* Saint Joan—too talky and upstart for her.

Because Joan was the role of her heart and her lifetime, she felt. And she had just had a six-month-long sold-out triumph in it on the Broadway stage (a Joan play within a contemporary one, Maxwell Anderson's *Joan of Lorraine*), where her performance (the play itself was critically panned) was not so much reviewed as venerated. "The cleanliness of her spirit is truly next to godliness," wrote the *Saturday Review* critic (John Mason Brown); "she makes innocence exciting and virtue interesting."

No one would claim that about the movie—which was dead on the screen from beginning to its far-off end. And her performance, though less risible than some of those around her (a collection of overly familiar character actors past their heydays in studio times), was precisely, even definitively, *not* interesting. Only radiant. It showed the limits in interest that effect can have.

She had tried something very different in her previous film, the much ballyhooed *Arch of Triumph* (1948), with Charles Boyer again. She was Joan Madou, a character supposedly based in the novel by Erich Maria Remarque on the real-life Dietrich: a café singer ("I sing in Russian, gypsy songs") in prewar Paris who is both irresistible and faithless and whom Nazi fighter Boyer both loves and survives (when another lover does her in). The early scenes with Boyer are remarkable: when, having prevented her from a jump into the Seine, he's trying to evade her sexiness, and you watch her watching him do that—as she waits for the surrender. But the movie (also an independent production) was a major botch, muddled and incoherent. (She was waiting her time through it to do her Joan on Broadway next.) It was a major flop.

If she wasn't Dietrich, no one expected or wanted her to be, least of all her fans. But she also wasn't Joan, it now seemed, and *that* was more serious. Some fiscal discipline (big studio style) might have saved these two pictures from their most disastrous losses (*Joan* did better in Europe than here), but such discipline was collapsing along with the big studios themselves. She had been named the most popular actress in the world in 1946. But now, it seemed, in 1948, that "popularity" was no longer a guarantee of much of anything: it couldn't even get people to go to her movies. Partly that was the movies themselves, of course—partly that they were bad, partly that they were formulaic, at a time when audiences, so it was said, were getting fed up with the old movie formulas—one reason, presumably, that they had been going in such surprising numbers, in the big cities at least, to foreign-language films like Roberto Rossellini's *Open City* (1945) and then his *Paisan* (1946), two opening salvos in what came to be called "neorealism" in the movies: gritty documentary-like films about the kind of war-at-home experiences that were unknown to Americans—films that seemed as if they might even change Hollywood movies—a little.

But that change was a ways off. And in the meantime Bergman—famously—went to Italy. She made the arrangements in the middle of filming yet another independent production, Alfred Hitchcock's *Under Capricorn* (1949)—yet another screwup, as far as she was concerned (a miscast leading man, Hitchcock's experiments with reel-length takes, and so forth), and as it turned out, another flop at the box office. After which she went to Rome to meet and quickly (it seemed) to fall in love with Roberto Rossellini. Who almost as quickly (it seemed again) made her pregnant, touching off a worldwide scandal. But especially in America—where she had been admired as much for her private life, for the chasteness of her celebrity, as for her screen one. Now it was this same Ingrid Bergman, whose most popular film in America had been *The Bells of St. Mary's* (we didn't know then about Gary Cooper or Robert Capa or Victor Fleming or the others, but then neither did her husband, so he said—those were the days), who had not only betrayed her young doctor husband of twelve years, with whom she had been publicly, even convincingly "happy," but her ten-year-old daughter, Pia, left behind and bewildered in Beverly Hills. An irony of all this, of course, is that if Bergman had done the usual thing and quietly terminated the pregnancy (they certainly considered doing that), there would have been almost no problem for the rest of us. As it was, she and Rossellini subsequently married, after their respective divorces. The baby was a boy, Robertino, followed later by twin girls, Isabella and Isotta.

Perhaps even more scandalously, the movie was a bomb—beyond forgiveness, really. What could they have been thinking of? *Stromboli* (1950), as it was called (after the island it was filmed on), was far beyond some folie à deux—it was execrable. You had to wait for the French critics—André Bazin and his New Wave followers—to save its reputation. But French audiences didn't want to see it any more than Italian or American ones did. Not after the first showings. Whatever else it was for her, or turned out to be, it was an incredible act of courage. Was there any other instance of such a star, at the peak of her fame, in spite of its recent setbacks, so radically uprooting herself to take on a whole new kind of filmmaking? Almost as if Garbo had run off with Robert Flaherty to make *Man of Aran*. Like that famous film, this one, too, was filmed with great hardship on a remote, barren, and treeless island and cast from the local population. She was not only the only star in the movie, she was the only actor (except for the man who plays the priest)—among people who hadn't even seen a movie before, let alone been in one. She later described how Rossellini, behind the camera, would tie a string to the toes of the other "actors" and then yank it when they were supposed to say their lines. Which were in English (another complication)—as was the film.

There was no script, only a rough scenario. Rossellini's method by this time was to put his performers into the fictional situations and the real locations both at once ("structures not their own," as Godard would put it later) and then film the results. Spontaneity, he said, was everything, and he would dispense with the usual preliminaries, like rehearsals or written dialogue. He could not finally determine his actors' moves or lines, he claimed, until their interaction with the real began to happen.

Bergman here is Karin—a war refugee who will do almost anything to get out of the displaced persons camp the movie starts in. If her early attempt to secure a visa for Argentina fails—as it does—she is going to marry the peasant fisherman from Sicily who's asked her. Even without really knowing him, except for the flirtatious language-impaired exchanges she's had with him through the barbed wire that imprisons her in the camp. He's just a boy, she says—and he looks it next to her. But they marry, in a church ceremony, and go across the water to his Stromboli home under the live volcano that gives the island its name—and its occasional excitement. She spends the rest of the movie trying to get off it, with or without her new husband. The marriage deteriorates, she gets pregnant, escapes their marital house, and climbs to the top of the volcano in an attempt to reach the other side of the island, where there are boats to civilization. It's here, with Karin on the volcano, that the movie ends. With stunning abruptness. Especially for those few audiences that saw the film in its American version, which was even more confusing than Rossellini's original, thanks to the studio's cuts and re-edits (it had been produced and bankrolled by Howard Hughes's RKO).

And those "raging passions" promised us by the lurid RKO ads proved nowhere to be found in the movie itself. The original treatments (as in Hollywood, there were several credited scenarists), all of them finally abandoned, had come closer to offering such excitements. They had Karin—according to Tag Gallagher, Rossellini's invaluable American biographer—"exciting the lusts of the island men" in order to repay the wrongs that men in general had done to her. In a second version, she tries to escape with another man and is chased up the volcano by her husband, whom she then attempts to kill by starting a rock slide. Both these unfilmed versions ended the same improbable way—with her chastened return to the husband. As does the final RKO version—by having a narrator (lacking evidence for it on the screen) simply tell us the reconciliation takes place.

But one of the oddest things about the movie—in all its versions—and most off-putting to audiences at the time was its lack of melodrama. Bergman's heroine, far from being a femme fatale, is rather drearily prosaic. Instead of inciting "raging passions," she decides—having just finished the last of the wine and then having a lounge on top of her bed—to put up some curtains. She even finds some paints and decorates one of her new home's bare stone walls with a floral design, and also gets some of the local men (all of them elderly) who are at least willing to talk to her (the local women will not) to help her with moving and repainting some furniture.

Stromboli: Karin (Bergman) shows some island wives how she has painted the walls of her home. They are not impressed.

Her husband, Antonio (Mario Vitale), returning from his fishing, doesn't really like what she's done to the place but tries to pretend that he does. You can see her irritation at this—after all her efforts. But where are the framed family pictures? he asks. And what has she done with the Madonna? "All right," she says, "I didn't throw it away. I just moved it." Out of sight, however. And this impasse is almost what makes for a big scene in this movie—this clash of solipsisms. (We're a long way here from the excitements of *Open City* or of *Paisan*.) Though he is trying, you notice (he will soon give up), and she is not.

Karin is almost doggedly self-centered. But you can't blame her much. She is trapped—on a "ghost island," as she calls it, among a community that is, for all its courage and hardiness, ignorant and suspicious, and mostly hostile (the women at least) to her. And her young husband, much as he seems to dote on her, is finally one of them, irredeemably. As when he berates her for humiliating him before the other men. But what had she done? She had been seen at the house of the local seamstress (those curtains), the island's official "bad woman." And then later, when he hears "talk" about her and the handsome young lighthouse keeper—the other young man on the island (both imported to it for the film, both nonactors)—he comes home and beats her up. And when she tries to leave, he nails the doors and windows shut. As it goes on, the film invites us to feel as alienated from these people as Karin is. And yet when one of them says to her—Karin has asked, just after hanging her new curtains, why the women don't visit her—"You are not modest," you don't just register narrowness and bigotry in this reply (and you do register those) but a kind of truth—not a light one, either, in this movie's apparent scheme of things.

Here, for the first time in her screen career, Bergman is not very likable. You must try to understand your husband, the local priest tells her. But who understands *me*? she replies. As far as she is concerned, she did what she had to do—failing Argentina. And now she thinks of seducing this priest (Renzo Cesana—the only other actor in the nonpro cast), especially when she learns that he has charitable funds at his disposal, more than enough to get her and her boy husband free of this island. Karin is, as we know (and have already seen), a practiced seducer. And in the wonderful scene between her and the priest in his humble rectory home, the film invites us to savor both her skill and her falsity, both of them extreme—as she appeals to the frightened little cleric's spirituality while trying to get a purchase on his arm, or a little lean against his chest, as he dances away, and the camera circles them both. No use there. Tend to your husband, he says again—and they part in anger.

The only spontaneous happiness this husband and wife ever display to us happens and then ends badly when he brings home a little rabbit. She exclaims in delight and takes it on her shoulder. But he's also brought home—to his own delight—a caged ferret. Which Karin doesn't see until he snatches the rabbit from her arms and gives it, laughing, to the now uncaged ferret—who not so promptly kills it, while Karin cries out in horror. And we see the cruelty of the kill in close shot, even after *she* has stopped looking at it.

It's a forerunner of the movie's most famous sequence—a mini-documentary about communal tuna fishing, a great gathering of small open boats forming a huge circle on the sea's becalmed surface, the men all together lowering a communal net, then hauling up a thudding and leaping tumult of great dolphin-sized fish, spearing them one by one, hoisting them into the boats and clubbing them—an event that seems less like "fishing" than a mass slaughter, rising to a kind of hysteria of thrashing, dying movement. Followed by a priest onshore blessing the result. Karin, who had been on the scene for all of this, having come out in a boat now to watch her husband, the future father, at his job of work (an impulse not unlike her hanging those curtains), is appalled and sickened. And more certain than ever that she cannot have her baby on this island.

She has already made a strong impression on the handsome young lighthouse keeper—letting him hold on to her well after he's caught and kept her from slipping and falling into the water, while the village harpies in their black scarves watch the scene from the cliff side above—and she consents to take the money he offers her to make her getaway with, to the island's other side. And later, escaping once again—not from barbed wire this time but through the windows her husband has nailed shut on her—she climbs down and sets forth, with only a pocketbook and a small suitcase, to cross the volcano. No longer the Bergman we once knew, by the way—it doesn't require lighting now to bring out the cheekbones. Her wholesome cherubic look (in *Gaslight*, Cukor could get away—briefly—with using that same face in close-up to stand for her as a little girl) has been replaced by Nordic handsomeness, becoming gaunter, more Garbo-like.

So would you believe it that she goes up that volcano and finds God there? Well, almost nobody else at the time did, either. But that is what happens next, more or less. In the 1950 U.S. version we never got to see this outcome, thanks to RKO, but in Europe they did. (It would take an Italian, said a French reviewer—to hear the voice of God in a volcano.) Here's how it goes, anyway: Overcome by smoke and heat and fumes (as Bergman herself nearly was), Karin cries out for God's help, then falls asleep on the ashen ground, waking the next morning to calm and sun and open sky. Moved, she exclaims over "the mystery," and invoking her unborn child, she prays for understanding. Then, turning away from the village below that she's left, she goes on—or seems to, at least. The last thing we hear is her voice repeating God's name—the last thing we see, under her voice, is a flight of birds against the sky.

Okay—but it all seems to come out of nearly nowhere. There have been offhand references before in the film to religious faith (including Karin's bitter remark to the priest that God had never been merciful to her) but no clue that that's where we've been heading. At least until we get there.

It is, of course, about grace. And the arbitrariness of it is part of what Rossellini wants us to register—the seeming disconnection here from what we take to be narrative realism or even ordinary plausibility. It is, after all, intrinsic to the idea of grace that it often be "amazing" as in the hymn—finding out the undeserving, or even the uninterested. (The epigraph in the opening credits to Rossellini's version of his movie is from Saint Paul to the Romans: "I was found of them that sought me not; I was made manifest to these that asked not after me.") Rossellini had tried something like all this just the year before in his *The Miracle* (1947) with his then mistress, Anna Magnani. She, too, ascends a mountainside on foot, much more protractedly, and not to a crater but to a hilltop monastery. But being a kind of holy fool or mad saint from the start, unlike Bergman's heroine, she essentially ends where she begins.

Karin starts on her climb almost casually, almost as if beginning a stroll, but then goes steadily upward, in low-angle shots that evoke the

OPPOSITE PAGE: The long and awful climb

heights ahead. And once she begins to struggle, blinded in the heat and fumes, abandoning her purse and suitcase, the camera doesn't so much seem to follow her, as it's done up to now, as to go on ahead, taking in the view on its own, waiting for her to enter the shot, from the bottom of the frame usually—or from the side when a panning shot comes to a halt, as if anticipating her arrival, waiting for her to catch up.

Though she never really seems to: she is too busy struggling upward, getting her hold on a rock just above in a close shot, then in a reverse shot emerging from behind it, falling back to lean against it. Then nightfall and level ground, where she falls asleep, under a view of the stars (hers and ours both). And the next shot of her, fading in after this one, is arguably the most beautiful one in the film (which studiously avoids such effects otherwise), showing her from the side, still sleeping, her face and upper body in the close shot foreground, the curve of her breast rising and falling under the shabby print dress, her body's outline reflected and inverted in the bleak-looking hills against the horizon beyond, behind which the sun is now rising. It's like another version of that friendly rock—a grandiloquent one, with a true dawn-of-time feeling. And it's followed—appropriately—by the movie's miracle, such as it is: the sun on her face, her hand raised to shield it, then her exclamation of wonder (in a close-up), "What mystery . . . what beauty," she says softly. Before she stands up and talks to God, asking him for insight and for courage—as the movie ends.

II.

"I DON'T NEED stars," Rossellini had ungallantly observed to reporters after Bergman first arrived in Rome (adding that he had "nothing against Miss Bergman because she is a star"). But he certainly needed her, or someone like her, to pull off a sequence like this last one. *Stromboli* sometimes feels like a documentary of a mythic event, of a goddess cast adrift among mortals, with a goddess's kind of problems in that situation—most notably severe isolation. Much like Bergman's own, it would seem. Rossellini's offscreen world was not like Hollywood, nor was it much like what she'd known in Sweden. It was not only theater and film people but intellectuals, writers and philosophers and theologians (a Dominican priest had coached her for her volcano epiphany). For a woman who had always shown a notable incuriosity regarding the world outside her own career (even Selznick had noticed that—having had to explain to her in 1939 that honoring a previous commitment she'd made to do a movie in Nazi Germany would be the finish of her career everywhere else), the new life was difficult. Even the jokes passed her by—and it wasn't just a language problem, Giulietta Masina later claimed. Nobody in the Rossellini circle then seems to have thought she was very bright or very interesting. The kinder ones called her naïve. Fellini, Masina's husband, was struck by "Ingrid's innocence"—even at home with her difficult husband "she was just like she always was in films, a queen, serene and pacific and saintly." But they all thought her out of place. So, it seems, did her husband. And he makes that out-of-placeness the controlling reality of his three most important films with her, even in a way their subject, not only in *Stromboli* but also in *Europa '51* (1952) and *Journey to Italy* (1953).

For me the most poignant single image of that mutual project—the scene that almost singlehandedly "explains" it—is in *Europa '51*, where she plays Irene, a well-to-do wife who, having lost her only child in an ambiguous sort of accident near the film's beginning, comes over the course of it to renounce her life of privilege altogether. But here she is, not yet midway into the movie, helping out a new working-class friend (Masina) by subbing for her on an assembly line, going to work with the masses as the factory whistles blow, and first spotted from above, in one of Rossellini's great panning shots of diverging crowds going forward. She is among the crowds of women, taller than most of them, including the little group of three flanking her, chatting among themselves as they guide her along, past the great smokestacks and metal sidings, the silos and railroad tracks, and into the yawning great doors of the factory building. She looks bemused, a little spacey, uncomfortable—in her stylish black cloth coat. And what is that in the crook of her arm? A package? Has Ingrid Bergman brought her lunch?

Because it's her more than the character (who's become increasingly hard to believe in) that you respond to here—at first at least. She had been inspired by *Open City*, Bergman later said, because nobody in it had looked or sounded like actors. Now the people around her don't even look like extras (this was a time long before we all became camera-ready). And the most "natural" of movie stars has never looked more like a star. A star, however, who has been caught slightly off

Europa '51: the dinner party, with Alexander Knox

guard—as if surprised, as it were, into the real. A screen star generally appropriates her role rather than disappearing into it (as an ordinary actor might do), but here with Bergman, at this moment, as she moves along towering above these dowdy-looking little women who seem at once taking care of her and hardly noticing her, it's as if something is appropriating her—and the effect is curiously moving.

Quite opposite to the way we see her in the movie's opening scenes—where she is like a society-lady version of the pre-epiphany Karin: driving herself home with her pug dog at her shoulder, arriving at the apartment house and getting out and hurrying into the lobby, being told that the elevator's not working ("As usual"), taking the stairs and letting herself in, proceeding down her hallway and greeting the servants, handing off the dog and leash as she passes ("Take care of this, will you?"), pausing to approve the dining room table set now for company, sweeping into her bedroom, talking through the doors to her husband (Alexander Knox), instructing the household staff as she sits at her dressing table getting herself ready—and fending off the sulky discontents of her twelve-year-old son, Michel (Sandro Franchina), who is wanting more of her attention than she can give him at this moment . . .

Later, presiding at the head of her dinner table, she is tense, full of gritted-teeth brightness, fingers circling without touching the stem of her wineglass, as she attempts to head off a looming (as she sees it) dispute between an airhead woman friend and a male guest who is also a Communist. "Yvonne, dear," she says, as she takes the soup bowl offered by her serving maid, "I think we'd better change the subject . . . André is slightly radical . . ." tipping her head to one side as she raises the soup spoon to her lips. "Oh!" says Yvonne, sounding pleased, "—a socialist!" "Worse than that, I'm afraid," mutters Irene into her soup. Then rallying with a little joke. "You see what a good hostess I am, a real diplomat? I put the dove of peace on my left"—the ascetic-looking André—"and the Marshall Plan on my right"—a beefy big-toothed American—"and somewhere in the middle"—with a fluttering hand gesture over the table—"I put a neutral buffer state like Switzerland." Then adding, the tenseness surfacing again: "And look what happens . . ."

But nothing *has* happened, really. We've all been to this party, or to some downscale version of it. What's powerful here is the sense—conveyed by her (and her director)—that there is something deeply wrong about all of it, familiar as it is. The worked-up high spirits, the chirping and chattering and exclaiming over nothing (Michel's new train is a special excitement). But most disquieting of all is her apprehension—unfounded as it seems to be—that meaning may break out. "Worse than that, I'm afraid . . ."

It has to be a strain having to sustain, even to enforce, all this emptiness—and Bergman here makes you feel it. So that later, when Irene partly responds to her son's accident, and to her own suspicion that he had been trying to kill himself, by exclaiming to her husband that "we must change our way of living—we have to, we can't go on like this any longer!" you're neither surprised nor unconvinced.

Irene: "We must change our way of living—we have to . . . !"

Then, after seeming to recover, Michel dies. And Irene does change her life after that. As this strange movie enjoins us to do as well, in fact. If she is right, says one of her improbable doctors near the end of the film, then we are all wrong: "Then like the fishermen of Galilee we should put up our nets and follow her." Forget *that* . . . They lock her up instead.

And what do you do after you've found God at the end of *Stromboli*? Rossellini knew, of course, that quick ecstatic flight of birds in the concluding shot had only finessed the question. So for a while after that he seems to try to answer it. First by doing a film about Saint Francis without Bergman and with a cast of nonactor Franciscan monks, the aggressively faux-naïf *Flowers of St. Francis* (1950). But in their next one, he had promised his wife—the story goes—*she* would be Saint Francis. Hence *Europa '51*, or, as it was also called in some of its versions, *The Greatest Love*. In which she is Joan again—the saint before her judges at the end. But a Joan less designed to edify us, as the Hollywood one meant to do, or to ravish us, as the Dreyer Joan certainly does, than to make us uneasy, to encourage our own self-questioning.

After Michel's death, Irene had turned first to the Communist André (Ettore Giannini), who more than willingly turns to her, of course. But she is less interested in him and in the class struggle than she is in the whole tenement community he introduces her to, including the family whose young son needs an operation they are too poor to pay for ("I can give them what they need," she says, and then does). Walking in the devastated neighborhood—expanses of rubble amid free-standing tower blocks in the background (like a neorealist Monument Valley)—she comes upon some ragged children who are watching a corpse being fished from the river. She follows them home to the rubble-dwelling young woman who takes care of them (Giulietta Masina, with a manically inflected English-dubbed voice). She has six, it turns out, three of them her own "and three I just picked up," but no husband and no job. Irene gets her one of the latter (through André again) but then has to go to it herself (as I described above). Another turning point for her: the dehumanization she witnesses at the factory of both work and workers appalls her, making her more determined than ever to reject her old life. But not in André's way, not for his hypothetical "paradise on earth" in the Marxist future. The paradise that she dreams of, she tells him, "is not only for the living but for the departed." It's for Michel, too—"something eternal."

And she prays—alone in an empty church, emerging one night to encounter a prostitute she knows from the tenement, Ines (Teresa Pellati)—who has just been ganged up on by the other street whores, since she is both ill and disagreeable. People back in the tenement shun her, too, even though she is dying—which she keeps announcing to them. So Irene starts to care for her, nursing her through her sickness—just as she will soon take responsibility for one of the place's young hoodlums, at the behest of his anguished family. And when he escapes the cops once again, she is charged with aiding and abetting him and is arrested herself. Her influential husband gets her free of the police but only to turn her over to the psychiatrists, who put her in their hospital, where she becomes a kind of ministering angel to the most disturbed of the other inmates.

Her doctors don't know what to make of her—any more than the lawyers and priests and judges also called in on her case: it would be one thing and perfectly okay, they all agree, if she had wanted to join a convent, or even a radical political movement. But she wants to be among *them* . . . Better to leave her where she is—indefinitely, it seems. And the movie's last shot shows her behind a barred window watching her husband's chauffeured limo drive away and looking down at her friends from the tenement who have gathered in the hospital court-yard to weep and call out to her.

It's a parable, of course. You stop even trying to take it literally shortly after Irene's dinner party. But that doesn't help you much with the dialogue. The endlessly talkative screenplay—by many writers (the English version was by celebrated wit and playwright Donald Ogden Stewart, living abroad because of the U.S. blacklists)—is numbingly bromidic. Like a play of ideas without the ideas. If you must blame something for your son's death, "blame our postwar society," says André. "Truth has become so relative," observes the psychiatrist, the result, in his view, of "too much corruption, too much propaganda." Irene talks this way, too, once she's begun "searching for a different path, a more spiritual path," as she puts it. "We must love one another as ourselves . . . Only that will bring us close, close to one another, as equals . . ." And so on.

All this was even more disheartening to Rossellini's audience than *Stromboli* had been—never mind Bergman's. The movie hardly appeared at all in America (I saw it at a Chicago grindhouse double feature in the midfifties). And even if it had circulated here, the atrocious English dubbing alone—of everyone but Bergman and Knox—sounding like voices from the crypt, would have doomed it.

For by this time it was clear, in Europe at least, that neorealism, as its great progenitor now practiced it, and especially in the films with his wife, would have very little to do with persuasive or plausible narrative, or even with the "real" as most people understood it. And to those who recognized *Europa '51*'s borrowings from the life of Simone Weil (who also worked in a factory and who embraced a voluntary poverty), Rossellini's Irene seemed even more egregious—devoid of Weil's "depth of culture" (Alberto Moravia), or of "the strength of her thinking" (André Bazin). But where most reviewers saw only, or mostly, in-

Irene in the mental hospital, comforting the afflicted

eptness and pretension, the *Cahiers* critics (again to the rescue) saw "lines of grace," even a "profound originality."

That last was Bazin again, despite his reservation about the central character. And he saw the "originality" in Bergman's performance especially, its revelation of her "moving spiritual presence." Because, in his view, "Rossellini does not make his actors *act*—rather he compels them only to be a certain way before the camera." The young Jacques Rivette, writing in *Cahiers* and like the others there then (Rohmer, Chabrol, Truffaut, Godard) on the brink of his own filmmaking career, described Rossellini—for whom his admiration (like theirs) was nearly unbounded—as a "fantastically simple" artist.

And so, you might say, is Bergman—unlike a Garbo or a De Niro. Take the moment when Irene encounters the slum children at the riverbank and squats down to give the tiniest girl a glancing kiss: "Little one," she murmurs, and rises again. It's tender, movingly so— but not engulfing (Garbo "engulfs," of course—both kids and flowers), so reflexive, so unself-conscious that it feels nearly selfless. Just as when she first walks through the open wards of her new hospital-home: the parade of intensely glaring female faces drifting in and out of their close-ups one by one—the definitive Hollywood cliché for such scenes—as she passes slowly among them. Her calm, her refusal of the intentionality that we see in such a heightened state on those other faces, almost redeems the filmic cliché. Which Rossellini offers here and elsewhere (like the extreme close-ups emphasizing her grow-ing spirituality) as unapologetically as he does all those platitudes in the script. Which she also redeems a surprising lot of the time (better than she could do for the *Joan of Arc* ones).

On the other hand, she must navigate more than one scene of in-tense emotionality. Yet the effect as she does is curiously remote. Even when her son dies—or even more so in Irene's grief over the death of Ines the prostitute. We've seen the development of their relation, nurse and patient, over several brisk scenes: Irene ordering the sick woman's meal from the store downstairs, then feeding her the soup, talking with the doctor, attending with others from the tenement at Ines's last sacrament and her last breath—and then sobbing uncontrollably, at a depth and persistence that leave the others at the bedside (and in the audience) bemused—Where did this come from? And then, why won't it let up?

We are never inside Irene here—and nothing in the scene quite helps us to be. Her emotion remains inaccessible. But you may find yourself persuaded by it nonetheless, and for just that reason. It's as if Rossellini is asking you to find the truth of it outside his movie—in your own relation to compassionate feeling. If the scene is going to work at all, you will have to feel however dimly, say to yourself however tentatively, that you recognize that experience of impersonal love, of connection to the suffering stranger (cf. Saint Francis—or Prince Myshkin). Almost as if the suffering itself—of the prostitute, of the leper, of whomever—were enough to inspire love. And in a way, it is—as Irene recognizes. While none of us could wish to become the object of such love (knowing we could be at any time, of course), Irene feels the fulfillment, even the happiness, of being its subject ("It feels good to be good," as the *Avenue Q* song says)—like a great light filling her, as she describes it to the priest at her hospital (he doesn't approve). When you're bound to no one, she tells him, you're bound to everyone: "It's just that the love we feel for those closest to us, for those who should be and maybe are dearest to us, suddenly isn't enough. It seems too selfish, too narrow. So that we feel the need to share it, to make our love bigger until it embraces everyone."

You could perhaps be persuaded by this, by its simplification even, possibly even moved by it (Bergman helps)—if it doesn't creep you out, that is. But the bluntness of the writing and filmmaking more or less forestalls the latter response. You can take it or leave it, the movie says. Exactly what Bazin and the New Wavers so much admired about Rossellini's neorealism (in contrast to De Sica's—who made the heart-wringing *Umberto D* this same year): the freedom it gives you—the personal involvement it asks of you but never compels. The same freedom that left—and still leaves—most audiences mostly puzzled.

III.

JOURNEY TO ITALY (1953) was puzzling in another way as well. At least *Europa* had been about Big Issues, however ham-fistedly. But what was this one up to? Less like a morality play than a low-energy soap opera—the high-flown talk replaced by the drone of marital bickering. With its stars seeming less to be *in* a movie than wandering around in one (Bergman's male lead, George Sanders, nearly had a nervous breakdown before the shooting was over). And the scenario, such as it was, seemed casual even for Rossellini: a collection of incidents that seem to lose meaning, to feel more incidental, not less, as they accumulate (one of the things Eric Rohmer liked about it—praising it for letting his mind wander).

Katherine and Alex Joyce (Bergman and Sanders) are an unhappy married couple from England who are touring in and around Naples—mostly separately. She sees the sights (relentlessly), museums and ruins and churches. He flirts with infidelity, or with the idea of it at least. But whatever they do or don't do apart from each other, they always return to their unending marital argument. Until they decide finally on a divorce. But then in the final sequence, in the midst of a surging crowd watching a religious procession, with a fishy-looking "miracle" (the obligatory cripple) in the far background of that action, they suddenly decide that they love each other after all. That's it, more or less—except for a final shot of crowds in the procession passing in front of two blank-faced carabinieri and the brass playing loudly off-screen. As if the movie were finally conceding that what we'd been watching was no big deal—so here's something else . . . Or so it all seemed to the audiences when it was first shown—it was an even bigger bomb than *Europa '51* had been. And it probably didn't help his case at the time that Rossellini had boasted so much in interviews about relying on accidents, the aleatoric approach, in making his movie. He just sort of came upon that Sorrowful Mother procession, he claimed—all happening in real time, the only fabrication being the insertion of two world-famous stars into the middle of it.

He had been lucky, too, with the sequence just before it—a real archaeological dig, which turned up (who knew?) a real pair of what seem to be husband-and-wife skeletons, locked in a deathly embrace, profoundly affecting the husband and wife in the movie (and becoming its most famous single episode).

But it was just this risk taking, this filmmaking on the verge of pointlessness, that so excited the young critics at *Cahiers*. And a movie like this one, they felt, freed the movies themselves into spontaneity, delivered them from the constraints of narrative realism and into "the very language of modern art itself" (Jacques Rivette). Free from story-telling as a first concern, film was able to explore and uncover reality—even to wander around in it. No other film of their own time had had such an intoxicating effect for them. Rohmer compares its impact to the Paris premiere of *Rite of Spring*. Bazin and Rohmer invoke Matisse—whose art is also "linear and melodic" (Bazin) rather than literal and detailed. Godard blazons *Viaggio in Italia* across a movie marquee in *Contempt*, and he borrows unmistakably from its sequence (see below) of Bergman at the archaeological museum. And so on. Unstoppably, it almost seemed.

And the implicit Catholicism in these films—as *Cahiers* read them—only spurred the enthusiasm for them. Being a left-wing Catholic—as Bazin was and the earlier critics at *Esprit* had been—in Paris (as elsewhere) in those days was not only fashionable generally but in film circles almost cutting-edge, yet another way of affronting the Tradition of Quality, of the old establishment atheists like Carné and Prévert, if nothing else. And this was reflected in the journal's criticism, often passionately. "Rossellini's genius is possible only within Christianity," proclaimed Rivette in 1955, citing Rohmer before him. "Rossellini, however, is not merely Christian but Catholic, in other words carnal to the point of scandal . . .

> What is it he never tires of saying? That human beings are alone, and their solitude irreducible, that except by miracle or saintliness, our ignorance of others is complete; that only a life in God, in his love and his sacraments, only the communion of saints can enable us to meet, to know, to possess another being than ourselves alone; and that one can only know and possess oneself in God.

Not what I meant at all, Rossellini would later claim—disowning "belief" in general—though he encouraged such readings at the time.

But what about the movie itself? The first shock it gives you is the way Bergman is made to seem—all traces of the goddess banished. Neither as formidable as Karin nor as glamorous as the early Irene. As the Englishwoman Katherine here, she even has a little trouble eating the pasta she's been served, using her napkin to cover her mouth in front of her affable Italian hosts, while her husband at the other end of the table lifts his wineglass to the company, all confident urbanity himself. Or look at her back at their hotel, half-reclining on a couch in a bed jacket playing solitaire and listening for the sound of his car returning—the aggrieved and waiting wife. (Her marriage with Rossellini was deteriorating.)

Their marriage seems hopeless. He is brisk and impatient. She is sensitive and "literary." She still remembers (their last name is Joyce)—like Gretta Conroy in "The Dead"—the boy who loved her who died young, a poet whose work she still quotes to Alex. She hates her husband's "cynicism"—he hates her "ridiculous romanticism." She wants to see Naples, he wants to go home to England as soon as their business here is done. Italy only makes him more impatient, it seems. And especially Naples—or rather *her* in Naples. So he goes to Capri by himself, where he reencounters a misty-eyed young woman with her foot in a cast (Maria Mauban) who seems receptive to him but who turns out to be in love with her husband, now absent but returning soon (and he, too, she tells Alex, has a gift for stinging remarks). Back to Naples, but instead of back to Katherine (who is waiting in that bed jacket), he tries picking up a prostitute (Anna Proclemer), who seems nice but is badly depressed and who starts talking about death (of another whore) almost as soon as she gets into his car (adjusting his mirror to look at herself)—never mind, he says, and drives her to her home instead. Back to his wife then. More exchanged slights, more failed moves to redress them, then to hell with it and good night (in separate rooms). And call-me-in-the-morning-will-you? In fact she doesn't—she forgets. And so on.

But for all the time we will spend watching this sort of thing, there is, and remains to the end as we do, the feeling that there is still too much we don't know about this marriage (did they ever get along?), and too much we are told and simply don't believe (that she was the one who refused to have children, for example). And even if that boy poet story isn't borrowed, it still feels that way. But we do know and believe (do we ever)—and it's a central fact for them, too—that they are married. And that circumstance has a weight for them (and for their movie) that perhaps belongs to their pre-sixties time (and to the Rossellinis' own marriage). But their off-again-on-again divorce decision (sure, *do* it, you want to say) has an urgency in the movie that doesn't feel faked. They don't do it, finally, it seems. And that, it seems, works out. It's not the love that sustains a marriage, Dietrich Bonhoeffer once wrote (in a letter from his Nazi imprisonment), but the marriage that sustains the love. (It may also disguise it, you might add to this, given the movie.)

Anyway what his movie was really about, Rossellini would soon say, was Naples itself: "the sense of eternal life" that both he and ultimately his heroine get from the place ("something that has completely disappeared from the world"). And the characteristic impassivity of his filmmaking—its lack of inflection or flourish—becomes then a way of getting at that "eternal life," of conveying the same "sense" of it to us. It's his own counterintuitive way, you might say, of breaking free from what Oscar Wilde called "the prisonhouse of realism," with its apparent commitment to ordinary reality, to "poor, probable, uninteresting human life" ("The Decay of Lying"). Not by reimagining the prisonhouse, as Wilde would seem to commend, but by refusing to, as Rossellini does: "Things are there—especially in this film—why manipulate them?" The miraculous in this view—the improbable, even—is what is around us always. If we could attend to it. As Katherine and Alex finally seem to do.

But long before that and from the movie's beginning, there is a recurring interest in different kinds of attention. Katherine, for instance, when she is first at the windows of their hotel suite, as she opens the shutters in the morning to the view of the bay and beyond it. She has to wake her husband in a minute, and her look outside here has the air of a reality check: It's all there, right? sea and hills and so forth?—as she would expect it to be, after all. And soon afterward we see that same look outward—of proprietary incuriosity—on her face and her husband's both, as they tour his late uncle Homer's Italian villa. They have come to Naples to sell it, and the young married custodians of the place are now showing them around it—in a tracking shot as long and elaborate as one of Max Ophuls's (but without his lyricism). Upstairs and down the caretakers lead them, in and out of the various rooms, showing them windows and hallways and objects, taking them onto the terrace to show them the view and then back in again and on. The tour is extended and brisk, punctuated by murmurs of concurrence and appreciation as blank as the faces and voices of the two visitors behind them, bestowing a kind of executive inattention: let's-look-at-this-now-okay-let's-go-on. And you feel a sort of uneasy surprise: Has anyone ever shown this to you before—this familiar bustling vacancy—with the kind of purpose and intentionality that Rossellini does here? As if asking you to look at the absence.

And at the not-seeing. Katherine drives to the Archaeological Museum the next day—it closes at four. "And I don't want to miss anything," she says to him as she claims the use of the car. And then as she drives, she proceeds to miss everything—all that we see, that is, just as she would see it if she were looking, as she passes slowly and windingly along the crowded streets muttering to herself about him and what a shit he is, how cruel and self-important, how she hates him in fact—past the teeming variety on the streets that we look at in her place. The point isn't subtle (Rossellini doesn't do subtle): though she truly wants to see Italy (unlike her incurious husband), she is in danger of seeing things only personally, only through her own unhappiness. What Bazin calls her "impoverished subjectivity."

"This must be it," she says, pulling up at the museum. Inside, a scruffy elderly guide approaches her—in long shot—and offers his imperfect English for the tour, and they go together into the sculpture galleries. And then on the soundtrack—instead of the canzones some unseen far-off tenor has been singing off and on through the movie's action up to now—a full orchestra launches itself (a score by Renzo Rossellini), opening with an eerie hovering flute trill. And suddenly we are looking at a statue, in close-up, a looming bronze likeness of a lounging Roman youth, as Katherine and her guide walk by below it. This time she is looking—gravely, steadily—as they go from statue to statue. So are we: at succeeding close shots of the sculptures, mostly at their faces, as the gabby little guide hustles her along, his chatter overridden now by the drifting dreamy music, by the slow dreaming camera movements, panning and circling the heads and bodies. A discus thrower's blank white eyes "looking" at us, Katherine looking back, seeming disturbed, struck. Then on: a group of dancing women hand in hand, a Venus (past her first youth, as the guide points out) with a missing hand, an athlete leaning against a pillar, a band of men with a dog subduing a wild bull, and so on—and again and again her, gazing raptly, wonderingly . . . The scene fades out on the dog.

It's a piercingly beautiful sequence (in *Contempt*'s homage to it, the blank white eyes are painted an oceanic blue). And you feel with some relief that it must make a difference now to the nagging wound her marriage has become—if only because this museum tour has seemed—and looked—epiphanic for her. And because this is, still, after all, a movie.

But it's a movie that seems bent on reminding us of such realities as that you may have an epiphany before a work of art, but (one of life's discouraging rules) that doesn't necessarily mean that you'll have a good day after that, now or later. Or that your marriage will improve. But she *is* improved in the next scene—back at the hotel, having cocktails with her husband and talking eagerly about the sculptures to him—about how living they seemed, all these long-ago people—and she herself seems newly alive, even gay, as they go in to dinner together. After all, says Alex, suddenly brightening himself, maybe we can enjoy ourselves here. Yes, she replies—then adds: If only you wouldn't be so mean all the time. And the chill has set in again.

And remains—into a posh party they go to next, given by some of Uncle Homer's high-end friends (Rossellini's as well)—one of whom seems to apologize for the luxury they all live in: "We are all ship-

Journey to Italy: at the museum (her elderly guide to the right),
Katherine locks eyes with a statue (of a fallen discus thrower).

wrecked," she says, in this postwar society. And Katherine, who has
become the object of a flirtatious duke's attention, laughs a little too
much—as Alex looks grimly on at her. Did you have a good time? he
asks her as they leave. *No,* she replies wearily—as if to say: Are you
crazy? And they quarrel again, even more bitterly (some progress there).
That's when he goes to Capri. And to yet another swank party there—
where a beautiful and sibylline divorcée informs him that "you love her
and you're jealous." He could have fooled us. For the moment, however, he has his eye on the dish with her foot in a cast.

Back in Naples, Katherine is back at the wheel of the car, on her
determined way to another unmissable sight—the remains of a Cu-
maean fortress on a cliffside over the sea—with another tiresome old
man guide. "Where is the Temple of Apollo?" she calls out to him.
"Too windy," he calls back—and deserts her. And she puts her dark
glasses on and looks out at the sea—ambiguously.

But now at least she is looking with us at the street scenes along
the way on these drives of hers—especially noticing the pregnant
women who seem to her to be everywhere in Naples. The hostess from
the villa takes her to the catacombs, especially wanting her to see the
great mound of ancient martyrs' skulls inside the church (reaching almost halfway to its ceiling). And the young woman prays before them,

as she tells Katherine, to have a child of her own, as Katherine stands gravely by and looks on.

But the final (and climactic) such excursion is the one she takes with Alex—at the behest of the villa's young host, who insists on their coming with him to Pompeii, where important excavations of the buried city are going on near the foot of Vesuvius. Neither of them wants to go—they have just had another fight (he'd wanted the car when she took it to the catacombs) and have finally, firmly resolved on a divorce—but they yield to the friendly pressure and go. Which leads to the movie's first—if only sort-of—dramatic moment, when the men digging, surrounded by rings of onlookers (including them), suddenly unearth not a single human skeleton, but a pair of them, a man and a woman ("perhaps husband and wife") lying together at their moment of death. Katherine is undone by this, breaking into tears, and asks Alex to take her back to their car.

"Is this the way out?" she says, going ahead of him. Concerned for her, he takes her arm—and she is almost apologetic. "I haven't told you about my day," she says (those skulls). Then: "There are so many things I haven't told you," she adds. And he admits that he, too, was moved by what they've just seen.

But soon they are quarreling again, hurting each other, evoking old grievances—as they walk to their car, on the long way out . . . Through and around the empty ruins of the ancient palace, down makeshift stairways, through crumbled archways and around half-standing pillars, past what look like abandoned restorations to another narrow stairway, up that and onto an open square, all stonework and sky—and they walk across it in a slow panning long shot, the soundtrack music swelling plangently, hauntingly, as they fall silent and draw apart and walk on. The sad sensuous music seems almost mourning for them, but its muffled, rhythmic urgency sounds like something preparing itself, too, something else—as the space between them widens on the bleak expanse they are crossing, in a long shot going away, then a reverse long shot coming toward us. And in the emptiness, on their own, but fatally together, too, they seem more deeply connected in these shots than they might if they were arm in arm. They reach their car and drive off down the highway as the mournful-tender music theme resolves itself. And we are left behind as the scene ends in a fade to black.

But then they're back again in the next shot, in the front seat of the car in the middle of a traffic-clogging religious procession and a thronging crowd. What's going on? Alex demands—as they start to bicker again about the divorce: he seems set on it, she is not so sure now. In the middle of this mass of people taking no notice of them, their car stalls at another roadblock.

They get out and strain above the heads around them to see what's going on—whatever it is, it's far from where they are. But then we see it—a statue of the Virgin in her Mother of Sorrows mode, borne aloft on men's shoulders, dressed in gold-flecked black with a sword through her heart (the way she still is when they carry her twice a year through my Italian American Brooklyn neighborhood). "How can they believe that?" says Alex, disgustedly. "They're like a bunch of children."

But Katherine is moved by children. "Alex, I don't want you to hate me," she says. "I don't want to finish this way." So what, exactly, he wants to know, does she want? "Nothing!" she snaps at him, "I despise you"—just as a cry from all around them wells up and the crowd presses forward in a great wave of excitement, sweeping her into their midst and away from him. They panic and call out to each other. He struggles forward, pushing and shoving, until he reaches her again, while off in the distance (in long shot) we see, briefly and indistinctly, a man in a circle of applauding onlookers walking and brandishing something that could be a crutch above his head—the obligatory "miracle," it seems. A moment of general confusion—which the couple are both looking toward, straining to see, as the surge of the crowd seems to travel through them and they hold each other tightly. Alex speaks first: "Katherine, what's wrong with us?" he says. "Why do we torture one another?" "You try to hurt me and then I try to hurt you back," says Katherine, holding onto his lapels and pressing against his chest. "But I can't anymore because I love you." He loves her, too, he tells her. And they smile and laugh together and tighten their embrace, burying their faces in each other's shoulders as the camera lifts off over their heads showing them in the center of the crowd from above, in the movie's penultimate shot.

No wonder Sanders almost had a breakdown—to spend three whole months just past the peak of your own career under the control of this putative "genius" who kept his "script" in notes in his pockets and his dialogue a secret until just before they had to speak it and so on, and

With George Sanders, straining to see the "miracle"—or
whatever the excitement's about

to wind up in the end with this, a Hollywood ending (complete with
the fadeout cliché) even feebler and more arbitrary than even Hollywood would have dared . . . (Probably he was just glad to be ending.)

What Hollywood would never have permitted was the frank and
unmediated improbability. As in *Stromboli,* the idea of grace is invoked
(just the part in *Stromboli* that RKO cut out for its American release)—
but more ambiguously. And as in *Stromboli* again, Rossellini doesn't
try to sell it to you (even that camera liftoff at the end is cut short in
midflight)—least of all by palliating its lack of motivation in any way.
Something that still seems daring even now. You may not believe that
ending when it comes (I didn't at first—sometimes I still don't)—but if
you do, it can seem powerfully moving, touching something that goes
beyond even an Antonioni, even at his most resonant. *This* "happy
ending" is a truly serious one—one that proposes itself not for resolution or relief, but for ecstatic belief. An affirmation of human mystery
suggesting something still beyond that. And it's what the film, almost
without our noticing, has really been preparing us for all along.

Especially, of course, by the sequence before it at Pompeii. And
even there, it seems to me, it's less the exhumation-of-the-buried-
lovers moment that counts in that preparation (that *is* conventional
motivation) than that scene's aftermath—that long walk that Alex and

Katherine take through the ruins "to the car." Where the sense of a god's-eye overview (for us) is so strong. A way of looking at both of them that feels both benevolent and impersonal at once. An imagery on the screen that suggests that there might be a kind of love that releases them not only from themselves, from their separate enclosed unhappinesses, but even from each other.

Because there is another scene after the "miracle"—the movie-concluding shot I described briefly above. Less exalted than the flight of birds that ends *Stromboli*—but even more dazzling in its way, if you're at all ready for it. It's those anonymous-looking cops standing and watching all the anonymous people (their heads mostly just above the frame) pass by right to left in front of them while the procession's oompah band blares away on the soundtrack. So it is that the movie with all its claustrophobic fixation on the couple (no scene without one or the other or both) ends not with them at all, but with their displacement by an image of the impersonal crowd—a final rebuke to their solipsism, their "impoverished subjectivities," even a clue to their redemption. With a to-hell-with-it kick to it: so you thought this was about *stars*—just *look* at all these people . . .

Wasn't that what "neorealism" was all about? Looking at these anonymous ones? (Or at stars more or less reduced to them?) For Bazin, that way of looking, especially in Rossellini and De Sica films, felt like love. Why not? Cinema itself, he also said, depends more than any other art form does on "a love for living creatures." And in De Sica, says Gilberto Perez, this love is not "eros, the love of the desirable, but agape, the kind of love God bestows on his creatures." Not "because they are good or beautiful or admirable, but because they are."

IV.

AFTER THIS FILM (which she never liked), Bergman would have still another go at Joan, in her husband's theatrical staging of the Honegger-Claudel oratorio *Joan of Arc at the Stake*. They toured Europe with it, attracting more crowds than critical acclaim (the Swedes were especially nasty: "She travels around and is shown for money," wrote one). In 1954, Rossellini adapted his production into a film—which attracted neither acclaim nor audiences. After that came *Fear*

(1954), which they made in Germany, in both German and English versions (badly dubbed in both), based on a Stefan Zweig short story, with Bergman as an adulterous wife to a vengeful husband. It was no worse than their other movies, said the reviewer in *Oggi* (in fact, most people thought it was), but after so many misfires maybe they should think about giving up on their collaboration: "once the world's unquestioned number one star and successor to Greta Garbo, Miss Bergman in her latest picture has become only a shadow of herself."

They were destroying each other's careers, Bergman was coming to feel—especially as the marriage seemed to be falling apart, too. The final break, she later said, came not with her film in Paris for her friend Jean Renoir, *Elena et les hommes* (1956), nor with her Hollywood film in London for mogul Spyros Skouras, *Anastasia* (1956, Academy Award, Best Actress), but with her appearance onstage in the Paris premiere of *Tea and Sympathy*. Rossellini had agreed to direct the production, had even signed the contract. But then he read the play. It was trash, he said, and pulled out, predicting its failure. But it was a huge success, especially for her. And it more or less marked—as did her "comeback" movie, *Anastasia*—the level of aspiration of the rest of her career as once again a major Hollywood star—though now of course Garbo was rarely invoked. Though Bergman's "very real inner goodness" (reviewer Clive Barnes) still was, at least on Broadway (her 1967 appearance in O'Neill's *More Stately Mansions*, with Colleen Dewhurst).

Rossellini, too, went on, of course—not only to a film project in India (*India Matri Bhuri*, 1957) but to another scandal there (his affair with a beautiful Brahmin wife and mother) and another new family (his third). And his long later filmmaking career was in some ways even more unbending and ambitious than the earlier one had been. Like his heroine in *Journey*, he had been overwhelmed by the livingness of history. And for the next two decades he would embark on showing that experience to us, in a series of neutral-seeming, would-be-objective historical reenactments, some of them quite remarkable—*The Rise of Louis XIV* (1966) and *Blaise Pascal* (1971) for two—others distended and inert, especially as their number increased. Climaxing (predictably) with a life of Jesus, *The Messiah* (1975)—made, he told the Pope (Paul VI), by a nonbeliever for other nonbelievers. It was about Christ's teachings, he said, and omitted the Passion. Indeed,

Rossellini's own passion seemed missing by then, worn down by money problems and critics' indifference and missing audiences. It was his last completed film.

But at least he hadn't done her career in after all. And the extraordinary films they made together (thanks to her courage as much as his), halting and unachieved even as they sometimes are, still seem— more than ever—like noble ones. Bergman of course had made wonderful movies before Rossellini (*Notorious*, *Casablanca*, and others), but it was only with him in the end—so it seems to me—that she made some nearly great ones.

12

Dreyer's Heroines

I.

THERE IS SOMETHING religious about the movie experience. Something that's been felt about it almost since movies themselves began—in front of their earliest awestruck watchers. And by now, as Phillip Lopate observes (in *Totally, Tenderly, Tragically*),

> It is, I suppose, a truism that the cinema is the secular temple of modern life. A movie house is like a chapel, where one is alone with one's soul. Film intrinsically avows an afterlife by creating immortals, stars. In its fixing of transient moments with permanence, it bestows on even the silliest comic farces an air of fatalism and eternity . . .

Arguably the preeminent "religious" filmmaker of our modern cinema time has been Carl Theodor Dreyer. Not that he would ever have wanted such a title, but the fact is that his late silent masterpiece *The Passion of Joan of Arc* (1928) alone could give him a solid claim to it.

And has there ever been a more overwhelming star turn in a movie than Maria Falconetti's as Joan? I never thought there would be for me, at least when I first saw the movie—or rather parts of it—in the early 1950s, when my friends and I were trying to start a film club at our college—a fairly unusual thing in those days (our first show was *Brief Encounter*)—and the film rental manager we were dealing with in his dingy and disarrayed little office said that he had a damaged print of it, unrentable because it was incomplete, without its music track, and worst of all no intertitles. But you could sort of tell what was going on—so did we want to borrow it to look at? So we did—screening it after hours on the wall of an empty university office, with no sound but the clattering projector. So here she is, I remember thinking at the time—and for the rest of my life.

Not Falconetti, whoever she was—but Falconetti's Joan. To Dreyer himself, I later learned, she had simply been "the martyr's reincarnation," in spite of the circumstances of how he first found her—a well-known actress doing a galvanizing Charleston each night on the Paris stage as the star of a boulevard comedy there. He interviewed her after that—without her stage makeup ("a work of art" in itself, he said)—screen-tested her the same way, and signed her. Filming in Paris began in May 1927, on an artful and elaborate world-to-itself medieval set, and went on for five intensive months, hewing to the historic records of the saint's trial (she had been canonized just seven years before) but compressing its eighteen-month length into a single day. The narrative, filmed in sequence and climaxing with her immolation, is one of almost relentless agony, interspersed with moments of exaltation. Much like the filming itself, by some accounts. And the movie was a commercial disaster. Apart from the other strikes against it, it was a silent—later critically acclaimed as the very "first *true* talking picture," but never mind—at a time when literal talking pictures in both Europe and America were taking over movie screens.

With shooting done, Falconetti went promptly back to the stage—the next day, according to Dreyer. And when the Nazis invaded Paris she moved with her daughter to Argentina, where she lived and acted on the Buenos Aires stage until her death in 1946. She never made another movie, for whatever reasons—probably no offers. But her single film became legendary and so did she.

It made Dreyer's reputation, marking his passage from a minor Danish filmmaker (eight silent features, mostly in the 1920s) to one with international cachet. And it would be the first of the five films—*Vampyr* in 1932, also made in France, then *Day of Wrath*, *Ordet*, and *Gertrud*, all made in Denmark and appearing at the rate of one a decade (his bankrolling was always tenuous) until his death in 1969—which would finally comprise, according to one academic critic (P. Adams Sitney), "the single most impressive oeuvre of sustained greatness in the whole history of cinema." And if not every film historian would agree with that statement, not one of them by now could be surprised by it.

Falconetti was thirty-four at the time—to Joan's actual eighteen. But even in relentless close-ups (making up nearly half of the movie) she is a convincing girl. At first she seems almost genderless—like a fairy tale's young hero, in her coarse peasant's jacket with its jaunty little flared shoulders, her short cropped hair curling up in a coil at the back of her neck. Her skin is dark and weatherworn, her eyes wide and staring, panic fighting with pride, then yielding to the purest, most piercing sort of sorrow. She is smarter and subtler than her tormentors, as the historic records show, but she is also naïve, as they are certainly not. It's the incredulity at the center of her terror (can these men be serious?) that makes her feel heartbreaking even early on. She is explicitly paralleled to Christ, of course—as when her lowlife jailers mock her, planting a crown of straw on her head and a mock-scepter in the crook of her arm. And she is repeatedly shown in attitudes of conventional piety: head tilted back, palms pressed together in prayer, tear-filled eyes lifted heavenward or closed in rapture as she receives the communion wafer—sights that impress and move even her judges by the end.

And that are saved from banality by the fierce yearning that Falconetti invests them with—a fierceness that you almost feel in your own flesh. And flesh is a major player in this spiritual film. Mostly because we see hers with such unsparing clarity (in Rudolph Maté's cinematography, also legendary)—the furrows in her brow, the roughness and pores of her skin, the eyelashes matted and clogged from weeping. Even the single tear that runs down her nose and hangs at its tip, the fly that lands there, the saliva that clings to the knuckles she's stuffed in her mouth to stanch her sobbing, the blood that jets from her arm when the physician cuts it (one ordeal Falconetti was excused from—it's a stand-in's arm), and so on.

But there's the same tactility in the way we experience her judges—in all their mortal decay, in extreme close-ups—or in group shots—against the white stone walls that background the action in the film's flat unmodulated light (no shadows). The majestic one's wattles, the reptilian one's glinting little eyes, the rabid one's fat pendulous lips—not a crease or a wart or a fold seems overlooked. And yet the feeling this brutal specificity also gives you is of a kind of beauty—engaging you the way that cathedral gargoyles do. But these are real faces of flesh—every pouch and seam and extrusion having an almost scenery-like presence and grandeur. Even the fat stupid monk who spits on her (it lands on her cheekbone—she touches it in disbelief with her finger) looks sort of magnificent in his close-up.

Bazin called it "a documentary of faces." But pressing against this tactility, this materiality of emphasis, is something else—an artful highly mannered semiexpressionist style that is often like a controlled delirium, full of jump cuts and elisions and extreme camera angles (they dug a ditch to get a certain one low enough). Enforcing the delirium is the absence of establishing shots—to tell you where you are, or even where the people on the screen are in relation to one another. And even the most fleeting cutaway shot tends to seem self-proclaimingly *composed*, if only in its eccentricity (e.g., the moving tops of marching soldiers' heads and helmets at the bottom of the frame in a shot of a white wall). And given the bewildering rate at which the images come at you (the film's average shot length is five seconds), it can feel at times like a succession of effects, like formalism in glimpses.

But at the center of it all is that continuing great close-up of her, of the yearning and suffering Joan, in all its shades and nuance—not a composed effect but a living presence—who seems not only to be enduring all this but at times to be watching it with us—as trapped in it as surely as she is in her "trial." Yet even her longest and most intense scenes can be inflected by those quick cutaway images. Like her climactic scene in her cell with Bishop Cauchon (Eugène Silvain), where she takes back her earlier recantation of her visions and thus finally seals her doom. "I denied God to save my life," she now tells him—in alternating close-ups between them, he above, she below, a cross-shaped window behind and above them both. No one among her judges wants her to die by now, least of all him, Cauchon, the chief one—but now she will. "Have you nothing else to say to us?" he asks—sorrowfully.

Before she can answer there's a cut to a medium shot of a group of the lesser judges (are they in her cell, too?—you're not sure). You recognize all three, of course (including the fat one who spat on her), but what you first register is the formal arrangement they make on the screen: one behind the other in a triangular outline there, a receding

Joan on trial

pyramid against the omnipresent white wall backdrop, the fat priest sitting at its base, the reptilian one standing behind him and turning to talk to the black-hooded monk behind him, who is facing right, and who then turns to go left and to walk out of the shot, which ends before he can. Back to Joan and Cauchon.

The shot itself is almost Felliniesque—with that director's interest in odd human outlines (especially among the clergy) in formal arrangements that shift and recompose (think of the post-orgy participants seen from the back walking to the beach at the end of *La Dolce Vita*) and his instinct for the way such shifts on the screen (especially in black-and-white) can be as stirring to watch as a brilliant dancer's movements. But in *Joan* such moments add up to much more, becoming in their recurrence not only oddly moving but forming a pattern of something higher and stranger at work within the movie—something that even the hollow men in that pyramid can be appropriated to. Just as Joan herself is.

There was something "indefinable" about Falconetti, Dreyer said— "something that was not of this world." And you could argue that it was just this mystery, as he sought it in his women stars, especially in their faces, that inspired his achievement from this film onward. More so than any other great filmmaker's, his close-ups of women are inquiries into the spiritual, into the "indefinable." And *The Passion of Joan of Arc* was essentially, he said, "a hymn to the triumph of the soul over life"— over those material limits the movie so insistently reminds us about.

But what sort of triumph? That is exactly what the young monk Massieu—played by Antonin Artaud, who has a close-up beauty here, long-faced and soft-eyed and stricken, that is almost equal to hers— wants to know from her finally. He has been her friend from the start of her trial. Back then she was defiant and hopeful, telling her inquisitors that she was a "daughter of God," who would soon deliver her from them by the "great victory" He had promised her. But now she is on the brink of execution, having abjured her abjuration, and Massieu has come to prepare her for her death. "Tell me," he says in his intertitle, his great gaunt face rising into the tilted low-angled close-up, "how can you still believe that you are sent by God?" His eyes are kinder than ever but the question is urgent—and she looks (in her close-up) up at him with an answering gentleness. Her head is now shaved and the hollows of her eyes are deeper—she looks skull-like,

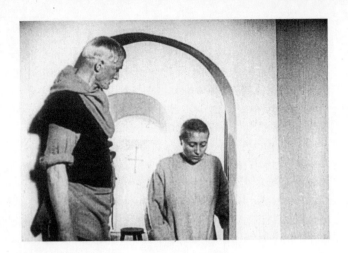

Joan at the stake

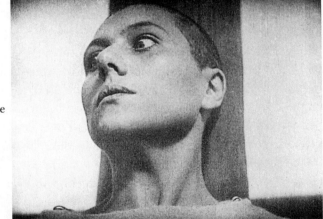

still eerily beautiful. There is a pause as we (and he) look at her. Then an answer: "His ways are not our ways," she says—her eyes lowered, a leftover tear going down her cheek.

Back to Massieu as he takes in this answer, his breath quickening, the thick burlap collar of his cassock rising and falling at the bottom of the frame as he stares fixedly at her. Then nods—as if answering himself ("of course"). Joan again, her eyes still lowered: "Yes," she says, as if responding to his unspoken thought, "yes, I am His child"—as if she herself is only just understanding. Massieu absorbs this, his breathing even quicker now. Then: "And your great victory?" he asks. She raises her head and looks at him, her eyes wide now, almost shining—an easy question: "It will be my martyrdom." He draws a breath for the last one, and the intertitle: "And your deliverance?" No answer at first, her gaze is still fixed on him, her head tilted back in the frame as if resting on the air there, a shadow of something like irony crossing her face—as if to say *Don't you know?* Then slowly lowering her eyes she gives the answer—"Death." And we look at her for a moment—looking at it. Then Massieu again, looking wasted, still gazing at her and sinking slowly below the frame line of his shot, like a torpedoed ship.

It's a justly famous sequence—the most famous one in the film, probably. The dawning wonderment of Falconetti's "Yes, I am His child" is like a revelation by itself into the nature of love, falling as it can like both a blessing and a doom. And the undefended Joan belongs to this love, as she now understands—not to the official church nor to her noisy fans in the courtyard nor even to the kindness of strangers like Massieu. She is alone with God now. And with us, as it happens—and overpoweringly—on the screen. Where she has gone by this point from hope to resignation, from pride to submission—even more significantly, perhaps, from calling herself "daughter of God" to being merely "His child," away from specification, even that of gender, toward the consent "to be as nothing," in William James's phrase, "in the floods and waterspouts of God."

One of the broader suggestions of Dreyer's achievement in this is both a paradoxical and illuminating one: a demonstration that the movie close-up in all its apotheosizing of the self may reach its fullest power—as it does through Falconetti's "performance" here—in a kind of selflessness. It's what Garbo often fails at—in her creaky vehicles apart from *Camille* (and the final image of *Queen Christina*)—though she tries. Where Dietrich, in her Sternberg films, evokes it only to put it in quote marks (see her praying scene in *Shanghai Express*). It's what Godard directly confronts Anna Karina with in *Vivre sa vie*, when he puts her in front of this same scene to watch it from the dark of an almost empty cinema, alternating close-ups of her tear-stained face with those of Falconetti—juxtaposing martyr with victim (the Karina heroine will die at the end, too), tragic beauty with its pathetic real-life counterpart, yearning replaced by malaise.

II.

BUT IF *The Passion of Joan of Arc* was like no other movie (it had no imitators, not even Dreyer himself),* what seems to me his greatest film, *Day of Wrath* (1943), was a lot like a Hollywood one. Apparently he thought so, too. Improbable as it might seem, Dreyer had always wanted to go to Hollywood. And in 1941 he tried to sell himself and the project (which was based on a popular Norwegian play) to Harry Cohn at Columbia. It had, after all, a dependable movie plot in the noir line of the time: sexy young woman with an elderly husband cheats with a young lover and ends up by doing all three of them in. But the story was set in seventeenth-century Denmark; once again the heroine was accused of being a witch and once again was burned at the stake at the end (though offscreen this time)—not exactly pluses, you imagine, for Harry Cohn. So the film was not made until two years later, in Nazi-occupied Denmark. Where it stayed, more or less (like *Joan*, it was also a flop with its first audiences), until the war was over, when it was released in Europe and the United States—to a mixed reception.

Anne Pedersdotter (Lisbeth Movin) lives in a provincial vicarage with her priest husband and his gorgonlike mother, in a village where literal witch hunts (and ensuing immolations) seem to happen a lot—

---

* *Vampyr*, the 1932 film that he made in France after *Joan*, was also unique and inimitable, though in a quieter mode, and without a centralizing heroine (though Sybille Schmitz as the vampire's victim is remarkable indeed).

and where the only one who is appalled by the cruelty seems to be Anne. Like an animal lover at the bullfights. When the old woman she attempts to save from the mob in the movie's first scenes (by letting her hide in the vicarage's attic) is burned alive in the following ones, Anne can only look away and sob. She is helpless, but she is from the start our ally in this film's world—the only reliably human figure in it. (Except for the one they burn.)

It's her husband, Absalon—played by Thorkild Roose, with eyes at once fierce and kindly—who aspires *beyond* the human, who recognizes, as Joan had done, that "His ways are not our ways." And in his rigor Absalon is a kind of saint—and is in that respect at least an unwitting corroboration of George Orwell's claim (re Gandhi) that "saints should always be judged guilty until they are proved innocent" (it's less likely, Orwell argues, that *we* are failed saints than that *they* are failed human beings). And Absalon's commitment to the divine (as he sees it) has led him, benign as his nature otherwise seems, to the burning of witches. Whereas the irreligious Anne instinctively makes quite other sorts of choices. As when she tries to save the old woman, or when she gives way to passion for her handsome stepson (Preben Lerdorff Rye) after he returns home from the seminary to meet his new "mother"—not a smart choice exactly (under the nose of her mother-in-law) but a sympathetic one. And Anne will soon become a Dreyer kind of saint, as single-minded an extremist of love as Joan had been. It won't take her long (the burning of the old woman is a help).

Even before his movie properly begins, Dreyer is concerned to place the action in a religious context for us: it opens not with opening credits, not even the movie's title, but with a sonic storm of clashing orchestral chords and blaring trumpets, the Dies Irae hymn rolling and crashing across the soundtrack as the hymn's awful words—with their promises of apocalyptic terror and final judgment—unscroll slowly before us on the screen, in a medieval style engraved text:

> *That Day of Wrath, that sulfurous day . . .*
> *Awake from clay to judgment . . .*
> *Day of Wrath, O see them stand*
> *Before His throne, small and grim,*
> *Clad in shame and rancid sin . . .*

And so on. It's a thrilling overture—not just the tumultuous music but the exultant cruelty. And it's the most *noise* the film will ever make again.

Unlike *Joan*, the pace here is slow and meditative—even when you might reasonably expect a little more excitement. As you might in the opening scenes when the accused witch, Herlofs Marte (Anna Svierkier), flees her pursuers—*slowly*, that is, since she is old and fat and moves with difficulty. And her cottage home (where she has just seen a neighbor woman who has come to her for herbs to cure her sick husband: "There is power in evil," Marte tells her) is cramped and dark and she has to get out by going the back way through the barn and the sheepfold and then squeezing through a gate in the pigsty. It takes some time, while the church bells and the cries of her persecutors ("Burn her!") sound in the distance—a long lateral leftward camera track following her as she goes.

And the same sort of slow lateral track (only rightward) will show her being apprehended at last in the dark of the vicarage attic. And later, when she is being tortured (offscreen), the camera will track along the walls of the chamber (only her cries are heard), past the assembled judges and witnesses—posed and lit here like a Rembrandt painting—until it gets to her and reaches what Truffaut would call "the most beautiful female nude in cinema, at once the least erotic and the most carnal." She is recovering, post-torture, sitting in profile on the edge of a table, bound and wrapped like a package that's come undone, the wrapping fallen around her waist, her cream-white flesh spilling down above it, looking pummeled and doughy, making a visual rhyme with the corona of wispy white hair around her face, which is like a wide-eyed little girl's and is now turned, tearful and defiant, toward Absalon, who is standing beside and above her.

People move slowly in this film, heavy with time and intention, usually to the ticking of a clock, in the dimly lit, sparsely furnished interiors. Freedom—or any hint of it—is outdoors, in nature: in a close-up of branches and leaves dancing in the wind under sunshot clouds; in a traveling shot that moves blissfully up an oak tree trunk to the effusion of leaf and bloom at its top; among the images that you see in the sequence where Anne and Martin first walk in the countryside together (Absalon wants the two "young people" to get to know each other) to the accompaniment of a gentle melody that you soon recognize

Day of Wrath: Herlofs Marte (Anna Svierkier) hiding from the witch hunters

as a benign transposition of the Dies Irae one. They walk and laugh and run—climbing a hill, petting a horse in a field, picking wildflowers, and so on—until they are brought up short by a passing reminder of the coming big event: a woodsman hauling logs for the burning.

But the camera keeps its distance (medium long shot) through this montage—freeing them for a time even from us, and in the more or less objective style of the whole film (in contrast to *Joan* again). There are no high- or low-angle shots, no extreme close-ups. And the close shots there are are those that tend to follow movement ("my floating close-ups," Dreyer called them) rather than trap and enclose it, giving more freedom to the actor, more neutrality to our relation to her or him. Though with Lisbeth Movin that neutrality isn't so easy to sustain—for us or for Dreyer.

Her beauty has an elvish cast—with her big eyes, long upper lip, and wide sensual mouth. More chorus girl than goddess—the kind of prettiness a hostile mother-in-law might be able to think of as "trashy." She is maidenly and timorous in the beginning scenes—but her first onscreen glance at that same mother-in-law, Merete (Sigrid Neiien-dem), tells us that the girl is less an obedient than a cornered one, and not at all the pushover she might have been taken for. Not even when she lets Absalon, her doting husband, console her in his arms for the old lady's harshness, then runs pettishly from the room away from both of them.

Merete is a fireplug of a woman—like a parade float in a shroud—whose mean little eyes soften only when they light upon her son or her grandson—and not always even then (the men often displease her), and certainly never when she contemplates her daughter-in-law, whose half-floating little run in this early scene, and in this hieratically paced film generally, has a dangerous life to it.

Soon after this, Anne comes through a heavy wood door into what seems an empty church (it's an early scene in the film) to some quietly agitated music on the soundtrack. She comes down a flight of steps, leaving the door ajar behind her, looking all around as she comes, turning and then walking urgently down a long pillared side aisle, the camera following her alongside but from behind the pillars as she goes—past stained-glass windows and stations of the cross—and then as she breaks into a light loping run—lifting her shoulders, touching her apron—a sudden ascent into graceful movement so seamless that it lifts your spirit with it: the easy stride, the hands clenched on the air, the lissome youthful body under the severe (but not unsexy) Puritan maid uniform—as she slows and then hurries, and then slows again and then *stops* . . . reaching out an arm and putting her hand on the last great pillar, standing and staring, as the camera pulls ahead of her and circles in front of her with an almost ceremonial gravity as she hesitates at the pillar, leaning forward and looking . . . Nice.

But looking at what? And where is she going? Not that you really ask just yet. The opaqueness, though temporary, is part of what makes the whole thing magical: you're *freed* from "reading" it. But then you watch her going to another door. She is going to eavesdrop on the church elders, including her husband, as they interrogate Herlofs Marte.

Her light loping run: Lisbeth Movin as Anne

The witch—as she certainly believes herself to be—has revealed to Anne that the girl's mother was one, too, though she was never publicly accused. And she has also accused Absalon (in private) of shielding the mother because he wanted the daughter for his wife. Marte has tried to use this accusation to save herself. But Absalon resists the blackmail, and Herlofs Marte is duly burned (he gives the command himself) before she can make good on it. But she leaves Absalon to his self-accusations—alone at the vicarage . . .

It's there, in those rooms with their low ceilings and dark woodwork, that the movie's subtly gleaming low-contrast cinematography (by Karl Andersson)—more film gris than film noir—makes its most powerful effect. The shadows in the subtle chiaroscuro seem especially congenial to Anne, who needs more and more to slip in and out of them, if only to conceal from the others the expression in her eyes. Have you ever noticed those eyes? asks Merete, up to her usual mischief with her troubled and resistant son—how they burn? Just like her mother's did in fact? But when Absalon looks into them—as he promptly does after this exchange—he sees (or tries to) something else: "Your wonderful eyes," he says tenderly, holding her by her arms, "so childlike, so pure and clear."

But Anne wants to know now about her mother: Is it true, she asks, that she had the power of "calling," the ability to summon both living and dead? Absalon dismisses the "childlike" question and leaves her, to go to his study. Alone in the parlor, Anne tries "calling" Martin. "I can do it!" she says to herself, as he seems to materialize out of the darkness behind her. And in the shadows and moonlight, the leaf patterns through the windows now on their faces, they embrace. "I can see you through my tears," she says. And he answers: "Tears which I am wiping away," touching her face, then adding: "No one has eyes like you." "Childlike, pure and clear?" she asks. "No—deep and mysterious. But with a trembling quivering flame." More like it. And closer to Merete—to whom "deep and mysterious" could hardly seem less offensive than "burning."

And so they go to the birchwood forest—a gentle lilting music on the soundtrack, beginning even before they leave, following them there and through a second idyllic montage, both graver and sweeter than the first: as they pause by a glittering stream and she cups her hands to drink and he kisses her mouth instead, their voices talking of love resonating in the forest stillness, as they spread their cloaks on the ground and lie down on them behind a slope, sinking below it and out of sight as the camera moves slowly in on it and stops. "What is that sound?" her voice asks. "It's the grass humming," he replies—we don't hear that hum, but we seem to see it as the moonlight dapples the grasses above them, and the sequence fades out.

But it's not entirely the way I describe it above—I left out the way Dreyer intercuts it again and again with shots of Absalon, now alone in his study, where he has gone ("I have lied to God") to pray and meditate—where we see him, between views of the lovers, and to the same gentle music, pacing slowly in the moonlight through the windows, or sitting heavily by the fire, in all his granitic and heartsore grandeur. And the effect surprisingly is less to underline the obvious point that Absalon is excluded from this idyll as to suggest instead that he is somehow mysteriously appropriated to it—less to underscore a tragic or ironic contrast, let alone a moral one, than to suggest an odd and moving harmony—a kind of hovering benignity.

Anne is transformed after this—from a Cinderella-in-the-ashes to the confident sensual presence we see the next morning at a family scripture reading—as she herself reads from the Song of Songs, reads to *him*, sitting across the table from her, reads pointedly, even impudently, as Merete sits glaring. The lovers are otherwise cautious, of course—scuttling like teenagers to different ends of the room when they think they hear someone coming. And then no one is. And Anne laughs. But Martin not so much. He is increasingly troubled by conscience. And as she waxes, he wanes—she becomes more and more not only the erotic initiator but the partner in control.

And then, on a wildly stormy night when Absalon has been called away to a sickbed and Merete has finally gone upstairs to bed, Martin is sitting alone in the parlor. With the wind now howling outside, Anne steals silently into the room behind him, looking both intent and wild, like something sent by the wind: her golden hair uncapped and loosened, falling to her shoulders, her eyes fixed on him, as she puts a *shhh* finger to her lips and goes silently, slowly around the room, holding him with her gaze, as she bolts the doors, first the one to the outside (the wind swells as she passes it), then the other to the upstairs . . . Now they're alone, her look says to him, as she comes, still slowly, toward him . . .

While Absalon, as we see, is now away at the bedside of his sick and dying friend—and as before, the lovers' separate activities are cross-cut with his. But to a different effect this time—a portentous one. "Whosoever believeth shall live though he die," Absalon says to the man (one of the judges who condemned Herlofs Marte), and assures him that he himself will soon be joining him. And he stays with him to his end.

Back at the vicarage, Anna is now resting her head in Martin's lap and dreaming out loud about the children they will have together—when they are free—especially about their son: "And the tenderness you gave to me," she says, "I will give back to him." A contrast to the sexy-jokey pantomime she's just performed for him (to the accompaniment of those winds), but a reminder that—as well as her being irresistible, inventive and ardent and vital—she is deeply in love, too.

And that pantomime was a knockout. But knockout or no, disturbing, too. Partly because of the sequence between them that has come before this vicarage one. One of their postcoital idylls, as she and Martin lie together in each other's arms in the reeds by a riverbank. He doesn't look happy—and what he comes out with next gives her an understandable turn: "Oh, Anne," he says, "if we could die together now." Die—what is he talking about? Why should they die? "To atone for our sin," he answers. "*Sin?*" she rejoins, hardly believing her ears. "Is it a sin to *love?*" How could that ever be so?

But if Anne has no sense of sin the movie she is in does. And she has become not only adulterous but toweringly and dangerously self-willed—seeming indifferent to her loved one's pain except as it touches hers. Her egoism is like Absalon's has been. Whose original inciting sin—as he comes finally to realize (his self-understanding precedes hers)—was not that he lied and so saved the mother but that he imprisoned the daughter in their marriage. As he confesses to Anne later: "I never asked you, I just took you to be married—a wrong I can never make amends for."

She agrees with him about that—in the movie's most brutally powerful sequence, after he has returned in the storm from that deathbed ministry. But his repentance only makes her more dangerous, as he sits broken-backed before her and she circles him like a prey animal gathering to pounce. He is old and exhausted and despairing, full of thoughts of death and a conviction that his own is near—even that it has been decided upon that same night, by someone else. "But who would wish you dead?" she says, standing and leaning over him out of the shadows, with her face and undone hair in the light, her hands flat on the table between them. Yes, who would wish that, he repeats mechanically—then takes another look at that face in the light above him. "Anne!" he cries—has she ever wished for his death? Why would she? she replies. Because I've done you such a great injustice, he replies.

And this confession only infuriates her the more—when even *he* sees what he's done to her! She not only tells him yes, that she has wished for his death, but that she has done it hundreds of times, and never more so than she is doing now—now that she and Martin— But she doesn't finish the thought, nor does she need to. Absalon rises from his chair, stricken, horrified. "Now you know!" she says, and then, savagely, wishes him dead again. As he staggers across to the stairs, calling out to his son—but then falls to the floor unconscious. Anne, in genuine terror now, screams. And the others come, to find him gone.

Not a bad night for a beginning witch. It seems to surprise even her (that scream and her panic). But "I was not responsible for his death,"

"But who would wish you dead?"

she swears to Martin later, as they stand watch together over Absalon's open coffin—meaning, of course, that when it comes down to it, she really doesn't believe in all that witchcraft stuff much more than we do. Any more than she can believe that it's "a sin to love." And especially not at this moment, with her agonized lover pressing her. She has already admitted to him that she wished for his father's death— but "did you wish it so that he *had* to die?" he demands of her now (*he* is a believer, at any rate). She kneels by the bier, placing her hand upon it, and says to Martin again that she was *not* the cause of his father's death—but with one of the film's omnipresent shadows now crossing her face.

Of course: Absalon died from heart disease (established beforehand). Martin came to her that first night when they made love not because of a witch's summons but because of his own itch for her. And so on. Anyway, in what serious movie in a realist mode—even a Danish one—could a heroine accused by a villain of being a witch then actually turn out to be one? Everything here is "explained"—of course.

Except for the fact that Dreyer keeps it from being so finally, not only in subtle ways—uneasinesses and ambiguities, not to mention shadows—but by at least one quite heavy-handed device. When Anne makes her first admission to her lover of wanting Absalon dead, her words are followed by a cutaway shot of Absalon traveling home in the night storm with his sacristan alongside and suddenly clutching his chest and staggering. Are you ill? asks the other. No, he answers—he just suddenly felt fearful, as if death had just brushed his sleeve.

The critic Robert Warshow—writing in 1948 when the movie first appeared in the United States—particularly deplored this sequence. He grants that "a psychological answer" to the movie's puzzles is "impossible" by this point. "But the supernatural one, which is the one [that Dreyer] chooses . . . is just as bad." Because "once the question of witchcraft is raised no one can be expected to believe in its reality."

But on the other hand, it's just that impossibility that Dreyer seems to be playing with. Because you've known all along, even if you're seeing the movie for the first time, that it's not a film that's going to tell you what you've known all along—it's not *The Crucible*, for example (though Arthur Miller may have seen and been influenced by it). And the supernatural answer here, far from seeming a bad late choice, as Warshow describes it, has in fact been implicit in the film from its start—and central to it. As its final powerful scene with Movin will confirm.

But before that, you must watch the trap closing round her. Worst of all to Anne is Martin's seeming to abandon her, seeming no longer to love her, lost to her in his own remorse. "Do you know, Anne," he says to her over Absalon's coffin, "we ought to go down on our knees and ask him to forgive us." "I have nothing to ask him to forgive," she says coldly—not surprisingly. But what she says next *is* sort of surprising:

ANNE: But I know that he would have forgiven us.

MARTIN (*staring at his father's face*): Now he is standing before God and accusing us.

ANNE: No, Martin . . . He is pleading for us because he sees how we suffer . . .

Counterintuitive as that may sound—given Absalon's last encounter with her—it still strikes you with the force of a truth, of an unexpected insight, confirmed by Movin's exhausted gravity as she says it. Of course—Absalon loved them both, we've seen that whenever we have seen him around them. And unrepentant as Anne may be, she has understood something about love, and about Absalon even, that his loving and guilty son may never do.

But it's Merete who wins in the end: she's lost her son but she reclaims her grandson and destroys her enemy. At the solemn service before Absalon's burial, while he lies still uncovered in his casket, she denounces Anne as a witch and accuses her of her husband's death. Martin rises to defend his stepmother. Of course you defend her, says Merete—before the Bishop and assembled elders—"with the Evil One's help she lured you into her power! With the Evil One's help she murdered her husband!" And to Martin, as it turns out, this reading of things proves irresistible. He falls silent—and ends up by his grandmother's side. "Let her deny it if she dares!" says the triumphant Merete.

She doesn't. She starts to, but then gives it up; sitting by his bier (they have uncovered his face for her testimony) in her hooded white mourning garment (the others all in black), she confesses, addressing Absalon directly. Not the Absalon who pleads for her but the one that she betrayed, the son of Merete and of the Church. "You have your revenge," she says to him. She confesses to luring the son and killing the father and husband, all with the help of the Evil One. "Now you know, now you know," she says to the dead man below her as she looks down at him. She looks up, with brimming eyes. "I see you through my tears," she says, "but no one comes to brush them away." Who is she talking to, though? To Martin?—harking back to their first night together? But now she seems beyond him—utterly alone now—in total abandonment. And she zones out—or so it looks. Then the muffled sound of a tolling church bell. Then silence. Then, as the camera stays on her, the faint sound of a distant music, a string threnody, can be heard. As she slowly raises her eyes, and with tears still flowing, she smiles—vaguely at first, then (unmistakably) beatifically. The film's

Martin's final abandonment of Anne

final moving surprise. It is as if someone or something has come to her after all—as if that benignity that has been hovering over the film has finally descended—as you look at her here. She will be burned, certainly. But she may also be redeemed.

It's like the climactic moments in Rossellini's Bergman films—the moments of grace's descent, of the final "miracle." But where Rossellini tends to distract us a little at such climaxes—the volcano and the flight of birds, the religious procession and the "cure"—Dreyer, a more rigorous artist, only focuses us more intently, more unwaveringly. On Anne's face—for the camera, as he once said, the face is the most fascinating of all landscapes. And her image on the screen then dissolves slowly into the same Dies Irae text we had seen at the movie's opening, unscrolling on the screen again, this time not to crashing chords but to the celestial sound, faint at first and then growing, of the boys' choir, singing that part of the hymn that seems to be about mercy:

> Day of wrath, for pity take
> My sins away from Satan's grasp
> And bear up my soul to heaven at last . . .
> Save us, Jesus, with your blood . . .

Then, as church bells toll, the shadow outline of a cross, against a gray-white background, fills the screen—and stays on it, turning into a grave marker, before the screen goes black, the bells still tolling.

III.

WHATEVER UNCERTAINTY THAT film might finally leave you in (not much, I think) about the reality of a divine grace, Dreyer's next film, in 1954—*Ordet (The Word)*—resolves categorically. Like a challenge thrown down: this time his heroine is literally raised from the dead at the end through faith in Christ—and by her brother-in-law, who believes that he actually *is* Christ. He is not (there are limits), but the miracle is real and literal, and is shown to us head-on, just as Anne's was, but with even less embellishment, no boys' choir or tolling bells. Inger simply wakes up in her husband's arms. An ordinary sort of miracle—the kind that the housewife Inger had herself professed to believe in.

Like *Day of Wrath, Ordet* was drawn from a contemporary Scandinavian play—this time a popular and well-known one (the improbable resurrection at the end helped that). Written by a Lutheran preacher, Kaj Munk, it was first staged in Copenhagen in 1932, the year that Dreyer first saw it. It was later adapted and filmed in Sweden by Gustaf Molander in 1943 (at that same time the playwright in Denmark was killed by the Nazis in retaliation for his sermons against them). Ten years after that, Dreyer wrote and filmed his own version—as he had been more or less planning to do, he said, since he had first seen the play. And *Ordet* would be the only one of his greatest movies to have any success in its own time.

The Borgs are a prosperous farming family in the 1920s in the remote Jutland islands. The family patriarch, Martin Borgen (Henrik Malberg—who had played the same role at the play's premiere in 1932), with his squat stolid frame and halting walk, his refulgent white hair, beard, and brows, is a passionate Christian believer, though a fairly enlightened one, putting him at odds with his less prosperous hellfire-and-damnation neighbors. He feels at odds with his three grown sons as well, all of them at home on the family farm: the eldest, Johannes, incurably insane; the youngest, Anders, in love with a girl from that other religion; the middle one, Mikkel, irreligious altogether. But married happily to Inger, who is the mainstay of the family. She is also the devoutest believer of them all. Pray, even if you think it won't help, she counsels her doting father-in-law, who is tempted by despair—about Johannes, mostly, his only "brilliant" son, whom he had sent off to the seminary to study, believing he would come back to be a powerful religious leader for the community—and not, as Johannes did instead, as this nutcase they can't even safely let out of the house.

The Johannes character (a more rationalized version of him) was the center of Munk's play. In Dreyer's film it's Inger (Birgitte Fedderspiel) who is. Blond (isn't everyone?) and homely-pretty, with big deep-set eyes, sculpted round cheekbones, a faint overbite, and an almost clownishly wide and radiant smile. She is far into pregnancy (as Fedderspiel herself was), rocking happily along behind her stomach as she walks, in her black bathrobe or her checkered full-length apron. She is for Dreyer another case, like Joan or Anne, of a mysterious female saintliness. But of an everyday kind—defined not by isolation (she is rarely shown in close-up, not even the floating ones). While the men around her seem mostly looking inside themselves, at their various unhappinesses—Anders at his lovelornness, Borgen at his family disappointments, Mikkel at his family resentments—she is looking out at them, with concern and tenderness. Even when she is challenging them. As she has especially to do with old Borgen, the most dominant and intransigent one.

He is wrong not to let his son Anders (Cay Kristiansen) see the girl he loves, even if she is from the Bible Belt, she tells the old man, over the biscuits she has made for him and that he especially likes. And she encourages Anders to go off to see the girl anyway, and so he does; Inger's voice on the soundtrack, singing in her kitchen (making those biscuits), follows him down the road through the dunes—in the movie's

Borgen, the family patriarch, with his sons—Mikkel at right and
Anders at left—and his daughter-in-law, Inger, with the coffeepot

only breach of its literal mode. But never mind: "I can do everything,"
she jokes to Borgen when he compliments her on the biscuits, and
then on her dexterity in filling his pipe for him. "Except," he ripostes,
mischievously, "have sons." (She and Mikkel have two little girls.) But
she will do that, too, if he wants—she promises him. Along with fried
eel for Sunday breakfast (another favorite).

But there is another magician in the house—who is also given to
predicting wonders: the Jesus impersonator Johannes (Preben Lerdorff
Rye—the actor who had been Martin in *Day of Wrath* ten years before), the character we first see at the movie's beginning, when he's
gotten out of the house in the middle of the night, forcing the rest of
them to go searching for him over the dunes, only to find him standing

on a bluff among the sea oats and facing the sea, preaching to an imaginary throng below, in his long greatcoat and thick sweater, his wispy little Savior's beard, his slicked-down hair pulled back and parted in the middle (the East Village look). "Woe unto you," he intones to the wind in his high whinnying voice, "ye hypocrites, because you believe not in me, the risen Christ, who has come unto you at the bidding of Him who made the heavens and the earth . . ." and so on. Until the unbelievers take him home again.

"Poor soul," says Inger to her husband when they are alone in their bedroom. "Oh, I don't know, perhaps he's happy as he is," replies Mikkel (Emil Hass Christensen)—who, as the family's official nonreligionist, inclines to this maddening contrary tone. With his rugged features, his brown skin and thick white hair, he seems nearly always in the family group shots to be situated at the edge of the frame, perched on the arm of a chair or sitting on the sill of a window, but assertively—as if to say: let the women and the old men sit *down*. It's only with her in their austere white bedroom, where the feeling of the deeply loving sex these two surely must have is so palpable, that he seems to find the composition's center. And it's there that he reminds Inger that he has never been able to stand "all the godliness" his father imposes on them. "But you believe in God, don't you?" says Inger, lovingly. But she knows how he feels about that, he replies—why does she even ask? "Then you have no faith?" she says. "No," he answers—sadly (like all of them, and how much more so, he would like to please her)—"not even faith in faith." It doesn't matter, she says—you have a good heart.

So does the movie. There are no Meretes in it—nor any fat expectorating monks. Even the intolerant hellfire fundamentalists are sort of sweet. Take the blissed-out young woman who gives testimony, in long luminous close-up, to the joy her religion has brought her, at Peter the Tailor's at-home prayer meeting. And though Dreyer gives a similar sort of attention to the congregants at this gathering—tracking slowly past the assembled faces—as he gave to the judges in his two witch-burning films, the effect, of course, is very different: these are Tolstoyan peasant faces, radiating their quotidianness, defeating both glamour and judgment.

But the accumulating blandness of all this comes to feel at times—and paradoxically—almost aggressive (not the sort of difficulty you'd expect a European art film to make). And your resistances to what

Mikkel called "all the godliness" are not only not appeased but close to being provoked. Mikkel is not the one who sets the movie's dominant tone: it's Inger who does that. And she is the simplest of simple believers. Whatever you pray for, Jesus will give you, she tells Borgen. And faith, when at last it comes to you, she promises Mikkel, will make you "feel warm through and through," just as it has done for her.

We are a long way here, almost needless to say, from either Joan or Anne. Closer to Rossellini's Saint Francis—but without the radical poverty (a crucial omission).

But then there are hitches, as the movie goes on, and they are hideous. Inger's baby does finally arrive—but "in four pieces," as the father announces with brutal offhandedness, as he comes out of the bedroom at the doctor's instruction to find a pail to put the pieces in. This "partial birth" abortion, as it's now called, has been done in the effort to save Inger's life. And even that fails. But such horrors will be offered not as setbacks to Inger's strength of belief but as roundabout confirmations of it. Johannes, after all, has foreseen them all from the start.

"A body in the parlor," he says early on, *before* all the calamities, making one of his hoo-ha entrances into the family's midst, "and so shall my Father in heaven be glorified." What did he say? asks Inger with a shudder. Who *listens* to what he says? replies Borgen (adding: "Johannes, dear, go back to your room").

Although Mikkel certainly does not set the tone of the movie, he does set its most interesting undertone: one of irritability, even exasperation. For the Borg family, it's not just the tragedy of Johannes's creeping-Jesus presence, but the monotony of it—the whiny voice, the nonsense talk, the stare that never looks at them, the live-in daily mockery that he offers to them all. Even his father is worn out by him in the end. "Is he dead?" he asks numbly, hardly turning to look as Anders and Mikkel carry the now collapsed prophet out of Inger's bedroom, where his first attempt to raise her from the dead has undone him. "His kind never dies," answers Mikkel.

And he becomes nearly as trying for us as he is for them. It's a performance that raises the question of what the film is up to. (*Ordet* "demands constant attention to the way meaning is being constructed," says *Time Out Film Guide*.) Johannes here has been made entirely less "human," less intelligibly motivated, than he was in the Munk play. But on the other hand, Lerdorff Rye's one-note style in the role

(Dreyer had him imitate the robotic singsong sound of an actual asy-
lum inmate they visited) suits the slow contemplative pacing, the sense
of formalist rigor—though in general that pace is due less to the actors'
tempos than to those of Dreyer's camera (Henning Bendtsen behind
it), with its patient deliberate tracking and turning from one performer
or speaker to another. The reaction shot here is usually something
you have to wait for until the camera reaches the "reactor." The shot-
countershot of classical movie editing is systematically contravened—at
least until it's suddenly reinstated, restoring us to the "realist" moviemaking we're used to, in the final sequence (the miracle). Before that,
Dreyer seems to be paying as much attention to the spaces between
them as to the people themselves. And no matter how agitated the
action—like the fight between Borgen and Peter the Tailor over their
lovestruck children, which ends in a near throttling (Borgen the would-
be throttler), there is the sense of this underlying calm.

You learn how it works (or doesn't) in the film's first long tracking
shot (three minutes of a six-minute take). It's the domestic scene that
follows upon the successful retrieval of Johannes from his sand dune.
The family gradually reassembles around their table. Borgen enters
first from the outside—to where Inger is waiting, in her robe with her
hair in a braid (they have all been roused from their beds), holding a
coffeepot at the ready. He passes her and goes rightward to where his
pipe rack hangs on a nearby wall. As he stops there, the camera leaves
him and continues rightward along the wall till it reaches a door that
opens and the rescued Johannes comes out, as if sleepwalking. He
goes, still moving rightward, to a dressertop where two candles in
holders sit. He lights both of them and turns around with one in his
hand. "What good does all that do . . . Johannes?" comes Borgen's
weary voice from offscreen. "I am the light of the world," Johannes intones, in his trancelike manner, "but the darkness does not compre-
hend it." Whereupon he turns and proceeds rightward again, picking
up the second candle with one quick unseeing gesture and bearing
both of them in front of him as he goes to a corner window with white
curtains. He raises the shade, bends and looks out, and places a candle in each corner. Then another voice from offscreen—not broken
and heartsore as poor Borgen's has just been (the catch he gave to "Johannes" when he pronounced it), but strong and deep. It's Mikkel's—
though we haven't seen him come into the room. "What are the candles

for?" he says offscreen. Johannes at the window executes a slow dazed turn toward the question: "That my light may shine in darkness," he says. Then staggers, his eyes rolling back in his head—seeming to lose his balance, but only to turn now and go leftward, back, to his room again, the camera following him, then, once he is inside, leaving him to go back to the window and the two burning candles.

Whereupon Inger enters the ongoing shot—from the frame's lower right—her back to us, with her long braid hanging down it. She goes to the window and takes up the candles, blowing first the one out, then the other, slowly and carefully, like a sacristan after the service. She turns and goes left, retracing Johannes's path, to the dresser where she replaces them—then continues left, thoughtfully, eyes looking down, one hand in her bathrobe pocket, the other in a fist brushing her nose, passing a second dresser and taking up the coffeepot she'd left there (with the same unseeing gesture Johannes just used) and returning with it to the family table—returning the shot (with still three minutes to go) to where it began.

"Every shot seems exactly right," said a recent review about a more recent and more conventionally made film (Paul Thomas Anderson's *There Will Be Blood*)—of course praising it. But that is not a sort of thing you could say about this film at any point in it—calling as it does instead for such absorbed, even apparently pointless, watching. But it's from the self-enclosure of such exact "rightness," of such triumphant control in the filmmaking, that Dreyer wants to deliver us—into something more like inexorableness, responsive to the characters but extraneous to them, too, an impersonal concern, a higher intentionality. And the more his camera's slow tracking movement becomes ingrained in our experience of the film, the more it comes to feel like another expression of the flow of sustaining tenderness (a thing in itself) between the characters that exists above everything else for them. So that when, much later on, with Inger in danger, Mikkel finds himself wondering at his old father's strength in the middle of loss, and Borgen replies to him, "Yes, but then I'm holding God by the hand, you see," his reply feels less like just more "godliness" than like a name for something you recognize yourself, however dimly, something you've been feeling from the accumulating force of the movie itself. That controlling tenderness.

It's while Borgen is at Peter the Tailor's house quarreling with him

"That my light may shine in darkness"

about their children's romance that he gets the news (Mikkel telephones him) that Inger has gone unexpectedly into labor and is now in mortal danger. He hurries back with Anders to find the doctor and midwife already there, hard at work—in the film's most overtly harrowing sequence. "I don't think I can bear it," says Mikkel—and you don't think he can, either, after what you've seen of the two lovers together. But then Inger gets well—out of danger now, says the doctor (a briskly confident presence), so let her sleep. And so he has a drink—and the pastor, also on hand, joins him. And the two worldly men take their ease and have a jocular discussion about the conflicting claims of religion and science, while Borgen, nearly ecstatic from relief now, plays their host, serving and kvelling over them.

And then she dies—slipping away just after the doctor has left. It's

Mikkel who announces it, coming from her room into the parlor. "So she's dead after all," he says tonelessly.

It's not exactly that we are unprepared for the miracle that soon follows this—in the final sequence. It starts being hinted at in Johannes's earliest ravings and becomes explicitly predicted when little Maren, Inger's daughter, starts coaxing her uncle about his promise to her to make it happen. He makes that first failed attempt (the one that undoes him)—with the disbelieving Mikkel standing beside him—and then disappears. Once again they search for him—but this time with no success.

Inger is laid out at home in an open casket, with candles lit and white sheets covering the windows in the custom of the time and place. And it's only when the coffin lid is about to be closed on her that Johannes, now inexplicably restored to sanity, returns. But even then it's only Maren's unwavering faith in his promise of the miracle that enables him to keep it: "Inger, in the name of Jesus Christ I say unto thee—arise!"

And so she does. A little slowly at first. And then after a pause she begins to stir, the hands clasped at her waist unfolding, her eyes opening. The room and mourners are silent. She breathes naturally now, and Mikkel draws her up and into his arms. She gazes at him, then throws her arms about his neck. "Morten," says Peter the Tailor (they have been reconciled over her death), "He is still the God of old—the God Elijah—eternal and the same." "Yes," says Borgen, "eternal and the same." Where is the child? Inger asks, as Mikkel holds her. "It lives with God," Mikkel replies—and when she looks at him wonderingly, says: "Yes, Inger, I have found your faith." She presses her face with hungry open mouth against his. "Now life is beginning for us," he says. "To live, to live," she murmurs. And the movie fades out.

So it's not of course the miracle that surprises you here at the end so much as your own "belief" in it when it happens. And that happens, I think, not in spite of its being flatly unbelievable but exactly because it is—the blatancy functioning almost like a subtlety in the result: "His ways are not our ways." It's the boldness that carries the conviction, mimicking the miracle of sudden faith itself. Something that Rossellini enacts for us in the Bergman films is something that Dreyer offers to enact *in* us. And we are to go away at the end of this film, as he said in his notes on it, "gripped and silent."

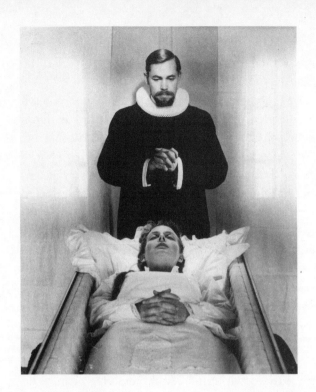

Inger: death and
transfiguration

IV.

DREYER COULD BE almost as interested, it seems, in "directing the audience," in Hitchcock's phrase, as the latter himself was, although in counterintuitive ways. Mostly by setting himself, and therefore us, some persisting central obstacle. If that obstacle in *Ordet* (and to a lesser degree in *Day of Wrath*) can be said to be a reasonable skepticism, in his final film ten years later, *Gertrud* (1964), it's at least partly the eponymous heroine herself.

"I must come before everything," she warns early on. And the issue of religious faith this time, almost for the first time in Dreyer, is irrelevant. Gertrud is an atheist. And it's she herself who becomes an object of veneration. Namely, to the besotted men around her. They have even provided her with a household shrine—a wall mirror in her parlor with candles in holders on each side, where, when we first see it, she appears out of the shadows into the light of her own image. You *are* beautiful, says her husband, coming up beside her there—but this only seems to make her sad as she turns away from both the mirror and him. The next time she will appear in it—again out of the dark behind her and this time wearing black—she is on her slow sad way to snuff out the candles that a visiting old lover has just lit there. Like Johannes at his window—and then Inger after him.

What he liked about the play (by Hjalmar Söderberg) that he adapted his movie from, Dreyer said, was that its tragedy was not "pathetic" but bitter—"the bitter tragedy of having to go on living even though ideals and happiness have been destroyed." Before this—even before *Ordet*—he had meant to make an epic life of Christ, preplanning it as he did over decades of historical research and study (among other things, he wanted to "exonerate" the New Testament Jews)—learning Hebrew, visiting Israel, sifting through records, preparing the lengthy screenplay. Which he first wrote, after the end of the war and after *Day of Wrath*'s European release, in Independence, Missouri (still a long way from Hollywood), at the invitation of a producer and money man (Blevins Davis) who lived there. The Christ of this screenplay (which was published after Dreyer's death) is, like Rossellini's, a humanist and political figure primarily. His miracles—unlike Johannes's—are ambiguous. And his resurrection—as with the Rossellini film—is

omitted. But the movie itself, which Dreyer was still planning and talking about up to the time of his death in 1968, never got made. Its prospects, whatever they were, surely can't have been helped by the advent of *Gertrud* four years before that, which was greeted at its Paris premiere—also meant to be a celebration of the filmmaker himself— with derision, even some speculation about senility. It dismayed even passionate admirers of *Ordet*.

Gertrud remains, I suppose, the most problematic of Dreyer's major films, but it is also in many ways the most fascinating—as problematic films often are. The heroine is an upper-class wife in turn-of-the-century Copenhagen, a concert singer, who decides to leave her husband, an important man in the government, for a younger man, an improvident musician-composer, while at the same time she resists the importunities of an old lover returned, now a famous poet. When the young composer eventually lets her down, she leaves her husband anyway, and the old lover, too, for what is apparently a bohemian but celibate new life in Paris. In an epilogue (Dreyer's invention) she is old and alone and visited by a male friend from the past, the one man in the story who has not been her lover. They both congratulate him on that. And he leaves her to her solitude, which seems finally and oddly to have fulfilled her.

Gertrud is in a sterner tradition of movie heroine than Inger is. Instead of being the woman who nurtures the man, Gertrud is in the line of the ones who judge him fatally—Joan Fontaine in Ophuls's *Letter from an Unknown Woman*, Sharmila Tagore in Satyajit Ray's *Days and Nights in the Forest*, Brigitte Bardot in Godard's *Contempt*— undoing him by their knowledge of him, exposing his shallowness by the contrast they inevitably offer to it. At the end they either move on from him, like Tagore, or become his victim in turn, like Bardot and Fontaine, done in by his emptiness.

This is more or less how Gertrud sees herself—before she, too, moves on. "Why do you torture me?" she says to her husband. She is the victim not only of the hollow men like him who want her to want them, but also of the one she herself wants—who turns out not to want her, or at least not enough. For him she becomes a passing adventure, for her husband merely an adjunct to his importance, for her old lover a distraction from his writing. The latter, however, was the one

OPPOSITE PAGE: Gertrud snuffing her candles

who had shown her long ago that love could be everything, as she later tells him. But then she had found out that for him it wasn't—and she left him. Just as she will now leave her current husband—whose love is also wanting in her view—for a man that she simply loves, and without conditions, but then who doesn't love her. As she later tells the writer, "Love is suffering, love is unhappiness." But she will never lose her conviction—carried even into her final solitude—that it is all that matters.

Nina Pens Rode is Gertrud, an austere heavy-lidded beauty with an upswept Doris Day haircut and a permanent heartsick look below it. Statuesque in long skirts, she moves as gravely and magisterially as the camera does. And it moves minimally, mostly to reframe slightly, or to follow the characters' almost equally minimal moves—mostly from chair to couch to another chair and so on, in rooms that seem at once luxurious and spare, in front of luminous grayish track-lit walls which sometimes disclose in pools of soft light an occasional hanging—a picture, a music score, a mirror (but unlike *Ordet*, where they are omnipresent, no clocks). The characters all talk a lot (he wanted to make "a film that was about *words*," Dreyer told the actor who complained about the length of his speeches), never brilliantly, often banally, and mostly in monotone—in head-on two-shots. So that instead of the movie cutting away (as in *Joan*) or traveling (as in *Ordet*) to the reaction shot, it now includes it, in longer and longer (up to ten minutes) unmoving takes in which two actors look mostly not at each other but half turned away, listening to the other as if to someone distinct but far away, while Dreyer makes sure we see them both at once. He was "not interested in cinema technique" in this film, he said later, while explaining its technique, but in "my actors' profoundest thoughts," in "their most subtle expressions." And so they turn themselves toward us. And they act in monotone, too—even the biggest emotions seem focused in nuances. Like Gustav Kanning's rage (Bendt Rothe) at his wife when she reveals her infidelity—shown by him not only in the cold, squidlike eyes, the bitten-off words of reproach, but the way he pinches the crease in his perfect trousers or fingers the watch fob hanging from his vest, staring fixedly ahead.

Why is this style so mesmerizing most of the time? It's often uncannily expressive, for one thing. Some of the film's most powerful single images are of those turned-away heads in the same close shot,

Gertrud at home with her prominent husband

in intensest connection there. (Gertrud even sits turned away later on from a statue in the park, a female nude who is also turned away from her.) But it's most powerful in those long sequences that might wear out your patience if they weren't so rich and full—so *intensely* static and slow. Take two successive but separate encounters during the film's most elaborate sequence—the big public celebration for Gertrud's returned ex-lover, Gabriel Lidman (Ebbe Rode), now a world-famous writer, who has returned to Denmark from his home in Rome and is now being feted at a banquet with speeches.

Lidman is, as we learn from those speeches—including a tribute from the young leader of an indoor parade of university students replete with song, banners, and torches—a sort of Nordic D. H. Lawrence, a poet whose work celebrates the erotic bond between man and woman as the center of meaning—who preaches, as the student orator puts it, that "in erotic ecstasy people find infinity and eternity" and that "to this idea of love all humanity is created and called." But these speeches—at just the point when her husband is in the middle of his less fulsome and more discriminating one (praising the poet's "inspirational stillness," a description that might also fit the film he's in)—have given Gertrud one of her headaches and caused her to repair to an upper room. Where Kanning soon joins her. She concedes to him that she was not at *Fidelio* (with its famous celebration of wifely loyalty) the night before but instead in the arms of her new love—Erland Jansson (though she doesn't reveal his name)—and they quarrel. She needs another rest after that and repairs to yet another room, leaving Kanning alone in this one, sitting on a couch near the door.

The door handle slowly turns and Gabriel Lidman enters—with the music from belowstairs, a string quartet, entering with him. He has been drinking too much at his tribute, as well as giving a rather too tentative acceptance speech, and he looks now less like a great erotic poet than like a Vegas comic between sets, slightly stooped with one hand behind his back and with a cigarette in the other, held very carefully between thumb and forefinger, as he stands and attends to the man on the couch with exaggerated alertness. Here you are, he says—and where is *she?*—as he leans forward to take in the other man's answer. Which is that she was ill before but is now somewhat better. Lidman makes a guttural sound—as if approving the reply. Kanning sits stiff-backed, unmoving, not looking at him: "Let's hear about you," he says in a dead voice, "how does it feel to be home again?" At which Lidman takes a long drag on the carefully held cigarette, eyes closing and brows rising, then adjusts his uncertain-looking stance towering over the other man and gives this wonderful answer:

> On your native soil? . . . Oh, yes . . . (*Gives a shuddering sigh*) The native soil of the fatherland is all well and good. I mean the earth—the air, the fields and forests. But the people, Kanning, the people— damn! . . . (*Another sigh*) I ended up in mixed company last night. Somewhat mixed company, one ought to say. Well . . . it doesn't matter. I was out to enjoy myself. So I shouldn't take it too seriously. Better to laugh it off . . .

And suddenly the music from below swells (as if someone had opened another door on it somewhere), sounding urgent and surging. They stop, they both look toward it . . . It dies down again. They resume. Gabriel: "What was it we were talking about?" he asks—with his ironic inflection. "Oh, yes," he answers—then almost as if talking to himself: "Listen . . . I want to go back to Rome. I can't work—." Breaking off— then gesturing with his cigarette, as if to say oh-you're-still-here . . . "I hear you'll be a cabinet minister?" "Yes," replies Kanning, "if you believe the newspapers." "You have to," says Gabriel—adamantly, again lifting cigarette to mouth. "You have to believe something in this world."

That "you have to" may be the film's only laugh line. But in a way the most telling thing in this dialogue of shared depression is the music that interrupts it. And that same music, going on, will also figure in the scene that immediately follows—when Gertrud comes back to this same room. This time it's Gabriel (Kanning has left) who is sitting alone on a couch. It is the first time he and she have been alone together since his return. "You look as young and pure as a bride," he says to her, as she gives him her hand and then sits next to him on the couch—but at its opposite end. "Gertrud, Gertrud, why did you leave me?" he says (more than once)—and eventually brings himself to tell her that her new young lover was among that "mixed company" of the night before, where he had been boasting to Gabriel and the others of his most recent conquest: "And he named her name, her beloved name," Gabriel says—as the music offscreen thrums away more urgently than ever. "What are they playing?" he then says, distracted in spite of himself, "what are we listening to now?" And you notice that his revelation about Erland's party behavior had been accompanied by a little roulade from the offscreen piano—and you're reminded that it's Erland's original composition that they are hearing, and Erland himself playing the piano. The music of youth—as the two comparative elders face their separate desolations, sitting on a couch and looking into the distance—with a space between them. (As one of David Ferry's "Found Single-Line Poems" puts it: "We're all in this apart.")

"Oh, Gabriel, help me to understand all this," she then says— meaning her suffering, meaning her impossible new love. She knew at the time that it was madness, just as she knows it now. Gabriel understands none of it any better, he tells her—he only knows now that his

"Oh, Gabriel, help me to understand all this . . ."

life was "shattered" the night before this when he heard "the woman whom I loved more than anything" casually traduced by "a reckless young man." (Old people take these things hard.) But then "nothing happens like we think it should," he adds. "How do you think it should, Gabriel?" Gertrud asks softly, turning to look at him, sitting back with hand resting on her chest—it's a genuine question, not a rhetorical one (she is readier to face the pain than he is). But then that still insistent music—the kid's music really—seems to preempt whatever his answer might have been: suddenly Gabriel's great dissolute-lion face begins to buckle and collapse with great heaving sobs in front of us—not turning away, that is, not until he feels her would-be comforting hand reaching out to his, when he rises and goes off.

Gertrud is a film of people reaching for meaning beyond their formulations of it. No surprise, then, that music—in its triumphant wordlessness—can seem like a corrective, even a rebuke. And if words seem inadequate to them, so, in a way, does reality—the reality of the present. "Give me your mouth," says Gertrud to Erland in one of their love scenes. She kisses him, then draws back and turns away, holding on to his arm and looking off: "Your wonderful mouth," she says—collecting an instant memory. And at the end she will live among those memories, as she tells her platonic old friend Axel (Axel Strobye) in the film's final sequence, and do so with a kind of happiness (her own private movies).

She is, of course, another of Dreyer's heroine saints. The ultimate one, in a way. She even does without God. But like most saints, from the Orwellian view at least, she is something of a pain in the ass—not fully human and not really trying to be. Not someone easy to live with, certainly (the long-suffering air, all those rests after headaches, and so on)—not even easy to tryst with. No wonder Erland decides to decide that she was just a good lay.

But before that he seems to approach her with the same reverence, the same awe even, as the other men do. Kneeling at her feet—in their precoital scene in his apartment—he puts his arm around her skirts, his face against her waist, while she touches his hair as if in benediction. "Strange woman," he murmurs, "who are you really?"

And you can tell by the way her eyes soften at this that she is more than ready for the question. She has just moved away from his embrace to sit on the piano bench in a close-up—in which he joins her, looking humble and boyish, like a supplicant consulting an oracle, his profile below and turned toward her, as he listens now to her answer—in what may be this movie's closest thing to a go-for-broke moment.

Gertrud with Erland—consenting to be his lover

They did almost forty takes of it, the actor who played young Erland, Baard Owe, later recalled (in his Criterion DVD interview). Even after the film had finally wrapped, Dreyer called the cast and crew back again, had the dismantled set rebuilt, and did sixteen more takes. It's not hard to imagine why. It's not only a scene that teeters on the brink of parody but one that ups the ante of the whole film, its daunting ambitiousness, its provoking strangeness. And does it flatly: "I am," she begins—looking tranced and distanced beneath the coquettish blond bangs, her head to one side, the shoulders of her frilly maidenly blouse at the bottom of the frame—"many things . . ."

> ERLAND (*beside her, looking off*): Who?
>
> GERTRUD (*raptly*): The morning dew, dripping from the leaves of the trees. White clouds sailing above, no one knows where . . .
>
> ERLAND (*undaunted*): Who else are you?
>
> GERTRUD: I am the moon, I am the sky . . .

And she goes on, in response to his prompting: she is also "a mouth, a mouth seeking another's mouth." "Sounds like a dream," he answers. "It is a dream," she answers. "Life is a dream." He seems disturbed by this idea, he looks up at her: "Life?" he says. "Life is a long, long chain of dreams," she replies, "drifting into one another . . ." And so on.

Dreyer, as his actor Baard Owe (Erland) said, "wanted to elevate this scene to the height of the famous ecstasy scene in *Joan of Arc*—he used that expression about it: she was to reach great heights. The director was especially concerned about Nina Pens Rode's lighting (the cinematographer again was Henning Bendtsen). And in the scene's general dimness, the softly focused brightness that floods her upper face, highlighting the expression in her eyes, is one of the things that gives her first close-up image here (when she first sits on the piano bench) its almost startling force. It's the rapt look, the one that she maintains (not looking directly at him) with slight variations—serenity, alarm, exaltation—throughout the take. And this magical lighting seems like another declaration of the "heights," of the transcendence she is meant to be reaching—and representing.

But it's also a reminder of how ambiguous, or at least ambivalent, even a "glamour" close-up can be. One of this movie's most stubborn integrities, after all, is that Gertrud, impressive as she is, is never moving or even likable. Dreyer himself, as he conceded, had decidedly mixed feelings about the character—especially about her self-absorption. And what partly signifies as her rapture in this scene also looks—startlingly—like self-intoxication, another more operatic inflection of that air of self-pity that this actor seems never entirely to quite lose (nor could Dreyer avoid registering it, it seems). Nor is that an impression that her I-am-the-morning-dew talk seems calculated to dispel. So that when there is at last a cut, and it involves her turning to kiss Erland in a reverse-angle shot, her face still in that transfiguring light but partly obscured by the back of his head as he presses his mouth to hers, it's almost a relief: so it is about him after all, about someone other than herself . . .

But of course it's not—in the end. When she reflects in her old age—in the movie's final sequence—that she has lived for love, you're reminded that it's not for love of him, nor for the love of Gabriel; it's not that she has known them, but that she has known love itself. "Am I beautiful? . . . young? . . . am I living?" asks the poem she has written and now shows to Axel—and answers each time in its refrain: "No. But I have known love." There will not even be her name on her gravestone, she tells him (she's already picked out the plot)—only the inscription "Amor Omnia."

Because of course love itself has a force, a presence, a reality of its own—as we all (hopefully) know. You can even love *it*, it seems—love yourself for feeling it even. Just as you can be moved by being moved—as Gertrud so often looks to be. But then how to escape this circle of self-absorption? In a world without God—Gertrud's world, and our own mostly, as well. It may have been Dreyer's, too. He kept his own counsel about that.

But there seems a kind of hope in this final sequence—where her old friend Axel is visiting her in her seclusion—in the light that suffuses the episode, almost bleaching out the two actors' faces at times, softening the outlines of walls and furnishings and objects around them, in what feels like an achieved serenity, almost. You recognize that light, however: it's been an emphatic presence in Gertrud's memories as they were shown to you (in the film's two flashbacks), and it's been there, too, as a kind of promise in the dappled walls and deep-

13

Balthazar

I.

ONE WAY TO avoid actors' self-consciousness is to avoid actors altogether—as Robert Bresson resolved to do after his first four films with professionals. He didn't believe in actors, he said. He didn't even believe in nonactors acting, as they did for Rossellini and De Sica and other neorealists. And he did all he could to keep that from happening with the amateurs in his own subsequent films—instructing his "models," as he called them, to play their roles without affect, to say their lines without overt expression, having them repeat them over and over again beforehand until they seemed devoid of either emotion or motivation. The result of such methods, of course (he made ten films strictly enforcing them), was a performing style that looked and felt impassive, uninflected, even narcoleptic at times. *All* acting is lying, he claimed. He wanted the authentic and mysterious human presence in front of his camera, not an impersonation—not "realism" but truth. In this way Bresson was probably the ultimate film artist of "watching them be"—at least its extremest, its most nearly literal exponent. Until Andy Warhol, anyway. (At least they were both Catholics.)

The result in his films for some viewers can seem less like "truth" than a higher artifice, a kind of imposed monotony. Pauline Kael, for one (not surprisingly)—who, although she admired Bresson's earlier, marginally more conventional films, *Diary of a Country Priest* (1951) and *A Man Escaped* (1956), found sitting through the later, more austere ones, she said—apropos of *Mouchette* (1967)—"like taking a whipping and watching every stroke coming."

Well, okay—you certainly know what she means. And that's certainly the risk that Bresson's method runs. But once you get used to it, once you give up such resistance, you're likely to find that as often as you see the "stroke coming," you're surprised by a feeling of revelation when it lands. Or else you're not.

He saw most other movies, he said, as "competitions in grimaces." And nearly alone, he did not at all admire Dreyer's *The Passion of Joan of Arc*. "I understand that at the time," he offered in a 1957 interview, "the film was a small revolution, but now I only see all the actors' horrible buffooneries and terror-stricken grimaces which you only want to flee." (If he later saw *Gertrud*, the most Bressonian of the Dreyer films, he never said.) And he particularly resented Falconetti's "way of casting her eyes to heaven." And in *his* Joan-on-trial film—which appeared some five years after that interview—Joan (Florence Carrez) would look downward a lot (to the fury of his cameraman, L. H. Burel—who thought Carrez had "marvelous, beautiful eyes"). *The Trial of Joan of Arc* (1962) is perhaps the most direly uninflected of all Bresson's films—adhering to the trial records (more closely even than Dreyer) in back-and-forth straight-on medium shots of Joan as she answers and of her inquisitors as they grill her, of various onlookers, both lay and clerical, faces as neutral as the voices. There are—as always in his films—memorable details: Joan's shackled bare feet almost skipping on her way to the stake; a lost-looking dog turning around in the crowd; a pair of doves flying up and away from the smoke and clamor; and the final image of the charred and smoking stake itself with a concluding drum roll on the soundtrack.

A Bresson film, nevertheless, depends crucially on the impassive "beings" he is centrally watching in them—what Susan Sontag called the "luminous presences" of his great "models." But not all his models are equal. And Sontag seems to have felt that the Joan film could have been saved by a more luminous presence than Carrez's in the lead. But I'm not so sure. Bresson's austerity—as happens there, I think—can sometimes register less as a reach toward transcendence than a personal rigidity, even stubbornness.

But if his asceticism of means didn't always work, it mostly did—and powerfully so, in films like *Pickpocket* (1959), *A Man Escaped*, and

Mouchette, among others, even his final one, *L'Argent* (1983). But the movie I want to talk about here is the one in which the Bressonian austerity works supremely. And then some.

II.

HIS *AU HASARD BALTHAZAR* (1966) is probably the greatest movie I've ever seen. I felt that when I first saw it almost four decades ago and I think so still. "More a miracle than a movie," Molly Haskell once said. "Really the world in an hour and a half," said Godard at its premiere. And both the miracle and the world are what Bresson, by whatever grace or dispensation, seems to have pulled off. By now most people who see it seem to agree about this. For director Michael Haneke, for one (who first saw it as a university student), it "remains the most precious of cinematic jewels." "No other film has ever made my heart spin like this one does." And so on.

And I'd almost like to let the whole thing go at that. It's always nice to pay a tribute to sublimity and then pass on. It's more daunting to confront it. But that's what I'll try to do here at the end of this book—however inadequately.

To begin with—a difficulty for some—it's about a donkey, the eponymous Balthazar. The humans in the movie—and there are many—are the ones who intersect his life from birth to death, the Deadly Sins incarnate, more or less, as Bresson had suggested. And they are played by the nonacting nonactors. As always, assembled for this movie only, and painstakingly chosen.

That the movie is going to be a curious experience is signaled from the opening credits—which start to unroll with an annunciatory roulade from a piano accompanying them—a passage from Schubert's A Major Sonata (D. 959). Which is suddenly interrupted for a moment, a strange and thrilling one, by a loud and sustained donkey's bray. It's over, and the piano resumes . . . but you're fairly warned: the sublime will keep strange company in this film. Like Titania with Bottom.

Then it begins. No more piano at first, very little dialogue, ambient sounds, a succession of mostly unexplained scenes, dissolving one into another as they go. First a close-up of a little donkey nursing at his mother's underside, sheep milling around them, their bells clangorous, the wind stirring the donkey's fur as he presses his head into his mother. Long delicate hands reach down into the frame from above and touch him. Give him to us, say the children, a boy and a girl. Impossible, says the father. And in the next shot he is leading the donkey with the children away down the hill. Close-up of the donkey inside a house; I baptize thee Balthazar, says the boy, in the name of the Father, the Son, and the Holy Spirit—as the baptismal water runs down the lustrous black fur onto the snow-white muzzle. Outside then with his keeper, the little donkey trots into a stall in the stable and stands looking out while it's locked. Next the children play with him in a hayloft. And then in a garden. The boy and the girl sit together in a swing while a second little girl (the owner of the hands in the first shot) pushes them. The two on the swing are head to head and tender. "Jacques," murmurs the girl. "Marie," says the boy.

It's at this point that you hear the piano again and the movie's central music theme, the poignant andantino melody from the same posthumous Schubert sonata, with its mixture of lament and acquiescence—a sound that will recur throughout the film and with increasing power and poignance ("the donkey's music," Bresson later called it). Balthazar goes to yet another little girl nearby, apparently very ill and lying on a pallet. She gives him some sugar and he goes off. Her nurse gives her some medicine in a spoon. The little girl covers her eyes and weeps.

Jacques and Marie (and friend) playing with Balthazar

The ellipses without explanation go on: dissolve to Jacques in a traveling coat kneeling on a wooden bench, carving a heart with his and Marie's names inside it. His father, stern by a car, standing in an overcoat, holding the car door open, calls to him. The nurse comes out of a doorway and looks at the father. In the reverse shot he looks distressed. The nurse goes inside again. He follows her. In the room is the sick girl, dressed for travel but sound asleep, stretched out on a cot. Hands again—the nurse's—reach down into the frame and lift her up, very gently.

Cut to a close-up of Marie kissing Jacques through the car window—he is inside, she is outside. She steps back and stands in front of the grown-ups' legs ranged on the porch behind her. A reverse close-up of Jacques in the car window. He will see her next summer, he says, and stretches out his arm to her. But in the reverse shot to this it's the little donkey who is standing in her place looking back at Jacques—not Marie, who is standing among the grown-ups' legs now and behind Balthazar, peeking out over him, as the piano reaches the resolving chord and the sequence—an idyll with a dying child in it—fades out.

And it seems to me that by this time in the movie—only minutes into it, after this delicate mordant lyricism, and especially with that final (and mysterious) who's-got-the-donkey? little joke—you're bound to feel that you're in the hands of a filmmaker like the sonata maker on the soundtrack: a master of inexplicable beauties.

And in a very different sort of animal movie, to be sure. The infant Balthazar flashes at least as large an "adorable" quotient as any other baby furry animal. You register that but you don't get to indulge it. Even as a baby (and another donkey "actor" presumably), he's too grave a presence—more moving than beguiling, his "baptism" less a children's game of grown-up than a solemn event, with its own backwash of mystery.

Next he is grown up himself—and the tone changes abruptly, even violently. In a sequence of rapid agitated cuts and dramatic low angles, we see him hauling and plowing and carting, blows raining on him as he is pushed and pulled and kicked. Until one of the overloaded wagons he's pulling turns over on a country road and he climbs out of the hay and escapes—with farmers in pursuit.

And he returns to his old place—a long trot up to and through rusted iron gates and past unweeded grounds and a For Sale sign on a tree, past a creaking door swinging in the wind and then around and through the garden furniture on the patio, past the bench where Jacques had carved his heart—then into the childhood stall. Where he stands and brays. He looks shabby now as well as big—a common work animal, grown into the halters and clinking chains encasing him. The sheen of childhood is gone—except for the white muzzle and underside, and his white-tipped ears.

He is discovered there, in his old stall, by Marie's father, a schoolteacher and tenant farmer, with his towering bird-of-prey handsomeness (Philippe Asselin). "Marie, Marie, come look!" he cries. And in the next shot, the marvelous and beautiful Anne Wiazemsky, with her oval face, stricken eyes, and softly pouting mouth, as the grown-up Marie, in her homely print dress, emerges from the stall with her arms around the donkey's neck. The camera tilts down to show his face, at peace between her hands.

She is in a way, after all, his leading lady. Later on, outside in the middle of the night and in her nightdress, alone with him, she crowns him ritually with wildflowers—a pagan counterpart to the baptism. While the two of them are being watched from hiding by the local bully and petty crook, the sinister satyrlike Gérard (François Lafarge), crouching in the bushes with a buddy. She's in love with him, Gérard whispers—and he with her. With a donkey? says the buddy, incredulous. Like in mythology, answers Gérard, trenchantly if improbably. (He also sings solo in the church choir.)

But Marie is not so sure it's love she feels for the grown-up and still faithful Jacques (Walter Green), who is as whitebread attractive as Gérard is creepily so. But she's enough attached to him that when her stiff-necked father drives the boy away (over a property quarrel with Jacques's father, who owns the place) she locks herself in her room in protest. Prompting her father—who prides himself on his self-taught modern farming methods ("That donkey makes us look ridiculous")—to sell Balthazar to a local baker.

This is how Balthazar ends up with Gérard, now the baker's delivery man. And how Marie encounters them both, stopping her little car on a country road when she recognizes the donkey, carrying sacks of baguettes. She runs to him: birds are chirping, leaves stirring in the wind and sun, and they are reunited again. But when she returns to her car, Gérard is inside it. With his cupped and upturned hand resting

Gérard (François Lafarge, at right) and his gang

obscenely, as it seems in the close-up, on the driver's seat she has just left. She tells him to get out. He lifts his hand and stays. She gets in. And he makes a pass at her, his hand on the back of her neck, that is like nothing so much as a doom falling. She runs from the car then, to where Balthazar stands by the road. She and Gérard, playing a game now, begin to feint and dodge and chase each other around the immobile animal, jostling but not budging him.

Then something astonishing: Bresson repeatedly cuts away here from the human actors, from the excitement between them, to the face of the donkey, as unreadable as the rest of him is unmoving—as if that face were somehow the point. You're surprised by this almost as much as you're convinced—which becomes the second surprise. As if

346 WATCHING THEM BE

the movie is anticipating your own deepest response—as if it knows not only more than you do but more than anyone does, making connections that go deeper than metaphor or paraphrasable meaning. In all the hectic feeling and action of the scene you look at Balthazar's stillness, even his remoteness—and that seems right. It's abetted by the Schubert theme, which sounds again here, very briefly—falling silent when Marie suddenly breaks away and falls and Gérard picks her up and they walk back to the car together. The sequence ends when—after a discreet ellipsis—the car drives off in the background of the shot, leaving Gérard behind on the road in the foreground. When he lifts his conch shell horn to his mouth (he uses it to announce his deliveries) and blows it loudly and exultantly, Marie, as we know then, has been *truly* fucked.

And so it goes from there. With the pair making out between deliveries, leaving Balthazar and his baguettes to wait outside in the rain and cold and snow, where he brays in distress. He is ill and about to be euthanized (the local vet comes with a mallet) when a homeless man named Arnold (Jean-Claude Guilbert) intervenes. He'll take him on the road, he says, and the animal will recover. Which he does. Arnold takes him and the other donkey he owns up into the hills to give rides to the tourists. But Balthazar's savior, kind as he is (Gérard likes to bully him, too), is a drunk who, when he is drunk, beats his animals even more savagely than Gérard does.

So Balthazar runs away—again. And this time—in one of the film's loopiest inspirations—he joins the circus. Hauling the meals for the circus zoo at first—until a trainer spots him as a "genius" (his kind knows everything, he says) and he becomes the show's star attraction, introduced over loudspeakers as "the mind of the century," fitted out with a coquettish little plume on his head and led into the center ring, where he proceeds to add and multiply sums on a blackboard by tapping out the answers with his front hoof, with his tuxedoed handler announcing and confirming the results. It's an act like the real-life Clever Hans, a showbiz horse in 1900s Germany who became famous for the same reputed skill. But Balthazar blows the act when he catches sight of Arnold in his audience one night, brandishing a wine bottle. Balthazar throws a tantrum onstage and is returned to his former owner.

Who will later die while riding him, falling to the ground between

The figure in the background (the grain merchant in the foreground)

his hooves—after being variously threatened by Gérard and then inheriting a fortune from an unknown and distant relation. Balthazar becomes part of the estate sale and is acquired by a miserly grain merchant (Pierre Klossowski), who plans on working him to death, mostly by withholding food from him. It's Marie's mother and father (Marie having gone off with Gérard and his gang) who buy him back—for his final days.

Marie is, as Godard first observed, the movie's other donkey—even passing through some of the same hands: her father's, Gérard's, even (a one-night stand) the grain merchant's. But unlike Balthazar, she bears the burden of human freedom. Where he embodies meaning, she must look for it. As she does: rejecting her father's rationalism and pride, resisting Jacques's romanticism, succumbing to Gérard's sensuality, even to his cruelty. What can I do? she responds to her mother's concern—it's love, and I would die for him if he asked me to. *"Pauvre petite,"* replies her mother (Natalie Joyaut).

Because it's also, as it turns out, emptiness and humiliation. And when she's had enough, finally she turns up one night at the grain merchant's door, looking for shelter and some food, but also genuinely wondering if it's really possible to live the minimal way that he does, without illusions or ideals, for only what you can hold and touch and own ("I love money and I hate death"). But she refuses his money and leaves the next morning.

Back home to the folks—where else? Balthazar is back again, too. And Jacques—waiting on "their" bench, still faithful, still vacantly handsome. He's the one she's been dreaming of, she tells him—the one who will love her and tell her that what's happened to her since they last met is not her fault. Except that it is, as she also tells him. She has learned about evil and Jacques never will. You live in make-believe, she tells him—in the world of their childhood vows and their games with Balthazar (who is grazing nearby). "Reality," she says, "is something else." For her it's mostly Gérard and coming to know that has been "like waking to a madness."

But madness trumps tepidity, it seems. Still, she will try: "I will love him, I will love him," she says, in Balthazar's stall feeding him some hay. Dissolve to a long shot of Jacques and herself, running hand in hand, Marie in the lead, up a hill toward the camera, coming to a stop in a medium close shot. And you are struck this time by Jacques, how strong and authoritative he looks here, in his tenderness toward her—it's really too bad he won't do. "Forget them," he says to her—and you realize she is going to meet Gérard and the gang. "I want to have it out with them," she says, like an addict's last rationalization—then stumbles forward into the close shot, falling at his knees and kissing almost greedily the hand that he holds out to steady her with. She rises and goes on alone, toward a stone house in the near distance below.

The next time we see her, when Jacques and her father go searching for her, she is inside the empty house. Gérard and the boys have gang-raped her and stolen all her clothes: she is found naked and crouched in the corner of an empty room, pressing herself into the wall. Thoroughly and finally degraded—at last. She is gone, says her mother when Jacques turns up to reclaim her later—and she will never return. And (the movie being nearly over) she never does.

At the hilltop, Jacques wants her to stop—instead, she
kisses his hand and goes on.

And there is more to the narrative than even all this—characters and complexities that I haven't even mentioned: Gérard's enabler, the baker's wife; Arnold's putative "crime"; the father's public humiliation and lawsuit; and so on. And we pass through it all sort of the way we do in life—through stories, even our own sometimes, that we only partly understand, with a feeling that we may be missing the point of it all, at least in the long run. But not quite so much as the people inside the movie are, since through all this we are aware of seeing what they are *not* exactly seeing—the figure of the donkey. Standing at least partly here—and not subtly (why should it be?)—for that world of unnoticed suffering that underpins all our lives, the more comfortable they are. When he is otherwise just being there—without any effect to speak of on the human destinies around him. Just a presence. In a way the film is about the mystery of presence—what it is and where it comes from. Partly, it would seem, from unawareness of itself.

He has to be the most beautiful donkey in the world, my friend claimed (she said she wished she could have been at his casting call). But he is also the way that Susan Sontag (writing before *Balthazar* was made) describes Bresson's human stars (in *Pickpocket* and *A Man Escaped*), as being plain before they (inevitably) become beautiful. And the truth is that it's not so easy to tell—for most of us—one donkey from another. It helps here that Arnold's other donkey is lighter-colored, and a little more bedraggled-looking, with an unruly cowlick on top of the head. You take her for a female if only because she is smaller, and possibly because the two of them trotting down the road together with matching burlap sacks swinging from their sides, or tied up together at the curbside waiting for Arnold, have a certain wearily conjugal air.

But no matter such impressions, Balthazar—unlike Bottom or Apuleius's Golden Ass or J. F. Powers's rectory cats or the "cast" of *March of the Penguins*—is *not* a virtual human being. Nor is he Christ, as many critics have read him—nor is he all-of-us or Everyman, as Michael Haneke claims. He is what you see—a donkey, if an exceptional one. Never mind that he gets so many of what look like classic reaction shots—his close-ups while standing between Marie and Gérard circling him in play, for example, or during his nocturnal crowning by Marie—if we could ever be sure what his "reaction" was meant to be. And the several human categories that people in the film assign him to—lover, genius, and finally saint—though clearly meant to be accurate in some way, are extravagant enough to remove him from our understanding even further.

So it's really a matter of *looking* at him in just the ways that Bresson directs us to. (You "must make yourself loved" by the spectator, he once said, by showing him "things in the order and in the way that you love to see them and feel them yourself.") Sometimes—as usual with this filmmaker—very indirectly. As when Gérard, when the donkey balks, ties a newspaper to his tail and lights it. You see Balthazar in long shot bucking and running off down the road with tail apparently smoking—then in a traveling close-up, his chain trailing slowly in the grass (the Schubert andantino theme here, too), starting and stopping and then moving again each time Gérard reaches his hand down to grasp it. A detail shot that's more eloquent about the aftermath of petty meanness than you can imagine any more frontal view of it ever being. Similarly, when Arnold's tourists are riding Balthazar and his donkey companion through the scenic hills, you hear the lordly male voices of the passengers discoursing about topics like action painting and guilt-and-the-unconscious while you watch the two donkeys' legs and hooves picking their careful beautiful way over the stones in the stream below with a delicacy that is nowhere to be heard in those offscreen voices. ("He sits on a clever donkey," Bresson said of one of the riders, "I make him talk nonsense.")

And then there are the frontal views. All those ambiguous reaction shots. And close-ups at times of such plain heart-stopping beauty that they're like meta-close-ups. As when Marie earlier on crowns the donkey with flowers in the middle of the night (see illustration on page 263). The sequence begins as you see her bare feet below her nightdress moving softly, soundlessly through the grass, with cicadas singing— then her hands reaching down gathering shoots and flowers, the camera following the hands as they rise into a two-shot of herself and Balthazar, with his white muzzle and white-ringed eyes. And you see then his incongruous crown, with idiot-looking daisies popping out of the leaves, and Marie in the same shot very tenderly adding the new bits. Then with a hand resting between his eyes she looks around— nobody watching now, right? Then, seemingly reassured, she lifts the enormous and beautiful head to her lips, the moonlight glinting in his eyes as she raises them out of the shadow, and kisses his muzzle, lingeringly, as the camera moves gently in and slightly *under* it—a camera movement like a caress, in the Bressonian style, both sensual and ascetic. You're moved but you keep your distance. And Balthazar, in his grave alert stillness, in his submission both to her and to the flowers, looks at once vulnerable and Olympian.

Next, Marie goes to sit on a bench nearby. Slumped against a tree behind, her forearm drooping across her lap, she contemplates her work. And you are struck by the way she looks not only touchingly girlish but incomparably and knowingly old, just the way much younger girls than she often can. The answering shot of Balthazar, however, is not her point of view but ours, looking at his eyes and upper head alone, bringing us closer in to him than we've been before—though you needn't be aware of that to feel the slight shock of it here, the slight sudden grandeur. His eye with its white ring is shadowed while the flowers above it and the white-tipped ears are lit by the moon—the ears twitching.

Gérard, as I said, is there, too, spying with a cohort from the bushes. And when he reaches his hand out from there to touch Marie's, she panics and runs into the house. She appears then at an upstairs window and looks down on Gérard and his buddy as they proceed to beat and kick the donkey below. She watches this, then slowly closes the shutter, withdrawing behind it.

Why doesn't she protest—call or cry out? It's what we want her to do (we are still, after all, at the movies). Is she afraid of waking her folks? Afraid of Gérard? Clearly she's already attracted to him. Probably all these things. But as usual in this film, you're likelier to know why a character *might* do or fail to do something than why she or he actually does it. But you are almost never unpersuaded—even when you're most surprised. One of the ugliest of those surprises is that closed shutter here. The horror of these scenes is not so much Gérard's gratuitous sudden cruelty to Balthazar as Marie's turning away from it.

Because in the end her failing spiritual fortunes through the film are charted less in terms of selfishness or recklessness or masochism, of filial ingratitude or the Deadly Sin of Lust, as in terms of her neglect of Balthazar, her growing inattention to him. The emphasis is on her passivity (the Deadly Sin of Sloth?). Her decline begins (as does his) with her forgetting to feed him.

If that seems improbable—well, just *look* at him. In the ways the film asks you to do. "The supernatural," Bresson wrote (echoing

Marie watches Balthazar in the moonlight while
Gérard reaches out from the dark.

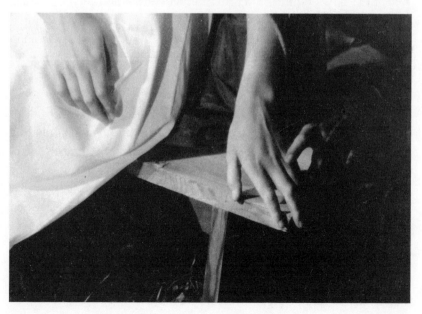

Rossellini, betraying his own neorealist roots) "is only the real rendered more precise," is "real things seen close up." At the circus, before his "discovery" and while he is still a menial, Balthazar is pulling the zoo animals' food cart. The sequence is a straightforward sort of montage, anchored in its recurring close-ups of Balthazar as a keeper leads him from cage to cage, chains clanking and cart creaking, stopping at each station in turn. Offscreen animal sounds at first—low-pitched growling, high-pitched chattering—sounding distant. As Balthazar is led into a close-up, where he stops and stands, shifting his weight in place. Then a fierce loud roar, sounding very nearby, and you see what he is looking at now: a majestic and magnificent tiger, very still and silent, reclining along his cage wall, head and shoulders up and alert, shadowed by bars, staring through them with transfixing, eerily luminous eyes. Balthazar's answering close-up (he's never in the same shot with the others) staring back. At the glamour, you suppose—unbelievable as it is. And then you see it again—again the tiger's stare, and a silence as if the world had stopped, as if *he'd* done it with that look alone. But then it resumes, and Balthazar is led off again.

To the next cage: a rather dingy, middling-sized white bear, neither silent nor serene but restive and growling, pushing disconsolately at his bars. Balthazar pricks up his ears at the complaining sounds: another look at the bear and he is led off again, leftward—and then rightward into the next shot, where he turns forward into his close-up, accompanied by sounds of monkeys screeching, and sees next a listless-looking chimpanzee, with a chain around his neck, seated before his bars with one arm raised and resting along the side wall, looking blankly back at him.

And whatever Balthazar may be or not be feeling through all of this, *we* are bound to register decline—from a tiger burning bright to a monkey in chains. But the next (and final) sight is something else altogether. It's preceded by Balthazar's closest close shot so far—almost nothing but his eye—which is matched in its intensity by the shot that follows it: a close-up of an elephant—or rather of its eye, the furrowed rough hide around it, the base of his trunk moving in the motions of eating. While the imponderable eye, small and translucent and unearthly, looks off. Without expression. But a witnessing eye, clearly. Like Balthazar's own. After registering it, he trots off (to stardom, ultimately, in the center ring, as it turns out).

But what are we watching here, anyway? Not "expressions," surely—the sort of thing we might watch for in people, and especially in people actors. What we are watching, in fact—as often we are at the intensest moments in all kinds of movies—is intense watching itself. Mostly Balthazar's. Just what Clever Hans was later revealed to be doing all along, rather than computing sums. (He never got the answer right if the questioner was out of his sight or didn't know it himself.) We're contemplating mystery, then—a community of it, in fact, a world of perception utterly beyond our own. And we're not just invited to look at it here but to be *still* in front of it, to refrain from trying to impose on it our own meanings, our own wills in fact. That injunction is one reason that the sequence, as impassive in its affect as its animal "actors" are, is so moving.

And the movie's people are nearly as affectless, of course. Thanks to Bresson's insistence on nonacting, the humans become only marginally more overt than the animals, and nearly as mysterious to look at. That, of course, is the underlying point in this movie. It's not the usual sentimental anthropomorphic one, that animals have human gifts, but rather that people have animal ones—the dignity, the purity and intactness, the final remoteness and inviolable beauty of animal nature.

Bresson rejects psychological analysis, and for much the same reasons that D. H. Lawrence did: as an affront to and a trivialization of human mystery. And acting, he felt—with its aim of making character intelligible—was another such affront. What he was after was the deeps, the essence of the human person—bypassing the will. Hence the stasis and automatism, the uninflected reading of lines. He compared filming a shot to "stealing" what his subject was hiding even from himself. He meant his "models" to rise above imitation, above intentionality, to achieve an animal purity on the screen that could also seem spiritual—transcending self-consciousness, their impassivity prompting us to watch them, this film's human figures, with something like the awe and respect—or at least the uncertainty—that we learn to give to Balthazar.

III.

"THAT WHICH IS beautiful in a film is the movement toward the unknown," Bresson wrote in 1962. And one of the most extraordinary things about this one, his masterpiece, is the way you feel that movement inside it, palpably, almost literally—progressing over its length and culminating in the final scenes.

Before that, the movie seems to have reached a point—familiar in life—where it feels as if everyone has gone away. Arnold has died, Marie has disappeared, her father, stubborn in his pride to the end, has turned his face to the wall and died. Gérard, of course, persists. And Marie's widowed mother—arguably the most generous spirit in the film—sits under a tree with her head in her hands with Balthazar grazing nearby. She says no when Gérard, with a sidekick, asks if they can borrow him. He's worked enough and he's old, she says, and he is all she has left. "Besides," she says, lifting a tear-streaked face from her hand to add a thought before they go, "he's a saint."

And the scene dissolves to the next: a close-up of Balthazar at the head of a religious procession outdoors, at the center of altar boys and incense fumes and swinging censers, with the communion host encased in a glass and silver tabernacle perched swayingly on his back, a priest and congregation following behind him. Then fadeout.

But his travail is not over. Gérard and the sidekick steal him that night for a smuggling run across the border. They load him with gunny sacks hanging from his sides, a blanket on top, and fill the sacks with stockings and perfume and gold trinkets, and then lead him with blanket and bags up into the hills, through trees and over rocks. The montage of this climb evokes the earlier religious procession—except that the "altar boys" now are two thugs who are beating and kicking him on the way, urging him on. Yet with the moonlight darting and sparkling over their movements and the Schubert theme suddenly on the soundtrack again, there is a feeling of exaltation, too—even though you know he's going to his end and you dread it.

They come to the crest of the hill at the edge of some trees overlooking a grassy plain below, and they stop to look and listen—in a frontal medium long shot. By now this shot or something like it feels very familiar: two intensely focused people, with the donkey between them, concerned about their own purposes, when we are only concerned about *his*, such as they are or may be. Now more than ever. It's a kind of summa moment—epitomizing the movie.

They crouch as some gunshots ring out. Far-off voices call out a warning. Then more shots, closer this time. Gérard and his friend run off down into the valley and disappear into the distance below. Close-up of Balthazar, his eyes and ears—listening, then starting as more shots ring out. He turns and leaves, going back into the wood behind.

The same one he is peering out from when daylight comes and birds are chirping. And we see in a close-up that he has been shot, with blood running out of a leg wound. Alone now for the first time since his early scenes, he walks out into the open, the burlap bags hanging like tumors from below his dark blanket. There are mountains in the distance. He stands and looks, framed against faraway chalk cliffs. Then a tinkling of bells, like the sounds that accompanied his infancy. And in the distance, in long shot, at the bottom of a great sloping plain, a flock of sheep are coming, with herding dogs barking and running them along, and a briefly glimpsed shepherd. The sheep graze and mill, the sheep bells sound, the dogs run and bark. All the sounds having the resonance of great spaces. And as the camera tilts down from above, there is Balthazar in their midst, partly lying on his side, partly sitting up, seeming to nod a bit, as the sheep seem to engulf him. The Schubert piano again now—as we watch his head declining, the sheep gradually and slowly departing. Next, he is stretched out among the stragglers, who move past and around him—with his halter and chains, his blanket and bulging sacks. A lamb in the shot's foreground sniffs at him and goes on. More milling and going off—and the soundtrack piano falls silent. Giving way to the increasingly clamorous sounds of the bells. As we see him finally, at a slightly lower angle, where he looks—the sheep are gone—both bloated, his white underbelly showing between the burlap folds, and weighted to the earth. Like a pile of old clothes. And the screen goes black.

This movie, one writer has observed (the novelist Gary Indiana in the liner notes to the Criterion *Pickpocket*) is "so painful to watch that if you can sit through it without weeping you deserve to be hit by a Mack truck when you leave the theatre." But for some people the movie—and particularly this ending—might *feel* like the Mack truck, it's so purely harrowing. And it may feel, too, like a rigged game. Balthazar is such a total figure of innocence (he doesn't even eat meat). And you see the "strokes coming" this time from very far off, again and again. You may even worry about what they were really doing to that donkey—as my friend who admired his beauty did. (Given the spirit of the film, I have to trust that he was largely well treated.)

Balthazar's death

But the rigged game goes beyond the film. It's more or less all around us. If we pay attention, that is. And in art at least we are attracted to pain as a subject—as in fact the truest, most finally satisfying subject of all. From the Greeks onward, the unhappy ending has been the only really and deeply convincing one. A phenomenon that not even Aristotle could quite explain. He might account for *Oedipus*, perhaps, but never for the mysteries of *Lear*, or of *Waiting for Godot* certainly. Or of *Balthazar*.

But—unlike *Godot*, where it is famously withheld—there is a sense of resolution here. It comes with death—as usual. A death that might well have seemed, for all its pathos, otherwise meaningless—a dumb animal meeting with an even dumber accident. If it weren't that the unknown that the film is moving toward didn't come clearer, and seem more and more deeply to be a religious one. There are fleeting if explicit hints to this on its surface: among them that Balthazar is named after one of the Magi, and that he is loaded for his final journey with the explicitly named gifts of perfume and gold. And if he is not himself a shepherd among sheep, he lives and dies in their neighborhood: he dies *from* our sins, not for them. But such allusions don't just decorate the film, they spring from its deepest impulses.

Like the feeling of exaltation that hovers over Balthazar's ascent into the hills toward what is clearly his final abjection. His blessedness, as you come more and more to feel about him, is like a fulfillment of the Beatitudes, of their radical unworldliness. Like Flannery O'Connor's image of Christ as he appears to Hazel Motes in *Wise Blood*—"that wild ragged figure who moves from tree to tree in the back of his mind"—Balthazar belongs to the back. But here things are reversed—like the meek and the poor inheriting the earth, the back becomes the foreground, even the world ("in an hour and a half," as Godard said).

Because the besetting human sins in this movie are inattention, even forgetfulness. A point that for me at least climaxes memorably in that long shot of Balthazar standing by the trees between the two smugglers, who are not aware as we are that something enormous is coming, not aware that it's *not* about them—guilty of the sort of un- consciousness that simply being human often entails: not only living in unnoticed suffering, but in unnoticed wonder, unnoticed mystery. Never mind that everyone dies alone and so does Balthazar. What you feel at his end—and the whole movie has worked to make you feel that this is important—is that his fall, like the sparrow's, is watched.

SELECTED BIBLIOGRAPHY

Affron, Charles. *Star Acting: Gish, Garbo, Davis.* New York: E. P. Dutton, 1977.

Baldwin, James. *The Devil Finds Work.* New York: Dell, 1976.

Barthes, Roland. *Mythologies.* New York: Hill and Wang, 1972.

Baxter, John. *De Niro: A Biography.* London: HarperCollins, 2002.

Bazin, Andre. *What Is Cinema?* 2 vols. Berkeley and Los Angeles: University of California Press, 1976.

Bergman, Ingrid, with Alan Burgess. *Ingrid Bergman: My Story.* New York: Delacorte Press, 1980.

Bloom, Harold. *Shakespeare: The Invention of the Human.* New York: Riverhead Books, 1998.

Bresson, Robert. *Notes on Cinematography.* New York: Urizen Books, 1977.

Callow, Simon. *Charles Laughton: A Difficult Actor.* London: Methuen, 1987.

Cardullo, Bert, ed. *Bazin at Work: Major Essays and Reviews from the Forties and Fifties.* New York and London: Routledge, 1997.

Cooke, Alistair. *Alistair Cooke at the Movies.* Edited by Geoff Brown. London: Allen Lane, 2009.

———, ed. *Garbo and the Night Watchman.* London: Secker and Warburg, 1972.

Dreyer, Carl Theodor. *Four Screenplays.* Bloomington and London: Indiana University Press, 1970.

———. *Dreyer in Double Reflection.* Edited by Donald Skoller. New York: Da Capo Press, 1970.

———. *Jesus.* New York: Dial Press, 1972.

Ferry, David. *Bewilderment: New Poems and Translations.* Chicago and London: University of Chicago Press, 2012.

Frayling, Christopher. *Sergio Leone: Something to Do with Death*. London: Faber and Faber, 2000.

Gallagher, Tag. *The Adventures of Roberto Rossellini: His Life and Films*. New York: Da Capo Press, 1998.

Godard, Jean-Luc. *Godard on Godard: Critical Writings*. Edited by Jean Narboni and Tom Milne. New York: Viking 1972.

———. *Masculine Feminine: A Film by Jean-Luc Godard*, ed. Robert Hughes. New York: Grove Press, 1969.

Greene, Graham. *The Pleasure Dome: The Collected Film Criticism 1935–40*. Edited by John Russell Taylor. London: Secker and Warburg, 1972.

Grier, Pam, with Andrea Kagan. *Foxy: My Life in Three Acts*. New York: Springboard Press, 2010.

Hiller, Jim, ed. *Cahiers du Cinéma—The 1950s: Neo-Realism, Hollywood, New Wave*. Cambridge: Harvard University Press, 1985.

Hollander, Anne. *Moving Pictures*. New York: Alfred A. Knopf, 1989.

Kael, Pauline. *For Keeps: Thirty Years at the Movies*. New York: Dutton, 1994.

———. *Conversations with Pauline Kael*. Edited by Will Brantley. Jackson: University Press of Mississippi, 1995.

Kazan, Elia. *A Life*. New York: Alfred A. Knopf, 1988.

Lambert, Gavin. *On Cukor*. New York: G. P. Putnam's, 1972.

Leamer, Laurence. *As Time Goes By: The Life of Ingrid Bergman*. New York: Harper and Row, 1986.

Leaming, Barbara. *Bette Davis: A Biography*. New York: Simon & Schuster, 1992.

Leonard, Elmore. *Rum Punch*. New York: HarperCollins, 1972.

Lopate, Phillip. *Totally, Tenderly, Tragically: Essays and Criticism from a Lifelong Love Affair with the Movies*. New York: Anchor Books/Doubleday, 1972.

———, ed. *American Movie Critics: An Anthology from the Silents Until Now*. New York: Library of America, 2006.

McBride, Joseph. *Searching for John Ford: A Life*. New York: St. Martin's Press, 2001.

O'Connor, Flannery. *Wise Blood*. New York: Farrar, Straus and Giroux, 1949.

Orwell, George. *A Collection of Essays*. London and New York: Harcourt Brace, 1946.

Perez, Gilberto. *The Material Ghost: Films and Their Medium*. Baltimore and London: Johns Hopkins University Press, 1998.

Pipolo, Tony. *Robert Bresson: A Passion for Film*. New York: Oxford University Press, 2010.

Quandt, James, ed. *Robert Bresson*. Toronto: Cinematheque Ontario, 1998.

Riva, Maria. *Marlene Dietrich*. New York: Ballantine Books, 1992.

Sternberg, Josef Von. *Fun in a Chinese Laundry*. New York: Macmillan, 1965.

Stuart, Jan. *The Nashville Chronicles: The Making of Robert Altman's Masterpiece*. New York: Simon & Schuster, 2000.

Tarantino, Quentin. *Jackie Brown: A Screenplay*. Los Angeles: Miramax Books, 1997.

Vieira, Mark A. *Greta Garbo: A Cinematic Legacy*. New York: Harry N. Abrams, 2005.

Warshow, Robert. *The Immediate Experience: Movies, Comics, Theatre and Other Aspects of Popular Culture*. New York: Atheneum, 1971.

Weil, Simone. *Waiting for God*. New York: G. P. Putnam's, 1951.

————, and Rachel Bespaloff. *War and the Iliad*. New York: New York Review Books, 2005.

Wiazemsky, Anne. *Jeune Fille*. Paris: Gallimard, 2007.

Wills, Gary. *John Wayne's America*. New York: Simon & Schuster, 1998.

Wilson, Robert, ed. *The Film Criticism of Otis Ferguson*. Philadelphia: Temple University Press, 1971.

ACKNOWLEDGMENTS

I DON'T SEE how I could have gotten through this book if I hadn't had the help of the friends who sustained me over its long writing time by their encouragement and support and criticisms—Sheila Biddle, David Ferry, Paula Fox, Anthony Giardina, Diane Jacobs, Phillip Lopate, Ron Overton, Joseph Pequigney, and Gilberto Perez. I am grateful to them all. And to Faber and Faber / Farrar, Straus and Giroux itself, for being such a good place to be a writer—but most of all for my magical editor, Mitzi Angel, whose care and perception are of the sort that a writer usually only hopes for, and who unfailingly improved my work. So did the labors of her exemplary young assistants, Will Wolfslau and Chantal Clarke. My gratitude as well to Denise Oswald, who first optioned the book; Stephen Weil, who publicized it; and Abby Kagan, who designed it. It was Howard Mandelbaum at his Photofest archive who supplied the book's photos—and Derek Donaldson at the same terrific place who supplied the dramatic image grabs (what would have been frame enlargements in the days of film) from the DVDs we watched together. And finally—very importantly—I need to thank Robert Cornfield, my friend and agent.

INDEX

Page numbers in *italics* refer to illustrations.

Abbott, Diahne, 170, 171
absurdism, 251, 252
Academy Awards, 33, 59, 83, 99, 115, 127, 149, 160, 172, 294
Adam Had Four Sons, 79
Affron, Charles, 28
Agee, James, 76, 159
Ager, Cecilia, 45
Alamo, The, 90
Algiers, 77, 80
All About Eve, 146–47
All This and Heaven Too, 138–39
Altman, Robert, 202–28; *Nashville*, 202–28
Ameche, Don, 70
Anastasia, 294
Anderson, Maxwell, *Joan of Lorraine*, 265
Anderson, Paul Thomas, 323
Andersson, Karl, 309
Angel, 68–69
animal films, 341–59
Anna Christie, 18–19, *19*, 20, 21, 80
Anna Karenina, 31, *32*, 33, 45, 49
Another Man's Poison, 147
Arch of Triumph, 266
Argent, L', 341

Arlen, Michael, *The Green Hat*, 11
Arliss, George, 124
Artaud, Antonin, 301
art films, 159–60
Arthur, Jean, 72, 98
Astaire, Fred, 180
Asther, Nils, 12
Astor, Mary, 139
As You Desire Me, 28, 169
Atwill, Lionel, 68
Ayres, Lew, 12

Bach, Steven, 69
Back to Bataan, 89
Bainter, Fay, 130, 133
Balanchine, George, 47
Balthazar, 251, 341–59; close-ups, 342, *343*, *349*, *350–52*, *353*, *354*, *356–57*; nonacting, 341, 355; scenes from, *263*, *342*, *345*, *347*, *349*, *353*, *358*
Bang the Drum Slowly, 172
Bankhead, Tallulah, 137, 149
Bardot, Brigitte, 329
Barnes, Clive, 294
Barretts of Wimpole Street, The, 150
Barrymore, John, 24, 26–27, 125

Barrymore, Lionel, 23, 24, 43, 125
Barthes, Roland, 5
Bates, Florence, 84, 86
Baxley, Barbara, 205, *206*
Bazin, André, 124, 125, 267, 280–84, 287, 293, 299
Beatty, Ned, 204, 207, *208*
Beery, Wallace, 24, 27
Bells of Saint Mary's, The, 87, 267
Bendtsen, Henning, 322, 336
Bennett, Joan, 77
Bergman, Ingmar, 251
Bergman, Ingrid, 76–88, 114, 124, 137, 265–95; in *Anastasia*, 294; in *The Bells of Saint Mary's*, 87, 267; in *Casablanca*, 80, 295; in *Dr. Jekyll and Mr. Hyde*, 80, *81*; in *Europa '51*, 275–76, *276*, 277–78, *278*, 279–81, *281*, 282–83; in *For Whom the Bell Tolls*, 76, 77, 80–82, *82*, 83, 84; in *Gaslight*, 77, 83, 84, 271; Hollywood career, 76–88, 266, 294, 295; in *Intermezzo*, 77–79, *79*, 82, 87; in *Journey to Italy*, 283–89, *289*, 290–92, *292*, 293; naturalness of, 76–79, 82, 83; in *Notorious*, 87, 295; Rossellini and, 265–95, 316, 325; in *Saratoga Trunk*, 84–85, *85*, 86–87, 131; Selznick and, 76–88, 275; in *Spellbound*, 87; stage career, 80, 265–66, 293–94; in *Stromboli*, 267–69, *269*, 270–72, *273*, 274, 280, 292, 293
Bertolucci, Bernardo, 173, 176
Beyond the Forest, 146
Bible, 153, 272, 311
Bickford, Charles, 21
Big Trail, The, 97–98
Birth of a Nation, 109
Black, Karen, 217
Blaise Pascal, 294
Blakeley, Ronee, 202; in *Nashville*, 202, 205–206, *206*, 207, 216–18, *218*, 219–24, *224*, 225–28
blaxploitation films, 234
Blondell, Joan, 124
Blonde Venus, 59–60, 63, 64, 65–66, *66*, 67
Blondie of the Follies, 26
Bloom, Harold, 37

Blue Angel, The, 53, 55, 72
B movies, 69, 79
Bogart, Humphrey, 80, 129, 138, 170
Bogdanovich, Peter, 73
Boland, Mary, 160, *162*
Boleslawski, Richard, 31, 151
Boorstin, Daniel, 227
Bordertown, 137
Borzage, Frank, 68
Bowen, Michael, 236
Boyer, Charles, 3, 4, 48, 83, 161–63, 266
Brando, Marlon, 18, 155–56, 169, 170, 172
Breathless, 262
Brecht, Bertolt, 154, 155, 251
Brennan, Walter, 106
Brent, George, 31, 131, 135, *136*, 138, 139
Bresson, Robert, 251, 338, 339–59; *Balthazar*, 263, 341–42, *342*, 343–45, *345*, 346–47, *347*, 348, *349*, 350–52, 353, 354–58, *358*, *359*; nonactor method, 339–40, 341, 355; *The Trial of Joan of Arc*, 340
Bride Came C.O.D., The, 139–40
Brook, Clive, 61
Brown, Clarence, 11, 20, 33
Brown, John Mason, 265
Brown, Johnny Mack, 16

Cabin in the Cotton, 137
Cagney, James, 124, 139
Cahiers du Cinema, 281, 284
Caine Mutiny Court-Martial, The, 153
Calvert, James Dan, 207, *208*
Camille, 4–6, *6*, 15, 21, 28, 33–34, *34*, 35, 36, 37–40, *40*, 41–42, *42*, 43–44, 44, 45, 46, 47, 48, 63, 137, 304
Capra, Frank, 31, 127
Carradine, Keith, 205, 209–10, *210*, 211–14, 226
Carrez, Florence, 340
Casablanca, 80, 295
Casino, 201
Chaplin, Charlie, 3
Chaplin, Geraldine, 204, *222*
Chase, Borden, 107
Chekhov, Anton, 251

Chevalier, Maurice, 179
Christensen, Emil Hass, *319*, 320
Cinemascope, 98
Citizen Kane, 202
Clift, Montgomery, 106, 177
close-ups, 4, 65, 78, 247–62, 271, 274,
282; Altman and *Nashville*, 212, 218,
225; Bergman and Rossellini, 271,
274, 282; Bresson and *Balthazar*, 342,
343, *349*, 350–52, 353, 354–57; of
Davis, 133, 138, 144, *145*, 146; of
De Niro, 197, 198, *200*; in Dreyer's
films, 298–99, *300*, 301, *302*,
303–304, 307, 316, 335–37; of
Garbo, 4, 5, *5*, 6, *6*, 9, 13–15, 24–25,
25, 28, 29, 30, 31, 36, 45, 46, 99, 197;
Godard and *Masculine Feminine*,
247–49, *249*, 250–55, *255*, 256–58,
258, 259–60, *261*, 262; Tarantino
and *Jackie Brown*, 233, 239, 240, *241*,
242, 244, 247; of Wayne, 90–92,
104, *104*, 105, 110
Coffy, 234
Cohen, Alexander, 73
Cohn, Harry, 304
Colbert, Claudette, 47, 98, 103
Columbia, 79, 304
comedy, 68, 150, 176; De Niro and,
176–87; Dietrich and, 68–69; Garbo
and, 48–51; Laughton and, 160–65;
musical romantic, 176–87; screwball,
69, 139, 161, 163, 176; slapstick,
160–62
Communism, 89, 277, 279, 280
Connolly, Jennifer, 194
Conqueror, The, 99
Conquest, 47–48, 50
Contempt, 284, 288, 329
Cooke, Alistair, 45
Cooper, Gary, 57, 91, 97, 139; Bergman
and, *82*, 84–85, *85*, 86–87; Dietrich
and, 57–59, *60*, 68
Coppola, Francis Ford, 170
Corn Is Green, The, 146
Cortez, Ricardo, 8
Cotten, Joseph, 83
Coward, Noël, 160
Crawford, Joan, 24, 83, 98, 103, 125
Crews, Laura Hope, 33, *34*
Crosby, Bing, 87, 177

Cukor, George, 33, 39, 41, 47, 83, 164,
271; Garbo and, 33–47, 51
Curtiz, Michael, 127

Dangerous, 127, 137
Daniell, Henry, 35, 41, *42*
Daniels, William, 53
Dark Victory, 137–38
David Copperfield, 164
Davies, Marion, 26
Davis, Bette, 83, 114–47, 163; in *All
About Eve*, 146–47; boldness of,
125–27, 130–46; in *The Bride Came
C.O.D.*, 139–40; close-ups, 133, 138,
144, *145*, 146; in *Dangerous*, 127, 137;
in *Dark Victory*, 137–38; early films,
124; eyes of, 115, 118, 120–23, 134,
140, 144; in *Jezebel*, 114, 129–33, *133*,
134–36, *136*, 137, 139; in *Kid Galahad*,
127–28; in *The Letter*, 114–17, *117*,
118–20, *121*, 122, 123, 139; in *The
Little Foxes*, 114, 139–42, *142*, 143–44,
145, 146; in *Marked Woman*, 128, *128*,
129; in *Mr. Skeffington*, 137, 146; in *Of
Human Bondage*, 125–27; Warner
Bros. and, 115, 124–29, 139, 146;
Wyler and, 114–47
Day of Wrath, 297, 304–307, *307*,
308–309, *309*, 310–13, *313*, 314–16,
316, 317, 319, 327
Dean, James, 156
Debord, Michel, 250, *255*
Deer Hunter, The, 188, 189
DeMille, Cecil B., 98, 149
De Niro, Robert, 169–201; close-ups,
197, 198, *200*; comedy and, 176–87;
gangster films, 187–201; in *Godfather*,
170, 172, 189; in *Jackie Brown*, 201,
229–31, *231*, 232; in *The King of
Comedy*, 170, 175–76; in *The Last
Tycoon*, 172–74, 183; in *Mean Streets*,
172, 174–75, 195; in *New York, New
York*, 170–72, 176–80, *180*, 181–82,
182, 183–85, *185*, 186–87; in *1900*,
173, *173*, 174; in *Once Upon a Time
in America*, 170, 174, 187–89, *189*,
190–97, *197*, 198–99, *199*, 200, *200*,
201; in *Raging Bull*, 169–70, 172,
183; Scorsese and, 169–87; smile of,

De Niro, Robert (*cont.*)
174, 183; in *Taxi Driver*, 169, 172,
174, 175, 176, 183, 200
Denmark, 297, 304–38
Denton, Donna, 208
Depardieu, Gérard, 173–74
Depression, 98, 225
De Sica, Vittorio, 283, 293, 339
Desire, 68
Destry Rides Again, 69–70
Devil and the Deep, The, 149
Devil Is a Woman, The, 67–68
Diary of a Country Priest, 339
Dieterle, William, 151
Dietrich, Marlene, 53–75, 98, 114, 123,
125, 188, 211, 266; in *Angel*, 68–69;
artificial beauty of, 57, 61–68; in
Blonde Venus, 59–60, 63, 64, 65–66,
66, 67; in *The Blue Angel*, 53, 55, 72;
comeback of, 69–70; comedy and,
68–69; in *Desire*, 68; in *Destry Rides
Again*, 69–70; in *The Devil Is a
Woman*, 67–68; in *Dishonored*,
54–55, 56, 60; in *A Foreign Affair*,
72; Garbo and, 53–55, 69, 76;
international concert years, 73–75;
in *Kismet*, 72; last films, 73; in
Manpower, 70; in *Morocco*, 53, 55–59,
60, 65; Paramount and, 53, 60, 68–69;
in *Pittsburgh*, 70, 71; publicity, 69, 72;
in *The Scarlet Empress*, 67; in *Seven
Sinners*, 70, 71; in *Shanghai Express*,
60–62, 62, 63, 304; in silent films, 53;
in *Song of Songs*, 60; in *The Spoilers*,
70; Sternberg and, 53–68, 75, 304; in
Touch of Evil, 72–73, 74, 232; war
service, 72; Westerns and, 69–70
Dingle, Charles, 141, *142*
Dishonored, 54–55, 56, 60
Disney, Walt, 160
Divine Woman, The, 10
Dolce Vita, La, 301
Donovan's Reef, 99
Doqui, Robert, 204
Douglas, Melvyn, 23, 49, *51*
Dreyer, Carl Theodor, 296–338; *Day of
Wrath*, 297, 304–307, *307*, 308–309,
309, 310–13, *313*, 314–16, *316*, 317,
319, 327; *Gertrud*, 297, 327, 328,
329–31, *331*, 332–34, 334, 335, *335*,
336–38, 340; *Ordet*, 297, 317–19, *319*,
320–24, *324*, 325, 326, 329–30; *The
Passion of Joan of Arc*, 296–99, *300*,
301, *302*, 303–304, 330, 336, 340
Dr. Jekyll and Mr. Hyde, 80, *81*
Duport, Catherine-Isabelle, 250
Durante, Jimmy, 26
Durbin, Deanna, 153
Duvall, Shelley, 204
Duvivier, Julien, 161

Eagels, Jeanne, 114, 127
Eastwood, Clint, 187
Eisenstein, Sergei, 67
El Dorado, 99
Eldredge, John, 127
England, 73, 83, 128, 149, 154–56, 160,
188
epic films, 188
Epstein, Julius, 80
Europa '51, 275–76, 276, 277–78, 278,
279–81, *281*, 282–83

Falconetti, Maria, 296; in *The Passion
of Joan the Arc*, 296–99, *300*, 301,
302, 303–304, 340
Faye, Alice, 70, 176, 177, 180
Fear, 293–94
Fedderspiel, Birgitte, 318, *326*,
Fellini, Federico, 301
Ferguson, Otis, 33
Feyder, Jacques, 12, 13, 20, 21, 24
Fields, W. C., 164
Fitzmaurice, George, 28
Fleming, Victor, 80, 265
Flesh and the Devil, 8–11, 14, 31, 49
Flying Tigers, The, 89
Flynn, Errol, 98
Fonda, Bridget, 229–31, *231*
Fonda, Henry, 89, 130, 132, *133*, 135,
148, 161
Fontaine, Joan, 329
Ford, John, 89–113; *The Long Voyage
Home*, 95–97, 105; *The Man Who
Shot Liberty Valance*, 99–101, *101*,
102, 105; *The Quiet Man*, 102–103;
Rio Grande, 99, 103–104, *104*, 105;
The Searchers, 92–93, 94, 95, 96,

105, *106*, 107–12, *112*, 113;
  Stagecoach, 90–91, *91*, 92, 95, 98,
  100, 105; Wayne and, 89–113
Foreign Affair, A, 72
Forster, Robert, 235; in *Jackie Brown*,
  235–40, *241*, 242–43, *243*, 244–45,
  245, 246
Fort Apache, 99, 105
For Whom the Bell Tolls, 76, 77, 80–82,
  82, 83, 84
Foxy Brown, 234
France, 35, 44, 49, 50, 63, 65, 73,
  247–62, 284, 297, 304
Francis, Kay, 137
Franklin, Sidney, 12

Gable, Clark, 3, 21, 70, 89; Garbo and,
  21–22, *22*
Galileo, 154
gangster films, 129, 170, 187, 189; De
  Niro and, 187–201
Garbo, Greta, 3–52, 76, 105, 114, 124,
  125, 137, 169, 267, 282, 294,
  303–304; in *Anna Christie*, 18–19,
  19, 20, 21, 80; in *Anna Karenina*, 31,
  32, 33, 45, 49; in *Camille*, 4–6, *6*,
  15, 21, 28, 33–34, *34*, 35, 36, 37–40,
  40, 41–42, *42*, 43–44, *44*, 45, 46, 47,
  48, 63, 137, 304; close-ups, 4, 5, *5*,
  6, *6*, *9*, 13–15, 24–25, *25*, 28, 29, *30*,
  31, *36*, 45, *46*, 49, 197; comedy and,
  48–51; in *Conquest*, 47–48, 50;
  Cukor and, 33–47, 51; Dietrich and,
  53–55, 69, 76; dying scenes, 45, *46*,
  47; early silent films, 7–14, 18;
  elusiveness of, 3–4, 6–8, 14, 22, 52;
  in *Flesh and the Devil*, 8–11, 14, 49;
  in *Gösta Berling*, 7, 10; in *Grand
  Hotel*, 24–25, *25*, 26–29, 33; in
  Inspiration, 21, 22; in *The Kiss*, 12,
  13, 20; last movie, 51–52, 69; laugh
  of, 14, 48, 50, *51*; in *Love*, 10, 14, 18,
  24, 31; Lubitsch and, 48–51; mask,
  48, 49; in *Mata Hari*, 21–24, 53–54,
  56; MGM and, 8–12, 21–29, 47,
  50–52, 53; in *The Mysterious Lady*,
  10, 14–15, *15*, 16, 535; in *Ninotchka*,
  3, 48–51, *51*; in *The Painted Veil*, 31;
  publicity, 29; in *Queen Christina*, 4,
5, *5*, 6, 28–29, *30*, 31, 197, 304; in
  Romance, 19–21; in *Susan Lenox*,
  21–22, *22*, 23, 28; in *The Temptress*,
  8, 13, 14; in *Two-Faced Woman*,
  51–52; voice, 18–21; in *A Woman of
  Affairs*, 11, *11*, 12, 16–17, *17*, 18, 63
Garden of Allah, 68
Garfield, Allen, *206*
Garis, Robert, 73, 232
Gaslight, 77, 83, 84, 271
Genthe, Arnold, 7; photographs of
  Garbo, 7–8, *9*
Germany, 7, 20, 53, 72, 294, 346; Nazi,
  72, 275, 297, 317
Gertrud, 297, 327, 328, 329–31, *331*,
  332–34, *334*, 335, *335*, 336–38, 340
Gibson, Henry, 203, *206*, 215–16
Gilbert, John, 8–9; Garbo and, 8–11,
  11, 12, 16–18, 28
Gish, Lillian, 3, 156, 158–59, *159*, 248
Glenn, Scott, 205, *222*
Godard, Jean-Luc, 247–62, 268, 281,
  284, 304, 329, 341, 347, 359;
  absurdism and, 251, 252; close-ups
  and *Masculine Feminine*, 247–49,
  249, 250–52, *252*, 253–55, *255*,
  256–58, *258*, 259–60, *261*, 262
Godfather: Part II, The, 170, 172, 189
Goldblum, Jeff, 204, 209
Gone With the Wind, 77, 131, *132*,
  234, 265
Gordon, Gavin, 19
Goulding, Edmund, 10, 24, 25, 26, 28,
  137–38
Goya, Chantal, 248–49, *249*, 250–58,
  258, 259–60, *261*, 262
Grandeur, 98
Grand Hotel, 24–25, *25*, 26–29, 33
Grant, Cary, 49, 63, 87, 181; Dietrich
  and, 63, *64*, 65–66, *66*, 67
Great Lie, The, 139
Green, Walter, 344, *349*
Green Berets, The, 90
Greene, Graham, 5, 47
Greer, Jane, 262
Grier, Pam, 232–46; blaxploitation
  films, 234; in *Jackie Brown*, *167*,
  234–35, *235*, 236–38, *238*, 239–40,
  241, 242–43, *243*, 244–45, *245*, 246
Griffith, D. W., 109, 156, 159, 248

Haller, Ernest, 133
Halliday, John, 21
Haneke, Michael, 341, 350
Hanson, Lars, 10
Harlow, Jean, 126
Harris, Barbara, 208
Haskell, Molly, 341
Hathaway, Henry, 99
Hawks, Howard, 31, 99, 105–107, 139
Hayward, David, 208, 222, 226
Hayworth, Rita, 161
Hellman, Lillian, 140
Hemingway, Ernest, 81–82, 84
Hepburn, Katharine, 125
Heston, Charlton, 73
Hitchcock, Alfred, 87, 267, 327
Hollander, Friedrich, 72
Hollywood, 3, 7, 52, 70, 76, 77, 266,
    282, 292, 294, 304; postwar, 99;
    Production Code, 129; wartime, 89.
    See also specific actors, directors, films,
    genres, producers, and studios
Houseman, John, 80
Howard, Leslie, 78, 125–27
Howard, Sidney, 152
Howe, James Wong, 77
Hughes, Howard, 268
Hunchback of Notre Dame, The, 151,
    155
Huston, John, 136
Huxley, Aldous, 48

If I Had a Million, 149
Informer, The, 95
Inspiration, 21, 22
Intermezzo, 77–79, 79, 82, 87
Italy, 266–74, 283–93
It Happened One Night, 127
Ivan the Terrible, Part One, 67

Jackie Brown, 201, 229–46, 247;
    close-ups, 233, 239, 240, 241, 242,
    244; leisureliness of, 232, 243–44;
    minimal characterization, 245–46;
    scenes from, 167, 231, 235, 238, 241,
    243, 245
Jackson, Samuel L., 229, 235, 236,
    239

Jezebel, 114, 129–33, 133, 134–36, 136,
    137, 139, 232
Joan of Arc, 265, 282
Joan of Arc at the Stake, 293
Jobert, Marlène, 252, 258
John Brown's Body, 153, 159
Jordan, Dorothy, 93, 94, 96
Journey to Italy, 275, 283–89, 289,
    290–92, 292, 293
Joyless Street, The, 7
Judgment at Nuremburg, 73

Kael, Pauline, 18, 125, 164, 201,
    339–40
Kanin, Garson, 48, 151–53, 155
Kazan, Elia, 18, 172–74, 176, 183
Keaton, Michael, 237–38, 238, 239
Keitel, Harvey, 174
Kid Galahad, 127–28
Kill Bill, 232, 245
King of Comedy, The, 170, 175–76
Kismet, 72
Kiss, The, 12, 13, 20
Klossowski, Pierre, 347, 347
Knight Without Armor, 68
Knox, Alexander, 276, 277, 278, 280
Koch, Howard, 120
Korda, Alexander, 68, 149, 150, 152
Kristiansen, Cay, 318, 319
Kurant, Willy, 247

Lady Eve, The, 132
Lady Takes a Chance, A, 98
Lady Tycoon, The, 172–74, 183
Laemmle, Carl, 124
Lafarge, François, 344, 345, 353
Lamarr, Hedy, 77
Lanchester, Elsa, 149
Laughton, Charles, 148–65, 169;
    comedy and, 160–65; directing
    career, 153–54, 156–60; in The
    Hunchback of Notre Dame, 151, 155;
    movie career, 149–55; Night of the
    Hunter and, 154, 156–57, 157,
    158–59, 159, 161; in Rembrandt,
    150–51; in Ruggles of Red Gap, 150,
    160–61, 162; in Sign of the Cross, 149,
    150; in The Suspect, 153, 154; in

Tales of Manhattan, 161–65; theatrical career, 148, 149, 153–55; in *They Knew What They Wanted*, 151–53; ugliness of, 151, 155, 162–65

Lawrence, D. H., 331, 355

Lawrence, Gertrude, 151–52

Léaud, Jean-Pierre, 247–49, *249*, 250–52, *252*, 253–55, *255*, 256–58, *258*, 259–60

Leigh, Vivien, 84, 131

Lemmon, Jack, 164

Leonard, Elmore, 229, 231, 243

Leonard, Robert Z., 28

Leone, Sergio, 187, 202, 253; *Once Upon a Time in America*, 187–201

Lerdorff Rye, Preben, 319, 321–22, *324*

Les Miserables, 150, 151

Lester, Bruce, *117*

Letter, The, 114–17, *117*, 118–20, *121–22*, 123, 139

Leven, Boris, 177

Lewis, Jerry, 175

Life magazine, 69

Little Foxes, The, 114, 139, 140–42, *142*, 143–44, *145*, 146

Lombard, Carole, 47, 151, 152

London, 73, 83, 149, 160

Long Voyage Home, The, 95–97, 105

Lopate, Phillip, 296

Love, 10, 14, 18, 24, 31

Loy, Myrna, 70, 128

Lubitsch, Ernst, 24, 28, 48, 68, 95, 149; Dietrich and, 68–69; Garbo and, 48–51

Lupino, Ida, 70

Magnani, Anna, 272

Malberg, Henrik, 318, *319*

Mamoulian, Rouben, 6, 28–29, 60, 67

Man Escaped, A, 339, 340, 350

Mankiewicz, Joe, 146, 147

Mann, Michael, 201

Manpower, 70

Man Who Played God, The, 124

Man Who Shot Liberty Valance, The, 99–101, *101*, 102, 105

March, Fredric, 32, 33, 45

Marked Woman, 128, *128*, 129

Marsh, Mae, 109

Marshall, Herbert, 31, 63, 115, *117*, 123, 141, 144

Marshall, Margaret, 23

Marvin, Lee, 100, *101*

Mascot, 98

Masculine Feminine, 247–62; close-ups, 247–49, *249*, 250–52, *252*, 253–55, *255*, 256–58, *258*, 259–60, *261*, 262

Masina, Giulietta, 275, 279

Mata Hari, 21, 23–24, 53–54, *56*

Maté, Rudolph, 298

Maugham, Somerset, 31, 114, 125

Mayer, Louis B., 7, 31

McCarey, Leo, 150, 160

McGovern, Elizabeth, 187, 188, 192, 196, *197*, 198

McQueen, Steve, 156

Mean Streets, 172–75, 195

memory, 105, 191, 338

Mendelsohn, Daniel, 245–46

Menjou, Adolphe, 57

Meredith, Burgess, 80

Merkel, Una, 69

Messiah, The, 294

Method, 155, 169

Methot, Mayo, *128*, 129

Metro-Goldwyn-Mayer (MGM), 4, 8, 24, 31, 47, 50, 72, 79, 80, 124, 137, 149, 151, 164; Garbo and, 8–12, 21–29, 47, 50–52, 53

Miles, Vera, 100, 101, 102, 108

Milland, Ray, 98

Miller, Arthur, *The Crucible*, 314

Minnelli, Liza, 170–72; in *New York, New York*, 177–80, *180*, 181–82, *182*, 183–85, *185*, 186

Miracle, The, 272

Mitchell, Thomas, 95, 161

Mitchum, Robert, 156, 157, *157*, *159*

Monogram, 98

Montgomery, Robert, 89

moon, 120–23

Moreno, Antonio, 8

Morocco, 53, 55–59, *60*, 65

Morricone, Ennio, 191, 193

Mouchette, 340, 341

Movin, Lisbeth, 304, 307, *309*, *313*, *316*

Mr. Skeffington, 137, 146
Muni, Paul, 124
Munk, Kaj, 317, 318
Murphy, Michael, 204
music, 57, 92, 123, 132, 161–62, 174, 191–93, 290; *Balthazar* and, 341, 342, 346, 351, 356–57; Dietrich and, 57, 63–64, 69, 70, 72; in Dreyer's films, 308, 310, 315, 332–34; *Jackie Brown* and, 232, 240, 244; *Masculine Feminine* and, 253–59; *Nashville* and, 202–28; *New York, New York* and, 170–72, 176–87
Mutiny on the Bounty, 150, 155
Mysterious Lady, The, 10, 14–15, *15*, 16, 53

Nagel, Conrad, 12, 14–15, *15*, 16
Nashville, 202–28; close-ups, 212, 218, 225; intercuttings, 203–204, 219, 221–22, 225; as "metaphor for America," 202, 216, 225–28; scenes from, *206, 208, 210, 213, 218, 222, 224*
Natwick, Mildred, 96, 97
Negri, Pola, 8
neorealism, 266–95, 339, 354
New Orleans, 63, 84, 129
New Republic, The, 33
New Wave, 247–62, 267, 283
New York, 7, 52, 63, 73–75, 83, 175–89, 265, 294
New York, New York, 170–72, 176–80, *180*, 181–82, *182*, 183–85, *185*, 186–87
New Yorker, The, 245, 246
New York Times, The, 12, 50, 110
Niblo, Fred, 13, 14
Nicholls, Allan, 211
Night of the Hunter, The, 154–57, *157*, 158–59, *159*, 161
1900, 173, *173*, 174
Ninotchka, 3, 48–51, *51*
Norton, Jack, *128*
Notorious, 87, 295
Novak, Kim, 262
Novarro, Ramon, 23, 54
Now, Voyager, 125, 146
Nugent, Frank, 50, 110

O'Connor, Flannery, *Wise Blood*, 359
Of Human Bondage, 125–27
O'Hara, Maureen, 102–104, *104*, 105, 153
Old Acquaintance, 146
Old Maid, The, 125, 139
Olivier, Laurence, 29–31, 129, 155
O'Malley, Rex, 38
Once Upon a Time in America, 170, 174, 187–89, *189*, 190–97, *197*, 198–99, *199*, 200, *200*, 201
O'Neill, Eugene, 18, 95, 294
On the Waterfront, 169, 172
Open City, 266, 270, 275
Ophuls, Max, 287, 329
Ordet, 297, 317–19, *319*, 320–24, *324*, 325, 326, 329, 330
Orwell, George, 305, 335
Out of the Past, 262
Owe, Baard, 335, 336

Pabst, G. W., 7, 8
Painted Veil, The, 31
Paisan, 266, 270
Paramount, 8, 24, 98, 124, 149, 161; Dietrich and, 53, 60, 68–69
Paris, 35, 44, 49, 50, 63, 65, 73, 259, 284, 297
Passion of Joan of Arc, The, 296–99, *300*, 301, *302*, 303–304, 330, 336, 340
Pasternak, Joe, 69
Pater, Walter, 7
Payment Deferred, 149
Peel, David, 205
Perez, Gilberto, 248, 293
Pesci, Joe, 175, 188
Petrified Forest, The, 127
Pickpocket, 340, 350
Pinter, Harold, 172, 173
Pittsburgh, 70, *71*
Porcasi, Paul, 55
Powell, William, 49, 124
Power, Tyrone, 70, 89, 176, 177, 180
Private Life of Henry VIII, The, 149
Private Lives of Elizabeth and Essex, The, 139, 140
Production Code, 129
Pulp Fiction, 232, 234

Queen Christina, 4, 5, *5*, 6, 28–29, *30*, 31, 60, 137, 197, 304
Quiet Man, The, 99, 102–103

Rage in Heaven, 79
Raging Bull, 169–70, 172, 183
Raines, Cristina, *210*, 211
Raines, Ella, 153, *154*
Rains, Claude, 87
Ralph, Jessie, 41, *42*, 45
Rathbone, Basil, 31, *32*
Ratoff, Gregory, 78
Ray, Nicholas, 111
Ray, Satyajit, 329
Reap the Wild Wind, 98
Red River, 99, 105–107
Reed, Donna, 105
Reid, Carl Benton, 141, *142*
religion, 153, 270, 272, 294, 296; *Balthazar* and, 342, 358–59; Dreyer's films and, 296–327; Rossellini's films and, 272, 274, 278, 284–85, 291, 294
Rembrandt, 150–51
Renoir, Jean, 153, 164, 169, 177, 294
Republic, 89, 98
Reservoir Dogs, 232
Reunion in France, 98
Rio Bravo, 99, 232
Rio Grande, 99, 103–104, *104*, 105
Rise of Louis XIV, The, 294
Rivette, Jacques, 281, 284, 285
RKO, 24, 125, 151, 152, 268, 269, 272, 292
Robertson, John S., 12
Robeson, Paul, 161, 163
Robinson, Edward G., 124, 128, 163–64
Rode, Ebbe, 331
Rode, Nina Pens, *328*, 330, *331*, 334–35, 336
Rogers, Ginger, 161, 180
Rohmer, Eric, 281, 283, 282, 285
Romance, 19–21
Rooney, Mickey, 125
Rossellini, Roberto, 265–95, 321, 327, 339, 354; Bergman and, 265–95, 316, 325; *Europa '51*, 275–76, *276*, 277–78, *278*, 279–81, *281*, 282–83; *Journey to Italy*, 283–89, *289*, 290–92, 292, 293; neorealism and,

266–95; *Stromboli*, 267–69, *269*, 270–72, 273, 274, 280, 292, 293
Rothe, Bendt, 330, *334*
Ruggles of Red Gap, 150, 160–61, *162*
Russell, Rosalind, 181

Saga of Gösta Berling, The, 7, 10
Sanders, George, 283, 291–92, *292*
Sands of Iwo Jima, 109
Saratoga Trunk, 84–85, *85*, 86–87, 131
Saturday Review, 265
Scarlet Empress, The, 67
Schrader, Paul, 169
Scorsese, Martin, 201; De Niro, 169–87; *The King of Comedy*, 170, 175–76; *Mean Streets*, 172–75; *New York, New York*, 170–72, 176–87
Scott, Randolph, 70, *71*, 91
screwball comedy, 69, 139, 161, 163, 176
Searchers, The, 92–93, *94*, 95, *96*, 105, *106*, 107–12, *112*, 113, 232
Seberg, Jean, 262
Selznick, David O., 31, 68, 76–88, 137; Bergman and, 76–88, 275
Seven Sinners, 70, *71*
Shakespeare, William, 37, 153–55
Shanghai Express, 60–62, *62*, 63, 304
Shearer, Norma, 125
Sheridan, Ann, 70
Sherman, Vincent, 146
She Wore a Yellow Ribbon, 99, 105
Shootist, The, 99
Siegel, Don, 99
Sign of the Cross, 149, *150*
Silence, The, 251
silent films, 7–13; Dietrich in, 53; end of, 10–11, 18; Garbo in, 7–14, 18; *The Passion of Joan of Arc*, 296–304
Silvain, Eugène, 299
Single Standard, The, 12
Siodmak, Robert, 153, *154*, 164
Sirk, Douglas, 111
Sjöström, Victor, 7, 10
Sondergaard, Gale, 116
Song of Songs, 60
Sontag, Susan, 340, 350
Spellbound, 87
Spiegel, Sam, 172–73, *174*
Spoilers, The, 70

Stagecoach, 90–91, *91*, 92, 95, 98, 100, 105
Stanwyck, Barbara, 124, 132
Steichen, Edward, 10
Steiner, Max, 92, 123, 132
Stephenson, James, 115, *117*
Sternberg, Josef von, 53–68, 188; *Blonde Venus*, 59–60, 63, *64*, 65–66, *66*, 67; Dietrich and, 53–68, 75, 304; *Dishonored*, 54–55, 56, 60; *Morocco*, 53, 55–59, 60; *Shanghai Express*, 60–62, *62*, 63
Stevens, George, 24
Stewart, Donald Ogden, 280
Stewart, James, 69, 89, 99–101, *101*, 102, 105
Stiller, Mauritz, 7–10, 13, 53
Stone, Lewis, 17, *17*
Stromboli, 267–69, *269*, 270–72, *273*, 274, 280, 292, 293
Sturges, Preston, 203
Superfly, 234
Susan Lenox, 21–22, *22*, 23, 28
Suspect, The, 153, *154*
Svierkier, Anna, 306, *307*
Sweden, 7, 8, 28, 76, 77, 96, 251, 317

Tagore, Sharmila, 329
Tales of Manhattan, 161–65
Tarantino, Quentin, 229–46; *Jackie Brown*, 229–46, *247*; minimalist approach to characterization, 245–46; *Pulp Fiction*, 232, 234
Taxi Driver, 169, 172–76, 183, 200
Taylor, Robert, 35, *36*, 40, 42, *44*, 89
Tea and Sympathy, 294
Technicolor, 82, 139
Temptress, The, 8, 13, 14
Thalberg, Irving, 8, 33, 48, 151, 172
There Will Be Blood, 323
They Knew What They Wanted, 151–53
They Were Expendable, 89, 105
This Land Is Mine, 153
Tiler, Scott, 194, 195
Time magazine, 76, 129
Todd, Ann, 79
Toland, Gregg, 78, 95, 97, 143

Tomlin, Lily, 202; in *Nashville*, 202–204, 207–208, *208*, 209–13, *213*, 214, 223–26
Tone, Franchot, 127
Torrent, The, 8
Touch of Evil, 72–73, *74*, 232
Tracy, Spencer, 70, 80
trains, 60–62, *62*, 63, 196–97, *197*, 198, *199*
Travolta, John, 234–35
Trevor, Claire, *91*
Trial of Joan of Arc, The, 340
True Grit, 99
Truffaut, François, 306
Turner, Lana, 52, 80
Twentieth Century-Fox, 98, 146, 161
Two-Faced Woman, 51–52
Tynan, Kenneth, 27, 29

Ulric, Lenore, 33, *34*
Umberto D, 283
Under Capricorn, 267
Universal, 69–70, 98, 124

Vampyr, 297, 304n
Vanity Fair, 7
Vertigo, 262
Viertel, Salka, 51
Vietnam War, 75, 221, 223, 227, 253
Vivre sa vie, 304

Waiting for Godot, 358
Walsh, Raoul, 70, 97–98
war films, 89–90
Warhol, Andy, 339
Warner, Jack, 139
Warner Bros., 70, 84, 115, 124–29, 139, 146, 188
Warshow, Robert, 314
Watts, Naomi, 31
Wayne, John, 70, 89–113, 123; *The Big Trail*, 97–98; close-ups, 90–92, 104, *104*, 105, 110; Dietrich and, 70, *71*, 72, 98; first starring role, 97–98; Ford and, 89–113; last films, 99; in *The Long Voyage Home*, 95–97, 105; in *The Man Who Shot Liberty Valance*,

99–101, *101*, 102, 105; in *The Quiet Man*, 99, 102–103; in *Red River*, 99, 105–107; in *Rio Grande*, 99, 103–104, *104*, 105; in *The Searchers*, 92–93, *94*, 95, *96*, 105, *106*, 107–12, *112*, 113; in *Stagecoach*, 90–91, *91*, 92, 95, 98, 100, 105; in *They Were Expendable*, 89, 105; Westerns and, 90–113
Weil, Simone, 280
Weld, Tuesday, 188, 196
Welles, Gwen, 204
Welles, Orson, 72; *Touch of Evil*, 72–73, *74*
West, Mae, 3
Westerns, 69, 70, 187; Dietrich and, 69–70; Wayne and, 90–113
Westmore, Perc, 139, 140
Wiazemsky, Anne, *263*, 344, *349*, 353
Wilde, Oscar, 286
Wilder, Billy, 48, 72
Wild Orchids, 12
Winters, Shelley, 156, 158
Without Reservations, 98
Witness for the Prosecution, 73

Woman of Affairs, A, 11, *11*, 12, 16–17, *17*, 18, 63
Wong, Anna May, 61, *62*, 63
Wood, Lana, *96*, 107
Wood, Sam, 84
Woods, James, 187, 188, 195
World War I, 149
World War II, 52, 72, 89
Wouk, Herman, 153
Wright, Teresa, 141
Wuthering Heights, 129
Wyler, William, 114–47; Davis and, 114–47; *Jezebel*, 114, 129–39; *The Letter*, 114–23, 139; *The Little Foxes*, 114, 139–46
Wynn, Keenan, 204, 208

Young, Loretta, 87
Young, Stark, 169

Zorina, Vera, 82
Zweig, Stefan, 294

PERMISSION ACKNOWLEDGMENTS

7/94